California 2nd Edition

Collect Your Court Judgment

By

Gini Graham Scott

Stephen R. Elias

Lisa S. Goldoftas

NOLO PRESS BERKELEY

YOUR RESPONSIBILITY WHEN USING A SELF-HELP LAW BOOK

We've done our best to give you useful and accurate information in this book. But laws and procedures change frequently and are subject to differing interpretations. If you want legal advice backed by a guarantee, see a lawyer. If you use this book, it's your responsibility to make sure that the facts and general advice contained in it are applicable to your situation.

KEEPING UP TO DATE

To keep its books up to date, Nolo Press issues new printings and new editions periodically. New printings reflect minor legal changes and technical corrections. New editions contain major legal changes, major text additions or major reorganizations. To find out if a later printing or edition of any Nolo book is available, call Nolo Press at 510-549-1976 or check the catalog in the *Nolo News*, our quarterly newspaper.

To stay current, follow the "Update" service in the *Nolo News*. You can get a two-year subscription by sending us the registration card in the back of the book. In another effort to help you use Nolo's latest materials, we offer a 25% discount off the purchase of any new Nolo book if you turn in any earlier printing or edition. (See the "Recycle Offer" in the back of the book.)

This book was last revised in: **January 1995.**

SECOND EDITION
Third Printing January 1995
ILLUSTRATIONS Mari Stein
Eddie Warner
PRODUCTION Stephanie Harolde
BOOK DESIGN & LAYOUT Jackie Mancuso
Toni Ihara
Terri Hearsh
PRINTING Delta Lithograph

Scott, Gini Graham.
Collect your court judgment / by Gini Graham Scott, Stephen Elias & Lisa S. Goldoftas ; edited by Lisa S. Goldoftas ; illustrations by Mari Stein. -- Calif. 2nd ed.
p. cm.
Includes index.
ISBN 0-87337-151-8
1. Executions (Law)--California--Popular works. 2. Judgments--California--Popular works. 3. Collection laws--California--Popular works. I. Elias, Stephen. II. Goldoftas, Lisa.
III. Title.
KFC1065.Z9S25 1991
347.794'077--dc20
[347.940777} 91-29147
CIP

Copyright © 1988, 1992 and 1993 by Gini Graham Scott, Stephen R. Elias, & Lisa S. Goldoftas
All Rights Reserved. No part of this publication may be reproduced, stored in a retrieval system, or transmitted in any form, or by any means, electronic, mechanical, photocopying, recording or otherwise without the prior written permission of the publisher and the authors.

Printed on paper with recycled content
Printed in the U.S.A.

DEDICATIONS

To Ann and Tobi, for their constant support and encouragement, and to Albin, whose generosity helped this book really happen.

—LG

To Ralph Warner, for the opportunity to do this book.

—SE

ACKNOWLEDGMENTS

The authors extend their heartfelt thanks to:

Attorney Michael Perna (of Marsh and Perna, Oakland, California) for his valuable suggestions and guidance in assembling the manuscript.

Attorney Sheldon Greene and the law firm of Greene, Kelley, Tobriner and Farren (San Francisco, California) for their generosity in allowing us to use forms and procedures that were developed for the law firm.

Attorney Irwin Eskanos (of Eskanos and Adler, Oakland, California) and Judge Allen Norris (Richmond, California) for their experienced and insightful overviews of the judgment collection process.

Attorney David Brown (Monterey, California) for his scrupulous review of the final manuscript and his many suggestions for improvement.

Tim Schooley, a small claims advisor, who read the first draft of this manuscript.

Keith M. Clemens, family law commissioner in the Los Angeles Superior Court, for contributing his time and expertise.

Ralph Warner, Mary Randolph, Albin Renauer, Robin Leonard and Steve Fishman for their excellent editorial assistance and legal contributions.

Paul Duguid for the many hours he spent with us sharing his knowledge of book design.

Jackie Mancuso, Terri Hearsh, Toni Ihara, Amy Ihara and Mari Stein for the book's design and artwork.

The many folks at Nolo without whose contributions the book would never see the light of day, especially: Stephanie Harolde, for her meticulous work and keen eye; Philip Ramsey, for his cheerful help in typing forms; Eddie Warner, for his excellent and patient work during his foray into production; and Ely Newman, for proofreading the manuscript.

CONTENTS

Chapter 1

How To Use This Book

THIS BOOK IS FOR PEOPLE or businesses who wish to collect a court judgment in California. Unfortunately, as readers who have attempted to collect judgments know, all too often it is a time-consuming and frustrating ordeal. But on a positive note, you can collect a judgment without an attorney and often without much additional expense. In this chapter, we introduce you to this book and help you determine the most efficient way to use it.

This book is only for people who already have a court judgment. If you have not yet obtained a judgment, you must do so before using this book. *Everybody's Guide to Small Claims Court*, by Ralph Warner (Nolo Press) will help for claims of $5,000 or less. *Everybody's Guide to Municipal Court*, by Judge Roderic Duncan (Nolo Press) is for claims of $25,000 or less.[1]

A. Nineteen Ways to Collect a Court Judgment

THIS BOOK COVERS 19 different ways to collect a court judgment. Each method is covered in a separate chapter or section. After this chapter, you'll only need to read portions of the book that are relevant to your situation.

The chart on the following page lists this book's 19 collection techniques and indicates how effective they typically are. Because people and situations vary, you'll have the flexibility to use whatever methods you decide are most likely to succeed.

Note: If the debtor has either died or filed for bankruptcy, your choices are greatly limited. Instead of reading the rest of this chapter, go directly to the specific chapter dealing with your situation: Chapter 16 for bankruptcy cases or Chapter 17 if the debtor has died.

B. Laying the Groundwork

YOU SHOULD IMMEDIATELY TAKE SEVERAL steps to put yourself in the best possible legal position to collect your judgment. These procedures will also help you get organized and:

- discover what assets are available for you to collect from
- be able to promptly proceed against assets to satisfy your judgment
- establish your priority vis-a-vis other creditors.

[1] These are the small claims and municipal court limits, respectively, as of 1991. These amounts may go up.

NINETEEN WAYS TO COLLECT A COURT JUDGMENT

PRELIMINARY STEPS

1	Place a legal claim (lien) on real estate	Chapter 4
2	Place a lien on business property	Chapter 4
3	Negotiate voluntary payments	Chapter 5
4	Conduct a debtor's examination; can obtain debtor's money and property at exam	Chapter 6

BASIC COLLECTION TECHNIQUES (least costly, generally most effective)

5	Seize (garnish) wages	Chapter 9
6	Seize (levy on) bank accounts and safe-deposit boxes	Chapter 8
7	Collect from business debtor's cash register (till tap)	Chapter 11
8	Collect money from business as it comes in, for a specified time (keeper)	Chapter 11
9	For debtors who file for bankruptcy, file a proof of claim	Chapter 16
10	For debtors who die, file a creditor's claim	Chapter 17
11	Collect (levy on) debts owed by third parties	Chapter 10
12	Suspend driver's license (special situations)	Chapter 1, Section D.2

ADVANCED COLLECTION TECHNIQUES (often expensive, usually least effective)

13	Seize and sell business assets	Chapter 11
14	Seize and sell vehicle	Chapter 12
15	Seize and sell personal assets	Chapter 13
16	Obtain a court order to seize property located in a private home	Chapter 18
17	Obtain a court order requiring the debtor to hand over specific property	Chapter 18
18	Obtain a court order requiring the debtor to assign (transfer) to you certain rights, such as the right to receive royalties or federal wages due the debtor	Chapter 18
19	Force sale of real estate	Chapter 14

1. Set Up a Case File

Organize a way to keep copies of all documents related to your collection efforts. You may want to use an accordion-type folder with separate file folders organized by category, such as court papers, letters, costs. If your collection efforts are extensive, you may choose to set up files by type of asset—such as vehicles, bank accounts, wages.

You should be able to easily lay your hands on any document or receipt you need. This is especially important when you compute the costs and interest which you are entitled to collect from the debtor. In Chapter 15 and the Appendix are instructions and worksheets to keep track of costs, payments on the judgment and interest that is legally due.

2. Establish Liens

Your next step should be to establish a lien—legal claim—against the judgment debtor's property. Liens give your judgment priority over other creditors and position you to get paid if the debtor declares bankruptcy or sells, refinances or transfers property. Chapter 4 discusses liens in detail and tells you how to create:

- real estate liens
- personal property liens—if the debtor is a business.

3. Know What You Can and Can't Do

Debtors have certain legal rights and protections. Read Chapter 2 to understand when you can start collecting. Read Chapter 3 for an overview of behavior you must avoid when collecting your court judgment.

4. Attempt Voluntary Collection

Now that the debtor has lost in court, she finally may be willing to pay you. If you work out a voluntary payment arrangement with the debtor, you won't need to take active collection measures. Chapter 5 gives suggestions for engineering voluntary payment of the judgment.

Even creditors who expect the debtor to pay voluntarily should create the liens mentioned above in Section B.2. If voluntary payment doesn't satisfy your judgment or the debtor declares bankruptcy, you want to be on record as a lienholder as early as possible.

5. Find Out What the Debtor Owns

If you don't already know where the debtor works and what assets he owns, use the routine asset-tracing procedures discussed in Chapter 6. That chapter covers debtor's examinations, subpenas and investigation of court files. Then you can pick and choose which assets to go after and how best to spend your time and money collecting.

It is often possible to find sources for payment even if that person is "judgment-proof"—virtually without assets and likely to remain so for the foreseeable future. This is discussed in more detail in Chapter 5.

6. Obtain Writ of Execution

You must obtain court permission to go after the judgment debtor's assets in each county where they are located. Chapter 7 tells you how to obtain this document, called a Writ of Execution.

C. Create a Collections Plan

NOW IT'S TIME to formulate your active collection strategy. This process depends almost entirely on you and your judgment debtor. In fact, it is impossible to uniformly recommend any one procedure for collecting your judgment, or even in which order the various procedures should be used.

For example, going after one debtor's wages may produce proceeds to satisfy the judgment, whereas going after another's wages may produce a bankruptcy petition. Trying to force the sale of a debtor's real estate is extremely costly, complex and usually requires a lawyer's help. Nonetheless, in some situations, this is the most cost-effective way of collecting, especially if the judgment is large enough to justify the incidental costs.

Collecting From Multiple Debtors

If a single money judgment has been issued against two or more defendants, the defendants are usually considered to be jointly and separately liable for the full amount of the judgment. This means that you are entitled to collect the entire judgment from a single defendant (separate liability), or parts of it from each defendant (joint liability).

With multiple defendants, it may be a good strategy to seek to collect from two or more simultaneously. Or, you might collect from whomever appears to be most accessible and most likely to have the money. If you collect more than an equal share from any defendant, it is up to him to go after the others for contributions, unless the judgment stipulates otherwise. If you inadvertently collect in excess of the judgment, you must return it immediately.

1. Make a Cost-Benefit Analysis

How do you assess how much time, money and energy you'll need to collect your judgment? The answer, of course, depends on variables peculiar to your situation and personality. And collection can be unpredictable: you may think it is going to be easy—then the debtor pulls out all the stops and turns your efforts into an ongoing paper chase. Or you may believe the matter hopeless, and a single letter can bring you a bonanza.

Keep these factors in mind when applying a cost-benefit analysis to your collection efforts as a whole:

- the size of the judgment
- the value of the debtor's assets, the legal accessibility of those assets and the possibility of the debtor coming into assets in the future through employment, inheritance, etc.
- the cost of collection methods and your ability to pay them up front
- competition from other judgment creditors seeking the same assets
- the time and energy you're willing to put into your collection efforts and
- any special circumstances affecting your likelihood of collecting.

2. Use Rating Charts

To help you choose among the collection procedures explained in this book, we have rated them at the beginning of the chapter covering each specific collection method. For instance, the chapter that covers selling cars contains the following chart:

COLLECTION FACTOR	High	Moderate	Low
Potential cost to you	X		
Potential for producing cash			X
Potential for settlement	X		
Potential time and trouble	X		
Potential for debtor bankruptcy			X

From this chart, you can immediately tell that this remedy can be very costly and moderately inefficient. On the other hand, you also learn that just going after someone's vehicle may produce a settlement, because of its coercive power. Knowing this, should you use this remedy? Suppose the debtor loves his BMW above all else. Simply by starting the process of having the car sold, you may get paid immediately, with no need to actually pursue the remedy to its expensive—and often frustrating—conclusion.

3. Select One or More Procedures

The best active collection remedies for most creditors are obviously those that carry a relatively low cost and a relatively high probability of producing proceeds to satisfy the judgment. Let's consider a couple of examples to see how this information can be used to formulate an overall collection strategy.

> **Example 1:** *Sheila obtained a small claims court judgment against her former friend, Fred, for $1,000. She wrote several demand letters, to no avail. Sheila knew that Fred was employed and owned a late model car and his home. She created a lien on Fred's home in case he decided to sell or refinance it. She decided not to go after his car and home because the potential cost of these remedies was likely to be greater than his equity. Sheila decided to go after Fred's wages, because she believed he was unlikely to leave his job or file for bankruptcy. Through the wage garnishment, Sheila's judgment was satisfied in three months, including collection costs.*

> **Example 2:** *Small Press, a book publisher, obtained a $5,000 judgment against Terry Wittgenstein and his small bookstore, Protos. Small Press knew that Protos did a brisk business and had a relatively extensive inventory. Owner Terry Wittgenstein owned a BMW automobile, a house and a 25-foot cabin cruiser, which he kept docked at a local marina. Small Press discovered that both the BMW automobile and the boat were heavily financed and that the costs of having them seized, stored and sold probably exceeded the amount of equity that Terry had in them. Small Press immediately created a lien on Terry's house, but decided not to force a sale, due to the cost and complexity of this remedy.*

> *Small Press then turned to Terry's business and decided to impose a "keeper" on the business, where a law enforcement officer stands by the cash register and collects proceeds as they come in. The fees for this procedure were approximately $60. When the sheriff phoned Terry at the bookstore and told him he was sending a deputy down to stand by his cash register, Terry quickly came to terms with Small Press, signing an agreement to pay off the judgment in installments over the next six months. Small Press knew that if Terry didn't comply with the terms of the agreement, it could follow through with the keeper and even have the sheriff seize and sell the inventory and assets to satisfy the judgment.*

4. Assess Likelihood of Bankruptcy

Keep in mind that a debtor has the option of filing for bankruptcy, even if she has filed for bankruptcy recently.[2] Once a bankruptcy petition is filed, all collection attempts must cease. Payments made during the 90 days preceding bankruptcy must be returned to the bankruptcy court, and you run a substantial risk that your judgment will be wiped out or paid off at a fraction of its worth.[3]

Obviously, you don't want to pursue such aggressive collection techniques that you push a debtor into bankruptcy. Nor is there any need to do so. Judgments last for ten years and are renewable for additional ten-year periods. If the debtor is having serious financial difficulties, it may benefit you to wait for his fortunes to change for the better.

Try to assess whether a debtor really is a candidate for bankruptcy or is just threatening to get you to back off. There is no foolproof way of telling, but generally the more established a person is in the community by virtue of employment or business ties, the less likely she is to go bankrupt. Collection attorneys often press ahead with collection efforts when faced with a debtor's threat of bankruptcy, concluding that there's no way to know for sure whether the threat is real. If you're pretty sure that the debtor will go bankrupt eventually because he owes a great deal of money to creditors, you may want to proceed full tilt at the outset, since someone else is sure to act if you don't act first.

Bankruptcy is discussed in more detail in Chapter 16, which covers creditors' rights and remedies in the bankruptcy court.

---

[2] A debtor can file a Chapter 7 liquidation bankruptcy only if she has not filed in the last six years. Chapter 13 repayment plan bankruptcies are always available to individuals.

[3] Some judgments, including those for child or spousal support, survive bankruptcy. (See Chapter 16.)

D. Special Situations

HERE ARE A FEW COLLECTIONS situations that require special mention.

1. Small Claims Judgments

Sometimes a judgment debtor is willing to pay up—but doesn't want to deal directly with the judgment creditor. A small claims court judgment debtor has the option of paying off a judgment directly to the court. The court can charge the debtor up to $25 for this service.

Once the court receives payment, it notifies the judgment creditor, who has three years to claim the payment.[4] After that, the state gets to keep the money. The court is responsible for filing a satisfaction of judgment. If the debtor pays by any means other than cash, money order, certified check or cashier's check, the clerk waits 30 days to enter the satisfaction of judgment.

2. Judgments Stemming from Auto Accidents

In certain circumstances, a judgment debtor's California driver's license may be suspended by the Department of Motor Vehicles (DMV) if the debtor doesn't pay the judgment.

- **90-day Suspension:** The judgment must be for $500 or less, arise from an accident on a California road and remain unpaid for more than 90 days from the date judgment was entered. After the DMV is notified, the debtor has ten days to pay or prove that insurance will cover the damage (CCP § 116.880, Vehicle Code § 16370.5).
- **Suspension Until Judgment Paid:** The judgment must be for more than $500 or for personal injury or death. It also must have resulted from an accident caused by an uninsured debtor's operation of a motor vehicle.[5] Suspension continues for six years, or until the judgment is paid or converted to a type of judgment under which payments are made in installments.[6] You cannot immediately renew the suspension after it expires. However, you can follow the suspension process again if you renew your judgment (Vehicle Code § 16379). (See Chapter 10.)

Remember that if the debtor needs to drive to work, license suspension may make her lose her job. The debtor could even become judgment proof or declare bankruptcy. If you intend to take such a drastic step—don't make idle threats—first negotiate with the debtor. You may be able to work out a payment plan.

To get the judgment debtor's license suspended, you must send to the DMV—or arrange for the court that issued the judgment to send:

- a certified copy of your judgment, or a docket entry showing the judgment
- the required fee—currently $20 and
- a simple one-page form available from the DMV titled Certificate of Facts Re Unsatisfied Judgment (Form DL-30).

Your court may have the Certificate of Facts Re Unsatisfied Judgment form, since it must complete part of the form. Or contact: Department of Motor Vehicles, Financial Responsibility/Civil Judgments Division, P.O. Box 942884, Sacramento, CA 94284-0001, 916-732-7119.

3. Victims of Crime With Restitution Orders

If you were awarded a restitution order in a criminal action, you can collect on that order as if it were a civil

[4]This is an important reason to keep your current address on file. (See Section E.1 of this chapter.)

[5]Unless the debtor had as much insurance as is required by state law, he is considered uninsured. If the debtor carried insurance at the time of the accident, and the insurance company won't pay the judgment, see an attorney.

[6]After three years, the debtor is allowed to have her license reinstated. She must file a Proof of Insurance (Form SR22) to accomplish that. If she doesn't pursue the reinstatement, the suspension will last up to six years.

money judgment (Penal Code § 1214(b)). Although probation officers are technically required to assist victims in collecting from criminal offenders, their caseloads usually don't allow time for that. Some victims' assistance centers are helpful, while others don't make collection of restitution a priority.

To collect, you must first obtain a certified copy of the criminal minute order or sentencing order, available from the court clerk at no charge. Present this certified order when you obtain an Abstract of Judgment (Chapter 4) or Writ of Execution (Chapter 7). Then you can collect using the techniques in this book.

4. Collecting From Married Judgment Debtors

Under California law, there are two categories of property owned by married people:

- **Community Property:** both spouses' income and most assets accumulated during their marriage.
- **Separate Property:** property that is owned by a spouse before the marriage, or accumulated after a permanent separation (even if the couple hasn't filed for divorce or legal separation), or property that is: (a) purchased during the marriage with separate property funds, (b) received by a spouse during marriage as a separate gift or inheritance, or (c) made into separate property under a written agreement between the spouses.

If your judgment is against only one spouse—meaning that the non-debtor spouse is not named in the judgment—be aware that the results of your collection efforts will be subject to these general rules:

- **Judgment debtor's wages:** You can always collect from the debtor's wages.
- **Judgment debtor's separate property:** You are always entitled to collect from the debtor's separate property.
- **Non-debtor spouse's wages:** The non-debtor spouse's wages cannot be garnished without a noticed court order (CCP § 706.109). For a debt incurred before marriage, you cannot collect from the non-debtor spouse's earnings if they are deposited in a separate bank account to which the debtor has no access.
- **Non-debtor spouse's separate property:** You can collect from the non-debtor spouse's separate property if the debt was incurred during marriage for food, clothing, shelter or other necessaries of life.
- **Community Property:** You can usually go after community property to collect your judgment. This is true even if the judgment is for a separate property debt, such as a debt incurred before marriage or after the parties separate. Thus, if you find out that the debtor and his wife own a grand piano, you can go after the whole piano even though the debtor's wife owns half as her community property share.

There are several exceptions to your right to pursue community property. The non-debtor spouse's share is exempt if the debt in no way benefitted the marriage—an issue that usually arises only if the spouses live apart. Finally, if the couple divorces, liens on community property will remain. For example, if a non-debtor spouse is awarded the family home as part of a divorce settlement, any real estate lien you have created will remain intact.[7] (See Chapter 4.)

5. Military Personnel

Active military personnel have certain rights that may restrict your collection efforts. See a lawyer if you're in that situation.

6. Debtors Under Conservatorship or Guardianship

Conservatorship and guardianship estates are under the jurisdiction of a probate court. You cannot use the collection methods described in this book. However, you may seek a court order from the probate court seeking payment of the judgment (CCP § 709.030).

---

[7] Community property is discussed in more detail in *California Marriage and Divorce Law* by Ralph Warner, Toni Ihara and Stephen Elias (Nolo Press).

7. Support Orders

The district attorney's office, or sometimes another agency, will provide free help collecting support orders. Unfortunately, backlogs prevent these agencies from getting to support collections in a timely manner. If you want an agency to take over the collection of your case, contact the district attorney's office in your county to make arrangements.

If you decide to collect your own support order, you may sometimes follow slightly different procedures from other creditors. Throughout the book, we point out such differences.

In addition to standard collections methods, you may be entitled to:

- use a court order that automatically deducts money from the obligor's paycheck
- suspend professional and business licenses if the holder is in arrears
- require the obligor to deposit a year's worth of child support payments in a special security fund
- require the obligor to post sufficient assets with the court to cover two years of support, if a payment is missed
- require an unemployed or underemployed obligor to prove he or she is looking for a job and to undergo job training if necessary
- file an action against a non-paying obligor for contempt of court
- be paid even if the obligor files for bankruptcy; once owed, support is owed for life, until paid in full
- receive 6% monthly interest on overdue payments, to a total of 72% of arrearage, and
- if the support judgment is in arrears, intercept the debtor's state taxes or lottery winnings. To initiate the process, obtain an Application for Notice of Support Arrearage and Notice of Support Arrearage from the court. Follow the instructions on those forms. (If you need more information, see *California Practice Guide: Enforcing Judgments and Debts*, published by the Rutter Group and available in most law libraries.)

Many of these collection methods require a court order. (See Chapter 23 for information on legal research, lawyers and independent paralegals.)

8. Judgment Against Licensed Contractor

If you sued a licensed contractor for a matter arising out of his contracting business, submit a copy of the judgment to the Registrar of the Contractor's State License Board, P.O. Box 26000, Sacramento, CA 95826. The Board will send a notice to the contractor, usually within a month. After the contractor is sent this notice, he has 90 days to pay the judgment, agree to installment payments in a written, notarized agreement signed by both of you (called an "accord") or post bond. If the contractor doesn't pay the judgment or file a judgment bond, his license will be suspended.

9. Judgment That Does Not Reflect Debtor's Correct Name

A potential stumbling block in the collection process is a judgment that incorrectly lists the judgment debtor's name or neglects to list all names by which the debtor is known.

Sometimes it is fairly easy to correct the problem, either by filing a document with the court (likely to be accepted in small claims), or by bringing a formal motion in court. You shouldn't have trouble correcting a clerical error ("Ham" instead of "Sam," for example). It's usually not a problem to add a fictitious business name (for example, "Dan Defendant, individually and dba Danny-Boy's Deli"). And if an individual shareholder is posing as a corporation, that shareholder can be added on—but a noticed motion is required.[8]

---

[8]See Chapter 18 for information on noticed motions and Chapter 23 for guidance on legal research. Sample forms are available in *California Forms of Pleading and Practice*, Corporations, Part II, "Alter Ego Liability" (Forms 41, 42 and 43) and *California Points and Authorities Law and Motion Practice*, Corporations, Part II (Form 43).

But your situation can get complicated in a hurry and will probably require a lawyer's help in situations such as these:

- You were aware of the different name but didn't use it when you filed your lawsuit.
- The new name reflects a change in entity—for example, a partnership rather than a corporation.
- The debtor gave you a false name or has informally changed her name.
- It has been more than three years since you filed your initial lawsuit.

A sample petition seeking an order to correct the name is below. It is unlikely that a municipal or superior court would accept this document without a formal motion, but a small claims court may—unless it has its own procedure.[9] (See Chapter 18 for information about preparing, and serving motions.)

Your name, address & phone

COURT NAME

PLAINTIFF	)	Case No.
v.	)	MOTION FOR
DEFENDANT	)	ORDER CORRECTING NAME
	)	IN JUDGMENT
______________	)	(CCP Section 473)

I am the judgment creditor in the above-entitled action. Judgment was entered on *(date)*. The defendant *(did/did not)* appear.

After entry of the judgment I discovered that the name of the defendant was incorrectly stated. I discovered the error in the following manner: *(state how error was discovered).*

The defendant was sued under the name of *(name appearing in judgment).* The correct form of the name is *(include all correct names).* I declare this is the name of the original defendant and not of a new and different party.

I move the court to amend the judgment nunc pro tunc to reflect the correct name of the judgment debtor: *(state all correct names). (Some courts may require documentation showing the old and new names, such as a DMV print-out, marriage certificate or court order.)*

I further declare that if the court grants this petition, no harm will result to the rights of anyone who is not now a party to the action.

I declare under penalty of perjury that the foregoing is true and correct.

Date:

____

Plaintiff's Signature

ORDER CORRECTING NAME IN JUDGMENT

It is so ordered.

Dated: Judge: ______________

[9] The procedure to amend a judgment to reflect a defendant's correct name(s) is specifically allowed in small claims court (CCP § 116.560(b)). In addition, a small claims court judgment may be amended to correct a clerical error (CCP § 116.725). Detailed instructions are contained in *Everybody's Guide to Small Claims Court*, by Ralph Warner (Nolo Press).

10. Collecting a Judgment Against a Public Entity

If you have a money judgment against a public entity in California, you'll need to follow special procedures to collect. Public entities include: the State of California, counties, cities, districts, public authorities, public agencies and any other political subdivisions in the state.[10]

As soon as you receive notice that the judgment has been entered, prepare the following:

1. A written declaration under penalty of perjury that specifies that you have a judgment, clearly identifies the public entity, states that you want to be paid as provided by law and indicates how much is owing. The sample declaration below contains all the required information.

2. A certified copy of the judgment or an Abstract of Judgment. You'll need to get this from the small claims court clerk and pay a small fee.

3. A small fee payable to the public entity (about $6).[11]

Take or send the three items to the agency you have the judgment against. By law, you're then supposed to serve notice of the filing on the judgment debtor, even though doing so is redundant. To play it safe, have a friend mail photocopies of the declaration and judgment to the public entity and sign a proof of service. Keep the original documents in a safe place.

The public entity must notify its controller, who will deposit the money with the court. Make sure that you have your current address on file with the court—otherwise, you may never get paid. (See Section E.1, below.)

Sample Declaration

I, (plaintiff's name), declare as follows:

1. *I have a judgment against the City of Los Angeles (Los Angeles Municipal Court case #11212).*
2. *I desire the relief provided by CCP Secs. 708.710-708.795.*
3. *The exact amount required to satisfy the judgment is (amount), plus interest at the rate allowable by law from February 16, 19__ until the judgment is paid in full.*

I declare under penalty of perjury under the laws of the State of California that the foregoing is true and correct.

Dated: February 16, 19__ ____________________
Plaintiff

E. Other Information About Collections

IN ADDITION TO THE BASIC PROCEDURES used to collect your judgment, you may need to:

- collect costs and interest on your judgment (Chapter 15)
- obtain a court order to assist your collection efforts (Chapter 18)
- transform an out-of-state judgment or support order to a California judgment (Chapter 19)
- renew your judgment (Chapter 20) or
- notify the court and offices where you placed liens on the debtor's property, once you have collected your judgment—or a portion of it if you agree to accept less (Chapter 21).

1. Court Must Have Your Current Address

Promptly report any change of your address to the court. This will ensure your notification if the debtor wishes to have a lien removed, wants to pay off the judgment, dies or files for bankruptcy. Also have the debtor served with a copy of the change of address form, either by mail or

---

[10]CCP Sec. 708.710.

[11]CCP Sec. 708.785(a).

personally and file a proof of service with the court along with your notice of change of address. We tell you how to have documents served in Chapter 22. Prepare your document on numbered pleading paper following the format in Chapter 18. Use the accompanying sample as a guide.

Your name, new address & phone

COURT NAME

PLAINTIFF NAME	)	Case No.
v.	)	NOTICE OF CHANGE
DEFENDANT NAME	)	OF ADDRESS
____________________	)	

To all parties and their counsel of record:

PLEASE TAKE NOTICE THAT *(name)* plaintiff in pro per in this case has moved to:

(new address, new phone number)

All communications to plaintiff in this case should be directed to such address.

Date: ____________________

Plaintiff's Signature

2. Fees and Deposits

Most collection procedures described in this book require money up front to cover costs, such as court fees, fees for serving papers and fees for making a property seizure (levy). Many also require an advance deposit to be made against the expected actual costs of making the levy. Because a fee or deposit is relevant to whether you should use the remedy, we often give an estimated amount in the text. Exact fees may be obtained from the levying officer (sheriff, marshal or constable) who assists in the collections process. Most costs may be added on to the judgment. (See Chapter 15.)

Fee Waiver Note: If you have a very low income, you may qualify for a waiver of some or all court fees and levying fees. Check with the clerk of the court that issued the judgment.

Legal Citations

Throughout the book you will encounter citations to California statutes. Most citations are to the California Code of Civil Procedure, which is abbreviated as CCP. Thus, CCP § 415.10 means Code of Civil Procedure Section 415.10. Chapter 16 of this book, which deals with bankruptcy, contains frequent references to the United States Code (USC). The citations are there so that you can look up the law for yourself if you desire. Chapter 23 briefly discusses legal research in the law library.

3. Forms and Court Documents

The Appendix contains most of the forms you will need to use the procedures discussed in this book. Make photocopies of any forms before you fill them in. Otherwise, you may find yourself empty-handed if you need to use that form again. Most of the forms are issued by the California Judicial Council, and are available from the court clerk's office or law library if you run out. We tell you how to obtain those forms we don't provide.

Los Angeles Superior Court Note: With the exception of pre-printed forms, all papers filed in the Los Angeles Superior Court must be attached to blue backing paper that identifies the parties, the court and the nature of the document being filed. Bluebacks—as they're called—can be obtained from most office supply stores.

4. Substitution of Attorney

If an attorney handled your case, you'll need to file a substitution of attorney document with the court. In this paper, your attorney agrees to withdraw from the case so that you can appear for yourself. Prepare your document on numbered pleading paper following the format in Chapter 18. Use the accompanying sample as a guide. Have the debtor served with a copy of the substitution of attorney. Service by mail or personal service may be used; see Chapter 22. Then file the original substitution of attorney and proof of service with the court.

Your name, address & phone

COURT NAME

PLAINTIFF NAME	)	Case No.
v.	)	SUBSTITUTION OF PARTY
DEFENDANT NAME	)	IN PROPIA PERSONA
	)	(CCP Section 284(1))
________________	)	

(Attorney's name), having represented me in the above entitled action as my attorney, I hereby discharge him/her and substitute myself in his/her place and stead.

Dated: ________________

Plaintiff's Signature

Consent is hereby given to the above discharge and substitution.

Dated: ________________

Attorney's Signature

5. Vocabulary

In this book we use the words "judgment debtor" and "debtor" interchangeably. We always mean judgment debtor when we say debtor. The same applies to "judgment creditor" and "creditor." We use feminine and masculine personal pronouns more or less randomly, preferring this approach to such cumbersome forms as "he or she."

We have done our best to define terms as we use them. Here are definitions of several terms that are central to the judgment collection process.

Exemption: Property that a debtor is allowed to keep, or receive a certain amount from if the property is sold. Exemptions allow people to keep a minimum amount of their property, even if they are in debt. (See exemptions chart in Chapter 13. A.)

Garnishment: When a regular payment owed to the judgment debtor by a third party is intercepted by a levying officer and given to the judgment creditor. The term is normally only used in respect to wage garnishments, where a portion of the judgment debtor's wages are diverted to the judgment creditor.

Judgment creditor: Any person or business that owns a judgment that has not been paid in full (or paid to the creditor's satisfaction).

Judgment debtor: Any person or business against whom a judgment has been obtained and who has not paid the judgment in full or to the satisfaction of the judgment creditor.

Levy: When a law enforcement officer (sheriff, marshal, constable) or registered process server acts under a Writ of Execution to obtain property or cash belonging to the judgment debtor for the purpose of satisfying a court judgment.

Levying officer: The law enforcement officer (sheriff, marshal or constable) who has responsibility in a particular county for making levies under a Writ of Execution. Most counties designate the sheriff as the levying officer. The term may also refer to the particular law enforcement officer (normally a deputy) who actually makes the levy (that is, travels to the place where the assets or cash are located and demands that they be turned over).

Lien: A legal claim against a specific item of property that must be paid before the property can be sold to someone else.

Registered process server: A private person in the business of serving legal papers. These people are also authorized to carry out levies on non-tangible personal property, but must work in conjunction with the levying officer for the county where the levy occurs.

Writ of Execution: A document issued by a court that permits a levy on the judgment debtor's property in a specific county.

Chapter 2

WHEN TO START COLLECTING

NOW THAT WE HAVE TALKED strategy in Chapter 1, you are probably anxious to get on with it. Not so fast. Strange as it may seem, the fact that you have a judgment in your hands doesn't mean you can or should immediately start collecting. Delays are sometimes imposed by law; and waiting can be a sound collection strategy. You can always use the waiting period—typically 20 days to six months—to prepare for your collection efforts.

A. Reasons for Delay

DELAYING IS GOOD for three major reasons:

- If you start enforcement procedures before the law allows, they will be invalid. In extreme cases, the debtor can sue you for damages.
- Even if you have a legal right to act immediately, it's often better to wait until the expiration of the debtor's right to set aside a default judgment[1] or appeal a contested case. You don't want to remind the debtor of an opportunity to contest your original judgment.
- The judgment debtor will be most likely to conceal assets around the time the judgment is entered. If you wait a little and let him relax, you may be able to collect more easily.

Exactly when you can begin your collection activities depends on when your judgment was entered.

B. Small Claims Judgments

IN SMALL CLAIMS COURT, wait 30 days before starting your enforcement efforts. The defendant has certain rights to contest the judgment, which are determined by whether the defendant showed up to contest the case.[2]

1. Small Claims Judgment After Contested Hearing

If the defendant showed up at the original small claims hearing and lost, or got a default judgment set aside and lost at a subsequent hearing, wait 30 days from the date the verdict is issued before you begin to collect. You

[1] A default judgment is obtained when the defendant fails to respond to the complaint in the time required. It is often possible for defendants to have default judgments set aside and be given a chance to respond if they had a good excuse for failing to file a response.

[2] For more guidance on small claims practices, see *Everybody's Guide to Small Claims Courts*, by Ralph Warner (Nolo Press).

cannot obtain or record an abstract of judgment until this time has elapsed (CCP § 116.810(a)). This delay gives the debtor a chance to file an appeal in the superior court asking for a new trial, called a "trial de novo." (Appeals are covered in Section D, below.)

2. Small Claims Default Judgment

If the debtor failed to appear, you received a Small Claims default judgment. Before collecting, wait 30 days from the date the clerk sends him notice of the judgment (CCP § 116.730).[3]

If the debtor files a motion to vacate (set aside) the judgment—a fair number do—you must be notified of when a hearing will be held. You must hold off collections until the motion is decided.

If the defendant's motion to vacate the default is denied, you can begin collection procedures. Although the debtor could appeal the denial of his motion and file papers to halt your collection efforts, it is unlikely—and even less likely for an appeal to succeed.

If the debtor's motion to vacate the default is granted, the court will either consider the merits of the case right then or, at the request of one of the parties, set another date for a hearing. If you win this contested small claims hearing, you must wait to see if the debtor appeals. (See Section D, below.)

Note: If a debtor who defaulted in small claims court asserts that she was not served properly, she must request a new hearing within six months of the date the default judgment was entered (CCP § 116.740). Because debtors rarely bring these motions (they are complicated and usually aren't granted), we recommend that you not wait for a full six months before starting collection activities. However, if you do wait six months, all potential thorns in your side will probably be eliminated.[4]

C. Municipal and Superior Court Judgments

IN MUNICIPAL AND SUPERIOR COURTS, you cannot collect until your judgment is properly entered in the court records by the clerk. Although you are then legally entitled to start collection proceedings, we recommend that you consider waiting until the deadline for the debtor to appeal the judgment has passed. If you start collection activities before the appeals period has expired, you may inadvertently push the debtor into filing an appeal that she might otherwise overlook. This is especially true if your judgment was obtained by default—meaning the debtor failed to appear in the case.

[3]Some judges are very lenient in allowing defendants who show up later to vacate the default judgment. Others vacate only if the defendant acts very quickly and has a super excuse.

[4]We say "probably" because courts tend to find a way to give a person her day in court if she really didn't know about a judgment, even if the time she discovers the suit is beyond the six-month deadline.

If you have information that other creditors are moving in or the debtor is selling a house, getting ready to move or taking some other action that will reduce your chances of collecting, you'll want to act immediately.

1. Judgment After Trial

If the debtor was present at the trial, he must appeal from most municipal or superior court judgments within 30 days from the date he is served with a Notice of Entry of Judgment, or 90 days from the entry of judgment if no service of the Notice of Entry of Judgment is made.[5]

2. Default Judgment

If the debtor wasn't at the trial, he gets 180 days to show up with an explanation that qualifies as "excusable neglect" (such as an unexpected serious emergency) and move to set aside the judgment.[6] When the defendant is represented by an attorney, judges are commonly willing to take the attorney off the malpractice hook and set aside the judgment. Even where an attorney isn't in the picture, some defendants may manage to file a motion of this kind and tell a good enough story to get a judge to set your judgment aside.

If you have reason to believe that the debtor disputes your version of the facts (even though he didn't file a response), you might be wise to wait until six months have elapsed before taking active measures to collect. Otherwise, the debtor might get an attorney to file a motion to set the default judgment aside.

There is a potential down side to waiting six months. Someone else may move more quickly than you and grab the debtor's assets or establish priority as a creditor. There is no pat answer to this dilemma, but here are some thoughts that may help:

- Consider waiting at least 30 days before starting collection efforts. The longer you wait, the harder it will be for the defendant to successfully file a motion to vacate.
- Check to see if the defendant was served personally with the original court summons. It is harder to set aside a default where there was personal service than one where the summons and complaint were left at the defendant's place of business or with someone at his residence and a copy mailed to him (since in these situations the defendant can always say he never got them).
- Think about what the defendant is likely to do. If the defendant clearly owes you the money and is not likely to go to court unless forced to, you're probably safe in going ahead with collection efforts.

D. What If the Debtor Appeals?

SUPPOSE THE JUDGMENT debtor files an appeal from your judgment. How you may proceed depends on which court awarded the judgment.

If yours is a small claims court judgment, wait 30 days, until the period to appeal expires. If the debtor files an appeal or motion to vacate, you must wait until the appeal is dismissed or decided in your favor before proceeding to collect (CCP § 116.810).

If you have a money judgment from a municipal or superior court, you may begin collecting while an appeal is pending unless the judgment debtor furnishes the court with an undertaking (a security similar to a bond) in an

---

[5]When a lawsuit is decided, the court normally informs each party of the date the judgment is entered (officially filed) in court records. The winning party is then supposed to prepare a document called Notice of Entry of Judgment and serve it on the other party to provide formal notice that the judgment has been entered (CCP § 664.5). If the notice isn't served, the judgment stands, but the time for the other party to appeal is lengthened to 90 days from the date of entry of judgment.

[6]In some very rare instances, a debtor may even have up to two years to move to vacate a judgment if he can show he wasn't served notice of the lawsuit and only recently learned of the judgment.

amount of one and one-half to two times the amount of the judgment (CCP § 917.1).[7]

There are both benefits and risks to going ahead when an appeal is pending. The benefits, of course, are that quick collection avoids the risk of losing any assets you know about now. They might be gone when you win the appeal (often several years later). The risk is that if you lose the appeal, you will have to pay back the money you collected, plus interest and costs incurred by the debtor as a result of the collection.

As a general rule, it is advisable to initiate collection efforts while an appeal is pending if you are willing to gamble interest and potential costs on the outcome of the appeal and:

- it appears that the appeal truly lacks merit
- you are concerned that assets currently available might disappear if you wait too long or
- other potential judgment creditors might grab all assets first if you delay.

Otherwise, we recommend that you wait until the appeal has run its course and your judgment is affirmed before you begin collecting.[8]

[7] If the debtor has an action pending against you, the court that issued the judgment can stay (delay) enforcement of the judgment (CCP § 918.5). This is normally done only if the court finds that: (a) the debtor is likely to prevail in the other action; (b) the amount in dispute in the other action is comparable to the amount of your judgment; and (c) you might not be able to pay the judgment in the other case.

[8] If you got the help of an attorney on the appeal, ask the attorney's advice on whether to start collecting your judgment while the appeal is pending.

Chapter 3

Behavior to Avoid When Collecting

THE LAW PROTECTS DEBTORS from undue harassment and public embarrassment by creditors. By and large, these laws are sensible compromises between creditors' needs and debtors' rights. Although some of these laws technically apply only to debt collection businesses and attorneys, it's best to follow them. Harassing a debtor is usually both unnecessary and counterproductive. It could even set you up to be sued by the debtor.

Because there are few things more unpleasant than having to pay money to a person who owes you a chunk in the first place, it pays to scrupulously honor the debtor's rights. Fortunately, for the most part, once you have a judgment, there is no need to contact the debtor, except to make a few requests for payment.

All right, let's get to specifics. If you want to know more about any of these prohibitions, consult an attorney or check out the law yourself in the law library.[1]

[1]The California laws governing debt collection practices begin in Civil Code § 1788. The federal Fair Debt Collection Practices Act, which regulates anyone who regularly collects debts for a living (usually collection agencies and attorneys) begin in 15 USC § 1692. If you're in doubt about a particular activity, look up the laws and judge for yourself. (Chapter 23 discusses basic research techniques.)

A. Communicating With Debtor

IF THE DEBTOR says not to contact her anymore, don't.[2] Given the number of collection remedies available, you seldom need to talk to the debtor if she doesn't wish to speak to you. If the debtor doesn't tell you to stop, and you continue to communicate with her, you may not:

- Threaten to publish the debtor's name as a person who does not pay bills. Here, publishing means "disseminate to the public." For example, if you list the names of people who have bounced checks to your business on the wall behind your cash register where customers can read it, you are in violation of the law.
- Suggest the debtor has committed a crime by not paying the judgment.
- Use obscene or profane language.
- Threaten to harm the debtor's family members, friends or the debtor's property.
- Threaten to do things that you have no intention of doing (for instance, selling the debtor's house when

[2]Use your common sense on this one. If the circumstances change and you are calling about something else (for example, you want to notify the debtor that you're going to seek a court order), make the call. The main idea is not to harass the judgment debtor over the phone or in person.

you don't intend to) or that you know can't be done (such as seizing 100% of the debtor's wages or having his welfare benefits cut off).

- Visit the debtor and refuse to leave when asked. If the debtor tells you to go away and you don't, you're both trespassing and harassing the debtor—and he can press criminal charges and file a civil suit for damages.
- Send the debtor collection notices that look like official court summonses or documents but aren't, or threaten to turn the judgment over to your "legal department" if you don't have a legal department.
- Falsely imply that you are an attorney or a federal or state governmental agent, or that you work for a credit reporting bureau or collection agency.
- Send the debtor a postcard mentioning the judgment or indicating anything on the outside of an envelope about the debtor owing you money. If you write to a debtor at work or anywhere else where a stranger is likely to open the mail (not a great idea to start with), mark it PERSONAL or PERSONAL AND CONFIDENTIAL to be safe.

Sample "No-No-Letter"

Date

Dear Mr. Defendant:

This letter will advise you that my judgment against you will stand for the rest of your life, wherever you go and whatever you do, unless you pay it off within one week.

You owe me $6,000 plus interest at the rate of 25% per year, and you're obliged to pay me in full before you make mortgage payments, buy food for yourself or feed the cat.

This judgment gives me the right to talk to your boss about you, and to let him know what a deadbeat you are. In fact, I've even set up an appointment to meet with him at the end of next week if I don't hear from you.

Why not just pay up now, before anything happens to you or your family? I'm sure you'd hate to see your microwave, stereo and car repossessed, or just happen to get smashed up. Furthermore, remember that I know where Barbie goes to nursery school.

I'm looking forward to talking with you soon, Danny-boy.

Sincerely,

Pam Plaintiff

Special Rules for Phone Calls

You may not:

- Call the debtor at work if the debtor or his employer tells you not to.
- Make repeated phone calls to the debtor or his family. You can only call more than once a day if it is necessary to reach the debtor. Obviously, if the debtor is "never in," there is some middle ground between legitimately trying to reach him and just plain harassing his family.
- Pretend you're different people on successive calls, so you can call again and again.
- Make calls very early in the morning or very late at night to the debtor's home unless you know he is a shift worker. (The usual policy is no calls before 8 A.M. or after 9 P.M.) You can call a business anytime during business hours, if other rules about contacting the debtor's business or place of employment are followed.
- Say why you are calling if you speak to members of the debtor's family or to employers or co-workers. The only time you can explain your reason for calling is if a person in the debtor's family brings up the judgment on his own initiative.
- Pretend you are someone other than who you are. You may use an alias, but you cannot suggest you are another particular person, such as a lawyer, member of the police force, local politician or government agent.
- Misrepresent the purpose of your call and cause the debtor to incur costs of long-distance phone calls or telegrams.

B. Talking About the Debtor

YOU MAY NOT LEGALLY:

- tell the debtor's employer about the debt or try to persuade him to urge the debtor to pay[3]
- tell the world how the debtor is a no-good so and so
- send around telegrams, pictures, photographs, cartoons, tapes or other materials to embarrass the debtor for not paying the judgment
- falsely claim the debtor has committed a crime.

C. Giving and Getting Information About Debtor

YOU MAY GIVE CREDIT or financial information to individuals and groups with a specific interest in obtaining this information. You may notify credit reporting agencies, credit interchange clubs, other creditors, and the debtor's bank or other lending institutions, unless the debtor has specifically asked you not to disclose this information. But stick to the facts you know ("I have a judgment against ABC Inc. which hasn't been paid for six months"). Avoid broad assertions ("Susan Smith is a hopeless deadbeat and pathological liar and you would be nuts to do business with her") and information you don't have or conclusions you can't prove ("He doesn't have very good credit"). If a credit bureau such as TRW should call you to verify the judgment, you can certainly acknowledge it. Just be honest about the amount due and stick to the facts.

---

[3] You can only contact the employer to verify employment or to initiate a legal enforcement measure to collect the debt, such as a wage garnishment. It is, however, common practice when trying to collect a judgment owed by someone on active duty with the military to contact the commanding officer and request assistance.

You may not, without the debtor's permission, look through confidential records about the debtor. This includes things like bank or school records, which are generally not open to the public. However, you are free to look through any record that is open to the public.

D. One Last Word

WE HAVE TRIED TO BE SPECIFIC in this chapter. However, don't get the idea that you are free to do anything we haven't listed as a "no-no." The examples above should be taken as a guide for the types of activities prohibited. As long as you are honest, reasonably sensitive of the debtor's rights, and interested solely in collecting your judgment in the least hostile way possible, you should do fine. Conversely, remember the old saying: He who seeks revenge should first dig two graves.

Editor's Note: On occasion, this book describes mildly deceptive but legal techniques used by bill collectors to obtain information (such as posing as a delivery service with a priority package to find out where the debtor works). The reason this is done, of course, is that there is often no other way to get the information. Nolo Press and the authors believe that most judgments can be collected without resort to deception of any kind, but that occasionally it may be necessary when dealing with judgment debtors who cynically use every subterfuge to avoid their legal and ethical obligations.

Chapter 4

Creating Liens on Debtor's Property

WE STRONGLY RECOMMEND that you create:

- real estate liens, whenever you are dealing with a debtor who either now owns or might eventually own real estate and
- business property liens, if the judgment debtor is a business that has equipment or inventory you can profitably go after.[1]

If the debtor files an appeal, you should wait until the appeal is decided before creating liens. You are prohibited from recording an abstract of judgment for 30 days after judgment is entered and while a small claims appeal is pending (CCP § 116.810). And for other judgments, creating liens while an appeal is pending could mean that you'll be stuck with significant costs later on if the defendant wins. See a lawyer if you're considering creating liens while an appeal is pending.

A. What Is a Lien?

THE CONCEPT UNDERLYING LIENS is really quite simple. A lien is a legal assertion that you have a claim of a specific value against certain property. Put another way, a lien changes your judgment against the debtor into a claim against whatever property is subject to the lien. Thus, even if the debtor sold the property, you would still be entitled to collect from the property.

> ***Example 1:*** *Joe Creditor places a lien for $10,000 on any real estate owned by Mary Debtor in Tulare County. If Mary sells her house to Fred, the lien will go with the property—thus Fred's ownership of the property will be subject to Joe's lien.*

---

[1] It is also possible to create a short-term lien against a judgment debtor's personal property (all property that isn't real estate, such as jewelry, stocks, pianos, precious metals, or computers). This type of lien is created primarily to prevent the property from being transferred to avoid collection, but also to protect you if the debtor files for bankruptcy. We explain how to create personal property liens in Chapter 6.

Example 2: *Arnold obtains a $2,000 judgment against ABC Rug Cleaning for damaging his Persian carpet. He places a lien against ABC's business assets. Prospective purchasers of ABC or its assets will learn that the property will come with Arnold's lien on it, and will probably require ABC to pay off the lien as a condition of sale. Again, this means that Arnold will have a claim against the property even if it is sold to someone as part of the sale of the business (a lien does not remain attached to property sold to customers in the normal course of business).*

It is important to realize that a lien is essentially passive—it doesn't get you your money right away. Instead, it gives you standing as a creditor to be paid from the proceeds if the property is sold or refinanced and the new owner or lender wishes clear title, which is almost always the case. Because real estate and business assets tend to eventually change hands—or at least serve as collateral for loans—a lien will typically eventually produce satisfaction of your judgment, including post-judgment costs and interest.

The Strategy of Liens

For both real estate and business personal property liens, follow these guidelines:

- It is usually wise to place liens on real estate and business assets, even though they might never produce proceeds to pay your judgment.
- By creating liens, you cover yourself in the event other creditors are in the picture.
- You normally must wait for the debtor to sell or refinance the property to realize any proceeds from your liens.
- If you place liens on the judgment debtor's property, you must immediately release them when your judgment is satisfied. (See Chapter 21.)
- Once you have placed liens on the judgment debtor's property, consider what more active measures are appropriate to your situation.

B. Two Types of Liens

LET'S TAKE A LOOK at the two types of liens a judgment creditor can place on a judgment debtor's property.

1. Real Estate Liens

Real estate liens are created by registering your judgment with the county recorder of a county where the debtor either owns real estate or might acquire it (instructions are in Section F below). This makes the lien a matter of public record.

A real estate lien may be created for any United States money judgment that is enforceable in California (CCP § 697.060(a)). That includes federal judgments and judgments from other states that are registered in California. (See Chapter 19.A.) It also applies to Workers Compensation judgments (CCP § 697.330).

There is no point in wasting your time creating a real estate lien if your judgment debtor is clearly unlikely to ever own real estate. But bear in mind that the lien lasts for the length of the judgment and can be renewed when the judgment is renewed. (See Chapter 20, Section B.)

a. Property Subject to Real Estate Liens

A judgment lien on real estate attaches to any real estate owned by the judgment debtor (whether the judgment debtor is a corporation, partnership, sole proprietor or individual) in that county at the time, and any real estate that is later purchased by the judgment debtor in that county while the lien is in effect (CCP § 697.340). For example, if you record an Abstract of Judgment in Alameda County and the judgment debtor later obtains title to real property in that county, a lien will automatically attach to that property.

b. Limits of Real Estate Liens

The fact that you have a lien against the judgment debtor's real estate doesn't necessarily mean you can get money out of the property. The property may already be mostly owned by a bank that holds a mortgage or deed of trust. If the bank forecloses on the property (which would happen if the payments on the mortgage or deed of trust aren't made), your lien only entitles you to what's left over after the bank takes its share.

Similarly, if other judgment creditors or holders of tax liens have recorded liens ahead of you, and one of these creditors forces an involuntary sale, you will only get paid after these "senior" lienholders, and your lien on that property then will be wiped out by the sale. In addition, if you record your lien first, a federal tax lien may have priority over yours if it was assessed first—even if the U.S. government didn't record a lien in the county's property records (*United States v. McDermott*, 93 C.D.O.S. 2102).

If the judgment debtor's real estate is her home, your chances of getting paid are further diminished. California law provides homeowners with the right to exempt from collection a portion of the equity in their dwelling (CCP § 704.720). This exemption, called a homestead, runs from $50,000 for individuals to $100,000 for elderly and disabled homeowners. Your lien does not attach to the portion of the debtor's equity that is protected by the homestead.[2] Thus, if an individual judgment debtor has $50,000 equity in a home protected by a homestead, and the property is foreclosed on and sold, $50,000 will go to the debtor rather than to creditors (exceptions are taxes, child support judgments and mechanics liens). We discuss homesteads in more detail in Chapter 14.C.2.

[2]Title companies routinely refuse to clear title until all judgment liens are paid, even though payment will necessarily have to come from the exempted amount. In other words, if anyone wants clear title to the property, your judgment will probably get paid despite the homestead laws.

c. *When Real Estate Liens Pay Off*

Although there are situations when a real estate lien may not result in payment of your judgment, often it will:

- **When clear title is desired.** At some point, the judgment debtor or someone who purchased the property from him will want clear title. To get it, all existing liens on the property, including yours, will have to be paid off. And if a new owner wants title insurance, a title company will not issue it unless the lien is paid off.[3]
- **When property is refinanced.** If the debtor wants to refinance the property or take out a loan on it, the lending institution will probably insist that the lien be taken care of.
- **If debtor dies.** Your lien will survive and remain on the deceased debtor's share of the property, with one exception. If the debtor owns property in joint tenancy (that is, with a right of survivorship) with someone other than his spouse, the property passes to any surviving joint tenants free of liens, including yours.[4] (See Chapter 17.)
- **If debtor declares bankruptcy.** A real estate lien puts you in the position of a secured creditor. This may help you get at least some money if the debtor files for bankruptcy. (See Chapter 16.)

2. Business Asset Liens

If the judgment debtor is a business—whether a partnership, corporation or sole proprietorship—you can create a

[3]There is no legal requirement that liens be removed before title to property is transferred or that a title company be hired to certify that title is clear. The lien simply remains on the property until such time as it is removed by the lienholder after the judgment has been satisfied. Thus, in some situations, such as transfers between relatives, the new buyer may take title to the property, liens and all. If, however, the new owner wants to transfer the property to a party who will need financing or who desires clear title, the lien will have to be cleared up. In the real world, judgment liens on real estate tend to get paid off sooner or later.

[4]If the surviving joint tenant is a spouse of the deceased, the property is treated as community property and the lien survives.

lien against some of its personal property assets. This includes tools, equipment, harvested crops, accounts receivable and valuable (over $500 unit value) inventory items (CCP § 697.350). The lien applies to any assets that are later acquired while the lien is in effect, as well as those owned when the lien is created (CCP § 697.510(b)).

You create this type of lien by registering your judgment with the California Secretary of State (instructions are in Section F, below). The lien lasts for five years, until the judgment is satisfied or the judgment creditor removes it, whichever happens first. The lien is most likely to pay off when the business is sold, since the new owner will want to acquire it free of liens. However, the problem with this type of lien is that it is extinguished if business assets are transferred in the ordinary course of business and the purchaser doesn't know about the lien—for instance, when inventory is sold to customers.

Since most types of business property don't carry title documents, it is very easy to sell business property without your being aware of it, and without the purchaser checking to see whether liens exist. Simply put, this type of lien is not as self-enforcing as is the real estate lien. Still, it makes sense to create one if the judgment debtor is a relatively large business with valuable personal property assets and/or inventory, because:

- If the business goes bankrupt, you will be treated as a secured creditor. (See Chapter 16.)
- If the business needs a loan, the lender may require the business to pay off the lien.
- If another creditor seizes the business assets to satisfy a judgment, you will be entitled to be paid in the order your lien was filed.

a. Property Subject to Lien

A judgment lien on business personal property attaches to:

- accounts receivable (money due the debtor as a result of a transaction involving her business)
- chattel paper (a document evidencing a monetary obligation and security interest in specific goods—such as an automobile lease)
- business equipment (machines, tools, computers, etc.)[5]
- farm products (crops that have been harvested)
- inventory with a unit value of over $500 (for example, most of the inventory of a car dealership would qualify, but only a few items in the inventory of a typical used book store would) and
- negotiable documents of title (such as a negotiable bill of lading or warehouse receipts).

The lien does not attach to the debtor's cars, boats or other vehicles registered with the Department of Motor Vehicles (CCP § 697.530 (d)(1)). It also does not apply to business fixtures that have been permanently attached to the office or building (a new roof, permanent walls, etc.), since these become part of the debtor's real estate.[6] But the lien does attach to all trade fixtures that can feasibly be removed, such as book cases, display counters and cash registers.

You can create this lien as an alternative to or in addition to any other liens you create in the course of your collection efforts. You can't, however, use this procedure if you have a superior court installment judgment, unless all of the installments under the judgment have become due and payable (CCP § 697.510(a)). On the other hand, the procedure can be used for municipal and small claims installment judgments, but the lien is only for the amount that has become delinquent, unless a court orders otherwise (CCP § 697.540).

b. Property Acquired After Lien Created

It does not matter whether the debtor owns business assets when you file your lien. If he later acquires them, the lien will attach to the new assets. For this reason, if

[5] If the judgment debtor is a sole proprietor, he may be able to exempt up to $2,500 in equity on the ground that they are tools of his trade. However, as we suggest in other chapters, your strategy should be to treat these assets as non-exempt and let the judgment debtor raise the issue.

[6] Things permanently attached to physical structures fixed on land, such as houses and mobile homes, are deemed by the law to become part of the structure and are accordingly treated as real estate. Real estate liens are discussed in Section B.1, above.

the judgment debtor has a long history of owning major businesses, it may pay to create a lien even if he does not now have a business. Then, if he does start or purchase a business, he might have to pay off your judgment as a condition of obtaining financing for his new endeavor. Since this lien only lasts for five years and is non-renewable, you may wish to wait until the debtor shows evidence that he might have these kinds of assets.

Example: *Frank owned and operated a business in which he built and sold small business computer systems. Emily bought a "lemon" computer from Frank for $8,000 and sued him when he refused to give her a refund. By the time Emily got a judgment against Frank, Frank had liquidated the business. However, Emily found out that Frank had long been an independent business person and had not worked for anyone else for over 20 years. Concluding that Frank would soon want to open another business, Emily created a judgment lien against Frank's (future) business assets. If Frank had not had this long history as a business person, Emily might have waited until Frank actually went back into business before creating the lien.*

C. The Zen of Liens

COLLECTING A JUDGMENT through the maximum possible use of liens involves little effort or expense, but a lot of patience. If you think in terms of years rather than months, a lien can become, in the words of a former judge, a "little money machine." One day, quite unexpectedly, it may produce full payment of your judgment because a purchaser of real estate or an ongoing business wants to own the property free and clear. As one collector puts it, your job is to outlast the debtor.

Throughout this book we caution against using overly aggressive collection measures that may push the judgment debtor into bankruptcy. The use of liens is the ideal way to minimize this risk. Of course, if you are looking for money right now, liens won't do you much good. But remember, impatience in trying to collect a judgment may cause its loss through a bankruptcy much the same way that impatience when trout fishing often spooks the trout, which hide behind rocks instead of snapping at your lure.

Then again—at the risk of overfishing a useful metaphor—if there are too many people trying to collect a judgment through liens, you may end up like the angler who tries to catch a trout while surrounded by others fishing the same stream. For real estate liens, it's a good idea to check the County Recorder's office in the county where the debtor owns real estate, and see whether other liens have been recorded on the debtor's property. (See Chapter 14.A.) For business personal property liens, check with the Secretary of State. (See Section F.3, below.) If other liens exist, don't count on being paid off through your lien. And after you create a lien, seriously consider pursuing one or another of the other collection techniques discussed in this book. If you want to force a sale of real property, see Chapter 14.C.

D. Lien Priorities

HAVING A LIEN can put you in a good position vis-a-vis other creditors. If other judgment creditors create liens, and the property is sold, creditors will be paid in the order their liens were created. If the debtor declares bankruptcy, your lien will put you in a better position to get paid.

The debtor's property is seldom adequate to pay multiple creditors. Accordingly, whether your lien was created first, last or in the middle can determine whether you get everything, nothing or something. This is true whether the judgment debtor owned the property at the time you created your lien or came into ownership at a later time (since the lien applies to after-acquired property). That's why it's wise to create liens even if the debtor doesn't currently own real estate or have normal business assets.

E. How To Create a Real Estate Lien

THERE ARE TWO STEPS to creating a real estate lien:

- Obtain an Abstract of Judgment for each county where the debtor may own or obtain real estate.

- Record an Abstract of Judgment with the County Recorder for each of those counties. (To find out whether the judgment debtor currently owns real estate in a particular county, see Chapter 14.B.)

1. Complete Abstract of Judgment

A blank Abstract of Judgment form is in the Appendix. Fill it in according to the following instructions.

Special note for child or spousal support judgments: If your judgment is for child or spousal support, you must file an Abstract of Support Judgment form. We provide a copy in the Appendix. The content of the form is essentially the same as the form shown below.

Caption: Follow the format of your earlier court papers. If an attorney handled your case, see Chapter 1.E.4. Check the box labeled "Judgment creditor."

Item 1: Check the "judgment creditor" box.

Item 1a: Enter the name and last known address of the judgment debtor.

Item 1b: Give the judgment debtor's driver's license number or check "unknown" if you don't know it.

Item 1c: Give the judgment debtor's Social Security number or check "unknown" if you don't know it.

If you check "unknown" for Item 1b or Item 1c, make sure these items really are unknown to you (for example, they do not appear on papers such as canceled personal checks, leases, rental applications or credit applications in your possession) and that there is no easy way to find them out (such as calling someone you know who does have the information). If later it can be established that you had this information or could very easily have obtained it, the effect of your lien may be destroyed if other creditors challenge its legitimacy (*Keele v. Reich* (1985) 169 Cal. App. 3d 1129, 215 Cal. Rptr. 756). See Section F.5, below, for instructions on amending your Abstract if you later find out you had access to the judgment debtor's Social Security number or driver's license number.

Item 1d: Put the address at which you served the judgment debtor with the summons and complaint in the underlying lawsuit leading to the judgment. This information can be obtained from the Proof of Service filed by you or your process server.[7] If you have misplaced your copy of the Proof of Service, you can get the information from the clerk of the court where you filed it.

Item 1e: If your judgment is against more than one judgment debtor and you want to impose a lien against the real property of any of these other debtors (generally recommended), check the appropriate box. Then list the name and last known address of each person on the back of the form. Remember to enter the plaintiff's name, defendant's name and case number on top of the back page.

Date and Signature: Fill in the date. Then print or type your name and sign in the spaces indicated.

Item 2a: Check this box.

Item 2b: Leave this item blank.

Item 3: Put your name here as judgment creditor.

Item 4: Put the judgment debtor's full name here *exactly* as it is shown on the judgment.

Item 5a: The date your judgment was entered goes here. Don't confuse the date of entry of judgment with the date it was filed or mailed, which may appear elsewhere on the judgment.

Items 5b-5c: If you renewed your judgment prior to its ten-year expiration date (see Chapter 20), put the date(s) here.

Item 6: Enter the total amount of the judgment (or renewed judgment).

Item 7: Leave this blank unless you obtained a prejudgment attachment of the judgment debtor's property (a complex process by which a plaintiff seeks to attach property so the defendant doesn't get rid of it before judgment).

---

[7] If your judgment was obtained in another state, you must have it properly entered in California to enforce it here (Chapter 19). Fill in the address at which you served the debtor with a Notice of Entry of Sister State Judgment, or, for foreign orders, the address you listed on the Statement for Registration of Foreign Support Order.

ATTORNEY OR PARTY WITHOUT ATTORNEY *(Name and Address)*: TELEPHONE NO.:

[ ] Recording requested by and return to:

Pam Plaintiff 415/999-9999
123 North Street
Berkeley, CA 94704

[ ] ATTORNEY FOR [X] JUDGMENT CREDITOR [ ] ASSIGNEE OF RECORD

FOR RECORDER'S USE ONLY

NAME OF COURT: San Francisco Municipal Court
STREET ADDRESS: City Hall, Room 300
MAILING ADDRESS: 400 Van Ness Avenue
CITY AND ZIP CODE: San Francisco, CA 94102
BRANCH NAME:

PLAINTIFF: PAM PLAINTIFF

DEFENDANT: DAN DEFENDANT

CASE NUMBER: 12345

ABSTRACT OF JUDGMENT

FOR COURT USE ONLY

1. The [X] judgment creditor [ ] assignee of record applies for an abstract of judgment and represents the following:
   a. Judgment debtor's Name and last known address

      Dan Defendant
      234 West Street
      San Francisco, CA 94118

   b. Driver's license No. and state: California #XXX000 [ ] Unknown
   c. Social Security No.: [X] Unknown
   d. Summons or notice of entry of sister-state judgment was personally served or mailed to *(name and address)*: 234 West Street San Francisco, CA 94118
   e. [ ] Additional judgment debtors are shown on reverse.

Date: February 1, 19__

Pam Plaintiff (TYPE OR PRINT NAME)

Pam Plaintiff (SIGNATURE OF APPLICANT OR ATTORNEY)

2. a. [X] I certify that the following is a true and correct abstract of the judgment entered in this action.
   b. [ ] A certified copy of the judgment is attached.
3. Judgment creditor *(name)*: Pam Plaintiff whose **address** appears on this form above the court's name.
4. Judgment debtor *(full name as it appears in judgment)*: Dan Defendant

[SEAL]

5. a. Judgment entered on *(date)*: 1/10/__
   b. Renewal entered on *(date)*:
   c. Renewal entered on *(date)*:

This abstract issued on *(date)*:

6. Total amount of judgment as entered or last renewed: $6,000.00
7. [ ] An [ ] execution [ ] attachment lien is endorsed on the judgment as follows:
   a. Amount: $
   b. In favor of *(name and address)*:
8. A stay of enforcement has
   a. [X] not been ordered by the court.
   b. [ ] been ordered by the court effective until *(date)*:
9. [ ] This judgment is an installment judgment.

Clerk, by ______________________, Deputy

Form Adopted by Rule 982
Judicial Council of California
982(a)(1) [Rev. January 1, 1991]

ABSTRACT OF JUDGMENT (CIVIL)

Code of Civil Procedure, §§ 488.480, 674,700.190

Items 8a-8b: Normally you will check Item 8a, as judgments are seldom stayed. If the court has ordered a stay of enforcement, check the box in Item 8b, and put the date the court-ordered stay will expire.

Item 9: Only check this item if your judgment specifies that the debtor can pay it off in installments over time. You are still entitled to an Abstract of Judgment and may use it to obtain a judgment lien on real estate. However, the amount of your lien at any given moment will correspond to the amount of money then due and not paid under the installment judgment, rather than the full amount of the judgment. In other words, as time goes by, if the judgment debtor pays you some money, the total amount due may decrease. If the debtor doesn't meet her obligations under the installment judgment, the lien will gradually increase.

Cost-Saving Note: When you record your Abstract of Judgment with the County Recorder, you will be charged by the number of pages. The Abstract of Judgment counts as two pages (front and back); however, it is only necessary to record the front side if you have a single judgment debtor (that is, you haven't added any judgment debtor information on the back side). Thus, you can save yourself a few dollars per abstract by typing or printing DO NOT RECORD THIS SIDE on the top of the reverse side of the Abstract of Judgment. Then you will only be charged for recording the front page.

PLAINTIFF: DO NOT RECORD	CASE NUMBER:
DEFENDANT: THIS SIDE	

You must record the back page if it contains information about additional judgment debtors.

2. Get Abstracts Issued by Court

Check with the court clerk to find out the correct fee for issuing an Abstract of Judgment—about $3.50. Make several photocopies and take or mail them to the court. A generic cover letter is included in the Appendix.

The clerk will first check the case file to make sure your figures and dates are accurate. Then she will sign in the space indicated, stamp your abstract form with the official seal, date it and hand the form back to you. This constitutes officially issuing the Abstract of Judgment.

Obtain separate Abstracts of Judgment for each county where the debtor could own property.[8] You can save yourself a trip or two to the courthouse by getting the necessary number of abstracts issued at one time. Since the information will be the same on all of them, you can simply fill out the form once and make copies as needed. Then sign each "original."

3. Record Abstracts of Judgment

Recording costs vary from county to county; they depend on the number of judgment debtors and the number of pages being recorded. It should cost you about $11 if you have one judgment debtor (plus $2 or $3 for each additional judgment debtor) and you follow our advice in Section E.1 above about putting "DO NOT RECORD THIS SIDE" at the top of the reverse side of the Abstract of Judgment. Check with the County Recorder for the precise fee.

Take or mail an Abstract of Judgment and one copy to the County Recorder's office for each county where you wish to create a lien. If the debtor may be selling or refinancing the property, or others may also be creating liens, go to the Recorder's office in person to speed up the process.

The County Recorder may first return your conformed copy, which has been stamped with recording information. Keep this copy until you receive the original

[8] You can record the same abstract in different counties. However, since it usually takes a number of weeks to complete the process, it's prudent to get separate abstracts.

Abstract of Judgment back from the Recorder, which usually takes at least several weeks. Then, keep the original with your other documents.

On the date the Recorder records your Abstract of Judgment, your lien will be placed on all the judgment debtor's real estate in that county. Ordinarily, the lien is effective for as long as your judgment remains valid (up to ten years from the date of entry of judgment and renewable in successive ten-year periods), or until you release it, which you are required to do when your judgment is satisfied. (See Chapter 21.)

Recording your abstract in one county results in a lien only on property in that county. Remember that when you record an Abstract of Judgment with a County Recorder it will create a lien against any real estate that the judgment debtor buys in that county during the life of the lien (CCP § 697.340). Thus, if the judgment debtor has significant contacts in several counties (perhaps she lives in one county, has a business in another county and a number of relatives in a third) you may wish to create liens in all three counties, even if the judgment debtor doesn't currently own property in any of them.

If you decide to create judgment liens in more than one county, be aware that lienholders have several ongoing responsibilities, which we discuss in Section E.5, below.

4. The Notice of Lien

After your lien is created by recording the Abstract of Judgment, the County Recorder will send the judgment debtor a Notice of Lien that informs her of the lien and gives her a chance to correct any mistakes that may have occurred.

Effect of Liens on Jointly Owned Property

How a lien on jointly owned real estate works depends on the form of joint ownership. To find out how property is owned, you can check the deed in the County Recorder's office. The property is held as a tenancy in common if it doesn't specify a method of joint ownership or if owners own unequal shares (for example, one tenant in common may own a 2/3 interest while the other tenant owns a 1/3 interest). Here's how the ownership affects your lien.

- **Tenancy in common:** Your lien attaches to the debtor's particular interest, and stays attached even if the judgment debtor transfers—or leaves in a will—the ownership to someone else.
- **Joint tenancy:** A judgment lien attaches to the judgment debtor's share of the joint tenancy and is still enforceable if the debtor transfers the share to a third party. If, however, the judgment debtor dies, your lien is wiped out (because under principles of joint tenancy ownership, the interest to which it attaches is legally extinguished by the debtor's death). The surviving joint tenants automatically take the property without the lien. A possible exception is when married couples hold real estate in joint tenancy: you may be entitled to a presumption that the property is really owned as community property.
- **Community property:** If property is held by a married couple as community property, your lien attaches to the entire property (that is, the ownership interests of both spouses) and will be enforceable against the property even if it is transferred to a third party. Basically, community property is property acquired by a married couple during their marriage, except for separate gifts to, and inheritances by, a spouse. (See Chapter 1.D.4, where we discuss community property in more detail.)

5. Continuing Responsibilities of Lienholder

As the holder of a judgment lien against the debtor's real estate, you have several ongoing responsibilities.

1. It is your responsibility to file any address change with the court from which you obtained your judgment. Then, if you move while the lien is in force, you can be easily contacted so you can be paid and the lien removed. (See Chapter 1.E.1.)

2. If you later realize that you knew or had access to the debtor's Social Security number or driver's license when you recorded the Abstract, you must prepare an amendment. Use an Abstract of Judgment form, but insert the words "Amendment to" before the title. Provide all the requested information, as well as the date, book and page where your Abstract of Judgment was recorded. Record the Amendment to Abstract of Judgment in each county where the original Abstract was filed. You will retain the lien priority of the earlier Abstract (CCP § 674(d)).

3. You must act quickly to release the lien once your judgment is satisfied (either through payment or settlement). Failure to take prompt action to release liens can subject you to liability for damages that result—for example, the failure to complete a sales transaction because of the lien. (Chapter 21 tells you how to release liens.)

4. If the judgment debtor has a common name, you may be contacted by other people who own property under that name to clarify that your John Smith judgment debtor is not the same as another John Smith. You must immediately and fully cooperate in clearing up the confusion and must provide your clarification in writing if it is requested. For instance, if due to a confusion of names, your lien was recorded against the property of the wrong person or entity, that person or entity may provide you with proof that he is not the judgment debtor and demand that you send a document releasing the lien. You then have 15 days to provide this release in a document suitable for recording (CCP § 697.410(b)); otherwise you could become liable for any damages resulting from continuing a lien against the wrong person (this is called "slander of title"), as well as a $100 fine. Also, the incorrectly identified person can request a court order to release the lien. (See Chapter 21 for how to release liens.)

F. How to Create a Personal Property Lien (Business)

TO PLACE A LIEN on business personal property, you must file a Notice of Judgment Lien with the California Secretary of State and serve a copy of it on the debtor. The lien will apply to existing and future assets of the business corporation, partnership or sole proprietorship. The lien lasts for five years from the date it is filed unless you collect your judgment or release the lien sooner.

Once the five-year period has passed, you can obtain another lien. However, the date the lien takes effect will be the new filing date, rather than the original date you created the lien (CCP § 697.510(c)).

1. Complete Notice of Judgment Lien

The Notice of Judgment Lien on Personal Property form and instructions for filling it out are in the Appendix. The instructions are straightforward and, except for two items discussed directly below, should present no difficulty.

Item 4F: Enter the total of your judgment, plus accrued interest and any post-judgment costs you have incurred. (See Chapter 15 for how to fill in and file a Memorandum of Costs and compute interest that has accrued since the judgment was entered.) When you are asked to release your lien, you can negotiate for any additional costs or interest.

Item 4G: Put the date you are signing the Notice. Make sure you mail the notice to the Secretary of State right away. If the Notice gets to the Secretary of State's office more than ten days after the date in this item, it may be rejected, and you'll have to file it again.

2. Filing and Serving the Notice

You must have the judgment debtor served with this notice—first class mail is sufficient. See Chapter 22 for how to have documents served by mail.[9]

---

[9] If the debtor doesn't receive the Notice of Judgment Lien on Personal Property for some reason, your judgment lien will still be valid.

MAIL TO:
Secretary of State
P.O. Box 1738
Sacramento, CA 95808

STATE OF CALIFORNIA
NOTICE OF JUDGMENT LIEN ON PERSONAL PROPERTY
(FOR FILING IN THE OFFICE OF THE SECRETARY OF STATE)
IMPORTANT—Read instructions on back before completing this form
REFERENCE: CODE OF CIVIL PROCEDURE SECTIONS 697.510, 697.550 AND 697.570

1. JUDGMENT DEBTOR (LAST NAME FIRST, IF AN INDIVIDUAL)
Defendant, Dan individually and dba Danny-boy's Deli

1A. MAILING ADDRESS OF JUDGMENT DEBTOR	1B. CITY, STATE	1C. ZIP CODE
234 West Street	San Francisco, Ca	94118

2. ADDITIONAL JUDGMENT DEBTOR (IF ANY) (LAST NAME FIRST, IF AN INDIVIDUAL)
--

2A. MAILING ADDRESS OF ADDITIONAL JUDGMENT DEBTOR	2B. CITY, STATE	2C. ZIP CODE
--		

3. JUDGMENT CREDITOR

NAME: Pam Plaintiff
MAILING ADDRESS: 123 North Street
CITY: Berkeley STATE: California ZIP CODE: 94704

4. ALL PROPERTY SUBJECT TO ENFORCEMENT OF A MONEY JUDGMENT AGAINST THE JUDGMENT DEBTOR TO WHICH A JUDGMENT LIEN ON PERSONAL PROPERTY MAY ATTACH UNDER SECTION 697.530 OF THE CODE OF CIVIL PROCEDURE IS SUBJECT TO THIS JUDGMENT LIEN.

A. Title of court where judgment was entered: San Francisco Municipal Court

B. Title of the action: Pam Plaintiff v. Dan Defendant individually and dba Danny-boy's Deli

C. Number of the action: 12345

D. Date judgment was entered: 1/10/__

E. Dates of subsequent renewals of judgment (if any): -- ; ______

F. Amount required to satisfy judgment at date of this notice: $ 6,050.00

G. Date of this notice: 2/12/__

5. *I declare under penalty of perjury under the laws of the State of California that the foregoing is true and correct.*

Dated: February 12 19__. (If not indicated, the date of declaration is the same as date in item 4G)

Pam Plaintiff
(SIGNATURE—SEE INSTRUCTION NO. 5)

FOR: ______

6. THIS SPACE FOR USE OF FILING OFFICER (DATE, TIME OF FILING AND FILE NUMBER)

7. ***RETURN COPY TO***

NAME / ADDRESS / CITY / STATE / ZIP CODE
Pam Plaintiff
123 North Street
Berkeley, CA 94704

NOTICE OF JUDGMENT LIEN—FORM J-1 (1/88)
PRESCRIBED BY THE SECRETARY OF STATE

FILING FEE $5.00

Mail the Notice of Judgment Lien to the UCC Division of the Secretary of State's office, P.O. Box 1738, Sacramento, CA 95808. (A generic cover letter is provided in the Appendix.) Include a copy of the Proof of Service showing that the judgment debtor received notice. Also send the fee (currently $5).

3. Effect of Lien on Business Property

Your lien on business personal property has priority over judgment liens that are filed later. However, if the debtor borrowed money to buy property and used that property as collateral, with the lender retaining legal title until the loan is paid off, the lender has a security interest in the property. The lender's interest will be satisfied before yours if it has taken the steps necessary to "perfect" its security interest in a timely manner. To do this, the owner of a security interest must file a financing statement (or UCC-1 form) with the Secretary of State. If the financing statement is not filed, your judgment lien may be entitled to preference over the security interest.

You can find out from the Secretary of State what sort of liens already exist against the person's property by sending a written request and fee (currently $11 per name search). Send a letter requesting a certificate showing all liens and perfected security interest statements for each business, and give the full, correct name of each business. The Secretary of State's office will issue a certificate showing whether there are any notices of judgment liens on personal property already on file. If there are, the certificate will also give the date and hour each notice was filed. This information could help you decide how likely it is your lien will result in payment of your judgment. If you have questions, contact the Secretary of State at 916-445-8061, or UCC Division, P.O. Box 1738, Sacramento, CA 95808.

Some potential glitches may affect your ability to collect through a business personal property lien. For example, once your judgment lien attaches to an item of property, it remains attached despite the debtor's sale, exchange or other disposition of the property. However, there is one extremely important exception. A buyer of the property in the ordinary course of business who doesn't know about the lien will generally receive this property free and clear. This means, for example, that the debtor can continue to sell his inventory (even though you have a lien against it because it has a unit of value of $500 or more) without legal consequence. However, if the proceeds of the sale remain with the debtor and can be separately identified, the lien continues on the proceeds. To enforce the lien under these circumstances you will probably need a lawyer. (See Chapter 23.)

G. Special Lien Situations

Several other types of liens may have a bearing on your collection strategy.

- **Mechanic's or materialman's lien:** This type of lien is created by someone who worked on a house or supplied materials and was not paid. For example, a mechanic's lien might be obtained by a carpenter or plumber. Due to time limitations, these types of liens are almost always created before a judgment is obtained.
- **Examination or execution lien:** A one-year personal property lien is automatically created when a judgment debtor is served with papers about a debtor's examination. (See Chapter 6.C.1.) A two-year lien is created when property is executed on. (See Chapter 7.C.)
- **Lien on pending legal action:** If the judgment debtor is currently involved in a lawsuit, divorce or other legal action, you can file a lien in that case. You would then be entitled to pursue any judgment the debtor wins—the debtor could not execute on the judgment in his favor until your claim is satisfied (CCP §708.440). It is easy to establish the lien—you can use the Judicial Council Notice of Lien form, available from the court or law library. Complete the form using the caption of the other case in which the debtor is involved. Attach an original issued Abstract of Judgment from your case to the Notice of Lien. The debtor and everyone involved in the lawsuit should be served with copies of both documents. The original documents and a proof of service must be filed in the other case. You may want to see a lawyer, especially if you wish to intervene in the other case.

Chapter 5

GETTING THE DEBTOR TO PAY VOLUNTARILY

YOU ARE PROBABLY READING this chapter because:

- you believe that the debtor is likely to pay your judgment voluntarily
- you want to preserve a personal, business or family relationship with the debtor and want to use legally coercive tactics only as a last resort
- you think that contacting the debtor to arrange voluntary payment will not result in the hiding of assets or
- you believe the debtor is judgment-proof and want to explore alternatives to cash payment.

If none of these statements is true, you may be better off immediately proceeding to the next chapter, where we get you started on finding out what assets the judgment debtor owns.

A. Relationship Between Judgment Creditor and Judgment Debtor

AT FIRST GLANCE, it may seem hopelessly optimistic to think that the debtor you have sued will now cheerfully pay you without further legal struggle. To understand why this is possible, let's take a moment to reflect on the basic relationship between judgment creditor and judgment debtor.

Before you obtained a judgment, you had only your own conviction that you were entitled to money. The debtor may have disputed the amount or even the existence of the debt. More likely, the debtor knew the money was owed, but also knew that without a judgment, you couldn't do much to collect it. Now, as the owner of a valid judgment, your status has changed dramatically. You have a legal right to subject the debtor to legal collection procedures for the foreseeable future (a judgment lasts for ten years and can be renewed for successive ten-year periods). And as long as any part of the judgment remains unpaid, you can prevent the debtor from having a good credit rating, which in the eyes of many credit grantors is the same thing as saying that the debtor is a deadbeat. As the judgment creditor you have a "one-up" position in relation to the debtor, both legally and ethically.

Although the debtor is "one down" in these respects, there's a good chance she has property necessary to satisfy your judgment.[1] And, as we discuss in detail in other chapters, by law some types of the debtor's assets are completely or partially exempt from collection. In short, the debtor still has a significant ability to frustrate your goal, and you are far better off if the debtor pays voluntarily.

To obtain voluntary payment of a judgment, concentrate not only on your strong points but also:

- be sensitive to the fact that certain aggressive collection efforts may cause the debtor to take refuge in bankruptcy, which generally causes a judgment to go up in smoke (Chapter 16)
- avoid illegal collection efforts that allow the debtor to invoke debtor protection laws (Chapter 3).

B. Ask for Your Money

ASSUMING YOU HAVE WAITED long enough to reduce or eliminate the possibility of the debtor appealing your judgment (we discuss these time limits in Chapter 2), remind the debtor that the judgment is due. Depending on the circumstances, you can do this with a brief letter or phone call.[2] If the debtor is likely to greet a phone call angrily or is a business with which you have no personal contact, send a letter.

The debtor should know about the judgment. Even if the judgment was obtained by default, the debtor received a notice of it in the mail. However, in our experience, the debtor will not always know the amount of the judgment, maybe because the debtor wants to avoid the situation and didn't read the court papers carefully. Thus, a reminder does three important things:

- lets the debtor know you are serious in your efforts to collect
- informs the debtor exactly what is owed under the terms of the judgment and
- opens a channel of communication with the debtor, so you can try to work something out without legal enforcement procedures.

Don't have overly high expectations that your first contact will produce immediate payment. It's unlikely unless you are dealing with a reputable business or individual who refused to pay before judgment because of a genuine dispute concerning the merits of your claim. Most debtors who have ignored your previous efforts to work things out, or have gone back on numerous promises to pay, will probably continue the pattern. It's best to view the reminder as simply an opening gambit in the negotiation process. You are notifying the debtor that you would like to work out a payment arrangement. Your tone should be firm, yet polite.

For example, if the debtor is a small local business, relative or someone else you know personally, you might make a call that goes something like this: "Hello, Fred (Mr. Smith)...As you probably know, I recently got a judgment against you in small claims court for $800. I'm calling to make arrangements for you to pay it off."

If the debtor is willing to talk to you, try to pin him down on what he's willing to do—for example, make full payment in the near future, make a series of installment payments, engage in barter or agree to some other arrangement satisfactory to you. If the debtor tries to put you off, come back with a counter-offer, such as, "I will accept part now and the rest in a post-dated check that I can cash in two weeks," or "How about a $200 payment each month, with the first check dropped by my office today?" Except in unusual circumstances, insist on being paid at least some money now, even though the debtor

---

[1] Sometimes, a judgment debtor's property is in the possession of third parties. We discuss how to go after that property in Chapter 10. Other times a judgment debtor has no property or income which can be legally collected. (See Sections G and H of this chapter.)

[2] Whenever you have a conversation with the judgment debtor, make a note of when the call was made and what was said. This type of documentation can be valuable if the debtor later accuses you of harassment.

gives you a song and dance about having no money. Even a small payment starts the payment process and thus gets the judgment debtor to decide that, yes, she will pay you the money she owes you. Getting a debtor over this psychological hump is extremely important.

Depending on the situation, you may wish to ruffle the debtor's feathers a little at this point and suggest that you "really don't want to start formal collection methods." However, it's often better, during your first contact, to see if a softer approach works. There will be time enough for heaviness later, if necessary.

If you write rather than telephone, consider adding a statement that you'd like to settle this amicably. If you are aware the debtor is having personal or financial problems that make immediate payment in full difficult, you may want to say that you are willing to take this into consideration if the debtor will get in touch with you promptly and work out a payment plan in good faith.

The following two sample letters illustrate this approach. The first is a brief reminder to a small business person who lost a judgment to another small business in a relatively routine contested matter. It is the sort of notice you might use if the debtor hasn't paid but has obvious assets and will probably cooperate. The second reminder letter assumes the same situation, with the very important difference that the creditor knows the judgment debtor is experiencing significant financial difficulties.

July __, 19__

Mr. Dan Franklin
ABC Company
1 East Street
San Francisco, CA 94110

Re: Racafrax Corporation v. ABC Company

Dear Mr. Franklin:

This is a reminder that I have not yet received payment of the final judgment of $3,500 which I was awarded in our contested court hearing on June 5, 19__, in San Francisco, California. Can you please send your payment now, so I can close this matter?

I appreciate your prompt attention to this matter, and look forward to receiving your payment within the next 10 days. Please feel free to contact me about arranging a schedule for payments if you cannot pay the judgment in full at this time.

Sincerely,

Pam Plaintiff
President, Racafrax Corporation

July 12, 19__

Mr. Jack Smith
XYZ Corp.
1234 Andrews Place
Oakland, CA 94121

Re: Racafrax Corporation v. XYZ Corporation

Dear Jack:

As you know, Racafrax Corporation has received a judgment against you for $3,301.26 from the Oakland small claims court for reimbursements, commissions, and other work done for you. This is a legal debt and we expect payment in full.

We understand that you have recently experienced some difficult financial times. While our strong preference is to collect our judgment promptly, we are willing to do so in a way which will leave you in the best financial condition possible under the circumstances. Accordingly, we are open to a regular payment plan to take care of this matter over the next few months.

In addition, let me say that we honestly feel our difficulty in getting together to resolve this matter prior to this judgment was due in part to your financial pressures. For this reason we are open to discussing working together on future projects, once the judgment is paid.

I hope we can work out a plan for you to pay off the judgment amicably. I look forward to hearing from you within the next 10 days.

Sincerely,

Pam Plaintiff
President, Racafrax Corporation

C. Send a Final Demand Letter

IF YOUR FIRST WRITTEN OR ORAL REMINDER doesn't produce a satisfactory response within ten days, be ready to follow up quickly with a more formal, written demand. Face up to the fact that your initial "good will and positive rewards" approach didn't work, and emphasize the arsenal of legal weapons you have available to collect if voluntary payment isn't promptly forthcoming. The very fact that you now display detailed knowledge about your legal rights may convince a debtor to pay rather than avoid you.

FINAL NOTICE

August 21, 19__

Ms. Susan Hernandez
P.O. Box 123
San Jose, CA

Dear Ms. Hernandez:

As you are no doubt aware, I received a judgment against you for $6,164 in the San Jose Municipal Court on June 19. A copy of the judgment was mailed to you by the court on June 20, but just in case you didn't receive it, a copy is enclosed.

This judgment is final. Accordingly, I hereby request that you pay it immediately. When payment is received, I will file a satisfaction of judgment with the court, which will close the matter. If payment is not received promptly, I will vigorously pursue my legal remedies.

As you should clearly understand, it's in your best interest to get this matter settled as quickly as possible. A judgment can go on your credit record and interfere with your ability to get credit. Also, the judgment gives me various legal collection powers, which include the right to recover my judgment from your wages (CCP § 706.010), personal property such as your motor vehicle (CCP § 700.090), and your house (CCP § 700.180).[3]

If I am forced to use formal collection methods, you will be liable for the costs as well as for the original judgment and post-judgment interest.

I will hold off formal collection efforts for the next 10 days to give you an opportunity to contact me about making payment. If I don't hear from you by then, I will begin the collection procedures allowed by law.

Sincerely,

Pam Plaintiff
President, Racafrax Corporation

To emphasize your tougher stance, start your formal demand letter with the words "Final Notice." Then go into the details, always remembering to stick strictly to legal rules. Don't threaten illegal actions or actions you don't plan to take. (See Chapter 3.)

---

[3] It is not a good idea to mention that you can go after bank accounts, since this could prompt the judgment debtor to change banks and hide this potential source of payment.

The accompanying sample letter lists a number of specific actions the creditor can take. Also, it notes the extra costs involved in formal collection efforts, as well as citations to the California laws authorizing these actions.

After a letter of this sort, you may get a phone call or letter from the debtor. Sometimes, of course, the debtor mainly wants you to listen to all of his reasons for not paying. Even if you believe you are being fed a line, it normally pays to be patient enough to open up communication with the debtor. We have also noticed that if you hear a debtor out, you sometimes get paid sooner.

Example: *Janice didn't appear in court when Jim sued her for nonpayment of some work he had done. After Jim got the judgment, he wrote asking for payment. Janice called Jim to explain in a long-winded way that she hadn't paid because she had had some objections to how Jim had done the project, and also because one of her big clients hadn't paid her (probably the real reason). Jim listened sympathetically but reminded Janice that she had never raised any objections about his work, either personally or in court, and that he was entitled to be paid under the judgment. After complaining a bit more, Janice finally admitted the sense of this, and paid up. Jim is convinced that listening patiently to Janice's face-saving explanation for the delay speeded up the collection process.*

D. The Debtor's Credit Rating as a Bargaining Chip

IF THE DEBTOR WANTS to keep a good credit rating, the fact that your unpaid judgment is a serious negative on a credit report will encourage him to pay. Of course, a few debtors may not be particularly concerned because they don't use much credit in the first place, or their rating is already so bad that your judgment won't make much difference.[4]

How does an unpaid judgment get in a credit report? Larger credit bureaus routinely check court records and enter information on newly recorded judgments in their computers. It is also perfectly legal to inform credit bureaus of the judgment—although some credit bureaus have a policy of only accepting information from members (who use their services regularly).

You can point out to the debtor that potential lenders, sellers of major property, potential employers and landlords commonly check credit records. If an unpaid judgment is on record, they regard it as a warning sign that the person may be irresponsible or may not have sufficient funds to pay them. A debtor with an unpaid judgment may find it difficult to get a loan, make a major purchase or rent an apartment.

Emphasize to the debtor that as soon as the judgment is paid, you will file notice with the court (see Chapter 21), and will be willing to communicate this fact to major credit reporting bureaus (whether they learned of the judgment from you or from their own monitoring efforts).[5]

Note on Judgments Against a Small Business: Small businesspeople, whether they be retailers, wholesalers, professionals, sales reps or whatever, are particularly dependent on their good credit reputation. Most routinely get goods and services on fairly generous credit, and many could not continue in business without it. In most fields, there is a strong and often amazingly efficient behind-the-scenes communication network through which businesspeople check up on each other. In addition, several national organizations, including Dun & Bradstreet, specialize in maintaining credit files on businesses. If you have a judgment against a business, you may wish to say in your demand letter that, as a matter of course, you forward a copy of all delinquent judgments to these organizations. However, do not threaten to publicize far and wide the fact that the debtor owes you money (remember, publishing a deadbeat list is illegal—see Chapter 3). You have a right to notify, and tell the debtor you plan to do so, all legitimately interested credit reporting agencies. You don't have the right to interfere with the debtor's business relationship by notifying customers and suppliers.

[4]For more about credit ratings from the debtor's point of view, see *Money Troubles: Legal Strategies to Cope With Your Debts*, by Robin Leonard (Nolo Press).

[5]If the debtor still hesitates, tell the debtor that you will tell the credit bureaus to remove the judgment from the debtor's credit file altogether.

E. Installment Payment Plans

LOTS OF DEBTORS EVENTUALLY TRY to work out installment payment arrangements. Typically, they claim they can't pay the amount due now, and ask for time to pay—often a lot of time. Use your best judgment in assessing what the debtor tells you. Do you think the debtor really is having financial difficulties? Or is he simply trying to delay paying you?

At this point, it's up to you to suggest a payment plan you can live with. Start by assessing the likelihood of collecting if you follow a more formal collection route. For example, if the debtor is working at a decent job and is unlikely to declare bankruptcy, you have the leverage to insist on fairly rapid and substantial payments.

Be wary of a debtor who proposes to pay nothing now, with the first payment to start in a few weeks or months. This sort of promise will very likely be broken. Also realize that a debtor probably expects you to be a fairly tough bargainer and will often make a first offer he thinks you will reject. You'll probably want to start your bargaining from a high end.

Of course, there is an exception to every rule, and if you feel the debtor is sincere and has some financial problems that will be cleared up soon, you may wish to wait a short but reasonable time. For example, a debtor asked one of the authors to wait three weeks for a first installment payment, stating a royalty check from her publisher would come at that time. The author agreed, sent a timely reminder and was paid the promised installment. Subsequent payments were also made, although it took a little additional prodding a couple of times.

1. Installment Payment Agreement

If the debtor agrees to make installment payments, draw up an agreement. One approach is to prepare a letter which says, "if you pay $___ per month, I will not actively seek to execute on the judgment except for recording an Abstract of Judgment." (See Chapter 4.) Send two signed copies to the debtor with the request that the debtor sign one and return it to you, keeping the other copy for her records. Keep the signed letter in your files, but don't file a copy with the court. If the debtor defaults on the agreement, you are free to immediately proceed to use the regular legal remedies just as if no agreement had been made.[6] Following is a sample letter.

August 13, 19__

Jane Lee
11232 First St.
Oakdale, CA 93221

Dear Jane,

This letter is to confirm your agreement to pay me the sum of $250 per month on the first of each month to pay off the judgment for $1,901 which I obtained against you on June 3, 19__, case number 854, plus post-judgment costs and interest.

As long as you make these payments, I will not undertake the collection remedies available to me under California law, other than recording an Abstract of Judgment against your real estate. However, if you fail to make a payment within five (5) days of the due date, this agreement will immediately become null and void at my option, and I may proceed with available legal remedies to obtain the full balance due.

Please sign a copy of this letter and return it to me in the enclosed envelope, along with a completed Income and Expense Statement.

Sincerely,

______________________	______________
Pam Plaintiff	*Date*

Agreed to by:

______________________	______________
Jane Lee	*Date*

[6] It is commonly better to do it this way than to add a formal stipulation of payment to the judgment. Formal stipulations need to be approved by the judge and, if the debtor fails to keep her word, you must obtain court approval to end the stipulation and initiate formal collection activities.

2. Income and Expense Statement

Commonly, collection agencies require debtors who want to make installment payments to first fill out a form under penalty of perjury that shows the debtor's assets, income and expenses. This statement is used by the agency to get information about the debtor and decide whether, and in what amount, installment payments should be allowed. It's a good idea to have the debtor fill out this type of form as a condition of any settlement. Then, if the judgment debtor defaults, you will have information about her income and assets which will support active collection measures.

If you want to use this approach, we provide a blank Income and Expense Statement in the Appendix. If the debtor doesn't complete and return the form, you have some indication of how successful an installment plan or other settlement agreement would be.

F. Accepting Less Than the Judgment as Full Payment

SUPPOSE THE DEBTOR SAYS that he is willing to pay you a portion of the judgment immediately if you will agree to drop your claim for the rest. Your first response may be "no way"; after all, you have gone to the trouble of getting your judgment, and you want to be paid in full. Slow down a minute. Sure you have the right to collect it all if you can, but people familiar with the process have learned the hard way that often your legal rights plus 75¢ will get you a cup of coffee. In other words, think before rejecting an offer that will produce at least some cash now. Examine the four variables set out below to make your decision.

1. The Likelihood of Collecting the Full Judgment

If the judgment debtor has income or assets which you believe can satisfy your judgment, there's not much point in compromising. On the other hand, if you are dealing with a recalcitrant and financially strapped debtor with no visible means of support, it may be a struggle to collect anything. In this situation, it often makes sense to prefer the proverbial bird in the hand to the possibly larger one that you still have to catch.

2. The Value of Your Own Time

When considering an offer of partial payment in full settlement for a debt, it makes sense to discount the amount of a full recovery by the value of the time it takes to get it. For instance, if you are a small businessperson and value your time at $25 an hour, and it ends up taking you a total of 30 hours to collect your judgment (remember, the value of your time can't be added to the judgment), you should sensibly subtract $750 from your judgment to determine its actual worth to you. Against this background, if the debtor offers to pay you $1,500 on a $3,000 judgment, you would probably want to refuse, since at your hourly rate you would have to spend 60 hours in collection activity before the debtor's offer would appear reasonable. On the other hand, if the debtor offers to pay you $2,300 on the $3,000 judgment, it may make sense to accept it, since it's easy to spend 28 hours (equivalent to the $700 shortfall) to fully recover a $3,000 judgment and costs if you have to use formal collection methods.

3. The Possibility of Losing More Money

If you spend money on futile collection techniques—bank accounts that are empty, cars with no value—you may end up throwing good money after bad, and coming up empty-handed.

4. Your Desire to Get the Last Dime

The basic collection approach advocated by this book is similar to the prayer that, roughly paraphrased, asks for the vision to seek what is possible, the courage to accept what isn't and the wisdom to know the difference. However, this basically pragmatic approach may not make sense to you if you are just so plain angry at the judgment debtor that you are willing to do whatever it takes to collect every penny owed you no matter how long it takes. You have the legal right to insist on full payment, and it's obviously up to you to weigh how much time and trouble you are willing to expend to achieve it. However, remember the words of one collections professional: "You'll have two choices. Either learn to take what you can with a smile, or go after every last nickel and be pissed off when you come up short."

G. If the Debtor Can't Pay

SO FAR, THIS CHAPTER HAS ASSUMED that the debtor has at least some resources to pay now, or a prospect of getting some in the future. But what about the situations—and there are some—where the debtor really doesn't have the means to pay your judgment and isn't likely to come up with any in the future?

There are three main ways to approach this problem. The first is to try to help the debtor find the money. The second is to see if the debtor can offer something besides money that you will accept as payment. The third is simply to forget about ever collecting and to expend your energy in a more creative way. In the next two sections, we look at the first two possibilities in some detail. If they don't work, you may have to admit that no payment will ever be forthcoming.

H. Helping the Debtor Find Money

SUPPOSE THE JUDGMENT DEBTOR seems like she wants to pay but sincerely believes she can't. We have learned that debtors often have more ways to pay than they originally think. You can help them identify potential resources.

Most of the sources listed below are applicable to both the debtor with personal debts and the debtor with a small business that's in trouble, though some are obviously more appropriate to one than the other. Some resources may be adequate to pay you in full, while others will help if the debtor is paying in installments. Obviously, also consider any additional likely resources not listed here.

When you first mention some of these possibilities, the debtor may resist. For example, she may not want to touch a particular savings account ("it's for medical emergencies only") or sell stocks ("they're for the kids' education and that's that"). Or she may not want to ask friends, relatives or a boss for a loan, because she doesn't want to take on more obligations or is reluctant to tell others about her financial problems. However, because you already have a judgment, you are in a fairly strong position to persuade the debtor to tap one or more of these resources. If you hit resistance in one area, suggest alternatives that might be more acceptable. If the debtor repeatedly turns down your suggestions, ask what other sources for payment she can suggest. The trick is to get the debtor involved in the problem-solving process, on the theory that if she really wants to find the money to pay you, she will.

This process can have an important side benefit. Even if your efforts don't produce results, you may have collected valuable information about the debtor's assets that can be used to actively collect your judgment.

One last word. Many of the suggestions that follow may initially seem inappropriate or naive. They are neither. We have learned from experience that human nature being what it is, there is no way to predict which suggestion will seem completely sensible to any given debtor. So, please suspend your disbelief and do not reject any of these suggestions out of hand. Instead, go through each one with the debtor until (hopefully) you find one that works.

1. Bank Accounts

This source may seem too obvious. After all, if the debtor has money in the bank, he wouldn't claim to be broke, would he? Leaving aside the fact that debtors can and do lie with regularity, others simply don't think of funds that they have earmarked for other purposes. They may have put money aside for a special purpose, such as the kid's education, a special trip, next year's Christmas presents or something else which in their minds is sacred.

Also, many people have thousands of dollars on deposit in retirement accounts (IRAs, Keogh plans) and other plans (certificates of deposit), under which the money can be withdrawn at any time, but at a penalty of higher taxes or loss of interest. Because of the withdrawal penalty, the judgment debtor may not consider these funds available. However, if you remind the debtor that those funds can be withdrawn, and perhaps offer to reduce the amount owed on the judgment to help offset any penalty suffered as a result of the early withdrawal, you may get paid.

2. Stocks and Bonds

Debtors may not think of securities as a source of ready cash. In fact, debtors sometimes choose to conveniently forget they have these resources. You may run into resistance, since stocks or bonds may provide a feeling of security. If so, you might suggest that the debtor keep the securities and use them as collateral to take out a bank loan—or better yet, a margin loan from the broker—to pay you.

Note: People who actively play the stock market often have large cash reserves on deposit with their broker so that stock transactions can be instantly carried out with a telephone call. These deposits are an excellent payment source for your judgment.

3. Income Tax Refund

The debtor may be entitled to a hefty income tax refund, which can be given to you as a relatively painless way of satisfying all or part of the judgment. Of course, this approach works best in the first several months of the calendar year, just before the refund is made by the IRS or California Franchise Tax Board.[7]

4. Loans from Credit Unions, Banks, Loan Companies

Credit unions tend to be liberal in making loans because they can often insist that the payments be deducted automatically from the employee's paycheck. Obviously, this approach only works with a debtor who works in a company with a credit union, or belongs to a credit union through a trade group or other organization.

A bank or savings and loan is another obvious source of a loan, particularly if a debtor has been a customer for some time. You might think that a debtor who otherwise has trouble paying wouldn't qualify for a bank loan. This isn't necessarily true if the debtor has some collateral, such as equity in a house. In some cases, a debtor may claim she can't get a bank loan because she already has one. The reverse is often true. If the debtor has a good payment record, she may well be able to refinance the existing loan and pay you with the extra funds.

If the debtor owns real estate of any kind, she can probably obtain an equity loan at a relatively low interest rate by executing a second deed of trust in favor of the lender. This suggestion is most appropriate if the debtor owes you a substantial amount of money and hasn't already encumbered the property with second or third deeds of trust. And there is even a small advantage for the debtor to do this, as interest paid on home equity loans is tax deductible.

If the debtor has trouble getting a bank loan, there are always loan companies. The interest is usually higher, but loan companies are often willing to take more risk in return.

---

[7] If you have a support judgment, you are entitled to intercept state tax or lottery winnings. (See Chapter 1.D.7.)

5. Credit Cards

A surprising number of debtors who claim to be destitute nevertheless have credit cards. If so, they can often request a cash advance on their MasterCard, Visa or other account, up to the limit of their credit. Then, they can pay this off on a long-term basis, by paying the minimum each month. Often debtors don't want to use their credit lines, but might if you convince them you are not going to settle for a hard luck story.

6. Insurance Policies

Some kinds of insurance policies—most notably life insurance—can build up a cash value. Then, if a debtor wants, he can cash it in or borrow against the policy at a reasonable rate of interest.

If your judgment is based on a tort claim, it's possible that the debtor's homeowner's or renter's policy will cover it. If the debtor overlooked this coverage, it's an excellent source of payment.

7. Bonding Companies

The debtor might be covered by a bonding company—likely if he works for or owns a state-regulated business. You can seek payment from that company if the judgment is based on a violation. Send a copy of the judgment along with an explanation of the business violation and a request for payment. If the bonding company won't pay, you may have to file a separate lawsuit against it. (For a judgment against a licensed contractor, see Chapter 1.D.8.)

8. Employer or Business Associate

Often debtors find their employers or business associates receptive to advancing them money against a salary or other money they expect (a bonus or pay for extra hours worked or vacation not taken). Some debtors may be resistant because they don't want others to know about their financial problems, but may be receptive if the alternative is a wage garnishment.

Be careful here. If you threaten to tell the debtor's employer about the judgment through a wage garnishment if payment isn't forthcoming, you may be crossing the illegal coercion line. Simply point out that if you have to actively collect your judgment, a wage garnishment will be one of your primary remedies and that the employer will find out about the judgment sooner or later.

9. Friends or Relatives

Family or close friends may be another good source of funds for debtors, although many debtors resist the idea, primarily out of pride. While understandable, this reaction often doesn't make much sense. Think of it from your perspective. Don't you feel good when a truly good friend or perhaps one of your children or a close relative asks you for needed help which you can give? If your answer is "yes," perhaps you can think of a way to help the debtor overcome his reluctance to ask his loved ones for help. If you can, both you and the debtor will be better off in the long run.

10. Sale of Household or Office Goods

A sale of unwanted household or office items can be an excellent and often almost painless way for the debtor to raise funds. A successful garage sale can raise several hundred dollars or more. One way to approach the debtor about raising money by selling things is to ask questions about what the person doesn't really need and might most easily sell. For instance, you might say something like, "Is there some older office equipment you aren't using very much, since you bought the new computer?"

Or if you are already sure a particular item is essentially surplus, you might suggest, "Why don't you put your video camera up for sale? You aren't using it anymore anyway. If you sell it now, you'll still get good value, but if you hold it a year or two, it will lose most of its value."

Barter Note: You may be interested in acquiring the debtor's property for your own use. We discuss that option in Section I, below.

11. Investors or New Business Partners

If the debtor has a basically sound business that is struggling, bringing in a limited partner or other investor is an obvious way to raise funds. And the additional capital might even give it an infusion of management skill.

If the debtor is receptive, and you know something about his business, you may even be able to suggest ways for him to do this. Help him see that even if he has been turned down for a loan, he may be able to raise money if he is willing to give an investor a share of the business. People are often willing to take a bigger risk if they stand to make a profit if the business does well. For example, personal friends or others in the same type of business who might not agree to make a simple loan might be willing to extend an investment, if they think the business has a chance of making them some money.[8]

[8] *How to Write a Business Plan*, by Mike McKeever (Nolo Press) gives information on how to organize and write a business plan for potential investors.

12. Business Income

Periodic polite personal reminders are also helpful if the judgment debtor gets regular income from a business. For example, one of the authors got a judgment against a former business associate (let's call him Farley) who genuinely was having financial difficulties. The author agreed to accept a small payment each month. After Farley made one payment and missed one, the author ran into him at a business networking event, spoke to him privately and reminded him of their agreement. Embarrassed, Farley paid the author a small amount on the spot, and reconfirmed the agreement, even though his financial problems hadn't eased. Farley did this for several months, then dropped out of sight for about a year. When he resurfaced, the author once again politely reminded him of the debt. Farley explained that his consulting business was kaput and he had no income. After thinking about this plight, the author got an idea about a job he might bid on and called him. Farley made the bid, got the job, thanked the author for helping and resumed making payments. We think the moral of this story is not only that it often produces better results to help people who are down on their luck, rather than simply dunning them, but that it almost always pays in the long run to stay in touch with people who owe you significant amounts of money.

13. Helping the Debtor Find Work

If the debtor is unemployed, a good way to get paid is to help her find work. If you have a business, you may even want to hire the person in exchange for a promise to repay you (this is obviously only a viable option where you and the debtor have a decent relationship, and the debtor has skills you can use). If you hire the judgment debtor, it's best to pay her what you would anyone else doing that job, but insist that you be paid a reasonable amount each pay period as an installment payment against the debt (usually 10% to 20% of the person's total pay is best for all concerned).

If the debtor has an independent business and you can make use of her services, negotiate to pay a lower than normal rate and subtract (from the judgment) the difference between what you would normally expect to pay and this artificially low rate. If you do this, be sure to put your agreement in writing. (See Section I, below.)

Another possible source of money is for the debtor to take on an extra part-time job. If the debtor is receptive but needs help with job hunting, offer suggestions. Perhaps you can help the debtor find extra work that will not only get you paid, but benefit him in the long run. If so, two good things have happened.

14. Turning Hobbies into Cash

If the debtor has a hobby, he may be able to get money from it. For example, a person who is a wiz with cameras might get jobs photographing parties or weddings. Someone who has a way with dogs might offer a dog sitting service. The possibilities are almost endless. And one nice thing is that if the debtor does develop a business from a hobby, he will not only be able to pay you, but his life may improve in the process.

15. Rental Income

Some debtors may be able to rent out part of their house or business building. Obviously, if the debtor leases or owns good business space, there is usually a way to lease or sublease part of it. As a judgment creditor with the power to use much more coercive collection techniques if need be, you are in a good position to insist that the debtor try this.

I. Barter for Goods or Services

IF THE DEBTOR IS NOT LIKELY to have money to pay you a meaningful amount any time soon, try to think of a nonmonetary way he can satisfy your judgment. The most obvious way is for you to accept goods or services instead of money. It seems strange today, but it wasn't too long ago that entire communities operated on a barter rather than cash basis. A carpenter might have little or no cash income but could and did trade carpentry work for food, shelter and even medical care. There is no reason why, when push comes to shove, you shouldn't encourage the debtor to embrace barter.

Perhaps the debtor owns some equipment or furniture that you could use. In some instances, the item may not be a priority on your wish list, but you may know someone you can sell or give it to. For example, we know a creditor who was owed money by a former client. The client had to move several thousand miles away, and suggested that he take her now surplus furniture as full payment. At first the creditor refused, not having any use for the somewhat battered furniture. Then, realizing his daughter was planning to move into her first apartment, and could use most everything, he agreed. It wasn't as good as full payment, but it was a lot better than getting nothing from a person who was likely to be judgment-proof for years to come.

If you consider barter, be flexible. Spend some time thinking about what the debtor reasonably can offer you that you are willing to accept. Agricultural produce, canned goods, artworks, handicrafts, camping gear, custom-made furniture (that rolltop desk you've been wanting) and sports, electronic or photographic equipment are among the many items a debtor may be able to offer you. If you have a business, maybe the debtor has some property which you could use, such as a table, desk, file cabinet, old computer or typewriter.

Even if the judgment debtor doesn't have goods you wish to barter for, he may be able to provide any number of valuable services. These could be anything from lessons (for example, music, art, computer repair or tennis) to home or car repairs. Here we are talking about specific, finite services. We recommend, however, that you not have the judgment debtor work for you on an ongoing basis without pay.

It's usually not a good idea to take a debtor's property with the idea of selling it and crediting the debtor with the proceeds. The price you get for the property will probably be far less than the debtor expects, which means you may have a new legal hassle on your hands. Either agree to accept specific property in exchange for a specific credit, or insist that the debtor sell the property and give you the proceeds.

If you come to an agreement, spell out what the debtor will do in order to satisfy all or part of the judgment. Be as precise as possible in describing the goods or services to be received as barter. Otherwise, the judgment debtor may interpret her obligations under the agreement differently than you do. Also, specify what happens in the event the agreement isn't fulfilled, so the debtor clearly understands that you will proceed against him legally if he doesn't comply with the arrangement you have reached. The agreement can specify, however, that the value of a part performance will be credited against the judgment. Finally, the debtor should indicate that he has entered into this agreement knowingly and freely and fully understands what the agreement says.

You can prepare your own agreement using the accompanying sample as a guide. When, when the debtor fulfills his part of the bargain, it's your legal obligation to file a satisfaction of judgment with the court. (See Chapter 21.)

Sample Agreement For Payment By Barter

Judgment Creditor Pam Plaintiff ("Judgment Creditor") and Judgment Debtor Dan Defendant ("Judgment Debtor") agree as follows:

1. *The judgment referred to in this agreement was obtained by Judgment Creditor against Judgment Debtor, entered in the San Francisco Small Claims Court on April 23, 19__, Case # 123, plus post-judgment costs which have been incurred, and accrued interest.*
2. *Judgment Debtor agrees to provide the following goods and services to Judgment Creditor, valued at a total of $700:*
   a. *One hour-long Jujitsu lesson per week for 10 consecutive weeks, beginning September 6, 19__ ($250, or $25 per lesson).*
   b. *One used Yamaha electronic keyboard, model Y315 ($200).*
   c. *One used oak computer work station ($250).*
3. *In consideration for making this agreement, Judgment Debtor understands that this judgment held against him/her by Judgment Creditor will be considered [ ] fully satisfied, or [X] satisfied for the amount described in paragraph 2.*
4. *Judgment Debtor understands that if he/she fails to deliver the goods and/or services described in paragraph 2 within one week of the date Judgment Debtor signs this agreement, this agreement will immediately become null and void at the Judgment Creditor's option, and the judgment can be enforced against Judgment Debtor to obtain the balance due on the judgment, less the value of any item or part of any item described in paragraph 2 that Judgment Debtor has already paid or provided to Judgment Creditor.*

Judgment Debtor and Judgment Creditor have entered into this agreement knowingly and freely, and fully agree to its terms.

Agreed to by:

______________________	__________
Judgment Creditor	*Date*
______________________	__________
Judgment Debtor	*Date*

Chapter 6

DETERMINING WHAT THE DEBTOR OWNS

IF THE JUDGMENT DEBTOR IS UNWILLING to pay your judgment, your main legal recourse (aside from creating liens as discussed in Chapter 4) is to go after the debtor's assets. It is often not that difficult if the judgment debtor has assets that can be seized, and you know where they are.

But what if you have no idea what the debtor owns? In this chapter, we explain several procedures you can use to discover a broad range of information about the debtor's assets, income and expenses so you can better judge where to direct your collection efforts. Later chapters provide methods for locating specific types of assets.

IF YOU WANT TO FIND	GO TO:
Bank and deposit accounts	Chapter 8.A
Where the debtor works	Chapter 9.E
Debts owed by others	Chapter 10.B
Motor vehicles	Chapter 12.B
Real estate	Chapter 14.B

A. Debtor's Statement of Assets (Small Claims)

IF YOUR JUDGMENT WAS ISSUED by a small claims court, the clerk should have given the debtor a form to complete and return to you within 30 days.[1] Unfortunately, most debtors don't complete this Statement of Assets form. You are entitled to ask the court to find the debtor in contempt of court for failing to complete and return it to you. Any sanctions, arrest fees or attorneys' fees may be added on to the principal of the judgment (CCP § 116.830(d)). Check with the small claims advisor or clerk about the procedure.

If you received a completed Judgment Debtor's Statement of Assets, you'll have information about the debtor's occupation, employer, pay, bank accounts, vehicles and other personal property.

[1] If the debtor files an unsuccessful motion to vacate or an unsuccessful appeal, he must return the form to you within 30 days of the date the court provides him with notice of the outcome.

B. Court Records

IF THE DEBTOR WAS RECENTLY INVOLVED in another lawsuit, has divorced or gone through a child or spousal support modification proceeding, the court file probably contains valuable information about her assets.[2]

You have a right to see these court files, which are public records. To do so, you usually must visit the court clerk's office in person. In many courts, the latest records are indexed on a computer printout or microfiche, so they're especially easy to find. Just look under the alphabetical listings for both the defendant and plaintiff by year, or by month for the more recent cases. If you know the debtor has used other names, check them too. With older cases, you may have to look through handwritten record books.[3]

If you find the debtor's name, the full listing will include the name of the opposing party in the case followed by the court docket or case number. Write down this number and give it to the court clerk to obtain the case file. You'll be able to review everything in the file—except in the rare circumstance when a document is sealed. You can ask the clerk to copy anything available for public viewing, or make copies yourself if the court provides a self-service copier. You cannot, however, take the court file or any documents in it out of the clerk's office for copying elsewhere.

C. The Debtor's Examination

UNDER CALIFORNIA LAW, as the judgment creditor, you may require the judgment debtor to appear at the courthouse and answer questions about his income and assets (CCP § 708.110(a)). This procedure is called a "debtor's examination." Its purpose is to provide you with means to find out how your judgment might be satisfied.

To set up this examination, you fill out a form called Application and Order for Appearance and Examination, have a copy personally served on the judgment debtor, and file the original with the court. The judgment debtor is then supposed to show up at court and answer your questions. If he is uncooperative, you can request the supervising official to order him to cooperate. If he doesn't show up, the supervising official can issue a bench warrant or order him to court to explain why he shouldn't be held in contempt of court.

You may also require the debtor to bring documents for your examination, such as bank account passbooks and statements, stock certificates, deeds and others. This is done by obtaining a Subpena Duces Tecum from the court and having the subpena served on the judgment debtor as well.

You can order third parties to appear at a debtor's examination if you have reason to believe they possess personal property belonging to the judgment debtor or owe the debtor at least $250. You may question third parties or examine documents related to the debtor's assets (CCP § 708.120 (a)).

Interrogatory Note: You may, instead of conducting a debtor's examination, send written questions (interrogatories) to the debtor (CCP § 708.020). The procedure costs very little and is easier than conducting a debtor's examination. The down side is that you help the debtor inventory his assets and give him time to figure out how to hide his non-exempt assets. Collection professionals almost never use interrogatories, since debtors seldom respond to them. Because this procedure is unlikely to produce useful results, we recommend against its use and don't go into it further. If you want to use interrogatories, see Chapter 23.A, where we tell you how to do your own research. Or, if the debtor is willing to cooperate, you can send an informal Income and Expense Statement for him to complete and return to you. That is covered in Chapter 5.E.2.

---

[2] In family disputes involving property and support, parties are required to submit detailed income and expense statements that give information about each party's financial affairs. And the judgment often specifies property that each party receives as a result of the divorce. Even if the parties agreed on all issues, their agreement will be in written form and incorporated into the final judgment of divorce.

[3] If a case is still open, you may be entitled to a lien (see Chapter 4.G).

1. Creation of Personal Property Lien

There is a potential side benefit to ordering the judgment debtor in for a debtor's examination. The law establishes a lien (see Chapter 4 for an explanation of liens) on the debtor's personal property the instant the Application and Order for Appearance and Examination is served on him (CCP § 708.110(d)). This examination lien attaches to all the debtor's non-exempt personal property[4] and remains for a year. The lien can be renewed by personally serving a new Application and Order for Appearance and Examination.

If the debtor sells or gives away personal property subject to this lien, you may still be able to reach the personal property if you can track it down.[5] The lien may also give you an advantage over other creditors should the judgment debtor file for bankruptcy more than 90 days after the lien takes effect. (See Chapter 16.)

2. Determine Court for Examination

The proper court for conducting the debtor's examination is usually, but not always, the court in which the money judgment was entered (in legal slang, the "judgment court"). You can use the judgment court if the judgment debtor:

- lives or has a place of business in the same county as the judgment court or
- lives or has a place of business within 150 miles of the judgment court.

If neither of these conditions applies, you must move the examination to a court in the same county as the debtor's residence or place of business.

How To Transfer Examination to Different Court

To conduct a debtor's examination in a different county from the judgment court, take the following steps (CCP § 708.160):

- Find the court in the county where the debtor lives or has a place of business.
- Fill out the Application and Order for Appearance and Examination (see Section C.4, below).
- Obtain an Abstract of Judgment from the judgment court (see Chapter 4).
- Prepare a declaration showing that the judgment debtor lives or has a place of business in the county where the Order of Examination is being sought.[6]
- Mail or take all of these papers to the new court along with the appropriate filing fee (currently $12 for the Abstract and $14 for the Application and Order of Examination).

That court is then authorized to issue the order. Once this is done, follow instructions in this chapter for having the order served and conducting the examination.

Note: People in the collections trade feel that it is usually a waste of time and money to conduct an examination if you have to travel a long way to do it. Debtors have a nasty habit of not showing up, and courts are often too busy with other matters to vigilantly protect your right to conduct the examination. Consider doing your own investigation along the lines suggested in the chapters on specific types of assets, or hiring an investigation agency if the judgment is large enough to warrant the cost. (See Chapter 23.D.3.)

3. Schedule the Examination

Before you complete the Application and Order for Appearance and Examination, contact the court clerk for a date and place for the exam. The clerk will tell you when debtors' examinations are scheduled at that courthouse, and will let you know the next available date.

---

[4] Many items of personal property are exempt from collection. (See Chapter 13.C.)

[5] If a third party bought the property for a price at or near its fair market value, and had no knowledge of your lien, you may not be able to reach it (CCP § 697.610 (a)).

[6] A declaration is a written statement made under penalty of perjury. See the samples in Section D.2, below.

ATTORNEY OR PARTY WITHOUT ATTORNEY *(Name and Address)*: TELEPHONE NO.: 415/999-9999

Pam Plaintiff
123 North Street
Berkeley, CA 94704

ATTORNEY FOR *(Name)*: In Pro Per

FOR COURT USE ONLY

NAME OF COURT: San Francisco Municipal Court
STREET ADDRESS: City Hall, Room 300
MAILING ADDRESS: 400 Van Ness Avenue
CITY AND ZIP CODE: San Francisco, CA 94102
BRANCH NAME:

PLAINTIFF: PAM PLAINTIFF

DEFENDANT: DAN DEFENDANT

APPLICATION AND ORDER FOR APPEARANCE AND EXAMINATION

[X] **ENFORCEMENT OF JUDGMENT** [ ] **ATTACHMENT (Third Person)**

[X] **Judgment Debtor** [ ] **Third Person**

CASE NUMBER: 12345

ORDER TO APPEAR FOR EXAMINATION

1. TO *(name)*: DAN DEFENDANT
2. YOU ARE ORDERED TO APPEAR personally before this court, or before a referee appointed by the court, to
   a. [X] furnish information to aid in enforcement of a money judgment against you.
   b. [ ] answer concerning property of the judgment debtor in your possession or control or concerning a debt you owe the judgment debtor.
   c. [ ] answer concerning property of the defendant in your possession or control or concerning a debt you owe the defendant that is subject to attachment.

Date: August 2, 19__ Time: 2:00 pm Dept. or Div.: 100 Rm.: 100
Address of court [X] shown above [ ] is:

3. This order may be served by a sheriff, marshal, constable, registered process server, or the following specially appointed person *(name)*:

Date: ____________________ *(SIGNATURE OF JUDGE OR REFEREE)*

This order must be served not less than 10 days before the date set for the examination.

IMPORTANT NOTICES ON REVERSE

APPLICATION FOR ORDER TO APPEAR FOR EXAMINATION

1. [X] Judgment creditor [ ] Assignee of record [ ] Plaintiff who has a right to attach order applies for an order requiring *(name)*: DAN DEFENDANT to appear and furnish information to aid in enforcement of the money judgment or to answer concerning property or debt.
2. The person to be examined is
   [X] the judgment debtor
   [ ] a third person (1) who has possession or control of property belonging to the judgment debtor or the defendant or (2) who owes the judgment debtor or the defendant more than $250. An affidavit supporting this application under CCP §491.110 or §708.120 is attached.
3. The person to be examined resides or has a place of business in this county or within 150 miles of the place of examination.
4. [ ] This court is **not** the court in which the money judgment is entered or *(attachment only)* the court that issued the writ of attachment. An affidavit supporting an application under CCP §491.150 or §708.160 is attached.
5. [ ] The judgment debtor has been examined within the past 120 days. An affidavit showing good cause for another examination is attached.

I declare under penalty of perjury under the laws of the State of California that the foregoing is true and correct.

Date: June 2, 19__

Pam Plaintiff *(TYPE OR PRINT NAME)* — Pam Plaintiff *(SIGNATURE OF DECLARANT)*

Form Approved by the Judicial Council of California AT-138, EJ-125 [New July 1, 1984]

APPLICATION AND ORDER FOR APPEARANCE AND EXAMINATION (Attachment—Enforcement of Judgment)

CCP 491.110, 708.110, 708.120

Some courts allow you to select your own date; others give you a particular date. Either way, make sure the date is far enough in the future that you can get the document issued from the court and get the debtor personally served at least ten days before the examination. As a general rule, allow at least 20 days for service, which means you shouldn't schedule the debtor's examination sooner than 30 days from when you start the process. It isn't uncommon to have an examination date set for six to eight weeks from the date the process is initiated.

4. Fill in Application and Order

A few courts have their own forms, so first call the clerk of the court in which you will be conducting your examination and ask whether it requires its own form or if it accepts the Judicial Council's Application and Order for Appearance and Examination form. If you use a local form, modify these instructions as needed.

Caption: Follow the format of your earlier court papers. Check the box before ENFORCEMENT OF JUDGMENT. Depending on whether you want the judgment debtor or third person to appear, check the appropriate box.

After ORDER TO APPEAR FOR EXAMINATION, put in the following information.

Item 1: Fill in the name of the person you want to appear.

Item 2a: Check this box if you want the debtor to appear.

Item 2b: Check this box if you want a third party to appear.

Item 2c: Leave this box blank.

In the long rectangular box, put information about where and when the examination will be held. (See Section C.3, above.)

Item 3: If the person who will be serving the papers is not a sheriff, marshal, constable or registered process server, put his name here. However, we recommend that you have one of these professionals carry out the service. (See Section E, below.)

After the words APPLICATION FOR ORDER TO APPEAR FOR EXAMINATION, fill in the following information.

Item 1: Check the box that says "Judgment Creditor" and put either the name of the judgment debtor or the name of the third party you want to examine. If you want to examine both, you must prepare two separate forms.

Item 2: Check the "judgment debtor" box if you want to examine the debtor.

If you want to examine a third party, check the box that says "a third person" and attach a declaration (statement under oath) showing that property worth more than $250 belonging to the debtor is in the possession of the third party. Fortunately, this information can be stated on "information and belief" (CCP § 708.120), meaning that you need not specify how you got the information—although we suggest that you provide as much detail as you can. Here is a sample "information and belief" declaration that you can modify to fit your situation. It should be typed double-spaced on numbered pleading paper.

I, Pam Plaintiff, declare as follows:

1. *I obtained a judgment against Dan Defendant from the San Francisco Municipal Court on Jan. 10, 19__ in case #12345.*
2. *The balance due on the judgment is $6,000, plus accrued interest and post-judgment costs.*
3. *On April 16, 19__ I conducted a debtor's examination of Dan Defendant. In the course of this examination, Dan Defendant stated under oath that he owns a variety of original paintings, valued at approximately $12,000. I am informed and believe that these paintings are in the possession of his agent, Arnold Florsheim.*
4. *I also determined from the debtor's examination that these paintings are the primary items of value owned by Dan Defendant which are subject to levy.*

I declare under penalty of perjury under the laws of the State of California that the foregoing is true and correct.

Date:

____

Pam Plaintiff

Item 3: Leave this blank, but read it to make sure you're seeking an examination in the right court.

Item 4: Check this item only if the court where you want the examination conducted is not the one that issued the judgment. In that situation, follow the procedure for transferring the examination outlined in Section 2, above.

Item 5: Skip this box if this is the first time you have tried to examine the judgment debtor or if you examined him more than 120 days ago. If you examined the debtor within the last 120 days, check this box and attach a declaration showing you have a good reason for another examination (CCP § 708.110 (c)). Here is a sample declaration that you can modify to fit your situation. It should be typed double-spaced on line-numbered pleading paper.

I, Pam Plaintiff, declare as follows:

1. *I obtained a judgment against Dan Defendant from the San Francisco Municipal Court on Jan. 10, 19__ in case #12345.*
2. *The balance due on the judgment is $6,000, plus accrued interest and post-judgment costs.*
3. *On April 16, 19__ I conducted a debtor's examination with Dan Defendant. In the course of this examination, Dan Defendant stated under oath that he owns a variety of original paintings, valued at approximately $12,000, which are in the possession of his agent, Arnold Florsheim.*
4. *I also determined from the debtor's examination that these are the primary items of value owned by Dan Defendant which are subject to levy.*
5. *On May 15, __ I conducted a third party debtor's examination of Arnold Florsheim to discover more about Dan Defendant's paintings. Mr. Florsheim told me that he possessed the paintings at one time but returned them to Dan Defendant in January 19__.*
6. *Although less than 120 days have elapsed since my last examination of Dan Defendant, I need to conduct another examination to discover the location of the paintings.*

I declare under penalty of perjury under the laws of the State of California that the foregoing is true and correct.

Date:

____

Pam Plaintiff

In the spaces indicated, type or print your name and the date, and sign the application.

You have completed the form if you are seeking to examine the debtor. If, however, you want to examine a third party, turn to the back of the form and complete Item (2) in the box titled "Appearance of a Third Person." In capital letters, fill in the amount of money you think the person owes the debtor, or describe the property you believe is in the third party's possession.

5. Have Order Issued by the Court

The completed Application and Order for Appearance and Examination must be signed by a judge. The court clerk will handle the details and either:

- return the original Application and Order to you so that it can be carried by the process server when service is made or
- retain the original for the court's files and provide you with a certified copy.

If you have the Order issued by mail, make four photocopies of the original document. Send the original and three photocopies (keep an extra copy for your records) to the clerk of the court issuing the Order along with a self-addressed stamped envelope and a cover letter explaining that you want the order issued and returned to you (a generic cover letter is included in the Appendix). The cost should be about $14.

D. Obtaining a Subpena Duces Tecum (Optional)

YOU MAY WANT TO OBTAIN a Subpena Duces Tecum for documents from the court. That way, when the judgment debtor or third party appears for the examination, she will have pertinent documents with her and won't repeatedly say "I don't know" to your questions. You will need to have the person you're examining served with the Subpena Duces Tecum prior to the examination date. The Subpena Duces Tecum will require that the person you're examining bring specified documents to the debtor's examination.

If you decide to obtain a Subpena Duces Tecum, it makes sense to do it at the same time as you get the Application and Order for Appearance and Examination. Here is how.

1. Complete Subpena Duces Tecum

A Subpena Duces Tecum form has been adopted by the California Judicial Council for general use. However, a few courts may use their own form instead, so you may have to adapt our instructions for that particular form. Also, many courts pre-issue subpenas—that is, they provide blank forms with the court's seal on them (often photocopied). Obtain a subpena form from your court.

Caption: Follow the format of your earlier court papers. Check the box before the words "Duces Tecum."

THE PEOPLE OF THE STATE OF CALIFORNIA, TO NAME: Enter the name of the judgment debtor or the third party you are examining.

Item 1: In the long box, fill in the date, time and place of your scheduled debtor's examination, listed on the Application and Order for Appearance and Examination (Section C, above).

Item 2: Check box "c"—because you are asking the debtor or third party to produce the documents at the examination. The records that are being subpenaed in this section will be described in the declaration that accompanies the Subpena (Section D.2, below).

Item 3: Fill in your name and telephone number. This identifies you as the contact person if the person being examined has questions.

Item 4: This states that witness fees and mileage must be paid upon service if requested then, and before the proceeding if requested later. Thus, if the subpena is directed to a third party, your server must be prepared to pay the fees and mileage on the spot.

Leave the proof of service on the back of the Subpena Duces Tecum blank for now. It will be completed after the document has been served.

ATTORNEY OR PARTY WITHOUT ATTORNEY (Name and Address): TELEPHONE NO.:	FOR COURT USE ONLY
Pam Plaintiff 415/999-9999 123 North Street Berkeley, CA 94704 ATTORNEY FOR (Name): In Pro Per	
NAME OF COURT: San Francisco Municipal Court STREET ADDRESS: City Hall, Room 300 MAILING ADDRESS: 400 Van Ness Avenue CITY AND ZIP CODE: San Francisco, CA 94102 BRANCH NAME:	
PLAINTIFF/PETITIONER: PAM PLAINTIFF DEFENDANT/RESPONDENT: DAN DEFENDANT	
CIVIL SUBPENA [X] **Duces Tecum**	CASE NUMBER: 12345

THE PEOPLE OF THE STATE OF CALIFORNIA, TO (NAME):

1. **YOU ARE ORDERED TO APPEAR AS A WITNESS in this action at the date, time, and place shown in the box below UNLESS you make a special agreement with the person named in item 3:**

a. Date: August 2, 19__	Time: 2:00pm	[X] Dept.: 100	[ ] Div.:	[X] Room: 100
b. Address: City Hall, 400 Van Ness Avenue, San Francisco, CA 94102				

2. AND YOU ARE
   a. [ ] ordered to appear in person.
   b. [ ] not required to appear in person if you produce the records described in the accompanying affidavit and a completed declaration of custodian of records in compliance with Evidence Code sections 1560, 1561, 1562, and 1271. (1) Place a copy of the records in an envelope (or other wrapper). Enclose your original declaration with the records. Seal them. (2) Attach a copy of this subpena to the envelope or write on the envelope the case name and number, your name and date, time, and place from item 1 (the box above). (3) Place this first envelope in an outer envelope, seal it, and mail it to the clerk of the court at the address in item 1. (4) Mail a copy of your declaration to the attorney or party shown at the top of this form.
   c. [X] ordered to appear in person and to produce the records described in the accompanying affidavit. The **personal attendance** of the custodian or other qualified witness and the production of the original records **is required** by this subpena. The procedure authorized by subdivision (b) of section 1560, and sections 1561 and 1562, of the Evidence Code will not be deemed suffficient compliance with this subpena.

3. **IF YOU HAVE ANY QUESTIONS ABOUT THE TIME OR DATE FOR YOU TO APPEAR, OR IF YOU WANT TO BE CERTAIN THAT YOUR PRESENCE IS REQUIRED, CONTACT THE FOLLOWING PERSON BEFORE THE DATE ON WHICH YOU ARE TO APPEAR:**
   a. Name: Pam Plaintiff b. Telephone number: 415/999-9999

4. **Witness Fees:** You are entitled to witness fees and mileage actually traveled both ways, as provided by law, if you request them at the time of service. You may request them before your scheduled appearance from the person named in item 3.

DISOBEDIENCE OF THIS SUBPENA MAY BE PUNISHED AS CONTEMPT BY THIS COURT. YOU WILL ALSO BE LIABLE FOR THE SUM OF FIVE HUNDRED DOLLARS AND ALL DAMAGES RESULTING FROM YOUR FAILURE TO OBEY.

Date Issued:

SUPERIOR COURT CITY & COUNTY OF SAN FRANCISCO, CAL.

DONALD W. DICKINSON
(TYPE OR PRINT NAME)

(SIGNATURE OF PERSON ISSUING SUBPENA)

COUNTY CLERK
(TITLE)

(See reverse for proof of service)

Form Adopted by Rule 982
Judicial Council of California
982(a)(15) (Rev. January 1, 1991)

CIVIL SUBPENA

Code of Civil Procedure, §§ 1985, 1986, 1987

2. Declaration for the Subpena

A Subpena Duces Tecum is not valid unless it is accompanied by a statement under oath to the effect that:

- you reasonably believe the records you are designating in the subpena are in the possession of the person to be served and
- the records you are seeking are material to your efforts to collect your judgment (CCP § 1985).

Prepare a declaration on lined pleading paper, using the accompanying samples as a guide. In Exhibit A, list any documents you want the person being served with the subpena to produce. You are permitted to infer that he possesses any document that would normally be in his (as opposed to someone else's) possession. For instance, the judgment debtor would normally be expected to possess bank books to his accounts, stock certificates issued in his name, bonds owned by him, deeds to real estate he owns and certificates of title to his automobiles. See the sample Exhibit A to the declaration for a basic list of documents you can request to be brought to the examination. In your declaration, make sure you cover the following.

- **Reason:** Why you want the person to produce these materials. This is almost always because you need them to enforce your judgment.
- **Relevancy:** Why you think this material is relevant to your case. These will almost always be because you need the information to levy on property available to satisfy your judgment.

There's no court charge for issuing a Subpena Duces Tecum unless you have to transfer the examination to another court. (See Section C.2, above.)

I, Pam Plaintiff, declare as follows:

1. *I obtained a judgment against Dan Defendant from the San Francisco Municipal Court on Jan. 10, 19__ in case #12345.*
2. *The balance due on the judgment is $6,000, plus accrued interest and post-judgment costs.*
3. *I am setting a debtor's examination of Dan Defendant for August 2, 19__ at 2:00 in Dept. 100 of this court. To provide information needed to levy on the judgment debtor's property, Dan Defendant will need to bring certain materials with him to the debtor's examination.*
4. *I believe that Dan Defendant has in his possession or under his control the documents or copies of the documents listed in the attachment entitled Exhibit A, as well as any other documents which provide information about Dan Defendant's assets. [If desired, the documents could be listed here instead of in Exhibit A.]*
5. *The materials indicated above are needed to enforce this judgment.*
6. *The materials indicated above are relevant to this case because they contain information which I need to levy on the judgment debtor's property in order to satisfy this judgment.*

I declare under penalty of perjury under the laws of the State of California that the foregoing is true and correct.

Date:

____

Pam Plaintiff

Exhibit A: Documents Requested in Subpena

1. Checkbook, deposit account pass book (bank savings, credit union, savings and loan), statements from banks, credit unions, savings and loans, brokerage firms (checking, savings, money market funds, mutual funds).
2. Stock certificates, certificates of deposit, bonds.
3. Title ("pink slip") to motor vehicles.
4. Promissory notes payable to judgment debtor and/or his/her spouse evidencing debts owed by others.
5. Receipts for property owned by judgment debtor or his/her spouse but held by third parties.
6. Deeds to real estate interest, deeds of trust.
7. Pay stubs (judgment debtor's and spouse's).
8. General ledger (for business debtors and independent contractors).
9. Invoices submitted for goods and services delivered by judgment debtor or his/her business to third parties.
10. Insurance policies.
11. Patents, copyright certificates, trademark registration certificates, royalty contracts for books, music, film, computer software, art, etc.
12. Certificates of title to personal property other than motor vehicle (such as valuable animals).
13. Bankruptcy papers (if petition filed within previous six years).
14. Leases which judgment debtor signed as a landlord or a tenant.
15. Applications for credit made within previous three years.
16. Copies of cancelled checks paid by tenants (if judgment debtor is landlord).
17. Trust instrument (if judgment debtor is trustee or beneficiary of a trust).
18. Statements from Keogh, IRA or other pension fund.
19. Copies of child or spousal support order (if judgment debtor is paying or receiving either).
20. Bill of sale for property sold within previous three months.
21. Copy of current occupational license(s), copy of occupational certification(s).
22. Receipts for funds placed in escrow.
23. Pawnbroker receipts.
24. Determination of Worker's Compensation eligibility and award.
25. Copies of judgments against judgment debtor, copies of judgments judgment debtor has against another party, copies of recent court filed papers in any cases in which judgment debtor or his/her business or spouse are a party.

3. Get Subpena Issued by the Court

If you aren't using a form that already has the court's seal on it, follow the same procedures described in Section C.5, above, for obtaining an Order of Examination from the court, but instead request that the Subpena Duces Tecum be issued. If you're obtaining the subpena at the same time as the Application and Order for Appearance and Examination, you can send these to the court together.

E. Examination Documents Must Be Served

YOU MUST NOW FIND SOMEONE to serve the Application and Order and Subpena, if any, on the judgment debtor or third party. Both documents must be served at least ten days before the hearing date. And the documents must be served correctly to establish a personal property lien (Section C.1, above).

1. Who Can Serve the Papers

Unless a judge signed an order allowing service by an individual, the Application and Order for Appearance and Examination must be served by a sheriff, marshal, constable or registered process server. (See Item 3 of the Order to Appear for Examination.)

If you think other creditors are also trying to get examination liens established, you may want to pay for a registered process server, since they normally act faster than a law enforcement officer.

2. Type of Service Required

If you are conducting an examination for the judgment debtor or third party, she must be personally served with an Application and Order for Appearance and Examination and any Subpena.

Examination Lien Note: Once you have the debtor served personally, the one-year examination lien is created even if the judgment debtor fails to show at the examination.

If you are examining a third party, you must have the third party personally served with an Application and Order for Appearance and Examination and any Subpena. You must also have the debtor served by mail with a copy of the Application and Order for Appearance and Examination. Since he is not being examined, but only being notified of the third party's examination (CCP § 708.120(b)(2)), the debtor need not be served personally.

Service is covered in Chapter 22. Give the server copies of the papers to be served. Hang on to the originals, since the server doesn't need them and you will have to apply to the court for duplicates if the originals are lost.

3. Fees

If you are serving only the judgment debtor, you technically don't need to tender fees at the time of the service.[7]

If, however, you're having a third party served with an Application and Order for Appearance and Examination, your server must offer mileage fees (currently 20¢ a mile). If you are also serving the third party with a Subpena Duces Tecum, you should give your server a check for $35 (witness fees) in case these are demanded at the time of service. A third party may also request reimbursement for documents photocopied for a Subpena Duces Tecum, at the rate of 10¢ per photocopy.

4. Filling Out Proofs of Service

Before you conduct your examination, you need to file a document, called a Proof of Service, with the court showing that the debtor or third party has been properly served. We tell you how to fill in a Proof of Service in Chapter 22, Section F. If you have a Subpena served, complete the Proof of Service on the back of that form.

---

[7] The judgment debtor, when served, could demand witness fees and refuse to comply with the subpena if the server doesn't pay the fees. There are two ways to deal with this possibility: equip your server to pay the fees if they are demanded, or stand on your rights and raise the issue when the debtor shows up for the debtor's examination.

5. File Documents With the Court

File these documents with the court:

- signed Proof of Service for the Application and Order for Appearance and Examination
- original Application and Order for Appearance and Examination (or a certified copy, if the clerk kept the original) and
- original Subpena Duces Tecum, if you are using one, with a signed proof of service.

The documents usually must be filed at least five business days before the examination is scheduled, though some courts only require a three-day advance filing, and a few will even accept filing the day of the examination. If you miss the deadline, the clerk may cancel the examination, and you will have to start all over again.

F. Prepare for the Examination

BEFORE YOU APPEAR at the examination, call the court clerk to check that the examination is still set to go at the scheduled time. The main reasons why the examination may have been taken off the court calendar are: (1) a proof of service wasn't filed on time, or (2) the judgment debtor or third party wasn't personally served at least ten days before the scheduled examination. Either way, you'll need to start all over again. If your purpose was to establish a lien (Section C.1, above), you might choose to drop the matter if the documents were properly served on time.

If the debtor shows up and answers your questions, you may obtain valuable information to assist you in your future collection efforts. This means you should plan what questions you want to ask. Generally, confine yourself to questions that you really need the answer to; don't read off a list of questions that are either beside the point or unlikely to get you good information on the debtor's assets. If you appear to be unnecessarily repeating yourself or wasting time, the debtor or third party may walk out or ask the supervising official to cut the examination short. Make your questions count.

To help you construct a good examination strategy, we provide a checklist of possible questions in the Appendix. Before appearing at the examination, go down the list, crossing out questions that don't apply to the debtor or to which you already know the answer.

One question you'll want to ask the debtor is how much cash he has on him, because you can have the judge order the cash turned over to you.[8] It's best to prepare, and bring to the examination, an order for the judge to sign. It is particularly wise to do this if the judgment debtor is the type who walks around with a big roll of $20s. A sample order is below; a fill-in-the-blanks form is included in the Appendix.

8 In one instance, a judgment creditor's attorney asked the judgment debtor whether he had any cash on him. It turned out he had $500 which a friend had just loaned him. The judge ordered the $500 turned over to the attorney (for the benefit of the attorney's client, of course).

Your name, address & phone

COURT NAME

PAM PLAINTIFF	)	Case No. 12345
v.	)	ORDER FOR DELIVERY OF
DAN DEFENDANT	)	PROPERTY AFTER EXAMINATION
________________	)	[CCP Section 708.205]

Examination Date: August 2, 19__
Time: 2:00 p.m.
Place: Dept. 100, Room 100

The examination of DAN DEFENDANT

(judgment debtor or third person) was conducted on the date and at the time set forth above. It appearing from this examination that:

☒ the judgment debtor has an interest in property in the possession or under the control of DAN DEFENDANT (judgment debtor or third person); OR

☐ a third person owes the judgment debtor $____________

(or property described as follows:____________________

____),

and that the property described above is not exempt from enforcement of a money judgment;

IT IS ORDERED THAT DAN DEFENDANT

(judgment debtor or third person) shall ☒ immediately/ ☐ within ___ days of entry of this order deliver to PAM PLAINTIFF (judgment creditor or levying officer of ________________ County at the following address:

____,

California) the following property: all monies and traveler's checks in his wallet and on his person which shall be applied toward the satisfaction of the judgment entered in this action on June 10 , 19__.

Dated:

____
Judge/Commissioner of
the Municipal Court

G. Conducting the Examination

ALTHOUGH IT IS COMMON for judgment debtors to not show up for an examination, let's assume that your debtor does. If our assumption is unduly optimistic, and your debtor is nowhere to be found at the appointed time and place, read Section H, below.

When you originally set the examination, you were informed where it would be held, usually in a courtroom. When you go to that location, you might be directed to another room. When you finally arrive at the designated location, you will find that a referee or judge is present, along with a bailiff. When your name is called, you and the debtor will be directed to an area nearby where you can discuss the matter privately. The process then occurs very informally, although the debtor is briefly sworn in first and agrees, under penalty of perjury, to answer your questions truthfully.

If you served a Subpena Duces Tecum, ask the judgment debtor for the documents requested. Examine each document before you begin asking questions, since some of your planned questions may be answered by the documents, and other questions will be suggested by them. Then ask your remaining questions from the checklist you prepared beforehand (Section F, above).

It's good strategy to avoid behavior that leads to your seeming like a hostile adversary who is maliciously asking lots of revealing and embarrassing questions. Try to present yourself as someone who is trying to help the judgment debtor find the money to pay you. Remember that the reason the debtor hasn't paid may be because she doesn't think she has the money or has other obligations she is putting first. Accordingly, if you explain that you need to ask some questions so that a reasonable payment plan can be worked out—while enabling the debtor to still carry on her regular work and business—she may be more likely to open up. You may want to work out a voluntary payment plan, with the understanding that you will only use formal procedures if the debtor doesn't live up to the agreement. Chapter 5 gives a variety of suggestions for how the debtor can come up with money to pay your judgment.

Another reason not to be pushy during this examination is that it could push the judgment debtor into declaring bankruptcy. After 120 days from the date of the first examination, you can schedule another examination and this time not be as concerned about the debtor's possible bankruptcy, since 90 days will have elapsed from the time your personal property lien was created.

Remember to obtain any money or property the debtor brought with him to the exam. (See Section F, above.)

If the Judgment Debtor Shows Up With an Attorney

Should you be concerned if the debtor shows up with an attorney? Not at all. First, explain that you are trying to work something out, so that you can arrange for voluntary payment. You want to make arrangements that the debtor can agree to and live up to on an ongoing basis. In other words, approach the attorney in the same reasonable way you would approach the debtor to get answers to your questions. Then, proceed to ask your questions.

The attorney will let the debtor know whether he should respond or not. However, as long as your questions are reasonable, such as the ones we have suggested, there is no reason the debtor shouldn't answer them. If you have any resistance from the attorney which you feel is not reasonable, you can always ask the referee to explain your situation to the judge, and then the judge may ask the attorney to have her client answer the questions the judge feels are appropriate. If you do ultimately work out a settlement, and the debtor reneges, you can nag the attorney who will, in most cases, come down on the judgment debtor.

If the judgment debtor failed to bring documents specified in the Subpena Duces Tecum, or you have problems getting him to answer your questions, or you feel the debtor is not responding honestly or thoroughly, you can go to the person supervising the examination. Usually, you will first speak to a referee about this, since the judge is often handling other procedures in the courtroom or in chambers. If necessary, the judge will take action.

Generally, a little assistance from the referee or judge is sufficient to get the debtor to cooperate. If the debtor has shown up at all, he is usually prepared to answer. But if he still refuses to answer when ordered to do so by the judge, the judge can cite the debtor for contempt of court, fine and even jail him. And you can have this done on your own; you don't need an attorney to help you.

Unfortunately for creditors, judges are often reluctant to throw the book at debtors who are in court unrepresented by an attorney. If this is the case, the judge may ask the person to either answer now or come in again with an attorney to represent him.

H. If the Debtor Doesn't Show

THERE ARE REMEDIES available to you if the debtor doesn't show up. When a debtor fails to show, most courts simply set another date for the debtor's examination. Most courts notify the debtor of the new date; otherwise you must. If the debtor doesn't show up the second time, and you do, the court will consider issuing a bench warrant if you apply for it and pay a fee for service—currently $20. Ask the court clerk to provide you with an application form.

If the judgment debtor is arrested on the bench warrant following an initial failure to appear, bail will be required before the debtor is released pending a future appearance on the warrant. You should be notified of the date set for the appearance on the warrant. If the judgment debtor appears at the hearing on the warrant and doesn't forfeit the bail, you can ask the judge to sign a turnover order as to the bail (see Chapter 18) or simply ask the judge to order the bail paid directly to you. In some counties you may be able to collect part of your judgment from this bail. We don't cover this procedure in this book.

Sooner or later, if you persist and the judgment debtor is located, you should be able to drag him in to answer your questions. And in some instances the debtor will simply get tired of having to deal with you and find a way to pay your judgment.

Chapter 7

How To Obtain a Writ of Execution

THIS CHAPTER TELLS YOU how to obtain a Writ of Execution (which we refer to interchangeably as a Writ), the key legal tool for actively enforcing a money judgment. It can be defined as court permission to go after the debtor's income or assets once you have a judgment.

Anyone who hears the dread phrase "Writ of Execution" can't help but conjure up visions of black-hooded hangmen presiding over medieval scaffolds. Once you get past the name, however, you'll find that obtaining a Writ of Execution is easy, and using it to collect the money you are owed involves mildly coercive (but not particularly uncivilized) remedies.

Should you worry about pushing the judgment debtor into bankruptcy by getting a Writ of Execution? The fact is, getting a Writ doesn't do anything to the debtor's assets. Only when you send it to a levying officer with instructions to take specific collection actions will the judgment debtor feel the bite. It is then that you want to consider whether your strategy is likely to cause the debtor to file bankruptcy.

Chapter 2 explains how long you must wait before initiating collections procedures. Once that time period has passed, you may wish to obtain a Writ so you can move quickly if you discover an asset that is worth going after. However, many collec-tion professionals only obtain a Writ when they have specific collection plans. Because a Writ of Execution is only good for 180 days from the date of issuance (you must get another one then), it does make sense to wait a bit if you don't plan on taking immediate steps.

Los Angeles County Superior Court Note: Before you can obtain a Writ of Execution from a Los Angeles County Superior Court, you must file an Application for Writ of Execution. Obtain this form from the clerk and fill it in. Then submit the application and your filled-in Writ of Execution to the clerk.

Sister-State Judgment Note: If you are seeking a Writ of Execution under a judgment based on an out-of-state judgment (see Chapter 19), you usually can't obtain a Writ until 30 days after the debtor is served with the Notice of Entry of Sister-State Judgment.

A. Fill Out Writ of Execution Form

THE WRIT OF EXECUTION form is in the Appendix. You must have one Writ of Execution issued for each county in which you are going after assets, even if you are pursuing more than one asset in a county.[1] You will need

---

[1] The court will only issue one Writ per county at a given time. It will not issue a new Writ until the issued Writ has been returned to the court by the levying officer who is handling a collection remedy for you. If you try to get a Writ and are told that it is "out," you'll need to contact the levying officer to find out why it hasn't been returned to the court.

a new Writ of Execution each time the old one expires. A Writ expires after 180 days.

Efficiency Note: If you anticipate needing more than one Writ, you can save yourself some time by taking the following steps:

- Fill in the front and back (as appropriate) of one Writ, except for Item 1 and Items 11-20.
- Make as many photocopies (front and back) as the number of original Writs you think you will need.
- Fill in Item 1 and Items 11-20 for each original Writ you need.
- Have each original issued as we instruct below.
- Save the rest of the copies in case you need more Writs later.

Keeping our efficiency note in mind, fill in the Writ as follows:

Caption: Follow the format of your other court papers. Where it says WRIT OF, check the EXECUTION (Money Judgment) box. Leave the rest of the boxes blank.

Item 1: Enter the name of the county where the assets are located.

Item 2: Skip this item.

Item 3: Enter your name exactly as it appears in the judgment and check the box that says "judgment creditor." You would check the box that says "assignee of record" only if someone assigned a judgment to you.[2]

Item 4: Enter the judgment debtor's name exactly as it appears in the judgment, and the debtor's last known address. If two judgment debtors are named in your judgment, list the name and last known address of the second judgment debtor below the first. If there are more judgment debtors, check the box for additional judgment debtors and enter their names in Item 4 on the back of the form. Remember, however, that if any of the judgment debtors have assets in a different county than the one you have specified in this Writ, you will have to obtain a separate Writ for that county to go after those assets. You must list all judgment debtors in each Writ.

Item 5: Fill in the date your judgment was entered, as indicated on the judgment or the Notice of Entry of Judgment which you prepared or received from the court. If you don't know the date, call the court clerk or look in the court file.

Item 6: This only applies if you have renewed your judgment before its ten-year expiration. If you renewed your judgment, fill in the renewal date(s). (Renewal of judgments is covered in Chapter 20.)

Item 7: A third party who has a security interest in the debtor's property may have requested that you send him a notice of sale should you decide to seize and sell that property. If so, check box 7b and enter the third party's name on the back of the Writ. If not, check box 7a.

Item 8: Skip this box unless you have amended your judgment to add additional judgment debtors. If you have, list the names of the additional joint debtors on the back of the Writ. If you originally obtained judgment against two or more parties, but didn't add them to the judgment later, this item does not apply to you.

Item 9: Skip this entire item. This only refers to a Writ of Possession or Sale.[3]

Item 10: This item applies only if you obtained a judgment against someone in another state and transferred it into a California judgment. (Instructions are in Chapter 19.)

Item 11: Enter the full amount of the judgment, which includes court costs and interest that were incurred before judgment and that have been granted by the court. This sum is on the judgment or the Notice of Entry of Judgment.

---

[2] An assignee of a judgment stands in the shoes of the original judgment creditor for purposes of enforcing the judgment. Collection agencies and attorneys may require you to assign your judgment to them in exchange for their agreement to pursue collection. Funds that you receive from the agency or attorney to whom you've assigned the judgment are basically your payment for giving them the judgment.

[3] A Writ of Possession is normally obtained in eviction actions, when a landlord sues to recover possession of the premises from the tenant, and in actions where a secured creditor seeks judicial authority to repossess personal property. A Writ of Sale is issued on a judgment for sale of real or personal property.

ATTORNEY OR PARTY WITHOUT ATTORNEY (Name and Address): TELEPHONE NO.: 415/999-9999

FOR RECORDER'S USE ONLY

☐ Recording requested by and return to:

Pam Plaintiff
123 North Street
Berkeley, CA 94704

☐ ATTORNEY FOR ☒ JUDGMENT CREDITOR ☐ ASSIGNEE OF RECORD

NAME OF COURT: San Francisco Municipal Court
STREET ADDRESS: City Hall, Room 300
MAILING ADDRESS: 400 Van Ness Avenue
CITY AND ZIP CODE: San Francisco, CA 94102
BRANCH NAME:

PLAINTIFF: PAM PLAINTIFF

DEFENDANT: DAN DEFENDANT

WRIT OF
☒ **EXECUTION (Money Judgment)**
☐ **POSSESSION OF** ☐ **Personal Property** ☐ **Real Property**
☐ **SALE**

CASE NUMBER: 12345

FOR COURT USE ONLY

1. **To the Sheriff or any Marshal or Constable of the County of:**
   SAN FRANCISCO
   You are directed to enforce the judgment described below with daily interest and your costs as provided by law.
2. **To any registered process server:** You are authorized to serve this writ only in accord with CCP 699.080 or CCP 715.040.
3. *(Name)*: Pam Plaintiff
   is the ☒ judgment creditor ☐ assignee of record
   whose address is shown on this form above the court's name.
4. **Judgment debtor** *(name and last known address)*:

   Dan Defendant
   234 West Street
   San Francisco, CA 94118

   ☐ additional judgment debtors on reverse
5. **Judgment entered** on *(date)*: 1/10/__
6. ☐ **Judgment renewed** on *(dates)*:
7. **Notice of sale** under this writ
   a. ☒ has not been requested.
   b. ☐ has been requested *(see reverse)*.
8. ☐ Joint debtor information on reverse.

[SEAL]

9. ☐ See reverse for information on real or personal property to be delivered under a writ of possession or sold under a writ of sale.
10. ☐ This writ is issued on a sister-state judgment.
11. Total judgment . . . . $ 6,000.00
12. Costs after judgment (per filed order or memo CCP 685.090) . $ -0-
13. Subtotal *(add 11 and 12)* . . . . . $ 6,000.00
14. Credits . . . . $ -0-
15. Subtotal *(subtract 14 from 13)* . $ 6,000.00
16. Interest after judgment (per filed affidavit CCP 685.050) . . . . . . $ -0-
17. Fee for issuance of writ . . . . . . $ 3.50
18. **Total** *(add 15, 16, and 17)* . . . . $ 6,003.50
19. Levying officer: Add daily interest from date of writ *(at the legal rate on 15)* of . . . . $ 1.64
20. ☐ The amounts called for in items 11–19 are different for each debtor. These amounts are stated for each debtor on Attachment 20.

Issued on *(date)*: Clerk, by ____________________, Deputy

— NOTICE TO PERSON SERVED: SEE REVERSE FOR IMPORTANT INFORMATION —

(Continued on reverse)

Form Approved by the Judicial Council of California
EJ-130 [Rev. September 30, 1991*]

WRIT OF EXECUTION

Code of Civil Procedure, §§ 699.520, 712.010, 715.010

*See note on reverse.

Item 12: Enter any collections costs and interest you have recorded on a Memorandum of Costs filed with the court. (We discuss how to fill in and file a Memorandum of Costs in Chapter 15.) If you have filed more than one Memorandum of Costs, enter the cumulative total. If you are getting a Writ for the first time, leave this item blank unless you are filing a Memorandum of Costs at the same time.

When To File Memorandum of Costs

Filing a Memorandum of Costs may alert the judgment debtor that you are planning active collection measures, since you need to send him a copy of these papers. If you wish to take the debtor by surprise, you may be better off claiming costs and interest later (but not more than two years after the costs are incurred). You may, however, want to file the papers simultaneously if the levying officer in your county does not serve papers. (See Chapter 15.D.)

The Memorandum of Costs must be filed a least two weeks before a Writ is issued, unless you include a special statement in the memorandum for a simultaneous filing. (See Chapter 15.D.)

Item 13: Add the judgment and costs claimed to date (Items 11 and 12) and enter the sum here.

Item 14: Enter the total payments you have received on your judgment.[4] (We provide a worksheet and instructions in Chapter 15.C.2 for keeping track of payments.)

Item 15: Subtract the payments (credits) in Item 14 from the subtotal (Item 13) and enter the difference here.

Item 16: Enter the post-judgment interest you recorded on your latest Memorandum of Costs. If you haven't filed a Memorandum of Costs, and you are proceeding shortly after judgment, don't worry about this entry; the interest will be minuscule and the levying officer normally adds interest. If enough time has elapsed since your judgment to make the interest significant, complete and file a Memorandum of Costs to account for the interest accrued since the date of the entry of judgment, and enter the amount here. (See Chapter 15.)

Item 17: Enter the fee for issuance of the Writ of Execution. You can obtain this figure from the court clerk. It should be about $3.50.

Item 18: Add the last subtotal, plus the interest and fee for the Writ (Items 15, 16, and 17) and enter the total here.

Item 19: Multiply the amount in Item 15 by 10%. Then divide by 365 to get the daily interest rate.

Item 20: This item applies only if you plan to ask the levying officer to collect different amounts from each debtor when there are two or more. If so, prepare an Attachment 20 and state the amounts.

Back of Writ of Execution Form: Normally you can skip filling in the back of the form. If, however, you do need to complete the back of the form, in the caption list an abbreviated version of the case name (for example, *Jones v. Smith*), and fill in the case number. See instructions for Items 4 and 8 on the front of the form. Skip Item 9, since you are seeking to collect a judgment for money.

B. Have the Court Issue Writ

NOW YOU NEED to get the Writ of Execution issued by the court clerk. First make at least three photocopies (back and front) of the Writ, plus one extra copy per additional judgment debtor. Keep one copy for your records.

When you give a copy of the Writ of Execution and the correct fee to the clerk, she will issue the Writ by affixing the official seal of the court and putting the date of issuance on the Writ. If you mail the Writ, send the original and copies to the court clerk (keep a copy for your records) along with the appropriate fee, a self-addressed stamped envelope and a cover letter asking for the Writ of Execution to be issued and mailed to you. (A generic cover letter is included in the Appendix.)

What happens if the clerk rejects your Writ? Usually you will be given an explanation. If you understand why

[4] You would also credit the value of services or goods that you received from the judgment debtor under a barter agreement—see Chapter 5.I.

it was rejected, correct the form and resubmit it. If you don't understand, reread this chapter and recheck your work.

C. How a Writ Works

A WRIT OF EXECUTION lasts 180 days. Only one Writ of Execution is issued by the court for a particular county at any one time.[5] The levying officer keeps the original Writ and serves copies on whomever you instruct the officer to levy against.

Sometimes, when a specific levy has been made (successful or unsuccessful), the levying officer will return the original Writ to the court rather than hold on to it for the entire 180 days. You should try to prevent this if your first execution was unsuccessful and you want to use the same Writ in that county again. You do this by stating in your instructions, that you want the Writ held for its entire life, absent a 100% successful levy. If, however, the levy does successfully satisfy your judgment, the levying officer will automatically return the Writ to the court. If, despite your instructions, the Writ is prematurely returned to the Court, you are entitled to obtain a new one. And, at the end of the 180 days, you can follow the instructions in this chapter to obtain a new one.

If property is levied upon or a wage garnishment is attempted, a two-year execution lien automatically goes into effect. This lien becomes effective as soon as the levy procedures are complete, regardless of the success of the levy. The lien is placed on the judgment debtor's interest in the property and expires two years from the date the Writ was issued (CCP § 697.710). (For more on liens, see Chapter 4.)

Note on Collections From Multiple Counties: If you limit your collection efforts to one county, you don't have to worry about overcollecting. The levying officer in charge of your file should make sure that you only receive what you are entitled to under the Writ. If, however, you give Writs to levying officers in two or more counties, there is an obvious risk that you'll get more than you're entitled to. Still, make each Writ for the total amount owing, following the instructions in this chapter. If too much is collected, you must promptly return the surplus to the levying officer, who will restore it to the judgment debtor.

If, after you have collected in full, there are any Writs of Execution still in the possession of levying officers, immediately instruct them to return the Writs to the court. Otherwise, you will not only have to return any money collected under these Writs, you also might give the debtor a basis to come back at you for overzealous collection practices.

D. What Do You Do Next?

YOUR NEXT STEP is to decide which assets you want to go after. Then, read the appropriate chapters for instructions on how to proceed. Chapter 1.A gives a chart listing the types of assets typically available for collection.

[5] Some counties will only make one levy at a time. If you want to attempt simultaneous levies in one county—such as a wage garnishment and bank levy—first check with that county's levying officer.

Chapter 8

SAVINGS, CHECKING AND MONEY MARKET ACCOUNTS

COLLECTION FACTORS	High	Moderate	Low
Potential cost to you		X ——	X[1]
Potential for producing cash	X		
Potential for settlement		X	
Potential time and trouble		X	
Potential for debtor bankruptcy		X	

IF YOU CAN FIND a pot of money that clearly belongs to the debtor and is not exempt from being taken under California's debtor protection laws, you are miles ahead in the collection game. A good bet is a savings or checking account in a bank, savings and loan, or credit union. Money market or deposit accounts controlled by financial or stock brokers are other great sources. Cash or other liquid assets, such as securities and gems, can sometimes be found in safe-deposit boxes, although it's rarer these days.

The judgment debtor can protect some types of funds from being taken to satisfy debts. No matter how large your judgment and how much is in these exempt accounts, the debtor may be able to keep this money, if she comes forward to claim the exemption—which is seldom the case. Thus, despite some problems, more often than not, deposit accounts can be a valuable source of funds for the collection of judgments. (Exemptions are covered in Section B, below.)

If you know where the judgment debtor has funds on deposit and have the account number, skip to Section B, below. If you need to find deposit accounts, we give you some tips in Section A.

A. Find Bank and Account Number

HERE ARE SOME SUGGESTIONS on how to find out where the judgment debtor banks and what her account number is. Although just the branch and correct account name are usually enough to levy on everything the debtor has in that branch, some levying officers require the account number. And having the account number allows you to find out the account balance and determine whether it to be worth going after.

If the debtor gets even a whiff that you are closing in on a deposit account, she will surely move it, and you will be back at square one with no money in your pocket. Also, if you speak to others, avoid mentioning the judgment. (See Chapter 3.)

[1] Unless you seize and sell the contents of a safe-deposit box, fees should be low–in the neighborhood of $20 per bank levy.

Note on finding money market and broker deposit accounts: There are two main ways to find money that is deposited somewhere other than a bank, such as certificates of deposit, money market funds or stockbroker accounts:

- Use the debtor examination and Subpena Duces Tecum in Chapter 6 to find out from the judgment debtor herself (remember, however, that the debtor may move these accounts once she gives you this information).
- Hire an assets tracing company. (See Chapter 23, Section D.)

1. Look at Debtor's Check

It's easy to find out the debtor's bank and account number if you have one of the debtor's checks. Many businesses regularly record this information before they cash checks. Or the information may be part of a credit application.

2. Write Debtor's Business a Check

If the debtor is a business, you (or better yet, a friend) can write the judgment debtor a check in the normal course of her business. It is usually possible to identify the debtor's bank from the stamp the bank places on the back of the cashed check.[2] Of course, this means you must physically examine the checks that have been returned to your bank for payment. If your bank doesn't routinely provide your cancelled checks to you, request a copy (usually for a small fee).

3. Ask Business Associates

If you know other people the debtor does business with, they may be willing to share information (the bank and account number on checks they have received from the debtor), in return for some helpful information from you. Technically, doing this constitutes sharing information about the debtor with third parties, a legal no-no, but no one is likely to complain if you do it discreetly. Of course, you should limit your contacts to people in your business network who you are pretty sure will be sympathetic to your situation, and won't immediately call the debtor and tip him off.

[2] If you are unable to interpret the back of the check, call or take it to a branch of the bank where it was deposited and ask for assistance.

Use of Pretexts

In Chapter 3, we emphasize that you should understand debtor protection laws and not make misrepresentations. However, you should also know that many professional bill collectors routinely get information from or about debtors by misrepresenting who they are. As long as the conduct doesn't violate any of the specific legal prohibitions set out in Chapter 3 and is not coercive or threatening, it is an accepted part of the bill collector's landscape.

Frankly, we prefer to get information about debtors by being strictly honest and above-board. Often, in fact, this approach works well. However, we must confess that when it comes to the most elusive debtors, we are tempted by some of the more creative bill collector ploys. These include:

- Coaxing the debtor to send you a check—perhaps by offering to sell something at a very low price. The amount makes no difference; you just want the account number. However, under no circumstances should you cash the check unless you promptly deliver the goods or services as promised.
- Calling the debtor's landlord and claiming that you need to verify some information the tenant gave you, and the landlord was named as a referral. As part of the routine verification, you ask where he banks. (See Chapter 14.B for information on how to locate the owner of real property. You'll need the debtor's address.)
- Calling the debtor and pretending to offer credit or a prize. Note, however, that some telemarketing schemes also use this approach. The debtor may, for good reason, be suspicious. Also, while there are no appellate court cases in the area, this approach may violate one or more of the statutes prohibiting deception in collection activities.

As we suggest elsewhere, you may want to hire an investigator to find this information. (See Chapter 23.D.)

4. Make an Educated Guess

If you can't find the bank or branch from one of the above sources, get out the phone book and look for banks and savings and loans near the debtor's home or job. You can use a map to find the streets near the debtor and run down the list of banks in the Yellow Pages. Small businesses that need to make daily deposits are particularly likely to use a branch within walking distance.

If the debtor works for a large company or state institution, or is in a labor union, check to see whether there is an affiliated credit union. The judgment debtor's account may be with a credit union rather than a bank.

5. Approach the Bank

In general, financial institutions are very secretive and protective of information about their depositors' accounts. Nevertheless, even if you don't know whether a debtor has an account at a particular institution or you don't know the account number, several techniques will often let you find out.

To learn if a debtor has an account in a particular bank branch, you can telephone (preferably just before closing, when things are hectic and bank people are less likely to do much checking), and ask to speak to someone who can give you account information. Say you're from a major store (such as a stereo or appliance store which is likely to get a lot of credit applications), and have a credit application that lists the bank's name as a reference. You want to check out that he does have an account there. Start to read off the account number and suddenly stop, saying something like: "Oh, you know what this person did. He put down his phone number instead of his bank account number. Can you do me a favor and look up the account number so I can correct this?" Sometimes, the bank representative will readily agree. However, the bank representative may ask to call you back. If so, remember how you identified yourself and attend to the phone until the call is returned.

An alternate strategy is to tell the bank that you're trying to verify an account number on a check that bounced, but can't read the account number because the check is torn, the bank punched a hole through it, or you have a bad photocopy. Finally, conclude by asking: "So, could you please look it up for me to see if the check will clear?" Often, they will.

B. Exempt Funds in Accounts

AS WE MENTIONED in the introduction, some money in financial institution accounts is exempt from attachment under California law. (If you want to oppose the debtor's claim of exemption, see Chapter 13.C.)

Child and Spousal Support Note: Most exemptions do not fully apply when the judgment is for child or spousal support. If this is what your judgment is for, inform the levying officer to help your levy go through smoothly.

1. Common Exemptions

If money in the account is comprised of exempt funds, the debtor has the right to keep it. These common exemptions apply to individuals only—not businesses:

- **Wages:** 75% of the debtor's wages deposited in a bank account are exempt. However, if the debtor's wages were garnished prior to the deposit, the ungarnished amount later deposited is fully exempt (CCP § 704.070(b)).
- **Assistance and benefits:** Money received from welfare or charitable organizations, Social Security,[3] the Veterans Administration, unemployment, disability and health insurance programs is completely exempt.
- **Public and private retirement pensions:** Funds received from a public or private retirement system (other than IRAs or Keogh plans) are completely exempt.[4]
- **IRA and Keogh plans:** Funds in these accounts, and funds that have been paid out of these accounts into a regular deposit account, are exempt to the extent they are necessary to provide for the support of the judgment debtor when she retires and for the support of her spouse and dependents (CCP § 704.115(e)). If the funds are payable on a periodic basis, the exemption is the same as if the payment were wages (roughly 75% —see Chapter 9).
- **Personal injury awards:** Personal injury awards[5] (either through settlement or judgment) are exempt to the extent they are necessary to support the judgment debtor and her family (CCP § 704.140).
- **Worker's compensation awards:** Funds paid for a worker's compensation claim are exempt.
- **Financial aid:** Funds provided for a student's expenses while attending an institution of higher education are exempt (CCP § 704.190).
- **Life insurance and annuities:** The exemption amount depends on whether the policy has matured. Unmatured policies usually have an exemption of $4,000 for an unmarried debtor, and $8,000 for a married couple. A matured policy's exemption depends on whether funds are needed to support the debtor and her family. An annuity will not be considered exempt unless it qualifies as insurance in the sense that it involves contingencies or risks.
- **Certain types of trusts:** Funds held in trust for the debtor under terms that strictly limit their use to the debtor's support (often termed "spendthrift trusts") are probably beyond your reach. If the debtor holds funds

[3] Funds in an account in which the judgment debtor's Social Security checks are directly deposited are automatically exempt in the amount of $500 for one debtor or $750 for two, or in excess of those amounts if funds consist of payments authorized by the Social Security Administration (CCP § 704.080). Additional amounts might not be exempt, but the judgment creditor must file an opposition within five days of being served by the levying officer with notice—10 days, if service was by mail (CCP § 704.080(e)(1)).

[4] CCP § 704.110(d). A public retirement system is basically any pension earned through employment with a governmental entity.

[5] Roughly, personal injuries include physical injuries, emotional trauma, property damage and damage to one's reputation caused by another's negligence or intentional acts. This exemption does not apply to a provider of health care services in connection with the claim on which the award is based.

as trustee for a third party, the exemption will depend on the terms of the trust. You'll probably need to see a lawyer if a debtor raises this exemption and you wish to pursue it.

- **Less common exemptions:** For more about exemptions, read Chapter 9.B and Chapter 13.A.2, or CCP §§ 704.010-704.210. You'll probably need to do this only if the debtor opposes your levy—see Section C.2, just below. (Chapter 23.A gives instructions on doing legal research in the law library.)

2. Strategy

The fact that funds in an account may be exempt shouldn't affect your strategy. Unless a court has ruled that a specific deposit is exempt, you are legally entitled to go after the funds without worrying about where they came from. In most situations, the law puts the burden on the judgment debtor to come forward and file a Claim of Exemption with the levying officer who collected the money. In the great majority of levies on a bank or deposit account, no exemption is filed. If, however, one is filed and you successfully oppose it, you will get the funds. If you are not successful, you'll have to return the money if it was distributed to you, but you can probably recover your costs. (See Chapter 15 for more on this.) In short, go after the money if you discover it.

C. Levying on Joint Accounts

IF THE ACCOUNT is in the debtor's name alone (whether the debtor is a corporation, a partnership or an individual), or is in the name of a sole proprietorship owned by the debtor, the whole account will be subject to your levy.[6] The entire account will also be subject to your levy if it belongs jointly to the judgment debtor and her spouse, but the spouse will be given an opportunity to object to the levy.

Example 1: *The judgment is against John Paul Jones. The account is in the name of John Paul Jones. You may levy against the entire account.*

Example 2: *The judgment is against John Paul Jones, Inc., a California corporation. You may levy against any account carrying the name of John Paul Jones, Inc. You may not levy against an account belonging to John Paul Jones as an individual unless you go back to court and amend the judgment to name him as an individual.*

Example 3: *The judgment is against John Paul Jones as an individual. The account is in the name of John Paul Jones, Inc., a solely owned corporation. You may not levy against the corporate account unless you amend the judgment to name the corporation as a defendant.*

Example 4: *The judgment is against Jones and Jones, a California partnership. You may levy against the Jones and Jones partnership account. If your judgment is against one of the partners as an individual, however, you may not levy against the account without a special order of the court (called a "charging" order).*[7]

Example 5: *The judgment is against John Paul Jones as an individual. The account is in the name of Jones Consultants, an individual proprietorship owned by John Paul Jones. You may levy against the Jones Consultants account if you provide the levying officer with a certified copy of the fictitious business name statement filed by John Paul Jones. This should be on file in the county recorder's office (in the county where John Paul Jones does business), or in the Sacramento County Recorder's office if the judgment debtor does business in more than one county.*

If the account is in the name of the judgment debtor's spouse, either alone or with others, you are permitted to levy on the account. However, you must provide the levying officer with a declaration showing that the parties are married (CCP § 700.160(b)). Also state the names you believe the account is in. The spouse and any third parties will have the opportunity to object to the levy. (Declaration samples are in Chapter 6.C.)

If the account is a joint tenancy account in the name of the debtor and someone else not her spouse, you are not permitted to levy on the third party's share of the funds (all joint tenants have equal shares). Also, you may

---

[6] If you need to amend your judgment to include a different name by which the debtor is known, see Chapter 1.E.5.

[7] This book does not cover charging orders. See Chapter 23 for how to research this question yourself.

be required to post a bond for twice the amount on which you are seeking to levy.[8]

D. How To Levy on Accounts or Safe-Deposit Boxes

NOW FOR THE NITTY-GRITTY, here-and-now instructions.

1. Obtain Writ

To levy on an account, you must first obtain a Writ of Execution. (See Chapter 7.) If there are accounts in more than one county, you will need a Writ for each county.

2. Determine Timing for the Levy

If you're going after a checking account, timing is important because the amount of money in it probably fluctuates rapidly. Unless you time the levy carefully, the account may not have enough funds to make your efforts cost-effective.

You can find out how much money is in the debtor's checking account at any given time by calling the bank and asking if a check for the amount of your judgment will clear. If the answer is no, try a little later, saying you have a check for a smaller amount. Keep trying until the bank reports that a check for that amount will clear. Before long, you'll get a rough idea of the balance in the account.

If you act when the bank account is at its low point, you not only collect little money, but also alert the debtor to your efforts. He will almost certainly move his account. There is an old saying: "If you shoot at the Emperor, don't miss." In the same manner, when you levy on a bank account, count on doing it one time and one time only.

Many people make deposits fairly regularly. Your monitoring should disclose the times of the month when the amount of the deposit is at its maximum. The levying officer, however will normally need a little lead time before making the levy. Thus, you should deliver your instructions well in advance of when you want the actual levy to occur. (See Section C.4, below.) Check with the levying officer to find out how far in advance they will need your papers; some may have a backlog. (See Section C.3, below, for instructions on finding the levying officer.)

Reality Note: Larger judgments normally can't be satisfied in full by levying on a checking account. The best you can do is to get a substantial portion of the money you are owed. Thus, if you have a $2,500 judgment and locate $800 in a checking account, you'll probably want to proceed with a bank levy and use other collection techniques to go after the rest.

Savings accounts and safe-deposit boxes are normally much less subject to fluctuations than are checking accounts. Indeed, these days many savings accounts (certificates of deposit, money market bank accounts, etc.) have penalties for early withdrawal, which encourage the debtor to keep the money on deposit for a considerable time.

3. Prepare Instructions

To find the levying officer for a county, call the sheriff's office in that county and ask if it levies on civil money judgments. If not, find out who does (marshal or constable). Call and find out the fees, how many copies of the Writ are required and whether local instruction forms are available.

It's best if you can arrange with the levying officer to have your Writ held until you phone in a request for it to be served on the bank, and have it served on the same

---

[8] In some cases, the bank will turn the entire joint account over upon a levy, figuring it is up to the non-debtor joint tenant to object. If you are required to post a bond, bonds can normally be obtained from title insurance companies or bonding companies. Give the bond to the levying officer, who will then complete the levy according to your instructions. The bond normally costs between 2% and 4% of its face amount. This cost is not recoverable from the bonding company, but possibly may be recoverable from the judgment debtor by claiming the amount on a Memorandum of Costs. (See Chapter 15.)

day of your request. This type of cooperation, however, is difficult to come by, especially in larger cities. If the levying officer is unwilling to hold the Writ for your phone call, ask whether you can specify the day and time of enforcement in your instructions. If neither of these methods works, ask how long it normally takes to serve a Writ, and get your paperwork to the officer that many days before you want it served.[9]

Prepare instructions for the levying officer, using the local form or Instructions for Levying Officers form letter located in the Appendix. State all of the following:

- the name, branch and street location of the financial institution holding the account or deposit[10]
- an account number, if available (some levying officers require this)
- the fact that the property (usually money) being sought is personal property
- the name or names the account or deposit is held in
- other relevant information, such as when and how to serve the levy, provided that the officer is receptive to specific instructions (call and find out). For instance, you may want to request the sheriff to levy at a given time of the month or week to coincide with the judgment debtor's pay period.

If you want the levying officer to take more than one levying action in a given county against a particular debtor, prepare separate instructions for each action. For instance, if you wish to have the levying officer collect from the debtor's savings account in bank X, and from the debtor's checking account in bank Y, you will need to prepare two sets of instructions and pay separate fees for both levies. Remember that if you collect more than the total balance due on your judgment, you must return the surplus.

The sample gives directions for a levy on all accounts and safe-deposit boxes in the debtor's name alone.

Date

To the Sheriff, County of Santa Cruz:

Enclosed please find:

1) an original Writ of Execution and three copies;

2) a check for $_____ fees; and

3) the following instructions for a levy on a deposit account.

Please serve the enclosed Writ of Execution and levy against any bank accounts and safe-deposit boxes belonging to Dan Defendant in the bank branch known as National Bank of Commerce, 567 Andrews Avenue, Santa Cruz. One account number is: 034-731078. In addition, collect from any other accounts owned by Dan Defendant at that branch. Please send any funds collected to me at the address shown below.

Please hold this Writ until I notify you by phone that I want it served, and then levy that same day or as soon thereafter as possible.[11]

If you levy on a safe-deposit box, ask the judgment debtor to open it voluntarily. If the box contains personal property other than cash that must be stored and sold, contact me first for further instructions. If force must be used to open the box, contact me first for further instructions. All property being sought in this Writ is personal property.

Sincerely,

Pam Plaintiff

---

[9] If you are in a county where the levying officer won't levy on bank accounts or is known to be inefficient, consider hiring a registered process server. (See Chapter 22.) Generally, we recommend against their use because of the potential for complications and because you need to prepare documents (such as the Notice of Levy) that are otherwise routinely prepared by the levying officer.

[10] Unlike banks, many money market managers and brokerage houses don't operate on a strict branch system, and you usually don't need to know in advance in which branch office the judgment debtor maintains his account.

[11] If the levying officer is unwilling to do cooperate with this type of request, you might put in language such as "Please perform this levy between the third and sixth day of the month."

Safe-Deposit Boxes

When levying on a safe-deposit box, the levying officer is faced with several choices:

- request the judgment debtor voluntarily open the box
- forcibly open the box if the judgment debtor refuses to cooperate or
- require you obtain a seizure order from the court allowing the box to be opened (Chapter 18, Section C).

If the safe-deposit box must be forcibly opened, you will first be required by the bank to post a deposit (usually $50-$100) to cover the associated costs.

A safe-deposit box may contain many different types of items (for example, insurance policies, stock certificates, bonds, title certificates, jewelry, cash). Some or all of this property will be seized by the levying officer. Cash and bonds can be given to you outright; tangible items such as jewelry must be stored and sold by the levying officer. For this, you will need to post a large deposit to cover storage and sales costs. If you don't wish to have the property sold (it may not be worth it), the levying officer will return it to the judgment debtor.

If the judgment debtor wishes to claim that some of the items seized are exempt, she must file a Claim of Exemption. For instance, family jewelry up to a certain value is exempt from seizure. (See Chapter 13.A.2.)

4. Give Instructions to Levying Officer

Make the necessary copies of the Writ and instructions, remembering to save one set for your records. Then mail or take the documents and correct fee to the levying officer. If you go to the levying officer in person, you can take your checkbook or cash for payment. Also, you may be able to have the clerk who accepts your documents review them to make sure that everything is clear and complete.

5. Notice of Levy Served

The officer uses the Writ and your written instructions to fill out a Notice of Levy, which he serves personally or by mail on the person in the institution who is in charge of the debtor's account. The debtor gets a copy. If more than one debtor is bound by the judgment, each should receive a separate Notice of Levy.

The Notice of Levy names the institution and branch being served, the property to be levied upon, and the amount necessary to satisfy the judgment. Also, it advises the institution that it has up to ten days to oppose the levy and that the funds must be put on hold in the interim. If the bank objects (which is unlikely, unless there are practically no funds in the account), we suggest you drop the matter or consult a lawyer.

The debtor may also object, by filing a Claim of Exemption. If either party opposes the levy, and you wish to pursue it, you will need to set a court hearing where the merits of the levy can be decided by a judge. See Chapter 13.E for instructions on opposing a Claim of Exemption filed by the judgment debtor.

6. Proceeds Are Distributed

Once the levying officer has collected the proceeds of the levy, he will disburse them to you. There is often a delay between the collection of funds by the levying officer and its disbursement to you. If you're concerned that your case has fallen through the cracks, call or write the levying officer.

Make sure that you keep track of all funds collected toward satisfaction of your judgment, as well as any costs incurred by you. We discuss this in detail in Chapter 15.

Chapter 9

PROCEEDING AGAINST THE DEBTOR'S WAGES

Collection Factors	HIGH	MODERATE	LOW
Potential cost to you			X
Potential for producing cash	X		
Potential for settlement	X		
Potential time and trouble		X	
Potential for debtor bankruptcy	X		

IF THE DEBTOR IS WORKING, you may be able to intercept a portion of his wages in order to satisfy your judgment. This process is known as a wage garnishment.[1] You can garnish wages relatively quickly and cheaply if:

- the judgment debtor works as an employee (not an independent contractor)
- the judgment debtor's job produces pay above the poverty line
- other wage garnishments aren't already in effect (unless your wage garnishment is for child or spousal support) and
- the debtor does not leave the job, contest the wage garnishment or file for bankruptcy.

A wage garnishment requires little effort from you. You give the levying officer information about where the judgment debtor works, provide a Writ of Execution and copies and pay a modest fee. Then you simply wait; the levying officer collects money from the employer and gives it to you. You can always lift the wage garnishment if you and the judgment debtor come to an agreement about voluntary payment of the judgment.

A wage levy can usually provide you with approximately 25% of the judgment debtor's disposable income. Naturally, if part or all of the debtor's income is determined to be exempt, you'll actually receive less.

Special laws govern child or spousal support wage garnishments. These garnishments can reach up to 50% of the judgment debtor's disposable income and have first priority. Thus, if a non-support levy is already in effect, you can supplant that levy if your judgment is for support and receive up to 60% of the debtor's wages.

Garnishing spouses' wages: If you have a judgment against someone who is married, you need a court order to garnish the spouse's wage (CCP § 706.109). Naturally, this restriction does not apply if both spouses are named as judgment debtors in the court judgment. (See Chapter

[1] As defined in Chapter 1.E.4, a garnishment is the process by which money owed the judgment debtor by a third party is intercepted and given to the judgment creditor.

23 for information on doing your own research and Chapter 18 for an overview of motions.)

A. Impact of a Wage Garnishment

YOUR POWER TO GARNISH a judgment debtor's wages is often a strong impetus for the debtor to pay off your judgment, since he may want to avoid the embarrassment and inconvenience of having his salary interfered with. Also, despite a federal law that prohibits employers from firing employees for wage garnishments that result from a single judgment, most employees rightly believe that a garnishment won't win them brownie points with their bosses. And they can be fired for multiple wage garnishments from different judgments. Thus, even the most uncooperative judgment debtor may be willing to pay voluntarily if faced with the prospect of a wage garnishment.

But a wage garnishment could push a debtor to leave her job, or propel a debtor toward bankruptcy. The loss of part of a paycheck, coupled with the embarrassment of having an employer know about her financial problems, may cause a debtor to look for a quick solution to relieve the pressure. If you choose to garnish wages, remember that you often walk a fine line between making great progress on collecting your judgment and closing off the possibility of collecting.

The debtor probably won't go bankrupt or quit his job if he has a lot at stake. This would probably hold true for a debtor who is a well established member of the community without a long list of other debts, an employee of an established corporate business in which he has a significant ownership interest or an owner of real property in which he has significant equity.

B. Limits on Wage Garnishments

FEDERAL DEBTOR PROTECTION laws limit how much of anyone's wages you can take at any one time. Unless your judgment is for child or spousal support, you may garnish up to 25% of the portion of the debtor's take-home wages, beyond a minimum.[2]

If your judgment is for child or spousal support, you are entitled to garnish at least 50% of the judgment debtor's disposal wages above the federal minimum. If the debtor is not currently supporting a child or spouse, it may be possible to get as much as 65% of a judgment debtor's wages taken for support (CCP § 706.052(c)).[3]

Here are some possible hurdles in the wage garnishment process:

Prior garnishment by other creditors: You can't garnish wages if they are already being garnished by another creditor, unless you are a former spouse seeking alimony or child support payments.[4] Normally, if your garnishment is second in line, it will be rejected by the employer, and you will have to file again when the previous creditor's garnishment ends. Bear in mind that an employee can be fired for two separate wage garnishments.

California exemption law: The debtor has the legal right to show that the portion of his wages that are above the federal minimum should be exempted because it is necessary to his own support or the support of a spouse or children. However, the debtor cannot qualify for this sort of exemption if the judgment itself comes from a debt that was incurred for the necessaries of life. We discuss this in more detail in Section D, below. Basically, this debtor remedy is most often a problem when the debtor has income just slightly over the minimum wage. Debtors with reasonably decent incomes are unlikely to get it all declared exempt.

Federal workers: Until February of 1994, you couldn't garnish the wages of federal employees (except

[2] A wage earner is entitled to exempt a portion of his weekly wages that is equal to 30 times the current federal minimum wage, which as of September 1994 is $4.25 an hour or $127.50 per week (CCP § 706.050).

[3] The court is entitled to order more or less than 50% withheld for support if it would be equitable to do so. The maximum that can be withheld (for example, 65% for delinquent debtors) is governed by federal law (15 U.S.C. § 1673(b)(2)).

[4] Support judgments are entitled to first priority, up to 50% of the judgment debtor's disposable earnings, or more with a court order.

Postal Service and Federal Housing Administration employees) or people in the military. You may now garnish the wages of federal workers (5 U.S.C. §5520a). Under interim federal regulations governing the federal garnishment process (5 C.F.R. 582), you may have the federal agency employer served with your Earnings Withholding Order (see Section C, below) personally or by certified or registered mail—return receipt requested. The service must be made on the official named by the agency to accept service; call the agency and ask. The agency itself need not be named in the order.

You must adequately identify the federal worker whose wages are being garnished, otherwise the Earnings Withholding Order will be returned to the issuing court. The regulations suggest that the following debtor information be provided:

- full name
- date of birth
- employment or Social Security number
- component of the agency for which the debtor works
- location of official duty station or work site, and
- home address.

The agency is supposed to respond to the garnishment within 30 days. The garnishment becomes effective as of the date it is served, but is subject to all other garnishments served before that date. Child and spousal support garnishments always get first priority.

The amount that can be garnished is based on the federal worker's salary after the following deductions are subtracted:

- mandatory deductions
- deductions for amounts owed the federal government
- withheld taxes
- health insurance premiums
- normal retirement contributions, and
- normal life insurance premiums.

If the amount that is left after all these deductions is $127.50 a week or less, then no garnishment will be made.

Military services note: Although the interim regulation described above for federal employees covers civilian employees of military employers, it does not cover actual members of the armed services. To garnish the wages of an armed services member, you will need to ask the particular service about its specific procedures.

Seamen's/longshoremen's exemption: You can't garnish seamen's, longshoremen's or harbor workers' wages. But see Chapter 18 for possible use of an assignment order.

Benefits and pensions exemption: Unless your judgment is for child or spousal support, you can't garnish unemployment benefits, worker's compensation claims or awards, relocation benefits, disability or health insurance benefits or most retirement plans.[5]

What does all this mean to you, the judgment creditor? Simply that the debtor may be able to contest your garnishment. Depending on the status of the debtor, the type of income and the amount of his pay, this may or may not be a problem for you. However, the fact that hurdles do exist means that many judgment creditors find it in their interest to contact debtors one last time to try to work out a settlement before initiating a wage garnishment.

C. How To Garnish Wages

HERE IS HOW you garnish wages.

1. Locate Debtor's Workplace

Skip to Section C.2, below, if you already know where the judgment debtor is working and have verified it (by calling). If you don't have a clue about the debtor's employment, following are some suggestions for how to find out. You'll need the company name and address for a wage garnishment.

---

[5] To directly intercept benefits and pensions for the payment of delinquent child or spousal support, you may wish to go through the district attorney's office.

When speaking with others, avoid mentioning your judgment. (See Chapter 3.)

- **Debtor's examination:** As discussed more fully in Chapter 6, a judgment creditor has the right to request that a debtor appear in court and answer questions concerning her employment and assets. The debtor's examination can be an excellent way to find out where the debtor works and how much she makes.
- **Debtor's statement:** If you are collecting a small claims judgment, the debtor is supposed to file a debtor's statement within 30 days. This statement should contain the name of his employer. Also see the Income and Expense Statement in Chapter 5.E.2.)
- **State employment:** If you think the person may work for the state, call the State Controller's Office Statewide Locator in Sacramento at 916-322-2760. They may be able to tell you if the person works for the state and where.[6]
- **Unions:** If you think the debtor belongs to a union, check with a branch of the local union. If you are asked why you want to know, and you believe the union won't cooperate if you tell the truth, have a good explanation ready. Possibly say you are trying to contact the person about employment, or that you previously worked with the person and just got back into town. You'll find a list of the labor unions in your phone book under "Labor Organizations."
- **Debtor's friends and neighbors:** If you know the debtor's friends, they may provide you with information about where the debtor works. If you know where the debtor lives, it may be productive to ask the neighbors where he works. If you don't want to knock on doors, you can usually locate the debtor's neighbors by use of a Haines or Polk Directory. (See Chapter 22.A.) These directories list most street addresses, except those with unlisted telephones.

When you believe you have located the debtor's place of employment, verify it by calling the work number. You can either ask if the debtor works there, or ask to speak to him. Or, if you don't wish to speak to the judgment debtor, call when you think he won't be there (lunchtime) and ask to speak with him. You should either get a "he's out to lunch" or a "no one by that name works here."

Use of Pretexts

In Chapter 3, we emphasize that you should understand debtor protection laws and not make misrepresentations. However, you should also know that many professional bill collectors routinely get information from or about debtors by misrepresenting who they are. As long as the conduct doesn't violate any of the specific legal prohibitions set out in Chapter 3 and is not coercive or threatening, it is an accepted part of the bill collector's landscape.

Frankly, we prefer to get information about debtors by being strictly honest and above-board. Often, in fact, this approach works well. However, we must confess that when it comes to the most elusive debtors, we are tempted by some of the more creative bill collector ploys. These include:

- Telling a neighbor or housemates that you are a long-lost relative and must locate the debtor quickly. Instead of pushing for the place of employment, simply ask for a work phone number. Then call that number to find out the debtor's place of employment.
- Calling the debtor at home and saying he is a finalist in a contest and then asking for routine information, including where he works.
- Calling the debtor and saying you are from an employment agency and you were given his name as a candidate for employment. As part of the routine interview, ask where he works now.
- Telling the debtor you are from a store or utility company, preferably one where you know he has an account, and asking him to update information for his credit file, including his employer.

As we suggest elsewhere, you may want to hire an investigator to find this information. (See Chapter 23.D.)

[6]There are limits on who the state keeps track of. Normally, only those directly employed by a state agency or department will be on the state's locator records.

2. Obtain a Writ of Execution

Before you can garnish wages, you must obtain a Writ of Execution directed to the county where the debtor is employed. Instructions are in Chapter 7.

3. Complete Application

You must give the levying officer instructions for serving the wage garnishment papers on the debtor's employer. This is done on a form entitled Application for Earnings Withholding Order. We provide this form in the Appendix.

Caption: Follow the format of your previous court papers. Leave the box for the levying officer's file number blank if you haven't levied in this county before. The levying officer will assign and enter the number. If you've done a levy on this debtor in this county (a previous wage garnishment, levy on a bank account or any other type of levy), the number will be on the papers connected with the former levy. Put that number in the appropriate box.

TO THE SHERIFF OR ANY MARSHAL OR CONSTABLE OF THE COUNTY OF: Enter the county where the debtor is employed (the same county as the Writ is directed to).

Item 1: Enter your name as the judgment creditor on the top line, exactly as it appears in the judgment. Just below, in the box on the left, enter the name and street address of the debtor's employer (a mailing address such as a post office box will not suffice). In the box on the right, enter the debtor's name, exactly as it appears in the judgment and home address (or last known address). If you know the debtor's Social Security number, include it.

Item 2: Check 2a to indicate that you want the money paid to you. If you want the money paid to someone else, check 2b and enter that person's name, address and telephone number.

Item 3a: Enter the date the judgment was entered. You can take this date from Item 5 on the Writ of Execution which you prepared (Section C.2, above).

Item 3b: Leave this blank unless you have agreed with the debtor for him to pay less than the full judgment. If so, put the amount you agreed to here. Also, if you have received payment from the judgment debtor since you obtained the Writ, subtract that amount from the total shown in Item 18 of the Writ of Execution and put the difference here (so you don't collect more than you're owed).

Item 4: Only check this box if you are seeking to collect a judgment for spousal or child support.

Item 5: If you have special instructions to the officer who will be serving the Earnings Withholding Order on the employer, check the box and put the instructions here. If you need more space, indicate that you have attached a page with instructions. Situations where you may want to give special instructions include:

- You know the debtor is working at the office under another name or nickname, and you want to have the levying officer call this to the attention of the employer.
- You are seeking less than 25% of the debtor's disposable income. You probably want to garnish less, for example, if you have previously garnished the debtor's wages, he filed a Claim of Exemption and the court determined a certain amount to be exempt. Rather than going through another Claim of Exemption contest, you are probably better off simply asking for the amount the court let you garnish.
- You are garnishing the wages of a federal employee and want to provide such identifying information as the debtor's full name, date of birth, home address and employment or Social Security number, as well as the component of the agency for which the debtor works and the location of the debtor's official duty station or work site. (See Section B, above.)

Item 6a: Check the box if you have not previously garnished the wages of the debtor.

Item 6b: Check the box if you previously obtained an order to garnish the judgment debtor's wages from this employer. Then check the appropriate box below.

- Check the first box if you attempted a wage garnishment before, but it was terminated by a court order. If so, you can't attempt another garnishment until 100 days after service of the Earnings Withholding Order on the employer or 60 days after the date

ATTORNEY OR PARTY WITHOUT ATTORNEY (*Name and Address*): TELEPHONE NO.: 415/999-9999

Pam Plaintiff
123 North Street
Berkeley, CA 94704

ATTORNEY FOR (*Name*): In Pro Per

LEVYING OFFICER (*Name and Address*):

NAME OF COURT, JUDICIAL DISTRICT OR BRANCH COURT, IF ANY:
San Francisco Municipal Court

PLAINTIFF: PAM PLAINTIFF

DEFENDANT: DAN DEFENDANT

APPLICATION FOR EARNINGS WITHHOLDING ORDER
(Wage Garnishment)

LEVYING OFFICER FILE NO.:

COURT CASE NO.: 12345

TO THE SHERIFF OR ANY MARSHAL OR CONSTABLE OF THE COUNTY OF SAN FRANCISCO
OR ANY REGISTERED PROCESS SERVER

1. The judgment creditor (*name*): Pam Plaintiff

requests issuance of an Earnings Withholding Order directing the employer to withhold the earnings of the judgment debtor (employee).

Name and address of employer	Name and address of employee
Ex-Corporation 1000 Industrial Street San Francisco, CA 94111	Dan Defendant 234 West Street San Francisco, CA 94118
	Social Security Number (*if known*):

2. The amounts withheld are to be paid to
   a. [X] The attorney (or party without an attorney) named at the top of this page.
   b. [ ] Other (*name, address, and telephone*):

3. a. Judgment was entered on (*date*): 1/10/__
   b. Collect the amount directed by the Writ of Execution unless a lesser amount is specified here:
   $

4. [ ] The Writ of Execution was issued to collect delinquent amounts payable for the **support** of a child, former spouse, or spouse of the employee.

5. [ ] Special instructions (*specify*):

6. (*Check a or b*)
   a. [X] I have not previously obtained an order directing this employer to withhold the earnings of this employee.
   —*OR*—
   b. [ ] I have previously obtained such an order, but that order (*check one*):
      [ ] was terminated by a court order, but I am entitled to apply for another Earnings Withholding Order under the provisions of Code of Civil Procedure section 706.105(h).
      [ ] was ineffective.

Pam Plaintiff
(TYPE OR PRINT NAME)

Pam Plaintiff
(SIGNATURE OF ATTORNEY OR PARTY WITHOUT ATTORNEY)

I declare under penalty of perjury under the laws of the State of California that the foregoing is true and correct.

Date: March 1, 19__

Pam Plaintiff
(TYPE OR PRINT NAME)

Pam Plaintiff
(SIGNATURE OF DECLARANT)

Form Adopted by the Judicial Council of California 982.5(1) (Rev. January 1, 1993)

APPLICATION FOR EARNINGS WITHHOLDING ORDER
(Wage Garnishment)

CCP 706.121

the Earnings Withholding Order was terminated, whichever is later. You can, however, attempt another wage levy if there has been a change in the debtor's employment circumstances (for example, he was promoted or given a raise).

- Check the second box if your wage levy was ineffective —for example, if the debtor was temporarily on leave from the job, and is now back, or another wage garnishment had priority over yours.

Type or print your name and sign the form twice. You are signing once in the role of the person requesting a Earnings Withholding Order, and once as the person who is stating under penalty of perjury that the Application is true and correct. Also, enter the date you sign the latter statement.

4. Give Instructions to Levying Officer

To find the levying officer for a county, call the sheriff's office in that county and ask if it levies on civil money judgments. If not, find out who does (marshal or constable) and call and find out the fees and how many copies of the Writ are required.

Make the necessary copies (remembering to save one set for your records), and mail or take the documents and correct fee to the levying officer.[7] A letter of Instructions to the Levying Officer is provided in the Appendix. If you go to the levying officer in person, you can take your checkbook or cash for payment. Also, you may be able to have the clerk who accepts your documents review them to make sure that everything is clear and complete.

[7] We recommend that you not use a registered process server for garnishing wages unless speed is a serious consideration or the levying officer doesn't garnish wages. This is for several reasons, the main one being that you will usually have to prepare additional paperwork that the sheriff, marshal or constable will normally prepare for you. (See Chapter 22 for use of registered process servers.)

Date

To the Sheriff, County of San Francisco:

Enclosed please find an original Writ of Execution and three copies, an original Application for Earnings Withholding Order and a check in the amount of $_____ to cover your fees.

Please proceed with a wage garnishment according to the Application for Earnings Withholding Order.

Please hold the original Writ of Execution for its entire 180-day duration or until the judgment has been satisfied, un less I contact you and instruct you differently.

Sincerely,

Pam Plaintiff

5. Levying Officer Serves Order

Based on the information in your instructions, the levying officer prepares an Earnings Withholding Order and serves it either personally or by mail on the employer or an agent in charge of the office or payroll. Along with the Order, the levying officer also delivers an Employer's Return form. The levying officer also serves the debtor with a notice informing the debtor about his legal options and a copy of the Writ.

6. Employer Completes Return

The employer must, by law, complete an Employer's Return and mail it back to the levying officer within 15 days. You should note on your calendar to watch for a copy of the Employer's Return, which you should receive four to six weeks after you send instructions to the levying officer. If you don't get a copy, ask the levying officer what is happening with your garnishment.

On the Employer's Return, the employer:

- corrects any wrong information about the name and address of the employer or debtor
- indicates whether the debtor is still employed and if so, any earnings in the last pay period and
- states when the debtor is paid (daily, weekly, every two weeks, twice a month, monthly or other).

7. If Employer Does Not Cooperate

If the employer doesn't return the Employer's Return form and carry out the order, you can bring a court action against her to recover the amount that should have been withheld, as well as attorney's fees. An employer could even be subject to criminal prosecution if she doesn't comply.

Fortunately, it is seldom necessary to go this far. Instead, as we indicate above, first check with the levying officer to make sure he has not received the Employer's Return. Then call or write the employer and inform him about your right to bring an action against him. This will almost without fail produce a cooperative employer, who most likely was simply negligent about returning the forms. See the accompanying sample letter.

April 25, 19__

Ms. Nina Heart
Ex-Corporation
1000 Industrial Street
San Francisco, CA 94111

Re: Pam Plaintiff v. Dan Defendant

SF Municipal Court Case No. 12345

Dear Ms. Heart:

On March 1, 19__ I sent instructions to the San Francisco County Sheriff to proceed with a wage garnishment in the above referenced case. They have informed me that they served you at Ex-Corporation with an Earnings Withholding Order on March 19, 19__.

By law, you were required to complete and forward the Employer's Return to the Sheriff within 15 days after ser vice, and to comply with the wage garnishment unless you filed a formal objection.

There are serious legal penalties for refusing to comply with a wage garnishment. You could be found liable for the amount due and owing on the judgment, and you could be subject to a separate lawsuit.

Rather than taking more formal steps at this time, I would appreciate it if you would immediately complete and return the Employer's Return to the Sheriff, and comply with the wage garnishment as required by law.

Sincerely,

Pam Plaintiff

cc: Sheriff, San Francisco County (Officer's File No. 1000)

California law also prohibits an employer from accelerating or deferring payments to the judgment debtor for the purpose of interfering with the judgment creditor's right to garnish the debtor's wages. If this occurs, the judgment creditor can sue the employer for the funds that should have been paid but weren't (CCP § 706.153).

If you have any problems with the employer, you can bring him in for a debtor's exam. (See Chapter 6.C.) You are also entitled to file a suit in small claims court, if the amount is $5,000 or less. For claims under $25,000, you can file in municipal court.[8]

Unless the employer objects, she must notify the debtor of the Earnings Withholding Order and provide him with a ten-day notice so the debtor can, at his option:

- see an attorney
- work out an agreement with you or
- file a Claim of Exemption and a financial statement to contest the requested wage garnishment. If the debtor files a Claim of Exemption, you will have an opportunity to oppose it.

If the debtor doesn't file a claim of exemption, and no other arrangement is worked out within the ten-day waiting period, the employer will begin sending a portion of the debtor's wages to the levying officer each pay period.

If you decide to lift or modify the garnishment, you must send a Notice of Termination or Modification of Earnings Withholding Order to the levying officer instructing him how to proceed. This easy-to-complete Judicial Council form is available from the court clerk or law library. Copies of the completed form should be sent to the employer and the judgment debtor as well as to the levying officer. If the levying officer is currently holding any money, you will probably want it sent to you, or perhaps even to the judgment debtor under the terms of your agreement.

---

[8] See *Everybody's Guide to Small Claims Court,* by Ralph Warner (Nolo Press) or *Everybody's Guide to Municipal Court,* by Roderic Duncan (Nolo Press).

Let us again remind you of the point with which we began this chapter: wage garnishments can push a debtor to file for bankruptcy, so carefully consider any offer by the debtor for a compromise or voluntary payments.

Note on Multiple Garnishment Orders: The Employer's Return instructs the employer on how to handle the withholding if she has received another wage garnishment order. Earnings Withholding Orders for child or spousal support judgments have first priority, and then orders for taxes. Should the employer get two orders of the same priority class on the same date, she should comply with the one with the earlier date of judgment; if the judgment dates are the same, the employer can select which order to carry out.

If the earlier garnishment (or wage attachment under the Family Law Act) is for support, and the amount being withheld is less than 25% of the debtor's disposable wages, you may garnish for the balance of the 25%.

8. If the Employer Objects

If the employer sends back the Employer's Return to the levying officer, stating a reason why he doesn't believe the wages should be garnished, the levying officer will send you a copy and ask you for further instructions. Common problems are:

- the debtor is not working there any more
- the debtor's wages have already been garnished by someone else or
- the debtor is working as an independent contractor, not as an employee.

Some problems are fairly easy for you to deal with. For example, if the debtor no longer works for that employer, and if you can find a current employer in the same county, you can send another Application for Earnings Withholding Order to the levying officer along with a new fee. The levying officer can use the same Writ of Execution. If you send no further instructions, the levying officer will automatically return the Writ to the court when it expires, which is 180 days after it was issued.[9]

If the problem is that the judgment debtor is an independent contractor, you can use procedures for a third-party levy (Chapter 10) or assignment (Chapter 18).

D. Opposing a Debtor's Claim of Exemption

SKIP TO SECTION E, UNLESS the judgment debtor contests your wage garnishment by filing a document called a Claim of Exemption with the levying officer. The procedure for filing the Claim of Exemption is included in the notice served on the debtor by the levying officer.

Real World Note: Roughly 85% of wage garnishments sail through without a Claim of Exemption being filed. This means the odds are you'll probably not have to deal with these procedures. However, if your luck runs the same as many of us, the odds don't count for much. Hence these instructions.

1. Claim of Exemption and Notice

The Claim of Exemption notifies you that the wage garnishment is being contested, and sets out the grounds for the objection. When the officer receives the Claim of Exemption from the debtor, she will mail you a copy, a financial statement (which the debtor must file with the Claim of Exemption) and a separate document called Notice of Filing of Claim of Exemption.

The Notice contains instructions for you, the judgment creditor. It also advises you that the Earnings Withholding Order will be terminated or modified to

[9]Some levying officers will return the Writ to the court before the 180-day period expires unless you instruct them differently. You should ask the levying officer to notify you in writing if and when the original Writ is returned to the court so that you will know to either obtain another one (assuming the 180-day period has expired) or obtain the original back from the court in case you want to attempt another levy.

reflect the amount of earnings claimed to be exempt unless you oppose the claim.

2. Deadline for Filing Opposition

You need to act quickly. You must file notice of your opposition with the levying officer and the court *within ten days after the mailing of the Notice of Filing of Claim of Exemption*. This means you may only have a few days from the day you receive the Notice to respond to it (this depends, of course, on the reliability and efficiency of the U.S. Post Office). The date the Notice was mailed is listed on that document. Your response must be served on the debtor at least 15 calendar days before the hearing date—20 days if service is by mail (CCP § 1005(b)).

3. Grounds for Claim of Exemption

Assuming your paperwork is sound, the only real basis for a judgment debtor to contest a wage garnishment is that her entire paycheck is needed to support herself and her family. If a court agrees (based on the debtor's financial statement), your wage garnishment either will not be allowed or, more likely, it will be reduced.

4. Grounds for Opposing Exemption

There are three exceptions to the debtor's claim of exemption.

Necessaries of life: The exemption doesn't apply if your judgment is based on a debt that was incurred for necessaries of life—shelter, food, utilities or medical care (CCP § 706.051(c)(1)). For instance, if you are a doctor who provided necessary medical services to the debtor and then obtained a money judgment for the value of these services, the debtor is not permitted to claim an exemption.

Personal services: The exemption doesn't apply if your judgment was obtained for the value of personal services you rendered the debtor as an employee. For instance, if you worked for the judgment debtor as a housekeeper and obtained a judgment against her for unpaid wages, the debtor cannot claim this exemption.

Spousal or child support: The exemption doesn't apply if your judgment is for child or spousal support.

If none of the three exceptions above applies, you will want to argue that the amount you wish to garnish won't prevent the debtor from adequately supporting her family. How do you prove that? If the debtor has a comfortable income, you will probably prevail, since 75% of the debtor's income is already exempt under the federal exemption. And if you can establish that the debtor is claiming unusual or dubious expenses, or that she is reserving an unreasonably high amount for living expenses, you should also prevail. If, on the other hand, the debtor is earning minimum wage and is barely scraping by, the debtor's Claim of Exemption will likely be granted.

It is important to understand that judges have almost complete discretion in deciding when this debtor's exemption is warranted, and the amount of wages to be exempted under it. Many judges are very sympathetic to debtors and will immediately take their side if you come across as too hard-nosed. Thus, if the debtor is offering to have somewhat less than the standard 25% withheld, whatever the reason, it might be worthwhile to accept his offer. Judges often persuade the parties to compromise.[10]

[10]Some judges take this opportunity to pressure the judgment debtor to agree to voluntarily pay a substantial portion of the judgment in installments. Then, the judge amends the judgment to make it an installment judgment (CCP §85).

Should You Oppose a Claim of Exemption?

People in the collection business have learned over the years to quickly decide whether a debtor's claim of exemption on the basis of need should be opposed or not. The main approach is to examine the financial statement, which the judgment debtor must submit with his Claim of Exemption, for any of the following items:

- an expense that seems out of line with common experience (such as $400 for utilities)
- an expense that should normally not be as high a priority as your judgment (for example, large payments on a note for an expensive or second car)
- failure to report income or assets that you believe to exist, on the basis of other information you have or
- omission of any other facts you think would sway a judge to deny the exemption, at least in part.

If any of these items is present, and the amount of wages or the size of the judgment makes it worthwhile to pursue the matter, by all means do so. Similarly, if the judgment debtor has an income well above the poverty level, the claim of exemption is unlikely to be completely honored no matter how many debts are listed. If, on the other hand, there is nothing in the debtor's financial statement that appears unreasonable, and the debt underlying the judgment is not for one of the exceptions discussed earlier, you may be better advised to think compromise.

5. Overview of How To Oppose a Claim of Exemption

If you decide to oppose the debtor's Claim of Exemption, follow the "Instructions to Judgment Creditor" on the Notice of Filing of Claim of Exemption form.

First, obtain several copies (the debtor's Notice says to get five) of two printed forms from the court clerk or library:

- Notice of Opposition to Claim of Exemption and
- Notice of Hearing on Claim of Exemption.

Because of the short filing deadline, we do not provide copies in the Appendix, in case the forms are updated and old forms would be rejected. Make sure you get the correct forms.

Second, fill out and file each of these forms with the clerk of the court and with the levying officer *within ten days of the mailing date* listed on the front of the Notice of Filing of Claim of Exemption. If you miss this ten-day deadline, your Earnings Withholding Order will be terminated, unless the debtor agreed in the Claim of Exemption to pay something out of her wages towards satisfaction of the judgment. In that event, if you agree to the reduced amount, you don't need to oppose the Claim of Exemption and the garnishment will proceed accordingly.

If your time is limited, you may need to either take these forms to the appropriate offices or send them by overnight mail. Remember, your filing deadline is *ten days from the mailing date* of the Notice of Filing of Claim of Exemption.

6. Complete Notice of Opposition to Claim of Exemption

This form is used to notify the debtor and the levying officer who sent you the Notice of Filing of Claim of Exemption form that you are opposing the judgment debtor's claim of exemption.

Caption: Follow the format of your previous court papers. Also enter the levying officer's file number, which will be on the Claim of Exemption papers you received.

Item 1: Enter your own name and address as the judgment creditor.

Item 2: Enter the name and last known address of the judgment debtor and his Social Security number if you know it. If you didn't know it before, it may be on the Employer's Return or the Claim of Exemption.

Item 3: Enter the date the Notice of Filing of Claim of Exemption was mailed. It should appear in Item 1 of that form.

ATTORNEY OR PARTY WITHOUT ATTORNEY *(Name and Address)*: TELEPHONE NO.: 415/999-9999

Pam Plaintiff
123 North Street
Berkeley, CA 94704

ATTORNEY FOR *(Name)*: In Pro Per

FOR COURT USE ONLY

NAME OF COURT, JUDICIAL DISTRICT OR BRANCH COURT, IF ANY:
San Francisco Municipal Court

PLAINTIFF: PAM PLAINTIFF

DEFENDANT: DAN DEFENDANT

NOTICE OF OPPOSITION TO CLAIM OF EXEMPTION
(Wage Garnishment)

LEVYING OFFICER FILE NO.: 1000

COURT CASE NO.: 12345

TO THE LEVYING OFFICER:

1. Name and address of judgment creditor

Pam Plaintiff
123 North Street
Berkeley, CA 94704

2. Name and address of employee

Dan Defendant
234 West Street
San Francisco, CA 94118

Social Security Number *(if known)*:

3. The Notice of Filing Claim of Exemption states it was mailed on *(date)*: March 22, 19__

4. The earnings claimed as exempt are
   a. [ ] not exempt.
   b. [X] partially exempt. The amount *not* exempt per month is $ 1,460.00

5. The judgment creditor opposes the claim of exemption because
   a. [ ] the judgment was for the following common necessaries of life *(specify)*:

   b. [X] the following expenses of the debtor are *not* necessary for the support of the debtor or the debtor's family *(specify)*:
   $1,000 rent (received by tenants; see declaration attached)
   $250 clothing
   $85 laundry and cleaning
   $125 entertainment

   c. [X] other *(specify)*:
   Please see declaration of Pam Plaintiff attached.

6. [X] The judgment creditor will accept $ 365 (per month) per pay period for payment on account of this debt.

I declare under penalty of perjury under the laws of the State of California that the foregoing is true and correct.

Date: March 26, 19__

Pam Plaintiff
(TYPE OR PRINT NAME)

Pam Plaintiff
(SIGNATURE OF DECLARANT)

Form Adopted by the Judicial Council of California 982.5(7) (Rev. July 1, 1983)

NOTICE OF OPPOSITION TO CLAIM OF EXEMPTION
(Wage Garnishment)

CCP 706.128

Item 4a: Check this box if you think none of the debtor's wages is exempt.

Item 4b: Check this box if you think only a portion of the wages is exempt. For instance, if the debtor claims his entire $400 weekly paycheck is exempt, and you think only $300 is exempt, check this box and put $100 in the space following it. (See accompanying sidebar, "Should You Oppose a Claim of Exemption?")

Item 5a: Check this box if your judgment fits within one of the exceptions to the exemption discussed in Section D.4, above—such as the judgment arises from a debt for necessaries of life, uncompensated personal services or for delinquent support.

Item 5b: Check this box if you think the debtor has overstated his hardship, and list which expenses (as shown on the debtor's financial statement) you think should be disallowed.

Item 5c: Check this box if you have any other reason why you think the exemption should be disallowed—for example, the debtor lied about his financial obligations or assets. If you need more room, add an attachment sheet.

Item 6: Put the amount of payment per pay period (listed on the Employer's Return) you are willing to accept.

Finally, enter the date, type or print your name and sign the form.

7. Complete Notice of Hearing on Claim of Exemption

This form is used to notify the debtor and the levying officer of a hearing to oppose the debtor's Claim of Exemption.

Caption: Follow the format of your previous court papers. Include the levying officer's file number.

Item 1: Fill in the name and address of the levying officer and the name and address of the judgment debtor (these items are on the Notice of Filing of Claim of Exemption). Skip the information for a claimant other than the judgment debtor.[11] Check the last box and fill in the name and address only if the judgment debtor has an attorney representing him.

Item 2: You normally check the box next to "judgment debtor" since this is the person claiming the exemption.

Item 2a: Ask the court clerk to give you a hearing date, time and location, and fill them in here. The hearing must be held within 30 days after the date you file your paper with the court. It is likely that the clerk will give you several alternative dates within the 30-day period. You can often obtain the court date, time and location over the phone, although in some cases it may be easier to visit the clerk's office in person. If you plan to mail your papers to the court (not recommended, in light of the tight time schedule), first get a hearing date on the phone.

Item 2b: Fill in the address of the court.

Item 3: Check this only if you don't intend to be at the hearing in person. You (and the debtor) have the option of attending the hearing or not. Normally, we recommend that you attend unless the matter is cut and dried (fot instance, the papers you or the debtor submit clearly indicate what the decision should be) and you have checked with the clerk to make sure nonattendance won't be held against you.

If you don't plan to attend, prepare a declaration (sworn statement) on lined paper and attach it to the Notice of Opposition and Notice of Hearing. In the declaration, explain why you won't be attending (perhaps you live far away from the court) and why you believe the debtor's Claim of Exemption should be denied. For instance, if you have knowledge that the debtor has other sources of income which are not indicated in the debtor's financial statement, state this and provide any supporting details and proof. An example of a declaration is shown below.

---

[11] There will not be another claimant unless you have sought an Earnings Withholding Order against the earnings of the spouse of the judgment debtor (which you can only do after obtaining a court order). Obtain the advice of an attorney if you want to garnish a spouse's wages. (See community property discussion in Chapter 1.D.4.)

ATTORNEY OR PARTY WITHOUT ATTORNEY (Name and Address): TELEPHONE NO.
Pam Plaintiff 415/999-9999
123 North Street
Berkeley, CA 94704
ATTORNEY FOR (Name): In Pro Per

FOR COURT USE ONLY

NAME OF COURT, JUDICIAL DISTRICT OR BRANCH COURT, IF ANY:
San Francisco Municipal Court

PLAINTIFF: PAM PLAINTIFF
DEFENDANT: DEFENDANT

NOTICE OF HEARING ON CLAIM OF EXEMPTION
(Wage Garnishment — Enforcement of Judgment)

LEVYING OFFICER FILE NO.: 1000
COURT CASE NO.: 12345

1. TO:

Name and address of levying officer
M. Levoff
San Francisco Sheriff
Room 333, City Hall
San Francisco, CA 94102

Name and address of judgment debtor
Dan Defendant
234 West Street
San Francisco, CA 94118

☐ Claimant, if other than judgment debtor *(name and address)*:

☐ Judgment debtor's attorney *(name and address)*:

2. A hearing to determine the claim of exemption of
[X] judgment debtor
☐ other claimant
will be held as follows:

a. date: April 10, 19__ time: 10:00 am [X] dept.: 200 ☐ div.: [X] rm.: 200

b. address of court:
City Hall
400 Van Ness Avenue
San Francisco, CA 94102

3. ☐ The judgment creditor will not appear at the hearing and submits the issue on the papers filed with the court.

Date: March 26, 19__

Pam Plaintiff
(TYPE OR PRINT NAME)

▶ Pam Plaintiff
(SIGNATURE OF JUDGMENT CREDITOR OR ATTORNEY)

If you do not attend the hearing, the court may determine your claim based on the Claim of Exemption, Financial Statement (when one is required), Notice of Opposition to Claim of Exemption, and other evidence that may be presented.

(Proof of service on reverse)

Form Adopted by the Judicial Council of California 982.5(8), EJ-175 [Rev. July 1, 1983]

NOTICE OF HEARING ON CLAIM OF EXEMPTION
(Wage Garnishment — Enforcement of Judgment)

CCP 703.550, 706.105

Finally, fill in, date, type or print your name and sign the form. Leave the Proof of Service on the back blank for now.

I, Pam Plaintiff, declare as follows:

1. *I obtained a judgment against Dan Defendant from the San Francisco Municipal Court on Jan. 10, 19__ in case #12345.*
2. *The balance due on the judgment is $6,000, plus accrued interest and post-judgment costs.*
3. *On March 1, 19__, I sent instructions to the San Francisco Sheriff for a wage garnishment of judgment debtor Dan Defendant. On March 22, 19__, a Notice of Filing of Claim of Exemption was sent to me.*
4. *I cannot attend the Hearing on Claim of Exemption which is scheduled for April 10, 19__. I plan to be away on a mountaineering expedition in Nepal during the entire month of April and will not be able to return for the hearing.*
5. *In Dan Defendant's Financial Statement, he indicates that he pays $1,500 in house payments. I am informed and believe that this is not true, but that he personally only pays $500 in house payments and receives $1,000 from two tenants each month. Dan Defendant did not claim this $1,000 per month income in his Financial Statement.*
6. *Dan Defendant claims that he needs $250 per month for clothing, $85 per month for laundry and cleaning, and $125 per month for entertainment. I believe that these expenses are excessive and unnecessary, and he should use those sums to pay off the judgment in this case.*

I declare under penalty of perjury under the laws of the State of California that the foregoing is true and correct.

Date:

Pam Plaintiff

8. Serve and File Opposition Papers

Within the ten-day deadline, proceed as follows:

Step 1: Make at least four copies of your documents. One is for your records, another is for the levying officer, a third is for the court and a fourth is for the judgment debtor. If there is an additional claimant (say, the debtor's employer), make an extra copy for this person.

Step 2: Have a set served on the judgment debtor, or on his attorney if he has one, at the address in Item 2 of the Claim of Exemption. This way, the debtor has full notice that you are opposing his claim, and he can either appear at the hearing or file additional papers with the court which the judge will look at in evaluating his claim.

You can have these papers served on the judgment debtor by mail or personally. In most cases, mail is the easiest and least expensive approach, as long as it allows the debtor at least 20 calendar days' notice of the hearing date. We cover service by mail and personal service in Chapter 22. The Proof of Service form is on the back of the Notice of Hearing form.

Step 3: Within the ten-day deadline, give or send the levying officer:

- the original Notice of Opposition to Claim of Exemption, with your original signature and
- a copy of the Notice of Hearing on Claim of Exemption.

If the levying officer doesn't get these documents within the ten-day period, he will tell the employer to terminate or modify the Earnings Withholding Order in accordance with the Claim of Exemption.

Step 4: Within the ten-day deadline, file with the clerk of the court:

- the original Notice of Hearing on Claim of Exemption form (with your original signature) along with a copy of the Notice of Opposition to Claim of Exemption stapled to it and
- an original Proof of Service, signed by the person who served the debtor with the Notice of Opposition to Claim of Exemption and the Notice of Hearing on Claim of Exemption.

9. The Hearing

If you decide to go to the hearing on the debtor's Claim of Exemption, you should sit down the day before and review your arguments. On the day of the hearing, try to get to the courtroom a little early. At the entrance, there may be a bulletin board with a list of the cases to be heard that morning. If your case isn't listed, check with the clerk.

Step forward when the name of your case is called. Be prepared to straightforwardly answer the judge's questions. Remember to call the judge "Your Honor." Don't interrupt the debtor if she makes statements you disagree with. The judge will give you a chance to state your disagreement at the proper time. Be prepared for the judge to actively get you and the debtor to compromise. While you are legally entitled to remain adamant and go for it all, that attitude may cause the judge to decide for the debtor.

If the court decides in your favor and denies the debtor's claim, the wage garnishment will go forward. Alternatively, if the judge decides that the Earnings Withholding Order should be modified or terminated, the clerk will send the judge's order to the levying officer, who will notify the employer. In either instance, you will soon receive a notice (Order Determining the Claim of Exemption) of what the court has decided.

If you lose the hearing on the Claim of Exemption, you can try another wage garnishment as soon as you can establish a material change of circumstances in the debtor's situation. For example, you could try again if the debtor gets a new and better job or a promotion. If the debtor's situation remains the same, you can try again either 60 days after the termination of the previous garnishment order or 100 days after the previous garnishment order was first served, whichever date is later (CCP § 706.105(h)).

Note on Appeals: Both you and the debtor can appeal from the judge's decision on the Claim of Exemption. But in the meantime, the Order Determining the Claim of Exemption of the judge is carried out. For example, if you lose and appeal, the exemption is allowed while your appeal is being decided. If you win on appeal, you can then begin collecting on your Withholding Order. If the debtor loses, appeals and wins on appeal, any money you have collected from the garnishment will have to be returned to the debtor either by you or by the levying officer if he is still holding the funds.

The appeals process is time-consuming, and few appeals are granted. We recommend that you not appeal should you lose the exemption struggle. It is much easier to simply wait a while and try again with another wage garnishment in which you might request less than 25% of the debtor's disposable wages. By the same token, the debtor is unlikely to appeal. In most cases, the debtor will simply accept his losses and that will be the end of it.

E. Get Your Money

ONCE YOUR EARNINGS Withholding Order is effective, the wage garnishment may last until you collect all your money or the order is terminated.

The levying officer collects the proceeds of the levy, then disburses them to you. There is often a significant delay between the collection of proceeds by the levying officer and its disbursement to you. While you should make reasonable attempts to ensure that your case hasn't fallen through the cracks, be patient. Levying officers often transmit collected funds in lump sum payments, rather than distributing them to you as they are collected. Some levying officers require that any requests for information about your levy be made in writing; others will give you information over the telephone or in person.

Make sure that you keep track of all funds collected toward satisfaction of your judgment, as well as any costs incurred by you. We discuss this in detail in Chapter 15.

If your judgment is satisfied except for uncollected costs and interest, you're entitled to seek a final earnings withholding order to recover those costs and interest (CCP § 706.028). (If service for a wage garnishment is performed by a private process server, see Chapter 15.D.)

F. If Your Order Is Terminated

IF YOUR EARNINGS WITHHOLDING ORDER is terminated by the court, you can apply for another order against the same employer after waiting either 60 or 100 days.

If the debtor leaves her job, the order will automatically terminate after a 180-day period during which no money is withheld (CCP § 706.032(a)(1)). If the debtor changes jobs, you can file against a new employer immediately.

If the employer gets an order of higher priority (such as for child or spousal support or taxes), your wage garnishment will be put on hold for up to two years; after that it will automatically terminate (CCP § 702.032(a)(2).

Finally, if you and the debtor work out a voluntary payment plan, you can terminate or modify the Earnings Withholding Order.

Chapter 10

Levying On Obligations Owed to Debtor By Third Parties

Collection Factors	High	Moderate	Low
Potential cost to you		X	
Potential for producing cash		X	
Potential for settlement		X	
Potential time and trouble	X		
Potential for debtor bankruptcy			X

ONE POTENTIAL SOURCE of funds for satisfying your judgment is debts and obligations that other parties owe the judgment debtor. The law gives you the right to require these third parties to pay what they owe to you instead of to the judgment debtor (CCP § 700.170).[1]

If a third party has the debtor's property in his possession, you can levy on this in much the same way that you levy on property in the possession of the judgment debtor (covered in Chapter 13). You must pay a fee and a deposit to cover the costs of collection and sale of the goods if necessary. If the property is at the third party's residence or other private place such as her office, you must also obtain a Seizure Order from the court (covered in Chapter 18).

[1] You generally can't levy on debts owed the judgment debtor by the government, including tax refunds (CCP § 699.720(a)(5)). However, if you have a support order, you may be able to intercept a state tax refund—see Chapter 1.D.7.

A. Introduction

COMMON AMONG THE MANY TYPES of obligations third parties may owe a judgment debtor are:

- accounts receivable, if the debtor is a business
- money due on a contract, or for services rendered by the debtor (common when the debtor is a professional, consultant or independent contractor such as a painter, carpenter or gardener)
- a judgment obtained by the judgment debtor against a third party and
- loans made by the debtor to the third party.

Third parties may also have temporary possession of property that belongs to the judgment debtor. For instance, a gallery may have an artist's or craftsperson's works on consignment, a stock broker may hold the debtor's stock certificates, and so on.

You can levy on the obligation by requiring a third party to pay to you what is otherwise supposed to be paid to the debtor. A third-party levy only reaches what is due the judgment debtor at the time of your levy. Thus, if the debtor is paid once a month as an independent contractor, you must levy each month to recover each monthly payment.

Alternative Remedy for Periodic Payments: If the judgment debtor receives payments from a third party on a regular basis (for example, royalties, some types of federal wages or steady payments as an independent contractor), you can require that the debtor assign these payments to you. This means that you, instead of the judgment debtor, will end up with the payments. The good side to the assignment procedure is that you don't need to make successive levies on payments as they become due, as is the case with third-party levies. The down side is that you will need to obtain a court order. We tell you how to obtain an Assignment Order in Chapter 18.

B. How to Levy on a Third Party

HERE IS THE PROCESS for going after debts owed or assets possessed by third parties.

1. Locate Third Parties Who Owe Debtor

If you have a reasonable belief that someone owes the debtor money or possesses her property, you are entitled to go after it. If there is a problem, such as the third party doesn't have the property or owe the debt in question, the third party can object in a Garnishee's Memorandum. All you really need to initiate a levy on third parties is their correct names and addresses, and the amount you think they owe the debtor or what property of the debtor you believe they possess.

The levying officer may only levy on property if it is someplace generally open to the public. (See Chapter 13.) If it isn't, you must convince a court to let the levying officer enter a private place to get the property. We tell you how to obtain and prepare a Seizure Order in Chapter 18. Getting the court's help in your collection efforts can be a little complicated, and we generally don't recommend it unless the amount of your judgment justifies the effort and you have unsuccessfully tried simpler procedures first.

Following are some types of third parties who commonly owe money or hold property belonging to others. Note that if you contact any of these people directly, you must follow behavior guidelines detailed in Chapter 3.

a. Third Party Hiring Debtor as an Independent Contractor

This can be one of the best sources for third party collecting if the debtor has a major and steady income source as an independent contractor. Strictly for the purpose of this book, an independent contractor is defined as someone who is in business for herself and who does not have a formal employer-employee relationship with the person who owes her money.[2] Some examples are people who:

- work for a business as an outside salesperson on commission
- are artists or writers who do projects on a contract rather than a salaried basis
- are small companies doing work for larger companies as independent contractors or
- do home repair or garden maintenance on a regular or semi-regular basis.

Carpenters, stoneworkers, plumbers, painters, pool service companies, roofers, electricians, housecleaners and many others fall into this category.[3]

It may be fairly obvious who the debtor is working for. A debtor who works as an outside salesperson may have a business card that identifies the principal company, and a writer or artist may list the names of major accounts on a publicity brochure.

Other times, you may need to do some checking to find out. One way might be to have someone, posing as a potential employer, call the debtor and ask for references. They may lead you to current customers, who in turn may provide you with information about the volume and frequency of business they do with the debtor. This will help

---

[2] Even though a person is paid as an independent contractor, state and federal governments may view the person as an employee for tax, unemployment insurance and worker's compensation insurance purposes. Whether a person is deemed an independent contractor by the government makes no practical difference to you. For the purpose of collecting your judgment, assume that a person paid as an independent contractor is an independent contractor.

[3] Although all of these people technically run small businesses, they often do so pretty much out of their hip pocket and don't have a business office. (See Chapter 11 for levies on a going business.)

you decide whether a customer is worth levying against. Or you may know people who have this information and are likely to tell you in the course of a casual conversation.

Another way to get information about third parties is to conduct a debtor's examination, along with a Subpena Duces Tecum, asking for copies of statements and books showing accounts receivable. (See Chapter 6.) A more down-home method might be to follow a debtor a few mornings to see where he goes, and then check a reverse directory to see who lives there. If these methods fail, consider hiring an investigator to get some information. (See Chapter 23 for how to find one.)

b. *Debtor's Clients*

If your debtor is a lawyer, business advisor, financial planner, medical services provider (doctor, acupuncturist, herbalist, etc.) or other "professional," his clients may be particularly good collection sources. For collection purposes, a client is in much the same position as a employer. Like an employer, the client hires the debtor to provide goods or services in exchange for a fee. And if the client is a major and steady source of income for the debtor, intercepting the payment may quickly lead the debtor into a payment plan that you can live with.

Remember that your levy is only good for the amount that the third party owes the debtor when you make the levy. If the account provides a relatively small sum each month, going after it through this procedure is probably not worthwhile.[4]

If you know the name of a regular, major client of the judgment debtor, it's probably fine to use this procedure. Otherwise, it's usually best to look for other payment sources. If you overuse this procedure with a lot of third parties who owe the debtor little or nothing, you may start to damage the reputation of the debtor, which could put you on the other side of a lawsuit. (See Chapter 3.)

[4]It may be worth your while to seek an Assignment Order from the court (Chapter 18). If you get it, you will automatically receive the payments from the debtor or third party as they become due until your judgment is satisfied or you cancel the assignment.

c. *Debtor's Landlord or Tenants*

If the debtor is a renter, it's likely that his landlord has a security deposit. Be cautious if you're contemplating a levy against that money. Landlords may not hesitate to evict a tenant who lacks a security deposit.

If the debtor is a landlord and owns either business or residential property, it is usually relatively easy to find out who rents it. You can ask the debtor in a debtor's examination (Chapter 6). You could use a reverse directory, which lists the names of people who have phone numbers at that address. (See Chapter 22.A.2, for how to use reverse directories.) If the property is nearby, you might go by and find out the tenants' names from their mail boxes or business signs.

A number of California cities have rent control ordinances that require landlords of covered units to register their buildings and provide information about the tenancies. If the debtor lives in a community with rent control laws, the rent control agency should have information about the debtor's rental income.

If the debtor is not a true landlord, but rather the primary or master tenant in a joint living arrangement (the tenant who is on the lease and responsible to the landlord), it is best not to attempt collection of payments paid to the debtor by the other tenants. They may claim the debtor is simply collecting their share of the rent to pass on to the real landlord and that it doesn't belong to the judgment debtor. Also, such subtenants tend to be somewhat less stable and more apt to move, so you're not likely to get a substantial amount from them.

d. *Someone Holding Debtor's Money or Property*

Finding out who has possession of the debtor's property can be difficult. However, if you know the debtor or his associates well, you may be able to get this information through general conversation. Or you might be able to track down some potential third parties from what you know about the debtor. For example, if the debtor has appointed a money manager to handle his funds, that person could be reached through a third-party levy. The same goes for a friend who is keeping a car or other personal property for a debtor.[5] Once again, however, levies on tangible personal property seldom make economic sense given the potential costs.

For instance, if the debtor is a craftsperson, artist or small publisher, he might have some books or artworks on consignment with a bookstore or gallery. A third party would be legally responsible to turn over to you any payments due the debtor at the time of the levy. You could also levy against the property itself, but the fees, storage costs and sales costs associated with levies on tangible personal property usually make a levy counterproductive. (See Chapter 13, Section A.)

e. *Broker or Institution Holding Debtor's Securities*

If the judgment debtor owns stock, the method you use to reach it depends on how the stock ownership is physically represented. For instance, if the ownership is manifested in stock certificates held by the judgment debtor, you can levy against the certificates themselves as tangible personal property (see Chapter 13). If, as is common, the certificates are held for the judgment debtor by a stock broker, you can levy against the stock in the manner explained in this chapter—that is, by a third-party levy against the branch office of the stock brokerage firm.

Sometimes stock ownership is not manifested in certificates. Rather, evidence of the ownership is in the computers of the company issuing the stock. In this case, it is possible to levy against the stock by making a third-party levy at a company's California headquarters. If the company's headquarters are out-of-state, you will need to obtain an Assignment Order directed to the judgment debtor. (See Chapter 18.)

f. *Someone Owing Business Debtor*

Businesses are commonly owed money for goods or services purchased by customers. In many types of businesses, payment is not even expected for 30 to 90 days from the date of invoice. For instance, a printing business is often owed large sums for printing jobs, a wholesaler for goods supplied a retailer and a clothing manufacturer for goods distributed to stores. These debts can be prime targets for levies.

Or, suppose the debtor is working out of her home selling mail-order products. You may not collect as you normally would from a going business (see Chapter 11), since a business in a home is beyond the reach of a levying officer absent a Seizure Order (CCP § 699.030). (See Chapter 18.) But if you find out the names of customers who have made purchases and haven't yet paid, you can legally obtain payments from them.

To find out whether such customers exist, you (or a friend) may wish to call the business debtor posing as a potential customer and ask for the names of other customers as references. When you call these other customers, find out what they have bought to estimate what they are likely to owe the debtor. Do not tell them that you have a judgment or say anything to damage her business or personal reputation. (See Chapter 3.)

2. Obtain Writ of Execution

Follow the instructions for obtaining a Writ of Execution in Chapter 7. You need one original Writ for each county in which a third party is located. If the third party is a natural person (as opposed to a business), this is generally the county where that person lives. If the third party is a business, it is the county where the business has its headquarters. If the business headquarters are in another state, you will not be able to levy against it and instead will have to obtain an Assignment Order directed to the judgment debtor. (See Chapter 18.)

[5] If you suspect that the debtor has hidden valuable assets by transferring them to third parties, and your attempt to levy against this property fails because the third party claims ownership, there may be a way for you to get the assets. However, this remedy involves a separate lawsuit against the third party and is not covered in this book. (See Chapter 23.)

Date

Re: Pam Plaintiff v. Dan Defendant

To the Sheriff, County of Marin:

Enclosed please find:

1) an original Writ of Execution and copies
2) a check in the amount of $_____ to cover your fees and
3) the following instructions for a levy on Careful Cat Catering.

Please serve the enclosed Writ of Execution and levy against any monies due and owing judgment debtor Dan Defendant by the third party, Careful Cat Catering, 100 Siamese Street, Sausalito, CA.

Dan Defendant should be owed approximately $1,100 by Careful Cat Catering for deli items delivered but not yet paid for. Since these sums are due and payable at the end of the month, please levy the week before June 30, 19__.

Please call me if you have any questions.

Sincerely,

Pam Plaintiff

3. Prepare Levying Instructions

To find the levying officer for a county, call the sheriff's office in that county and ask if it makes levies on civil money judgments. If not, find out who does (marshal or constable). For each county where you want to make a levy, prepare instructions for the levying officer. If the levying officer provides his own form for instructions, you should use it; otherwise, use the Instructions to Levying Officer provided in the Appendix.

a. Levying on a Debt Owed by a Third Party

To levy on a debt owed by a third party to the debtor, include the following in your instructions:

- the third party's name and address
- the amount of money you believe the third party owes the debtor at the time the levy is being made and
- when you wish the levy to be made (often near the end of the month, since this is likely to be when the maximum amount will be owed by the third party).

Following are sample instructions.

b. Levying on Tangible Personal Property Held by a Third Party

Tangible personal property is all property, except real estate, that has a physical nature. Examples are pianos, jewelry, cameras, computers, stereos, furniture and stamp collections.[6]

To obtain tangible property held by a third party, you must instruct the levying officer to take, store and sell the property. Also, you need to pay a substantial deposit (probably several hundred dollars), as well as the statutory fee, to cover the associated costs. (See Chapter 13 for a discussion of levies on tangible personal property.)

Following are sample instructions for levying on property being held by a third party.

[6]Examples of intangible personal property are accounts receivable, stock, bank accounts, copyrights and trademarks.

Date

To the Sheriff, County of Alameda:

Enclosed please find:

1) an original Writ of Execution and four copies

2) a check in the amount of $______ to cover your fees and

3) the following instructions for a levy.

Please proceed to levy on (remove, store and sell) the following tangible personal property belonging to Dan Defendant, which is in the possession of Miguel Fast:

a) One Steinway baby grand piano and

b) Full set of 12 crystal goblets.

This property is located at the Space Studio of Miguel Fast, 2001 Space Street, Berkeley, CA, 94704. The Space Studio is generally open to the public.

Please keep me up updated as to the status of this levy. I would like to attend the sale, so let me know when that will be.

Please call me if you have any questions.

Sincerely,

Pam Plaintiff

4. Give Instructions to Levying Officer

Call the levying officer to find out the number of copies of the Writ needed, the correct fee and deposit. Send the original and copies of your documents, fees and cover letter to the levying officer for the county where the third party is located.[7]

5. Levy Takes Place

The levying officer will serve the third party with copies of your papers, a Notice of Levy and a blank Garnishee's Memorandum for the third party to fill out. The third party must complete this if she wishes to contest the levy, or doesn't turn the property or funds sought after to the levying officer within ten days. The judgment debtor will also be mailed a Notice of Levy.

Unless the third party has a good reason for refusing to fork over the money or personal property, she must give the levying officer what is due to the debtor at the time of the levy. If the third party has any of the debtor's property which you instructed the officer to collect, she must turn it over to the officer along with any documents necessary to make the transfer.

a. *If Third Party Doesn't Comply*

A third party who does not turn over the money or property sought in the Writ must explain her reasons to the levying officer within ten days and provide complete information about the nature of any obligation owed to the debtor. She does this by using a Garnishee's Memorandum form. One common reason for non-payment is that someone else has beat you to the punch and already gained rights to the money due the debtor. Another common reason is that the third party doesn't owe anything to the debtor.

If the levying officer gets a copy of the Memorandum of Garnishee back from the third party, you will get a copy, along with information about any payment the third-party debtor has made. In some instances, the Memorandum will explain that the obligation to the debtor is due but not yet payable, but that payment will be forthcoming. However, in other cases, the Memorandum will indicate that nothing is due or can be expected.

The penalties for a third party who doesn't comply with a levy as required by law are severe. The third party can be liable not only for the amount of the levy, but also for the costs and reasonable attorney's fees you spend to

[7] If you are levying against money only, a process server could be used to speed up the process. That will require additional work on your part. (See Chapter 22.)

establish that he is liable.[8] Given these possible penalties, an informed third-party debtor commonly pays after being notified of your levy. You can help this process along with a letter something like the sample provided.

If the third-party still doesn't comply, you can file a suit in small claims court, if the amount is $5,000 or less. For claims under $25,000, you can file in municipal court.[9]

September 10, 19__

Re: Pam Plaintiff v. Dan Defendant
SF Municipal Court Case No. 12345

Miguel Fast
2001 Space Street
Berkeley, CA 94704

Dear Mr. Fast:

On August 1, 19__ I sent instructions to the Alameda County Sheriff to proceed with a levy on property which belongs to Dan Defendant, but which you have in your possession. The specific property in question is:

1. One Steinway baby grand piano and

2. Full set of 12 crystal goblets.

The Sheriff has informed me that you were personally served with levying papers on August 13, 19__, but to date you have not responded by returning the Garnishee's Memorandum or turning the property over to the Sheriff.

By law, you were required to complete and forward the Garnishee's Memorandum to the Sheriff within ten days after service, and to comply with the levy unless you filed a formal objection.

There are serious legal penalties for refusing to comply with a sheriff's levy. You could be found personally liable for the amount due and owing on the judgment, and you could be subject to a separate lawsuit.

Rather than taking more formal steps at this time, I would appreciate it if you would immediately complete and return the Garnishee's Memorandum to the sheriff, and comply with the levy as required by law.

Sincerely,

Pam Plaintiff
cc: Sheriff, Alameda County (Officer's File No. 1000)

b. If Anyone Objects

If the judgment debtor files a Claim of Exemption, use the procedures outlined in Chapter 13.C. If the third party objects to your levy and you wish to pursue the

---

8 CCP § 701.020. You will need to go to court to establish this third-party liability. If you do, you can then collect from the third party instead of the original debtor. (See Chapter 23, Section A, for how to research this procedure in the law library.)

9 See *Everybody's Guide to Small Claims Court*, by Ralph Warner (Nolo Press) or *Everybody's Guide to Municipal Court*, by Roderic Duncan (Nolo Press).

matter (which usually is not recommended), you will probably need to consult with a lawyer. (See Chapter 23.)

6. Get Proceeds From Levy

The levying officer will disburse the proceeds of the levy to you. There is often a significant delay between the collection of proceeds by the levying officer and its disbursement to you. While you should make reasonable attempts to make sure your case hasn't fallen through the cracks, be patient. Some levying officers require that any requests for information about your levy are made in writing; others will give you information over the telephone or in person.

Keep track of all funds collected toward satisfaction of your judgment, as well as any costs incurred by you. We discuss this in detail in Chapter 15.

Chapter 11

LEVYING ON A GOING BUSINESS

COLLECTION FACTORS	High	Moderate	Low
Potential cost to you	X—	—	—X[1]
Potential for producing cash	X		
Potential for settlement	X		
Potential time and trouble		X	
Potential for debtor bankruptcy		X—	—X[2]

IF YOU HAVE A JUDGMENT against a going business—whether it is a corporation, partnership or individual proprietorship[3]—you are entitled to have the levying officer do any or all of the following:

- make a one-time collection of cash and checks in the cash register (called a "till tap")
- remain on the premises, collecting receipts as they come in, and make an inventory of the business assets (called a "keeper")
- seize all visible personal assets (not real estate) of the business and hold them for sale.

An important value of these procedures is their coercive effect: many business owners would rather pay your judgment than face the prospect of a deputy sheriff standing by the cash register or seizing business assets.

Real World Note: Levying officers can be very good at shaking money loose from businesses with as little energy as possible. One sheriff reported great success in extracting payment by calling a debtor business and graphically describing what the levying officer would do ("Do you really want one of my deputies, with his police special on his hip, standing next to your cash register all day making your customers nervous?"). In the overwhelming number of cases, the business owners found a way to pay the judgments voluntarily, the sheriff reported.

A. Choosing a Procedure

LET'S LOOK AT THE AVAILABLE PROCEDURES for levying against a going business, so you can choose whatever seems to be most promising in your circumstances.

---

[1] There are two types of levies on a going business: levying on the assets of the business, which is expensive, and levying on cash coming into the business, which is not.

[2] Again, it depends which collection method you employ. Seizing and selling a business's assets has a greater likelihood of pushing a debtor into bankruptcy than levying on incoming cash.

[3] This assumes that the business entity is named in the judgment. If your judgment is only against an individual, you will probably need a court order to levy on the business even if the individual owns it lock, stock and barrel.

1. Levying Against Receipts

As we mentioned, there are two ways to go after receipts of a business: by till tap or keeper. Some restrictions apply to both methods:

- You cannot levy against receipts received by a home-based business without a court order allowing a levying officer to enter the home. (See Chapter 18.)
- You can't levy against a business's credit card receipts or receipts on sales that are not yet final, such as a down payment or layaway deposit.
- Some levying officers refuse to collect checks because of the problems involved in getting them cashed.

a. The Till Tap

If you request a till tap, the levying officer makes a single trip to the business and picks up all the money in the cash register or cash box (taps the till). It is the quickest method of going after business receipts, and can be imposed as many times as you want. If the storeowner uses his wallet rather than a cash register to store his receipts, a till tap probably won't work.

You must pay an advance fee and deposit, which should be in the neighborhood of $60. If the deputy doesn't complete the procedure for some reason—for example, the business is closed—you may get some of it back. If there is enough money in the till, the levying officer will collect enough to pay for his fees and costs as well as the amount of the judgment. If so, you get the amount of your judgment, plus the amount that you advanced. (See Chapter 15.)

b. The Keeper

If you instruct the levying officer to place a keeper on a business, a deputy remains at the business and is authorized to collect all cash that comes in. This is a particularly good approach for a retail business, which receives money throughout the day.

A keeper is also a good way for you to find out about the assets of the business, since you can instruct the levying officer to take an inventory of equipment, furniture and merchandise.

Usually, keepers can be authorized to remain on a business's premises for daily increments, up to ten days. After that, the assets and/or inventory must be seized and sold. In the real world, a keeper rarely stays anywhere this long. Unless the debtor objects, the officer stays until he has collected the balance specified in your Writ, plus the amount needed to cover the levying officer's costs. The officer will give you what he collects, less his costs (you might even be entitled to a refund on part of your deposit). Anything left over should have gone back to the debtor.

An officer may not remain while the business is operating if the debtor expressly objects. However, if an objection is raised, the levying officer is authorized by law to immediately seize, store and sell business assets regardless of the debtor's objections (CCP § 700.070; see Section D, below).

Kinds of Keepers. You have several choices when you request a keeper:

- An eight-hour keeper. You can instruct the levying officer to collect both incoming cash and (possibly) checks and also conduct a quick inventory or examine business records at the business.
- A 24- or 48-hour keeper. The procedure is much the same as in the eight-hour keeper arrangement—the deputy just stays longer, and it costs more.[4] It may make sense to use a longer keeper if you're dealing with a business that has unusually long hours or operates around the clock (say, a convenience food store). Also, because a keeper will prevent assets or inventory from being removed from the business if you so instruct, it may be a good idea to have at least a 24-hour keeper if you fear this happening.
- An open-ended keeper (up to ten days). As we mentioned, if your judgment is fairly large, and the business does not take in enough cash each day to satisfy the judgment in a day or two, it is a good idea

[4] Not all sheriffs, marshals or constables offer this arrangement. For example, the San Francisco sheriff charges the same for anything over eight hours, based on its 48-hour keeper fee.

to be prepared for a long-term keeper, if you can afford it. An open-ended keeper provides the maximum incentive for the debtor to settle with you.

The open-ended keeper is potentially the strongest of your remedies but also runs the greatest risk of driving the debtor out of business or into bankruptcy, which will severely diminish your chances of collecting your judgment. An 8- or 24-hour keeper is often the most effective remedy.

Cost. How much do keepers cost? The fees set by statute are relatively low—approximately $55 per keeper for an eight-hour shift. However, because the levying officer has a right to collect in advance for potential costs, you are commonly required to deposit $75 to $150 for an eight-hour keeper and about $850 (but $2,500 in one county) for a keeper that lasts for ten days, depending on the county. Part of this deposit may be refunded if the costs don't run that high. The costs you pay may be recovered from the judgment debtor, either from that levy or from a subsequent levy. (See Chapter 15.)

2. Seizing Business Assets

Having business assets seized and sold is an expensive, time-consuming and economically risky procedure. The forced sale of property typically brings only a small percentage of its true market value. You must also pay substantial costs up front for conducting an inventory, transporting and storing the assets and holding the sale. (You should be reimbursed for the costs if the sale brings enough cash.) Also, the property you try to seize and sell may already have been used by the business as security for other debts, or may be legally exempt from sale. Accordingly, levying against business assets is normally not recommended unless:

- you have a hefty judgment and you feel sure the sale will bring in more than the cost of having the property seized, stored and sold or
- you want to acquire the property for your own use.

Section C, below, contains instructions for having the assets of a business seized and sold to pay a judgment.

B. How to Levy Against Receipts (Till Tap or Keeper)

HERE ARE THE STEPS to levy against the receipts of an ongoing business (till tap or keeper).

1. Obtain Writ of Execution

Obtain a Writ of Execution for the county in which the business is located. We tell you how to do this in Chapter 7.

2. Obtain Levying Information

To find the levying officer for a county, call the sheriff's office in that county and ask if it makes levies on civil money judgments. If not, find out who does (marshal or constable). Call the levying officer and ask:

- the amount of the deposit for a till tap and for keepers lasting different lengths of time and
- whether or not the levying officer provides a form for instructions for levies against an ongoing business. If so, obtain a copy.

3. Decide on Till Tap or Keeper

Based on the deposit amount and your willingness to pay it given the likelihood of collecting, decide which type of levy you want to use (till tap, eight-hour keeper, etc.).

4. Prepare Levying Instructions

Prepare appropriate instructions. If the levying officer does not provide a form, use the following samples as guidelines. A blank Instructions for Levying Officer form letter is in the Appendix.

Date

Re: Pam Plaintiff v. Dan Defendant

To the Sheriff, County of San Francisco:

Enclosed please find:

1) *an original Writ of Execution and copies;*
2) *a check for $_____ fees; and*
3) *the following instructions for a levy (till tap) on a going business.*

You are hereby instructed to seize the following personal property: enough cash and checks in the possession of the following business to satisfy the sum specified in the accompanying Writ of Execution.

Danny-boy's Deli
234 West Street
San Francisco, CA 94118
415-999-8888

Please levy on or before the end of the business day on a Friday (the debtor makes weekly deposits at approximately 3:30 on Friday afternoons). Thank you.

Sincerely,

Pam Plaintiff

Note: If you believe that a company is likely to have a substantial amount of cash or checks on hand at a certain time (normally at the end of the business day if you are dealing with a retail concern, but perhaps in the afternoon just before the daily bank deposit is made), instruct the levying officer to visit the business then.

Here are sample instructions for an eight-hour keeper. To arrange for a keeper of more than eight hours, follow the sample provided for an eight-hour keeper, but change the time the keeper is to last. Note the specificity of the instructions regarding what the officer is to look for while at the premises.

Date

Re: Pam Plaintiff v. Dan Defendant

To the Sheriff, County of San Francisco:

Enclosed please find:

1) *an original Writ of Execution and copies; and*
2) *a check for $_____ fees.*

You are hereby instructed to place an 8-hour keeper at the following business by virtue of the accompanying Writ of Execution.

Danny-boy's Deli
234 West Street
San Francisco, CA 94118
415-999-8888

In addition, please make an inventory of the personal property in Danny-boy's Deli, including all equipment, appliances, machinery and utensils used for food preparation, silverware and china (this may be in a back storage room along with other catering supplies), linens, catering supplies, and all other personal property on the premises.

Please call me if you have any questions.

Sincerely,

Pam Plaintiff

5. Send Instructions to Levying Officer

Make the number of photocopies of your Writ and instructions required by the levying officer, plus one set for your file. Send the original and copies of the Writ along with your instructions and fees to the levying officer for the county where the debtor's business is located.[5]

6. Get Proceeds From the Levy

The levying officer will follow your instructions and proceed with either a till tap or keeper. He may advise you in writing about the outcome of the levy. If there was any problem with the levy—such as the business being in a private home, or the business having moved—the levying officer may contact you.

Once the levying officer has collected the proceeds of the levy, he will disburse them to you. There is often a significant delay between the collection of proceeds by the levying officer and its disbursement to you. While you should make reasonable attempts to make sure your case hasn't fallen through the cracks, be patient. Some levying officers require that any requests for information about your levy are made in writing; others will give you information over the telephone or in person.

Keep track of all funds collected toward satisfaction of your judgment, as well as any costs incurred by you. We discuss this in detail in Chapter 15.

C. How To Seize Business Assets

IF YOU DECIDE you want to take the physical property or assets of a business, not just the incoming cash receipts, the levying officer will seize the property if he can (by hiring a moving company, at your expense, to pick up and store the property) and conduct a sale. Remember that this is a costly and time consuming process. (See Section B.2, above.) However, it has extreme coercive value, and may result in partial or full payment of the judgment midway through the process. In addition, if you want to purchase the physical property or assets of the business, you can probably obtain them at a very low price.

[5] If you are levying against money only, a process server could be used to speed up the process. That will require additional work on your part. (See Chapter 22.)

1. How to Approach Exempt and Other Nonreachable Property

Not all business property can be seized to pay off your judgment; some is off-limits. The normal approach is to ask that everything be seized. The levying officer then decides which property to seize and which to stay away from. You are not liable for his mistakes, and you have little alternative but to rely on his judgment.

The main types of off-limits property are:

- Property belonging individually to the debtor owner of the business that is exempted by law. For instance, if the owner of a business keeps his personal motorcycle at the business, the motorcycle cannot be seized as a business asset, and the owner may claim an exemption for this motorcycle as a motor vehicle. And the debtor can claim as exempt up to $2,500 worth of necessary tools, materials or equipment.[6]
- Business property that doesn't actually belong to the business (property borrowed or leased from a third party, such as typewriters, expensive furniture and copying machines.)
- Inventory held by the business on consignment. For example, this might be jewelry on consignment by local artists.
- Partnership property, unless the property actually belongs to the judgment debtor or you can clearly specify in your instructions to the levying officer which property belongs exclusively to the debtor.[7]
- Inventory, furnishings, equipment and other items that are subject to a security interest that has been perfected through filing a financing statement with the Secretary of State. (See Chapter 13.A.2.b.)

[6] If exempt property is seized, you may end up having to give it back and even pay the associated costs if the debtor challenges them. (See Section C.3.e, below.)

[7] To get a partner's share of the partnership interest, you would need a "charging order" from the court. (We don't provide instructions for this procedure; see Chapter 23 for how to do your own research).

2. Property in a Private Home

You cannot reach business property located in a private home unless the debtor consents or a court issues an order permitting the entry or seizure. Judges are understandably reluctant to issue such an order. A court might allow you to levy against a home business if:

- you have exhausted other methods of collection and can't find any other assets to levy against
- the judgment is big enough to justify your reaching a little further than is normally permitted or
- the debtor conducts a substantial business out of her home.

Example: *If Joanne, the debtor, just does some professional writing or part-time selling out of a room in her house, this would probably not justify a court order allowing you to enter and seize property. If, on the other hand, Joanne uses a substantial part of her home for a suite of offices, has clients coming and going on a regular basis, and has several employees, a court might allow a levying officer to enter. This might also hold true if you could show that the debtor is conducting a substantial mail order business from her home.*

What about the many businesses that are run out of a store front connected to living quarters in the back or in a second story? Most likely, the levy will go through without a court order, since the store is physically separate from the residence. However, it is up to the discretion of the levying officer.

If you think you have a basis for collecting from a business in a private home, you must obtain a Seizure Order with the court where you got your judgment. (Chapter 18 contains instructions.) If your motion is granted, you will get a court order permitting the levying officer to use your Writ of Execution against the debtor's business in his home. You can then take or send this court order, along with your Writ of Execution, instructions and fees to the levying officer, who will carry out your levy just as if it were against a regular business.

3. Instructions for Seizing Business Assets

To go after the property of a business, you may first need to arrange for a keeper, depending on the requirements of the levying officer in the county where the business is located. Instructions for a keeper are explained in detail in Section B, above. Here are the steps for levying against the personal property of a business.

a. Obtain Levying Information

To find the levying officer for a county, call the sheriff's office in that county and ask if it makes levies on civil money judgments. If not, find out who does (marshal or constable). Call the levying officer and find out:

- the procedure for seizing and selling tangible personal assets of a business (do they require a keeper first, and if so, for how many hours)
- the deposit amount required, and whether there will be an additional deposit once the business has been inventoried ($400 to $1,000 could be on the low end of the deposit scale) and
- whether or not the levying officer provides a form for instructions for levies against an ongoing business. If so, obtain a copy.

b. Obtain Writ of Execution

Obtain a Writ of Execution for the county in which the business is located. We tell you how to do this in Chapter 7.

c. Prepare Levying Instructions

Prepare appropriate instructions. If the levying officer does not provide a form, use the Instructions for Levying Officer in the Appendix.

Date

To the Sheriff, County of San Francisco:

Enclosed please find:

1) an original Writ of Execution and copies

2) a check for $_____ fees and

3) the following instructions for a levy on the assets of a going business (48-hour keeper and seizure and sale of business assets).

Subject to the instructions and limitations in these instructions, you are hereby instructed to seize, advertise for sale and sell by virtue of the accompanying Writ of Execution the following business personal property: all monies, debts, credits and effects, all goods, wares, merchandise, stock in trade, equipment, inventory, fixtures and furniture in possession or under the control of the following persons, firms or corporations located at:

Danny-boy's Deli
234 West Street
San Francisco, CA 94118
415-999-8888

Please place a keeper in charge for a 48-hour period. (Do not let the keeper stay into the weekend.) [8] *As soon as possible, please inventory the premises, obtain an estimate of the moving and storage costs, and contact me at the telephone number provided below before taking further action. If I then desire to continue with the levy, and no settlement with the judgment debtor has been made, this is your authority to remove enough property and/or merchandise from the premises to satisfy the amount of the claim specified in the Writ of Execution.*

Finally, if a sale is held, please advise me in advance so that I can attend the sale.

Sincerely,

Pam Plaintiff

You need to understand several points about these instructions:

- They require the levying officer to give you an estimate of the potential cost of seizing the assets. This gives you a chance to back away from this remedy if it appears too expensive.
- They specify that the property to be seized is personal property. (If you wish to go after real estate owned by a business, see Chapter 14.)
- They allow the levying officer to seize less than all of the assets if, in his judgment, they are sufficient to satisfy your judgment. Remember, however, that as little as 30-50% of the property's market value is sometimes realized from a forced sale. Overkill is definitely in order when it comes to seizing assets for sale, especially if they are old and not worth much to start with.

d. *Send Instructions to Levying Officer*

Make the number of photocopies of your Writ and instructions required by the levying officer, plus one set for your file. Send the original and copies of the Writ along with your instructions and fees to the levying officer for the county where the debtor's business is located.[9]

The levying officer will follow your instructions and proceed with a keeper and/or the seizure and sale of business property. He may contact you about posting further fee deposits, to let you know the outcome of the levy, or if there was any problem with the levy—such as the business lacking seizable assets, or the business having moved.

e. *If Off-Limits Property Is Seized*

If the business is open to the public generally, and not located in the debtor's home, the levying officer can seize pretty much anything of value he finds there. As mentioned, however, some business property can't be seized. (See Section C.1, above.)

The officer usually goes on the assumption that the debtor owns or is in charge of everything present, unless

[8] This sentence is clearly optional. For many retail businesses, Saturday is the busiest day and you might say that the keeper shouldn't run into Sunday. Another reason you may want to delete this sentence is if you are worried that the judgment debtor will remove assets during the weekend and you want the keeper on the premises to prevent that.

[9] If you are levying against money only, a process server could be used to speed up the process. That will require additional work on your part. (See Chapter 22.)

the debtor shows him evidence to the contrary. The officer will use his judgment in deciding if the evidence is convincing. If there is a substantial question of ownership, the officer normally will leave the disputed property with the business, letting the parties fight it out in court.

If the business wants to get back any seized property or protest the levy, it must file a Claim of Exemption with the levying officer within ten days, giving a reason why this property should not have been taken—for example, because the property belongs to someone else or is exempt. Similarly, if a third party wishes to claim ownership of property seized in the levy, it can make a third party claim.

If either the business debtor or a third party contests your levy, you will be notified and given an opportunity to contest the claims. We discuss this in Chapter 13.C.

f. Sale and Distribution of Funds

If the debtor doesn't file a successful Claim of Exemption, the levying officer will sell the property. He will notify the debtor at least ten days in advance and post other notices in the city or district, telling where and when the sale will take place.

Such sales are rare, since they are so expensive and the returns are so little. More commonly, the debtor works out a settlement to get the property back without a sale. Up to the time of the actual sale, the judgment debtor can settle with you—which means paying you as much of the balance owing on the judgment, costs and interest as you demand.

If you wish to attend the sale, you can do so. If you pay cash for the business assets, the status of your judgment will not be affected; you will still be able to collect the full amount of your judgment if you can find other property to collect from. However, it is also possible to use your judgment as a credit in the bidding process (contact the levying officer on this one) and only have to put up cash (or certified check) if you bid higher than the unsatisfied amount of your judgment.

After the sale, the officer will turn over the proceeds to you, up to the balance of your judgment, less any fees and costs you still owe the levying officer for conducting the sale. If you have already paid all fees and costs, you should be reimbursed for these as well. If anything is left over, it goes to the debtor.

Once the levying officer has collected the proceeds of the levy, he will disburse them to you. There is often a significant delay between the collection of proceeds by the levying officer and its disbursement to you. While you should make reasonable attempts to make sure your case hasn't fallen through the cracks, be patient. Some levying officers require that any requests for information about your levy are made in writing; others will give you information over the telephone or in person.

Keep track of all funds collected toward satisfaction of your judgment, as well as any costs incurred by you. We discuss this in detail in Chapter 15.

Chapter 12

LEVYING ON MOTOR VEHICLES

COLLECTION FACTORS	High	Moderate	Low
Potential cost to you	X		
Potential for producing cash			X
Potential for settlement	X		
Potential time and trouble	X		
Potential for debtor bankruptcy			X

CALIFORNIA LAW PERMITS a judgment creditor to go after a debtor's motor vehicles to satisfy a judgment. This includes a debtor's car, truck, motorcycle, boat, plane or recreational vehicle (RV).[1]

Note: If your judgment stems from a car accident, see Chapter 1.D.2.

To the uninitiated, going after a debtor's motor vehicle to satisfy a judgment seems like a good idea. In reality, a forced sale of a motor vehicle nets little or no cash for the judgment creditor. It usually makes sense to levy on a vehicle only if:

- the vehicle is valuable and the debtor has substantial equity in it (ownership interest free and clear from loans)
- you want the vehicle for your own use (you can force a sale and buy the vehicle yourself for much less than its market value—see Section B, below) or
- you think the debtor will be scared into settling with you. Because nobody in California wants to be without wheels, an indication that you are actively considering seizing and selling her vehicle may give the debtor an adequate incentive to pay the judgment. Anyone who has been around the collection business for any length of time knows that when a person feels threatened with the loss of his precious wheels (or wings or keel) he often pays off a debt with money that he claimed absolutely didn't exist the day before.

A. Problems With Vehicle Levies

THERE ARE SEVERAL PRACTICAL REASONS why going after a debtor's vehicle is often fruitless (and why you should think carefully before using this approach). Here are the principal ones.

1. Debtor May Not Own Vehicle

If the vehicle is valuable, chances are a lot of money is owed to a lender—a car dealer, bank or credit corporation. If so, that lender must be paid off before you are.

[1]Generally, a motor home is capable of routinely traveling the highways (it has wheels) and must be registered with the DMV. By contrast, a mobile home is usually attached to the ground permanently or semi-permanently and does not travel the highways unless it is moved by a commercial mobile home mover. A mobile home need not be registered with the DMV and is not a vehicle for purposes of this remedy; it should be treated as real property for the purpose of making a levy. (See Chapter 14.)

Because sales seldom net what the vehicle is really worth, usually there is little or no money left for you.

2. Vehicle May Not Be Worth Much

If the judgment debtor is the legal owner of the vehicle (it's paid for), it's probably an older model or has greatly depreciated in value, and will be worth too little to warrant the cost of sale.

3. Vehicle May Be Partially Exempt

If you seize a debtor's only motor vehicle (as shown by DMV records), the debtor is automatically entitled to receive from the sale proceeds the first $1,200 of his equity in the vehicle. If the debtor owns two or more vehicles, he may still be entitled to the $1,200 exemption, but he must come forward and claim it. And if the debtor uses the motor vehicle you seize in his business, and doesn't have a vehicle that both qualifies for the $1,200 exemption and is fit for the business use, he may exempt $2,500. In short, for you to receive cash from the sale of a motor vehicle, the debtor's equity in the vehicle must be substantially over the applicable exemption amount.

Note: If you want to seize a boat or RV that is the judgment debtor's principal residence, a homestead exemption may come into play. (See Chapter 14.) If it does, your chances of realizing any proceeds from a forced sale are almost nil.

4. Vehicle Will Sell for Less Than Value

Anyone who has sold a used vehicle knows that what it fetches depends greatly on how it is sold. For example, a car that can be sold for $5,000 through a newspaper ad may only bring $2,500 as a trade-in.

Cars that are levied on are sold by the levying officer at an auction, which tends to bring in even less for the car than a trade-in. As a general rule, cars sell for approximately two-thirds of their low blue-book value (the low value listed in the *Kelley Blue Book* for cars utilized by California dealers or *Edmund's Used Car Book*). Most levying officers will not consider going after a car with a low blue-book value of less than $1,600.

5. High Costs of Levy

One major problem with levying on a judgment debtor's vehicle is that the costs of seizing, storing and selling it can run from $600 (the typical cost for levying on a car) to over $2,000 for boat and plane levies. These costs must be paid to the levying officer in advance of the levy, in the form of a deposit. If the levy is unsuccessful or doesn't produce any proceeds, you will have thrown a lot of good money after bad (although you may be able to recover these costs if you satisfy your judgment from other assets–see Chapter 15).

Example 1: *Rory obtained a $1,500 small claims judgment against Terry. Rory had Terry's Honda Prelude seized and sold, after paying the levying officer a $500 deposit. At auction, the car sold for $9,000, even though its market value (if sold privately) was probably closer to $12,000. Out of that money, the legal owner of the Honda, Gulp Acceptance Corporation, had to be paid the amount still due on the note, $7,700. Next, Terry received his $1,200 exemption, leaving $100. After deducting the costs of seizure, storage and sale ($400), the sheriff gave Rory $200 of his deposit back. Rory ended up losing $300 out of pocket as a result of the levy.*

Example 2: *Joshua obtained a $5,000 judgment against Berta. He found out that Berta owned an old model RV which she stored at her mother's house except when she used it for vacations. Joshua did a little asking around and determined that the RV had a market value of $5,000. He had it seized and sold by the sheriff. It sold for $2,500 (half of the fair market value, typical for a forced sale) and the costs of seizure, storage and sale amounted to $1,000. Joshua realized $1,500 from the sale.*

6. You May Need Court Order

Normally, a vehicle can only be levied on if it is in a public place, such as a street. If it is in a garage or other private place, you must first get a Seizure Order from the court. (See Chapter 18.)

B. How To Levy on a Vehicle

LET'S CONSIDER in more detail each of the steps for levying on a vehicle.

1. Get Vehicle Information

When you initiate the levy, you will need to provide the levying officer with a description of the vehicle, license or vehicle ID number and location where the vehicle can be found (a public place or on the street). You will also want to know what ownership the debtor legally has in the vehicle (legal owner, registered owner, joint owner). That way, you won't initiate a levy on a vehicle owned by a financial institution, for example.

Other than the obvious—going to the debtor's home or place of business to see where he parks his vehicle—here are some ways to get vehicle information:

- Debtor's examination and Subpena Duces Tecum (Chapter 6). To keep the debtor from concealing the vehicle, we suggest that you ask questions about it in a routine manner, not as though you are seeking to levy upon it
- Judgment debtor's Statement of Assets (Chapter 6.A)
- Court records (Chapter 6.B)
- Use a pretext (Chapter 9.C.1 and Chapter 8.A). Make modifications to obtain the information you need
- Data search firms, asset tracing firms, investigators (Chapter 23.D).

Another source of information is the Department of Motor Vehicles (DMV), which maintains information on all vehicles registered in California. Bear in mind, however, that the DMV will send a copy of your request to the judgment debtor or actual owner, who will have 10 days to object to your request. The only way to restrict the debtor's right to object arises if you're also seeking to serve the debtor with legal papers. (In that case, see Chapter 22.A.6 and use form INF 1129.)

If you decide to take your chances with the debtor objecting or hiding the vehicle, use Form INF 70, titled Driver License or Vehicle/Vessel Registration Information Request. You can use this form for two types of requests.

- **Vehicle/Vessell Registration Information:** This will provide information about what cars, boats, trucks, RVs and motor homes are registered under the name of the judgment debtor. You can also find out information about legal owners of the vehicle(s).
- **Asset Search:** The form does not give this option, but you may write the words "asset search" under Type of Request/Fees (the charge is currently $5.00), and again in Part C: Reason For Requesting Information and the Intended Use. You'll need to attach a copy of your judgment to the form.

The DMV's notice will alert the debtor that you are inquiring about his vehicle. You might gainfully follow up a license search by contacting the debtor and suggesting a settlement (see Chapter 5) before you initiate a levy.

You can get a copy of form INF 70, Driver License or Vehicle/ Vessel Registration Information Request, by stopping by or calling your local DMV office or by requesting one from the central DMV office at Registration Records/ Histories Unit, P.O. Box 944247, Sacramento, CA 94244-2470 (916-657-6474). The form is a two-part carbon form (the second part is sent to the debtor to advise him of your request). Bear in mind these factors when completing the form:

- The DMV checks for an exact match of the name you provide. Thus, if you specify John Smith, and DMV records show the judgment debtor as Jon Smith, the search may turn up a blank. Your best bet may be to submit several requests with variations of the debtor's full name (John P. Smith, John Paul Smith, J.P. Smith, J. Paul Smith). However, you must pay for each name search.

- Fees depend on what information you request—see the DMV form for a fee schedule.

2. Determine Debtor's Ownership

If you sent in a DMV vehicle registration request, look on the DMV printout to see who is listed as the legal owner (L/O). The registered owner is indicated by the code R/O. If the debtor is neither the legal owner or registered owner, you may have reached a dead end.[2] If the vehicle is in the name of a business owned by the debtor as an individual proprietor, ask the levying officer how to proceed next. Similarly, if the vehicle is jointly owned, ask the levying officer what additional documentation is needed for the vehicle to be levied on.

[2]If you discover (through a debtor's examination or the DMV full vehicle history) that the vehicle was very recently transferred, you may be able to seize the car from the new registered or legal owner. To do this you will need the help of an attorney.

Legal Owners, Registered Owners and Lienholders

New cars and boats are typically purchased by making a down payment and obtaining a loan for the balance. The lender retains legal title to the vehicle or boat, in the form of a purchase money security interest, until the loan is paid off. Accordingly, when the vehicle is registered with the DMV, the registration shows the purchaser as the **registered owner** and the lender as the **legal owner** until the legal owner files a release (after full payment of the loan).

Until the release is filed, the legal owner is normally entitled to repossess the vehicle if payments on the loan are not kept current. If the vehicle is sold to satisfy other debts, the legal owner is entitled to be paid the full value of the outstanding loan. Thus, if you have a debtor's vehicle sold to pay off your judgment, the legal owner must be paid before you get any money. The legal owner can also ask the court to prevent the property from being sold and have the property released to the registered owner.

Certain liens may have been placed on the vehicle, such as labor liens, tax liens and attachment liens. These liens entitle their **lienholders** to be paid before anyone else if the car is sold—except for the legal owner, who is always paid first.

When a motor vehicle is levied on, the levying officer must send a Notice of Levy to all legal owners, if different than the judgment debtor, as well as to all lienholders. This notice gives them an opportunity to protect their interests in the vehicle. If the property is repossessed and sold by the legal owner, you are theoretically entitled to receive any proceeds from the sale that are left over (after the judgment debtor receives his exemption), but such insider sales almost always bring less than is still owed on the vehicle.

a. If Debtor Isn't the Legal Owner

Commonly, you will discover that the debtor is the registered owner, but a bank or financing company is the legal owner. In this situation, it is extremely unlikely that you will come out ahead by forcing a sale. The amount of money owed on a car is often as much as (or more than) what the car can be sold for at a forced sale. Unless you are prepared to gamble the amount of the deposit on being able to force the judgment debtor into settlement, or you want to purchase the car for yourself at a forced sale, you should abandon this particular levy.

If you do choose to continue with the levy, you next want to determine the debtor's equity in the vehicle—that is, the value of the debtor's interest in the vehicle after the amount owed on it is subtracted from what the vehicle is likely to fetch at a forced sale. The way you do this is to start with the low value of the car as reflected in current used car or vehicle guides utilized by California dealers, such as the *Kelley Blue Book* for cars or *Edmund's Used Car* book. The vehicle will probably sell for about two-thirds of that amount at a forced sale.

If you are going after a boat or plane, the same type of information can normally be obtained from dealers. If you are unable to obtain access to a used vehicles price guide, check advertised prices in the newspaper and use the lowest sales price offered for the year and type of vehicle.

Once you determine the probable forced sale price for the vehicle, subtract the amount the debtor owes on it. This information must be obtained from the legal owner, or from the debtor himself in a debtor's examination. (See Chapter 6.) If you have difficulty getting this information, remember that the probability of your coming out ahead is slim when a third-party legal owner is in the picture.

If the judgment debtor has some equity in the vehicle (there is something left over after the amount owed is subtracted from two-thirds of the vehicle's low value), then subtract $1,200 (the judgment debtor's personal exemption in the vehicle) and $600 (the normal cost of a vehicle levy). If the debtor still shows some equity in the vehicle after these subtractions, and there are no liens on the vehicle (other than that held by the legal owner) it may be worthwhile going after it.

b. *If Judgment Debtor Is the Legal Owner*

If the judgment debtor is the legal owner, this makes the situation much easier to deal with. To find out whether the vehicle is worth going after, subtract $1,800 ($1,200 exemption plus $600 costs) from two-thirds of the low value shown for the car. If your remainder is positive, you may be able to get some cash from the forced sale. Otherwise, forget it unless, as we mentioned earlier, you want the car for your own or you are willing to spend $600 in hopes of inducing a settlement.

3. Obtain Writ of Execution

To initiate a motor vehicle levy, you need a Writ of Execution for the county where the vehicle is located. Don't get fooled into thinking that the vehicle is automatically in the same county as the debtor's residence. Rather, find out where the vehicle is physically located—for instance, on the street or public parking garage near where the debtor works. Instructions for obtaining a Writ of Execution are in Chapter 7.

4. Prepare Instructions

To find the levying officer for a county, call the sheriff's office in that county and ask if it makes levies on civil money judgments. If not, find out who does (marshal or constable). Call the levying officer and ask:

- the deposit amount required for a vehicle levy
- whether the levying officer has form instructions and
- if the vehicle must be worth a certain minimum amount.

For a car, you need the license plate number, the make and year. The vehicle identification number helps provide positive identification, in case the license plates have been put on a different car, but it isn't required. Include the car's color and known identifying factors (dent in right rear fender, two-tone, convertible, etc.).

Get as much detail as you can as to where and when the officer is likely to find the car. An officer can't go into a private garage or warehouse to get the car unless the owner invites him in. But as long as the vehicle is parked on the street or in a public place, it's fair game. For instance, if you know the car is likely to be within a block or two of the debtor's home at certain times in the morning or night, say so in your instructions. Or if the debtor takes his car to work and parks his car on the street or in the company parking lot, advise the officer accordingly, and give him the times when the debtor is at work.[3]

For boats, planes, motorcycles and RVs, give the same type of identifying information, including the manufacturer, license number, color and type of vehicle or craft.

Finally, if someone other than the judgment debtor is either the legal owner or a lienholder of the vehicle, you must provide the levying officer with their names and addresses so that they can be served with a Notice of Levy. This is where you will need the information from DMV records. The levy will be ineffective if you don't provide this information.

The levying officer may have his own form instructions for levying on a vehicle. If so, use them. If not, use the Instructions to Levying Officer form letter located in the Appendix. Here is a sample:

Date

Re: Pam Plaintiff v. Dan Defendant

To the Sheriff, County of San Francisco:

Enclosed please find:

1) Writ of Execution and copies and

2) check in the amount of $_______.

Please proceed to levy on (seize, store and sell) the following vehicle belonging to Dan Defendant:

1985 Saab 900 Turbo
Silver/rose color
Has a stuffed monkey hanging from the rear-view mirror
License Number XXX41
Vehicle ID No. DUUUUUUUUUH999

The vehicle is always parked in the street in front of the Dan Defendant's place of business between the hours of 9:00 a.m. and 5:00 p.m., located at:

Ex-Corporation
1000 Industrial Street (at Financial Way)
San Francisco, CA 94111

Please keep me up updated as to the status of this levy. I would like to attend the sale, so let me know when that will be.

Sincerely,

Pam Plaintiff

Note: If you think the officer may have trouble finding the vehicle, or the debtor may have it in a private place, this might be a good time to use a registered process server. Since they get paid for getting the vehicle, they tend to be more creative than sheriffs when faced with difficulties. A private process server is likely to spend more time trying to figure out where the debtor may have hidden the car on a public street and go a little further to locate it. For instance, a common ploy is to park a car two or three blocks away when the debtor knows that someone is likely to come get it. (Information about private process servers is in Chapter 22.)

Should you become convinced that the debtor is carefully keeping his car on property that a levying officer is not permitted to enter (for example, a garage, carport or other secured area belonging to the debtor, friend or relative), your only alternative may be to seek a court

[3]If the car is parked in a lot that has controlled access, the lot's owner may or may not let the levying officer enter.

Seizure Order permitting an officer to enter this property. See Chapter 18 for instructions.

5. Opposing Claim of Exemption or Opposition

After the debtor is notified of your levy, he can file a Claim of Exemption. If the levy is on the judgment debtor's only motor vehicle, the judgment debtor need not file this document to receive the automatic $1,200 exemption.

If the judgment debtor owns at least two motor vehicles, a Claim of Exemption must be filed for the exemption to take effect. If the judgment debtor claims that the motor vehicle is a necessary tool of his trade—and thus entitled to the $2,500 exemption—he must file a Claim of Exemption. The Claim of Exemption should be denied if the judgment debtor doesn't have another vehicle that would be reasonably adequate for the debtor's business purposes and that could be covered under the $1,200 personal vehicle exemption. In other words, if the judgment debtor has two cars, he can't take this exemption unless one of the cars is totally unfit for his business purposes (for example, he has a VW beetle as a second car, but needs to haul pipe for his plumbing business).

If a Claim of Exemption is filed, follow the procedures outlined in Chapter 13.C to oppose it. There is little you can do to contest a Claim of Exemption for $1,200, but if the car is claimed as a tool of the trade, you can oppose the Claim of Exemption by showing that the debtor is only entitled to the $1,200 exemption and the debtor's first car is reasonably adequate for use in the business.

Third-party objections: Third-party owners can also object to your sale. If a third-party owner files a claim, and you fail to file an opposition to it, which involves posting a deposit equal to the approximate worth of the car, the car will be released back to the debtor. As a general rule, you should only oppose a third-party claim if you are convinced you can prevail legally. You'll probably need to see a lawyer.

6. Attend Sale If You Want Vehicle

After you send your papers and fees to the levying officer, he will follow your instructions and proceed to seize and sell the vehicle. He may contact you about further fee deposits, to let you know the outcome of the levy, or if there was any problem with the levy (such as the vehicle being in a garage, or the debtor wanting to work out a settlement).

Sales of vehicles and the distribution of the proceeds are governed by CCP §§ 701.510 through 701.830. If you are contemplating buying the vehicle yourself, we recommend that you read these statutes to get an idea of what is involved (see Chapter 23 for more on legal research) and then ask the levying officer about the specific procedures used in that county.

You and the debtor will be given notice of the time and place of the sale. You should strongly consider attending if you think you could use the vehicle. The sale is conducted like an auction, with the vehicle sold to the highest bidder. As mentioned, the price normally obtained for vehicles in these auctions is far below their value in an unforced sale. You may be better off buying it yourself than letting it go for an amount that most likely will get you little or nothing in satisfaction of your judgment.

If you pay for the car, the status of your judgment will not be affected; you will still be able to collect the full amount of your judgment if you can find other property to collect from. However, it is also possible to use your judgment as a credit in the bidding process (contact the levying officer on this one) and only have to pay any additional amount if you bid higher than the unsatisfied amount of your judgment.

7. Get Proceeds From Levy

Assuming you did not attend the sale and the levying officer has collected the proceeds of the levy, she will disburse them to you. There is often a significant delay between the collection of proceeds by the levying officer and its disbursement to you. While you should make reasonable attempts to make sure your case hasn't fallen through the cracks, be patient. Some levying officers require that any requests for information about your levy are made in writing; others will give you information over the telephone or in person.

Make sure that you keep track of all funds collected toward satisfaction of your judgment, as well as any costs incurred by you. We discuss this in detail in Chapter 15.

Chapter 13

Levying on Tangible Personal Property

COLLECTION FACTORS	High	Moderate	Low
Potential cost to you	X		
Potential for producing cash			X
Potential for settlement			X
Potential time and trouble	X		
Potential for debtor bankruptcy			X

IN THIS CHAPTER, we discuss levies against tangible personal property—physical objects having value. This includes stock certificates, bonds, cameras, stamps, coins, computers, expensive musical instruments, video equipment, stereos, jewelry, tools, recreational equipment, weapons, luxury clothing (such as a mink coat), art, precious metals and the like. The property must be owned by the debtor and be in his possession.[1]

Seizing personal property should usually be a last resort. Prying personal property loose from a debtor is difficult and often not worthwhile. The main impediments are:

- The amount realized from a forced sale of personal property is usually not worth the effort and expense, except for items which have a ready market value, such as securities, precious metals and pianos.
- California law allows the debtor to keep many types of property. These are called "exemptions."
- The property may belong to someone else, or someone may have priority over you to collect from the property.
- A levying officer may not enter a debtor's residence without the debtor's consent or a court order—often difficult to get.

A. How To Levy on Tangible Personal Property

FOLLOW THESE INSTRUCTIONS to levy on tangible personal property.

1. Find Assets To Pursue

To start a levy, you must know whether the debtor has tangible personal property that is really worth this cumbersome procedure. You can use some of the techniques discussed elsewhere in this book:

- Debtor's examination and Subpena Duces Tecum (Chapter 6). To prevent the debtor from concealing

[1] Personal property owned by a business is covered in Chapter 11. Motor vehicles sales are covered in Chapter 12. Obligations held by a third party are discussed in Chapter 10.

property, ask questions about property in a routine manner, not as though you are planning a levy.

- Judgment Debtor's Statement of Assets (Chapter 6.A).
- Court records (Chapter 6.B).
- Use a pretext (Chapter 9.C.1, and Chapter 8.A.3). Make modifications to obtain the information you need.
- Data search firms, asset tracing firms, investigators (Chapter 23.D).

Once you know what the debtor owns, you must decide if it's worth going after. Make your decision based on these factors:

Value at forced sale. At a sale held by a levying officer, most personal property brings in a small fraction of the its fair market value. For example, a dining room table that might bring $1,000 in an antique store might sell for $250-$300 in a forced sale. Common exceptions to this diminished value rule are gold, gemstones, coin collections, pianos and securities (stocks, bonds, etc.).

Cost of storage and sale. The levying officer must store seized assets for a while to give the judgment debtor a chance to file a claim of exemption and to give notice of the sale. If a sale does occur, the cost of conducting it is substantial. In short, there are significant costs associated with levies on personal property. When these costs are deducted from the proceeds (which already are artificially low), often there is little or nothing left over to pay the judgment. So, let us emphasize: Before you send the sheriff out to levy on personal property, make sure you have identified at least one really valuable asset which you think has a reasonable chance of producing significant proceeds.

2. Determine if Property Is Off-Limits

Property you believe belongs to the debtor may be unreachable because it is exempt, belongs to someone else or is subject to another party's lien. Let's examine those possibilities.

a. Exempt Property

Debtors are allowed to keep some basic items of property, referred to as exempt property. Debtor protection laws are an attempt to strike a balance between the judgment creditor's right to collect and a human being's right to avoid sinking to the level of the many homeless people who haunt American cities.

Before we list the most important exemptions, you should understand how exemptions work. There are really two types of exemptions:

- those that return to the debtor a specific monetary allowance if the exempt property is sold
- those that protect certain property against sale.

Exemptions apply to individuals only, not businesses. The exemptions discussed in this chapter come into operation only if the judgment debtor comes forward and claims them (by filing a Claim of Exemption). However, as discussed in other chapters, some exemptions operate automatically.[2]

If a debtor has to claim an exemption to qualify for it, why not grab the exempt property and hope for the best? In many instances this makes sense, especially since few judgment debtors actually file Claims of Exemption. If, however, you have exempt property levied on, and it must later be returned to the judgment debtor because of a successful Claim of Exemption, you will lose temporarily, and maybe permanently, the costs and fees of the levy. While you are legally authorized to collect these from the judgment debtor (see Chapter 15), you may collect nothing at all. In short, by going after exempt property, you may throw good money after bad.

Here are the main exemptions applicable to the debtor's tangible personal property items that are not covered in other chapters in this book.

Household furnishings and personal effects: The judgment debtor is entitled to exempt all household furnishings and personal effects that are "personally used," "located at his principal residence" and "ordinarily and

---

[2]Certain funds in bank accounts are automatically exempt (Chapter 8), as are a portion of the debtor's wage (Chapter 9) and $1,200 worth of a motor vehicle (Chapter 12).

reasonably necessary." There is no particular dollar limitation. However, a court could determine that a particular item is too valuable or unusual to be "ordinarily and reasonably necessary." The court may let the item be sold if the debtor gets back part of the proceeds for a replacement item. For instance, if a judgment debtor has a $5,000 antique dining room table, the court might allow the table to be sold but allow the debtor the first $1,000 from the sale. Pianos and expensive electronic equipment are often treated in this way. Most other types of household furnishings are not; that is, the blanket exemption is upheld if the judgment debtor claims it.

Jewelry, heirlooms and works of art: The debtor's jewelry, heirlooms and works of art can be seized and sold; however, the debtor gets the first $2,500. It makes little sense to go after these types of assets unless they will bring in considerably in excess of $2,500. Also, the judgment debtor may claim that some items of jewelry or heirlooms are personal effects, which are exempt without regard to value if they are "ordinarily and reasonably necessary."

Health aids: The debtor is allowed to keep health aids necessary to help him work or live comfortably, such as a wheelchair.

Building materials: The debtor can keep up to $1,000 in building supplies if they were purchased to repair her home.

Tools of the trade: If tools of the debtor's trade are sold, the debtor gets the first $2,500 of the proceeds. A tool of the trade is anything used by the judgment debtor—or a spouse—in carrying out an actual business activity, such as:

- tools, business-related equipment, musical instruments, cooking implements
- materials such as paper, cloth, wood and hardware
- uniforms
- office furnishings
- books and manuals
- one commercial motor vehicle[3] and
- one fishing boat or other vessel used in the business.

Computer equipment needed to do desktop publishing, word processing or information searching also probably fits within the tools of the trade exemption. If the debtor and her spouse are in the same trade, business or profession which is also their livelihood, they are each entitled to a $2,500 tools of the trade exemption, for a total exemption of $5,000.

Researching Exemptions

A number of other exemptions apply to a judgment debtor's personal property. The most important of them are dealt with in other chapters. Following is a complete list of all exemptions and the citations to the Code of Civil Procedure sections where they are found.

If you want to read about how courts have interpreted any of these exemptions, visit your nearest law library. Locate the section in an annotated version of the Code of Civil Procedure (West's Annotated California Codes or Deering's Annotated Codes) and read the case summaries that follow. Chapter 23 gives more information on legal research.

[3] See Chapter 12.B.5, for more information about vehicle exemptions.

EXEMPTIONS FROM THE ENFORCEMENT OF JUDGMENTS

The following is a list of assets that may be exempt from levy.

Exemptions are found in the United States Code **(USC)** and in the California codes, primarily in the Code of Civil Procedure **(CCP)**.

Because of periodic changes in the law, the list may not include all exemptions that apply in your case. The exemptions may not apply in full or under all circumstances. Some are not available after a certain period of time. You or your attorney should read the statutes.

If you believe the assets that are being levied on are exempt, file a claim of exemption, which you can get from the levying officer.

Type of Property	Code and Section
Accounts *(See Deposit Accounts)*	
Appliances	CCP § 704.020
Art and Heirlooms	CCP § 704.040
Automobiles	CCP § 704.010
BART District Benefits	CCP § 704.110
	Pub Util C § 28896
Benefit Payments:	
BART District Benefits	CCP § 704.110
	Pub Util C § 28896
Charity	CCP § 704.170
Civil Service Retirement Benefits (Federal)	5 USC § 8346
County Employees Retirement Benefits	CCP § 704.110
	Govt C § 31452
Disability Insurance Benefits	CCP § 704.130
Fire Service Retirement Benefits	CCP § 704.110
	Govt C § 32210
Fraternal Organization Funds Benefits	CCP § 704.130
	CCP § 704.170
Health Insurance Benefits	CCP § 704.130
Irrigation System Retirement Benefits	CCP § 704.110
Judges Survivors Benefits (Federal)	28 USC § 376(n)
Legislators Retirement Benefits	CCP § 704.110
	Govt C § 9359.3
Life Insurance Benefits—	
Group	CCP § 704.100
Individual	CCP § 704.100
Lighthouse Keepers Widows Benefits	33 USC § 775
Longshore & Harbor Workers Compensation or Benefits	33 USC § 916
Military Benefits—	
Retirement	10 USC § 1440
Survivors	10 USC § 1450
Municipal Utility District Retirement Benefits	CCP § 704.110
	Pub Util C § 12337
Peace Officers Retirement Benefits	CCP § 704.110
	Govt C § 31913
Pension Plans (and Death Benefits)—	
Private	CCP § 704.115
Public	CCP § 704.110
Public Assistance	CCP § 704.170
	Welf & I C § 17409
Public Employees—	
Death Benefits	CCP § 704.110
Pension	CCP § 704.110
Retirement Benefits	CCP § 704.110
Vacation Credits	CCP § 704.113
Railroad Retirement Benefits	45 USC § 228l
Railroad Unemployment Insurance	45 USC § 352(e)

Type of Property	Code and Section
Benefit Payments (cont.)	
Relocation Benefits	CCP § 704.180
Retirement Benefits and Contributions—	
Private	CCP § 704.115
Public	CCP § 704.110
Segregated Benefit Funds	Ins C § 10498.5
Social Security Benefits	42 USC § 407
Strike Benefits	CCP § 704.120
Transit District Retirement Benefits (Alameda & Contra Costa Counties)	CCP § 704.110
	Pub Util C § 25337
Unemployment Benefits and Contributions	CCP § 704.120
Veterans Benefits	38 USC § 3101
Veterans Medal of Honor Benefits	38 USC § 562
Welfare Payments	CCP § 704.170
	Welf & I C § 17409
Workers Compensation	CCP § 704.160
Boats	CCP § 704.060
	CCP § 704.710
Books	CCP § 704.060
Building Materials (Residential)	CCP § 704.030
Business:	
Licenses	CCP § 695.060
	CCP § 699.720(a)(1)
Tools of Trade	CCP § 704.060
Cars and Trucks (including proceeds)	CCP § 704.010
Cash	CCP § 704.070
Cemeteries	
Land Proceeds	Health & S § 7925
Plots	CCP § 704.200
Charity	CCP § 704.170
Claims, Actions & Awards:	
Personal Injury	CCP § 704.140
Worker's Compensation	CCP § 704.160
Wrongful Death	CCP § 704.150
Clothing	CCP § 704.020
Condemnation Proceeds	CCP § 704.720(b)
County Employees Retirement Benefits	CCP § 704.110
	Govt C § 31452
Credit Union Shares	Fin C § 14864
Damages *(See Personal Injury and Wrongful Death)*	
Deposit Accounts:	
Escrow or Trust Funds	Fin C § 17410
Social Security Direct Deposits	CCP § 704.080
Direct Deposit Account — Social Security	CCP § 704.080
Disability Insurance Benefits	CCP § 704.130
Dwelling House	CCP § 704.740
Earnings	CCP § 704.070
	CCP § 706.050
	15 USC § 1673(a)
Educational Grant	Ed C § 21116

(Continued on reverse)

EXEMPTIONS FROM THE ENFORCEMENT OF JUDGMENTS
(Continued)

Type of Property	Code and Section
Employment Bonds	Lab C § 404
Financial Assistance:	
Charity	CCP § 704.170
Public Assistance	CCP § 704.170
	Welf & I C § 17409
Student Aid	CCP § 704.190
Welfare *(See Public Assistance)*	
Fire Service Retirement	CCP § 704.110
	Govt C § 32210
Fraternal Organizations Funds and Benefits	CCP § 704.130
	CCP § 704.170
Fuel for Residence	CCP § 704.020
Furniture	CCP § 704.020
General Assignment for Benefit of Creditors	CCP § 1801
Health Aids	CCP § 704.050
Health Insurance Benefits	CCP § 704.130
Home:	
Building Materials	CCP § 704.030
Dwelling House	CCP § 704.740
Homestead	CCP § 704.720
	CCP § 704.730
Housetrailer	CCP § 704.710
Mobilehome	CCP § 704.710
Homestead	CCP § 704.720
	CCP § 704.730
Household Furnishings	CCP § 704.020
Irrigation System Retirement Benefits	CCP § 704.110
Insurance:	
Disability Insurance	CCP § 704.130
Fraternal Benefit Society	CCP § 704.110
Group Life	CCP § 704.100
Health Insurance Benefits	CCP § 704.130
Individual	CCP § 704.100
Insurance Proceeds — Motor Vehicle	CCP § 704.010
Jewelry	CCP § 704.040
Judges Survivors Benefits (Federal)	28 USC § 376(n)
Legislators Retirement Benefits	CCP § 704.110
	Govt C § 9359.3
Licenses	CCP § 695.060
	CCP § 720(a)(1)
Lighthouse Keepers Widows Benefits	33 USC § 775
Longshore & Harbor Workers Compensation or Benefits	33 USC § 916
Military Benefits:	
Retirement	10 USC § 1440
Survivors	10 USC § 1450
Military Personnel — Property	50 USC § 523(b)
Motor Vehicle (including proceeds)	CCP § 704.010
	CCP § 704.060
Municipal Utility District Retirement Benefits	CCP § 704.110
	Pub Util C § 12337
Peace Officers Retirement Benefits	CCP § 704.110
	Govt C § 31913
Personal Effects	CCP § 704.020
Personal Injury Actions or Damages	CCP § 704.140
Pension Plans:	
Private	CCP § 704.115
Public	CCP § 704.110
Prisoner's Funds	CCP § 704.090
Property Not Subject to Enforcement of Money Judgments	CCP § 704.210
Prosthetic & Orthopedic Devices	CCP § 704.050
Provisions (for Residence)	CCP § 704.020
Public Assistance	CCP § 704.170
	Welf & I C § 17409
Public Employees:	
Death Benefits	CCP § 704.110
Pension	CCP § 704.110
Retirement Benefits	CCP § 704.110
Vacation Credits	CCP § 704.113
Railroad Retirement Benefits	45 USC § 228l
Railroad Unemployment Insurance	45 USC § 352(e)
Relocation Benefits	CCP § 704.180
Retirement Benefits & Contributions—	
Private	CCP § 704.115
Public	CCP § 704.110
	Ins C § 10498.5
Segregated Benefit Funds	Ins C § 10498.6
Social Security	42 USC § 407
Social Security Direct Deposit Account	CCP § 704.080
Soldiers & Sailors Property	50 USC § 523(b)
Strike Benefits	CCP § 704.120
Student Aid	CCP § 704.190
Tools of Trade	CCP § 704.060
Transit District Retirement Benefits (Alameda & Contra Costa Counties)	CCP § 704.110
	Pub Util C § 25337
Travelers Check Sales Proceeds	Fin C § 1875
Unemployment Benefits & Contributions	CCP § 704.120
Uniforms	CCP § 704.060
Vacation Credits (Public Employees)	CCP § 704.113
Veterans Benefits	38 USC § 3101
Veterans Medal of Honor Benefits	38 USC § 562
Wages	CCP § 704.070
	CCP § 706.050
	CCP § 706.051
Welfare Payments	CCP § 704.170
	Welf & I C § 17409
Workers Compensation Claims or Awards	CCP § 704.160
Wrongful Death Actions or Damages	CCP § 704.150

b. Property Securing a Third-Party Debt

You can't, as a practical matter, reach property that is subject to a perfected security interest or that is subject to liens that have priority over yours.[4]

> **Perfected Security Interest Defined**
>
> A security interest in property is normally created when the purchaser of the property borrows money for the purchase and gives the lender title to the property until the loan is paid off. This arrangement is common in purchases of expensive equipment, jewelry and household furniture.
>
> For the lender to assert her rights to the property as title owner, she must "perfect" her title by registering it with the California Secretary of State. Once a security interest is perfected, the security interest owner can prevent others (including you as a judgment creditor) from seizing the property until the loan has been paid and the security interest released.

Generally, we recommend that you check to see whether property is subject to a security interest before you instruct the sheriff to seize and sell it. You can find out by checking with the Secretary of State, who keeps a record of all perfected security interests. We discuss this procedure in Chapter 4.F.3. Or, you can pay a data search firm to do it for you. (See Chapter 23.D.)

What happens if you try to levy on property in which a security interest is owned by a third party? Basically, if the third party learns of the proposed property sale in time, he can file a third-party claim of ownership against you to stop the sale. If he learns of the sale after it has occurred, he can file a claim to get what the debtor owes him from the proceeds of the sale. If you've already spent the proceeds, he can sue you for the value of the property or even move directly against the property itself (which would lead to the sale purchaser coming back against you). You could be liable for any losses or damages suffered by the third party in his efforts to collect.

[4]In Chapter 4, we discuss two common liens and explain there that when property is sold, the senior lienholder is entitled to be paid first.

c. Property Subject to an Examination Lien

If another creditor has served the debtor with notice of a debtor's examination, all his personal property is automatically subject to a one-year examination lien. (See Chapter 6.C.) If you attempt to levy on property subject to such a lien, the fruits of your effort may end up in the lienholder's basket.

If you believe other judgment creditors exist, check the court records for each county where a debtor's examination may have taken place. (See Chapter 6, Sections B and C.) If you find a case against the judgment debtor, examine the file to see if a Proof of Service was been filed for an Application and Order for Appearance and Examination. If so, and the date of service is within the past year, all the judgment debtor's personal property is subject to the other judgment creditor's lien for the amount reflected in the judgment and any Memoranda of Costs in the case file. If you are faced with this situation, you can either:

- proceed with your levy in the hope that the lienholder has given up and won't find out about your levy or
- wait until the lien expires and then go after the assets.

> **Checking for Other Judgment Creditors**
>
> Court records may give you an idea of what previous attempts to collect, if any, have worked and which have not. These records can steer you away from an asset which a previous creditor was unable to reach because the debtor successfully claimed it as exempt, or because it is subject to a perfected security interest held by a third party.
>
> You might also be able to find out about other creditors' collection attempts from the levying officer where the debtor or her assets are located. Call the levying officer and ask for details. It makes sense to find out if there are other active creditors, because levying officers must levy on writs in the order received.

d. Considerations for Married Judgment Debtor

In general, you can go after a married debtor's separate property and community property, but usually not the separate property of a nondebtor spouse. Community property rules are covered in detail in Chapter 1.D.4.

Without a complete history of a married couple's property acquisition history, it is virtually impossible to tell how property is owned. So how should you proceed? As we mentioned earlier in regard to exemptions, one sensible approach is to go after valuable property and let the chips fall where they may. If the property is worth enough, it may justify your time and the risk of ending up with a bag full of costs and no proceeds.

3. Obtain Seizure Order for Assets in Debtor's Home

If the property is located in the judgment debtor's house or other private location, you'll need a court order permitting the levying officer to enter. To obtain such a Seizure Order, you must tell the judge what you expect to find there. The judge will not allow the levying officer to go on a fishing expedition.[5] See Chapter 18 for how to obtain a Seizure Order. Obtain certified copies from the court.

4. Obtain a Writ of Execution

Obtain a Writ of Execution for each county where the property is located. We tell you how to do this in Chapter 7.

5. Prepare Instructions

To find the levying officer for a county, call the sheriff's office in that county and ask if it makes levies on civil money judgments. If not, find out who does (marshal or constable). Then call the levying officer and ask:

- the amount of the deposit you must put down for making the levy
- how many copies of the Writ, instructions and, if applicable, a Seizure Order are required and
- whether or not the levying officer provides a form for instructions for levies against a debtor's tangible personal property.

If the levying officer provides a form, get a copy and use it. Otherwise, follow the guidelines in the accompanying sample. A blank Instructions for Levying Officer form letter is provided in the Appendix.

Date

To the Sheriff, County of San Francisco:

Enclosed please find:

1) an original Writ of Execution and copies

2) a check for $____ for fees and deposit

3) a certified copy of a Seizure Order.

Please proceed to levy on (remove, store and sell) the following tangible personal property of Dan Defendant which is located in his home at 234 West Street, San Francisco, CA 94118:

a) Original signed lithograph set by artist DeChing

b) Camera equipment

c) Mink coat (kept in hall closet)

d) Antique bedroom set (in guest bedroom)

e) Coin collection (kept in Dan Defendant's study)

f) Steinway baby grand piano.

Please keep me updated as to the status of this levy. I would like to attend the sale, so let me know when that will be. Thank you.

Sincerely,

Pam Plaintiff

---

[5] Even if the levying officer will attempt a levy and desist only when the debtor refuses to allow him into the house, we recommend getting the court order first. If the debtor keeps the officer out, she will have time to relocate valuable property before you can get a Seizure Order.

6. Send Instructions to Levying Officer

Make the number of photocopies of your documents required by the levying officer, plus one set for your file. Send your documents and fees to the levying officer for the county where the debtor's property is located.

The levying officer fills out a Notice of Levy, which she serves personally on the judgment debtor. The Notice of Levy names the person being served, the property to be levied upon and the amount necessary to satisfy the judgment.

7. If Debtor Files Claim of Exemption

When the debtor receives a Notice of Levy, she has ten days to respond from the date the notice was served on her. To object, the debtor must file a Claim of Exemption describing the property claimed to be exempt and the reasons for this claim, citing the section of the Code of Civil Procedure permitting the exemption.

If the debtor files a Claim of Exemption, the levying officer will serve you with a copy of it and a Notice of Claim of Exemption. This document officially states that unless you take proper steps to oppose the Claim of Exemption, the debtor's property will be released to her. Instructions for opposing a Claim of Exemption are covered in Section C, below.

8. Sale by Levying Officer

The levying officer posts a notice of sale and serves the notice on the debtor either personally or by mail. The notice states the date, time and place of the sale and describes the property to be sold. It is also posted in three public places in the city or judicial district where the property is to be sold.

The property is sold under auction rules to the highest bidder (CCP § 701.570(b),(d)). If you want the property yourself, you can use the judgment as a credit against your bid (CCP § 701.590(b)), but you'll need cash or a certified check to pay for a bid higher than the judgment. Call the levying officer and find out about the auction and your options as a judgment creditor.

The levying officer distributes the sale proceeds as required by law. Your share of these proceeds depends on the total fees due the levying officer (CCP § 687.050), applicable exemptions, the existence of third-party owners who must be paid and the priorities of any other creditors with claims.

9. Get Proceeds From Levy

Assuming you did not attend the sale and the levying officer has collected the proceeds of the levy, she will disburse them to you. There is often a significant delay between the collection of proceeds by the levying officer and its disbursement to you. While you should make reasonable attempts to make sure your case hasn't fallen through the cracks, be patient. Some levying officers require that any requests for information about your levy are made in writing; others will give you information over the telephone or in person.

Make sure that you keep track of all funds collected toward satisfaction of your judgment, as well as any costs incurred by you. We discuss this in detail in Chapter 15.

B. If Third Party Claims Property

A THIRD PARTY WHO HEARS about the levy may claim to own some of the property by claiming that the debtor:

- is storing it for him as bailee[6]
- is keeping the property on consignment
- borrowed the property from the third party
- has already sold or signed over the property to the third party, but not yet delivered it or
- pledged the property as security, either in the course of purchasing it (a purchase-money secured interest), or for a loan unrelated to that particular property (a non-purchase-money secured interest).

---

[6]A bailee is someone who stores property for another.

If you encounter a third-party claim, the procedure for opposing it is similar to that described for claims made by the debtor, with some procedural differences. If the amount of your judgment justifies bringing in legal help at this point, then by all means do so. However, usually, you are better off not contesting a third-party claim.

C. How To Oppose a Claim of Exemption

TO OPPOSE A CLAIM of Exemption, you must act fast. You must respond, in writing, within ten days from the date the Notice of Claim of Exemption was personally served on you, or 15 days from the date the Notice of Claim of Exemption was mailed to you, if notice was sent by mail to an address in California (CCP § 703.550, 684.120).

You must fill out and file with the court two forms, which are available from the court clerk or law library:

- Notice of Opposition to Claim of Exemption and
- Notice of Hearing for Order Determining the Claim of Exemption.

Because of the short filing deadline, we do not provide copies in the Appendix, in case the forms are updated and old forms would be rejected. Make sure you get the correct forms.

1. Fill out Notice of Opposition to Claim of Exemption

This form states that you oppose the debtor's Claim of Exemption.

Caption: Follow the format of your other court papers. Fill in the levying officer file number, located on the Claim of Exemption.

Item 1: Enter your name and address as the judgment creditor.

Item 2: Enter the name and last known address of the judgment debtor and his Social Security number, if you know it.

Item 3: Skip this unless the Claim of Exemption was made by someone other than the judgment debtor. This generally occurs only if you have levied on property in the debtor's possession that belongs to someone else.

Item 4: Enter the date the Notice of Claim of Exemption was mailed (it's on that form).

Item 5: Here you explain why you think the items claimed in the exemption should not be exempt. You may check one or more of the following boxes.

Item 5a: Check this box if you think the debtor's claim is incorrectly based on the statute cited for the exemption. (See Section A.2 above, and Chapter 23 on doing legal research.) For instance, if the debtor is claiming her expensive camera equipment should be exempt as tools of the trade (CCP § 704.060), you may want to argue that she is not really using these items as tools of her trade. You might state that the debtor is employed full-time in another capacity, and photography is really just her hobby.

Item 5b: Check this box if you think the debtor's property shouldn't be exempt because his equity in the property is greater than the amount allowed by the exemption. In other words, you think the value of the property is more than the deductible amount.

For example, say the debtor is claiming his works of art as exempt under CCP § 704.040, because they are only worth $2,500. However, you know or suspect these paintings in his home and office are really worth much more. As long as you can show this at the hearing on your motion of opposition, the value over the allowable exemption will be found not exempt.

Reality Note: Obviously, it is difficult to contradict a debtor's statement as to the value of his property, since you have no independent means of appraising it. Your argument is likely to work only if the property's value is obviously much greater than that claimed. This might be the case, for example, if you are going after a big 24-karat gold ring, and you know that day's price for gold.

Item 5c: Skip this item unless you can think of other reasons why the debtor's claim of exemption should be denied, such as your belief that the debtor is making untrue statements.

ATTORNEY OR PARTY WITHOUT ATTORNEY *(Name and Address)*: TELEPHONE NO.: 415/999-9999

Pam Plaintiff
123 North Street
Berkeley, CA 94704

FOR COURT USE ONLY

ATTORNEY FOR *(Name)*: In Pro Per

NAME OF COURT: San Francisco Municipal Court
STREET ADDRESS: City Hall, Room 300
MAILING ADDRESS: 400 Van Ness Avenue
CITY AND ZIP CODE: San Francisco, CA 94102
BRANCH NAME:

PLAINTIFF: PAM PLAINTIFF

DEFENDANT: DAN DEFENDANT

NOTICE OF OPPOSITION TO CLAIM OF EXEMPTION
(Enforcement of Judgment)

LEVYING OFFICER FILE NO.: 1000
COURT CASE NO.: 12345

— DO NOT USE THIS FORM FOR WAGE GARNISHMENTS —

The original of this form and a Notice of Hearing on Claim of Exemption must be filed with the court.

A copy of this Notice of Opposition and the Notice of Hearing *must* be filed with the levying officer.

A copy of this Notice of Opposition and the Notice of Hearing must be served on the judgment debtor and other claimant at least 10 days *before* the hearing.

TO THE LEVYING OFFICER:

1. Name and address of judgment creditor

   Pam Plaintiff
   123 North Street
   Berkeley, CA 94704

2. Name and address of judgment debtor

   Dan Defendant
   234 West Street
   San Francisco, CA 94118

   Social Security Number *(if known)*:

3. [ ] Name and address of claimant *(if other than judgment debtor)*

4. The notice of filing claim of exemption states it was mailed on *(date)*: September 8, 19__

5. The item or items claimed as exempt are
   a. [X] not exempt under the statutes relied upon in the Claim of Exemption.
   b. [X] not exempt because the judgment debtor's equity is greater than the amount provided in the exemption.
   c. [X] other *(specify)*: Judgment debtor Dan Defendant states that the Steinway baby grand piano belongs solely to his wife. In fact, he received the Steinway as a personal inheritance in 1987.

6. The facts necessary to support item 5 are
   [ ] continued on the attachment labeled Attachment 6.
   [X] as follows: The lithograph set by artist DeChing is worth at least $5,000 as a similar set recently sold for $6,500. The camera equipment is not tools of the trade, since both Dan Defendant and his wife work full-time in a deli/catering business. The Steinway baby grand was received by Dan Defendant as a personal inheritance.

I declare under penalty of perjury under the laws of the State of California that the foregoing is true and correct.

Date: September 15, 19__

Pam Plaintiff
(TYPE OR PRINT NAME)

▶ Pam Plaintiff
(SIGNATURE OF DECLARANT)

Form Approved by the Judicial Council of California
EJ-170 [New July 1, 1983]

NOTICE OF OPPOSITION TO CLAIM OF EXEMPTION
(Enforcement of Judgment)

CCP 703.550

Item 6: Check the first box if you need extra room to support your reasons in Item 5.

Check the second box if you can set out your facts in the space provided. For example, if you checked item 5a because you think the debtor is not using the equipment claimed to be exempt for his trade, enter your reason. See the sample.

Finally, date the form, type or print your name and sign it.

2. Fill Out Notice of Hearing on Claim of Exemption

This form is used to notify the debtor and the levying officer of the hearing on the debtor's Claim of Exemption. This same form is used for opposing a claim of exemption for a wage garnishment.

Follow the instructions in Chapter 9.D.7, to complete this form, with the following modifications:

Item 1: Fill in any third-party claimant.

Item 2a: The hearing must be held within 20 days of the date you file your opposition papers with the court. You must have the debtor served at least 15 days before the hearing, if service is by mail, or ten days before, if service is personal.

Item 3: If you don't plan to attend the hearing, see the sample declaration below to complete this item.

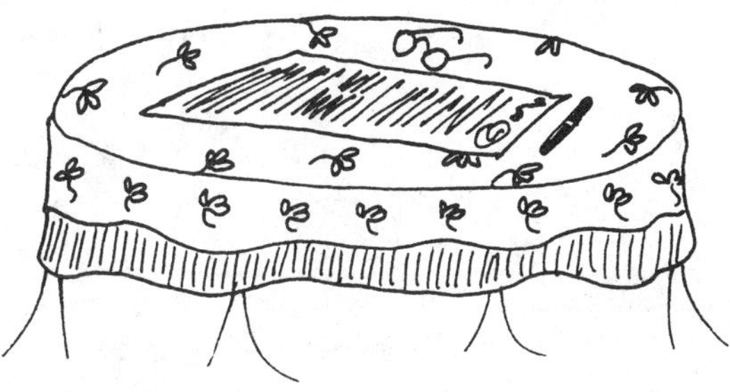

I, Pam Plaintiff, declare as follows:

1. *I obtained a judgment against Dan Defendant from the San Francisco Municipal Court on January 10, 19__ in case #12345.*
2. *The balance due on the judgment is $6,000, plus accrued interest and post-judgment costs.*
3. *On August 5, 19__ I sent instructions to the San Francisco Sheriff for a levy against tangible personal property owned by and in the possession of Dan Defendant. On September 8, 19__ a Notice of Filing of Claim of Exemption was sent to me.*
4. *I cannot attend the Hearing on Claim of Exemption which is scheduled for September 28, 19__. I will be in Boston, Massachusetts for my sister's wedding from September 16 through October 14, and the claim of exemption must be heard during this time.*
5. *Dan Defendant states in his claim of exemption that the lithograph set by artist DeChing is worth less than $2,500 and therefore is exempt pursuant to CCP Section 704.040. I am informed and believe that the lithograph set is worth more than $5,000. A similar lithograph set by artist DeChing was recently sold by the 20th Street Art Gallery for the sum of $6,500. The owner of the art gallery told me over the phone that all of DeChing's lithograph sets are worth "at least $5,000 and probably much more."*
6. *Dan Defendant states in his claim of exemption that the camera equipment is exempt pursuant to CCP Section 704.060 inasmuch as he uses it as tools of the trade. I am informed and believe that this is not true since Dan Defendant and his wife Martha own and work full-time at Danny-boy's Deli, a delicatessen and catering business.*
7. *Dan Defendant states in his claim of exemption that the Steinway baby grand piano belongs solely to his wife Martha. I am informed and believe that this is not true because Dan Defendant received it as a personal inheritance from his mother.*

I declare under penalty of perjury under the laws of the State of California that the foregoing is true and correct.

Date:

____
Pam Plaintiff

3. Serve and File Your Papers

Within the ten- or 15-day deadline, take these steps:

Step 1: Make at least four copies of your filled-in documents. One is for your records, another is for the levying officer, a third is to be sent to the court and a fourth is for the judgment debtor. If there is an additional claimant (say a third party who contests your levy), make an extra copy for this person.

Step 2: Have copies of these two documents served on the judgment debtor (or on his attorney, if he has one), at the address indicated on Item 2 of the Claim of Exemption. You can have these papers served on the judgment debtor by mail or personally. Usually, mail is the easiest and least expensive approach, as long as it allows the debtor at least 15 days' notice of the hearing date. Only ten days' advance notice is required if service is made personally. We cover service by mail and personal service in Chapter 22.

Step 3: Within the ten- or 15-day deadline, file with the clerk of the court:

- the original Notice of Opposition to Claim of Exemption (with your original signature)
- the original Notice of Hearing on Claim of Exemption (with your original signature) and
- an original Proof of Service, which is on the back of the Notice of Hearing form. The Proof of Service is filled out by the person who serves the Notice of Opposition to Claim of Exemption and Notice of Hearing on Claim of Exemption on the debtor. We provide a sample proof of service in Chapter 22.

Step 4: Within the ten- or 15-day deadline, give or send the levying officer:

- a copy of the Notice of Hearing on Claim of Exemption and
- a copy of the Notice of Opposition to Claim of Exemption.

Step 5: Once the levying officer receives your papers, she files with the court the Claim of Exemption sent to her by the debtor. If you don't get these notices to the levying officer by the deadline, she will immediately release any property claimed to be exempt back to the debtor or other claimant.

4. Claim of Exemption Hearing

It's generally a good idea to go to the hearing. Sit down the day before and review your arguments, as well as the papers submitted by the debtor. On the day of the hearing, try to get to the courtroom a little early. At the entrance, there may be a bulletin board with a list of the cases to be heard that day. If your case isn't listed, check with the clerk.

Step forward when the name of your case is called. Be prepared to straightforwardly answer the judge's questions. Remember to call the judge "Your Honor." If the judgment debtor shows up, don't interrupt her even if she makes statements you disagree with. The judge will give you a chance to state your side at the proper time. Be prepared for the judge to actively get you and the debtor to compromise. While you are legally entitled to go for it all, a stubborn attitude may prompt the judge to decide for the debtor.

5. After the Hearing

You will be notified of the judge's decision at the hearing or by mail. You and the debtor have the right to appeal the decision, just as in any other court proceeding, but appeals are rare.

If the finding is in your favor, the property can be sold and the proceeds applied toward satisfaction of your judgment. If the debtor prevails, any property found exempt must be released by the levying officer. Or a judge may order a variation of these two themes. For instance, the judge might determine property to be partially exempt but require it to be sold and replaced with a less costly item, with part of the proceeds of the sale going to the judgment creditor.

Until a decision is made on the Claim of Exemption, the levying officer will hold the property, and cannot release, sell or otherwise dispose of it. You will be charged the costs of this storage (which can be very expensive but which may recoverable from the judgment debtor–see Chapter 15).

Chapter 14

LEVYING ON REAL ESTATE

COLLECTION FACTORS	High	Moderate	Low
Potential cost to you	X		
Potential for producing cash		X	
Potential for settlement	X		
Potential time and trouble	X		
Potential for debtor bankruptcy			X

WHILE REAL ESTATE is often the most valuable asset the judgment debtor owns, collecting from it can be time-consuming and expensive.

The procedure for grabbing and selling someone's real estate is so convoluted that it usually requires a professional's help. We don't take you through each step of the process, but do give you a broad overview of the steps, along with enough detailed guidance to get you started. To continue, you will probably either need to do some research in the law library , or get professional assistance (Chapter 23). Of course, simply by initiating the process you may quickly get the judgment debtor to pay, or at least to agree on an installment payment plan.

A. Ways to Collect From Real Estate

THERE ARE TWO basic ways to collect from real estate:

- obtain a lien on the property and wait until the debtor wants to sell or refinance it
- force a sale of the property and collect from the proceeds.

Let's examine each of these methods.

1. Create a Lien and Wait

Fortunately, you rarely have to force a sale of a judgment debtor's real estate to collect your judgment if you obtain a lien against the property and are willing to wait—unless there are substantial creditors who created liens before you. You should create real estate liens even if you plan to sell the property. (Complete instructions for creating real estate liens are in Chapter 4.)

Liens on real estate are on file at the county recorder's office. When the owner wants to sell or refinance the property on the open market, your lien must be paid off for the purchaser to receive clear title. And you can maintain a lien for decades if you renew your lien each time you renew your judgment. (See Chapter 20.)

2. Force a Sale

Forcing a sale of real estate is a complicated process that may not net you much money. The difficulty is primarily due to several factors:

- If the real estate is the judgment debtor's home, homestead laws may entitle the debtor to keep $50,000 to $100,000 of the proceeds of a sale, depending on his age and family status.
- If the real estate is someone's dwelling (someone other than the debtor), a special order of sale must be obtained—a fairly complex court proceeding.
- Real estate tends to be heavily encumbered with deeds of trust (mortgages) which must be paid off before you can realize anything from a forced sale.
- The property may be subject to liens senior to yours, state liens or materialmen's liens (liens of contractors or laborers who worked on the property).
- The cost of selling real estate eats up a chunk of the eventual proceeds.
- Forcing a sale of real estate is complex and time-consuming, and requires a number of court appearances.

You may wish to consider one other possibility. If you want the real estate for your own use, you can get it cheap by forcing a sale and bidding on it yourself. While you may not realize any cash from the sale (from the standpoint of satisfying your judgment), you probably will get a good deal on the real estate and still be eligible to collect your judgment by other means. A forced sale of real estate rarely produces anything like the full market value of the property. Partly because of the scavenging nature of the process, forced sales often produce as little as 50% of what the property would fetch if sold conventionally.

Section C, below, provides an overview of the homestead laws and the process of forcing a sale. If you wish to undertake this process, you will probably need assistance from a knowledgeable attorney at some point.[1] However, you should be able at least to initiate the procedure yourself, which may prompt the judgment debtor to pay rather than fight.

[1] If you use an attorney, try to find one who has forced a property sale before. You don't want to pay for the attorney's learning curve. If you hire an attorney, this chapter will give you a good idea of what you are paying for.

B. Find Debtor's Real Estate

IF YOU DON'T KNOW what real estate the debtor owns, the methods outlined in Chapter 6 may be helpful. Or one of the following sources may yield the information.

1. County Tax Assessor's Office

Each county's tax assessor has listings of every property owner and piece of property in the county. This information may be contained in microfiche, a computer printout, or handwritten records, depending on the county.

If you have the debtor's correct name (check under the spouse's name and any business names as well), you can locate all real estate he owns in any county you check. You won't be able to tell whether the debtor owns the property alone or with someone else, but it's easy to find that out by looking at the deed (Section B.2, below).

If you have the debtor's address, you can find out if he owns the place. If he rents, you will learn the name of his landlord, who may give you some other useful information.

The tax assessor's listing also contains the address where the assessor mails the owner's tax bills. If the mailing address is different from the address of the property, it may be helpful for serving the debtor/owner with court papers. The mailing address also may provide you with another potential source of property to satisfy your judgment.

The assessor's listing may also include the assessor's parcel number (APN) of the property. That may be useful to have for cross-referencing, and will tell you whether a Declaration of Homestead has been filed on the property.

Some assessor's offices give out information by phone. If not, you can visit or write the office. If you write the tax assessor, an example of a letter requesting information is shown below. There should be no fee for this information, but enclose a self-addressed, stamped envelope with each request.

> *Date*
>
> *Assessor's Office, San Francisco County*
> *City Hall*
> *San Francisco, CA 94102*
>
> *Dear Assessor:*
>
> *Please provide me with the following information:*
>
> *1) Who owns the property located at 234 West Street, San Francisco, California 94118? Please provide me with the current names and addresses of the owners of record, the APN, indicate when the property was acquired and whether a declaration of homestead has been filed on the property.*
>
> *2) Does Dan Defendant own any property in San Francisco? If so, please provide me with the date the property was acquired, the property addresses, APNs, and indicate whether a declaration of homestead was filed.*
>
> *Enclosed is a self-addressed, stamped envelope for the return of this information. Thank you for your assistance.*
>
> *Sincerely,*
>
> *Pam Plaintiff*

2. The County Recorder's Office

For detailed information on ownership of the property, you must look at the deed itself. Copies of deeds are recorded at the county recorder's office. This search generally must be done in person. You can find out several important things about the property by looking in the county recorder's public records:

- whether the debtor owns the property by himself. It's important to know what share of this property he owns, because your judgment lien might attach only to his share. Other property owners can separately sell their interests in the property without worrying about your lien.[2] If the debtor decides to sell his share, however, or if the whole property is sold, the new owner will probably not purchase the property unless your lien is paid off.
- whether a bank owns a large portion of it.
- whether other judgment creditors and lienholders have already obtained liens against the property.

Deeds are usually indexed by name of the owners (all parties to a deed–grantors and grantees–are cross-indexed). The indexes are usually on microfiche, microfilm, or may even be handwritten. The indexes are generally alphabetical, and cover a certain number of years. Thus, for example, you may need to check on several microfiche cards to locate all property listings for a judgment debtor for a given 20-year period. When you visit the county recorder's office, ask for instructions on how to find the information you need.

3. Title Companies

Another way to find out where the judgment debtor owns property in is to check with a title company. Title companies provide a large range of services to buyers and sellers of real estate, such as title searches, title insurance and escrow transactions.

Many title companies have an alphabetical list of property owners compiled by a private source. While some title companies may have access to the entire list, which includes listings in every county, many only have listings for their particular area. This means you may have to check with title companies in several counties if you suspect the debtor has property in more than one place. (In that case you might be better off paying a data search firm to find out the information.)

Title companies may have more detailed information—often called a property profile—on a particular piece of property. Besides listing the owner of record, a profile may include some of the following information:

- year the deed was filed
- size of the property
- mailing address
- zoning restrictions

[2] But if husband and wife own the home as community property or in joint tenancy, you will probably be entitled to reach both spouses' interests. (See Chapter 1.D.4).

- estimated total value of the property
- value of any existing deed of trust (mortgage)
- amount of taxes assessed, whether taxes have been paid and to whom the tax bill was sent
- assessed value of the property
- current vesting or grant of the deed and
- a copy of the last deed and latest open deed of trust.

Title companies vary in their willingness to give out information. Some let you come in and look through their records. Others give out some information over the phone if you give them an address or the name of a property owner. Still others won't give any information to the public. Check with title companies in your area; you can find them listed in the Yellow Pages. When you call, ask to speak to customer service or an escrow officer.

4. Data Search Firms

For approximately $25-$35, you can have a data search firm conduct a statewide search for real estate owned by the judgment debtor. In many instances, it is worth your while to have one of these companies do your search rather than do it yourself. We discuss data search firms in Chapter 23.D.

C. Forcing a Sale of Property

FORCING A SALE of real estate is a time-consuming and expensive proposition that will probably require the help of a lawyer. Here, we explain how to determine if a forced sale appears worthwhile and, if so, how to start the process on your own.

1. Is It Economically Worthwhile?

Before levying against real estate, you want to know whether the judgment debtor has sufficient equity in the property to justify the effort. If, for example, the debtor is a 1/6 owner of a heavily mortgaged piece of real estate, you'll throw a lot of good money after bad if you go after the property. Even if the debtor is sole owner of a $200,000 home, chances are the deeds of trust on the property, homestead exemption and costs of sale will leave little or nothing.

To determine the judgment debtor's precise ownership interest and equity in real estate, use the sources described in Section B, above.

2. Understanding Homestead Laws

An important step in determining whether a forced sale is worthwhile is to find out whether the property is covered by the California homestead exemption. If a residence qualifies for a homestead exemption, you cannot force its sale unless the proceeds, after all liens, mortgages and costs of sale are paid, are likely to be more than the amount protected by the homestead laws (CCP § 704.800(a)).

Most often, judgment debtors have far less equity in their homes than the amount protected by the homestead exemption. That means the homestead laws normally will prevent you from forcing a sale of a home occupied by the debtor (whether it be a house, a boat that is lived on or a mobile home). And, if a formal Declaration of Homestead is on file, residential real estate owned by the debtor but rented out to a third party is also protected.

If you attempt to force a sale but receive no bid that is sufficient to pay off the homestead, mortgages, liens and costs of sale, you will not be able to recover your costs from the judgment debtor. In short, you will lose money if you unsuccessfully levy on property covered by a homestead (CCP § 704.840).

How It Works. If you force a sale of residential real estate subject to a homestead exemption, the homeowner receives from the proceeds at least the amount of the exemption before a judgment creditor is entitled to receive a penny. There are three exemption amounts: $50,000 for individuals, $75,000 for families, and $100,000 for the elderly or disabled.

Important Exceptions. The homestead exemption does *not* apply if:

- the judgment is for child or spousal support or
- the debtor or a member of his family isn't living in the residence (unless a Declaration of Homestead was filed before you recorded your judgment lien).

Also, delinquent property taxes and materialmen's liens (liens created by people who worked on the house) must be paid before the exemption is applied.

Eligibility. A judgment debtor's property is eligible for homestead protection if either of the following is true:

- the property is a residence (for example, house, condo, coop, houseboat, mobile home) and lived in by either the judgment debtor or a member of his family (no Declaration of Homestead need be recorded; protection is automatic) or
- the property is residential real estate and is covered by a Declaration of Homestead (which you can discover by a search at the county recorder's office).

A property owner may have only one homestead at a time.

> ***Example:** Davae and Andrenae, a married couple, record a Declaration of Homestead on their home in Petaluma. Two years later they decide to rent the house out to someone else and buy a new home in Santa Rosa. They decide to maintain the homestead on the Petaluma home and accordingly don't record a new Declaration of Homestead on the Santa Rosa home. Davae and Andrenae can claim the homestead exemption in the Petaluma home (the one covered by the Declaration of Homestead) but may not claim an exemption in the Santa Rosa home.*[3]

All of this can be a bit confusing. If you need to know more, see *Homestead Your House*, by Warner, Sherman and Ihara (Nolo Press).

[3] If Davae and Andrenae decide to file for bankruptcy, they will be entitled to claim a homestead exemption in the Santa Rosa home (the one they are living in) but not in the home where the Declaration of Homestead is on file (since they are not living in it). In other words, the written Declaration of Homestead has no effect in bankruptcy proceedings—it's where the judgment debtor is living that counts in the bankruptcy court (*In re Anderson*, 824 F.2d 754 (9th Cir. 1987)).

3. Sale Procedures

As we mentioned, you will probably need the help of an attorney before you are finished. We tell you in Chapter 23 how to locate collections attorneys.

Research Note: If you plan to initiate a levy on the judgment debtor's real estate, first become familiar with the laws governing this process. For real estate that is not being used as a dwelling and/or is owned by a partnership or corporation judgment debtor, these are CCP § 700.015 and §§ 701.540 through 701.680. If the real estate is a dwelling, you must also read CCP §§ 704.710 through 704.850. (See Chapter 23 for more on doing research in the law library.)

Here are the basic steps to force a sale when the property is a real estate dwelling (any real estate where a person resides).[4] For real estate that is not a dwelling and/or is owned by a partnership or corporation, the steps which entail court hearings are not required.

Step 1: Obtain a Writ of Execution (Chapter 7).

Step 2: Prepare written instructions for the levying officer. What should go in these instructions varies from county to county. To find the levying officer for a county, call the sheriff's office in that county and ask if it makes levies on civil money judgments. If not, find out who does (marshal or constable). Call the levying officer for the county where the real estate is located and obtain the following information:

- the deposit required for a real estate levy
- whether the office provides its own form instructions for making a real estate levy
- what documents you must provide with your levy instructions (these may include a filled-in Notice of Levy, a legal description of the property and a list of lienholders) and
- how many copies of each document are required.

Step 3: Deliver the required papers, required number of copies and deposit to the levying officer.

[4] The procedure outlined here is for real estate dwellings (CCP § 704.740). If the judgment debtor's dwelling is a boat or motorhome, see Chapter 12.

Step 4: The levying officer serves the Writ of Execution and Notice of Levy on the judgment debtor.

⚠ We anticipate that from this point on you will obtain the help of an attorney for residential property, and accordingly only provide a bare-bones outline of the remaining steps. Even if you decide not to go any further, the judgment debtor may already be willing to settle.

Step 5: Within 30 days after Notice of Levy is served on Judgment Debtor, you must give the levying officer a list of all lienholders and owners of deeds of trust and mortgages on the property. See Section B, above, for how to obtain this information.

Step 6: You must file a formal noticed motion in the county where the property is located and obtain an Order of Sale within 20 days after the Notice of Levy was served on the debtor.

How to Obtain an Order of Sale

Before you obtain an Order of Sale, you must get the property independently appraised, obtain a title report that reflects all encumbrances and liens and determine whether the home is subject to a homestead exemption. To obtain an Order of Sale, you must give the court:

- the fair market value of the property
- amounts of liens and encumbrances on the property (including mortgages, deeds of trust, liens senior to yours and, in some cases, liens junior to yours[5]) and
- amount of the homestead exemption, if one is applicable.

Step 7: The court sets a hearing within 45 days after the motion is filed and issues an Order to Show Cause (why the property shouldn't be sold) to the debtor.

Step 8: The Order to Show Cause and certain other papers must be served on the debtor and occupants of the dwelling within 30 days of the scheduled hearing.

Step 9: If the debtor doesn't attend the hearing, she is entitled to request a second hearing.

Step 10: At the hearing, the court determines and issues an order containing the amount of any homestead exemption, the fair market value of the property and the amount of sale proceeds that must be distributed to holders of liens and encumbrances.

Step 11: A sale is held by the levying officer (no sooner than 120 days after the Notice of Levy was served) after giving notice to the judgment debtor, lien and encumbrance holders, and the occupant of the dwelling (at least 20 days before the sale), stating the date, time and place of sale and the address and a description of the property. The property may be sold only if the winning bid is at least 90% of the property's fair market value as determined by the court in its Order of Sale or the court orders otherwise. If a high enough bid is not received, the court can order a new sale one year or more later.

Non-residential property. No special Order of Sale is required. However, the sale cannot occur until 120 days after the Notice of Levy is served on the judgment debtor, and the proceeds must still exceed the amount of existing encumbrances and liens on the property.

[5] Senior liens are those which were created before yours, or which are given priority by law (such as tax liens). Junior liens are those created after yours. When property subject to liens is forcibly sold, senior liens are paid off first; the junior liens are only paid if there is enough left over. After the forced sale, all liens are extinguished.

Chapter 15

COLLECTING POST-JUDGMENT COSTS AND INTEREST

WHILE SOME COURT JUDGMENTS are paid in full right away, others take months or years to collect. You are entitled to interest on the judgment until it is paid. And you may also collect most of the costs incurred to collect the judgment—such as court filing fees and levying officers' costs. Of course, like the judgment itself, being entitled to collect post-judgment interest and costs and actually recovering them are horses of a different color.

It is important to carefully keep track of what you collect and what is due you. If you collect more than is owed you, you must return the overpayment to the judgment debtor immediately. You could inadvertently collect too much if, for example, you simultaneously attempt both a wage levy and a bank levy in different counties.

In this chapter, we show you how to keep track of payments on the judgment, costs and interest. We also show you how to file papers with the court to claim your costs and interest.

When the Debtor Pays By Check

Always make copies of checks written by the debtor to pay the judgment. Should you later want to levy on a bank account, you'll have information on where the debtor has been banking. If the debtor's check bounces, make a demand on the debtor by certified mail, requesting payment on the bounced check within 30 days. Keep photocopies of the bounced checks, your demand letter to the debtor and the original signed certified receipt.

If the debtor does not make the check good, you can take either of these steps:

- Sue in small claims court (or in municipal court if there is no small claims court in your area), for the original amount of the bounced check plus three times that amount—with a minimum of $100 and a maximum of $500 as "treble damages" (Civil Code § 1719).[1]
- See if your county's district attorney's office has a check diversion program. To avoid criminal prosecution, the person who wrote a bad check must make the check good and comply with other rules. You cannot seek damages if you enlist the district attorney's help—but you'll be spared the hassle of another lawsuit.

[1] For more information, see *Everybody's Guide to Small Claims Court*, by Ralph Warner (Nolo Press).

A. Post-Judgment Costs

VARIOUS COSTS ARE SPECIFICALLY collectable according to statute and can be added to your judgment with a Memorandum of Costs (CCP § 685.070). They include all of the following:

- clerk's filing fees (such as for obtaining a Writ of Execution or Abstract of Judgment)
- statutory fees charged, and costs incurred, by the levying officer for attempting a levy under a Writ of Execution
- statutory fees charged by a process server for serving the Application and Notice of Order of Examination or Subpena Duces Tecum, if they are approved by the court in which the debtor's examination is conducted (Chapter 6)
- fees charged to have a bench warrant issued and served if the debtor doesn't show up at the debtor's examination, if the judge approves them (Chapter 6)
- fees expended for recording an Abstract of Judgment to place a lien on the debtor's real estate (Chapter 4)
- fees for filing a Notice of Judgment Lien on Business Personal Property (Chapter 4)
- notary fees incurred in the collection process (if, for instance, you file a partial Satisfaction of Judgment)
- fees connected with bringing a motion, if approved by the judge (Chapter 18) and
- attorney fees, if the judgment called for attorney fees on the basis of a contract or statute (CCP § 685.040).

Note that you cannot add in lawyers' fees, fees for your own time or miscellaneous out-of-pocket expenses such as parking costs. If you want to recover these kind of expenses, you need to file a motion with the court. (See Section A.2, just below.)

1. Costs of Levies

When a levy is made against the judgment debtor's assets, the levying officer is authorized to collect the amount remaining on the judgment (shown in the Writ of Execution) and the costs of that particular collection. These costs include:

- the statutory fee for issuance of the Writ of Execution under which the levy is made and
- the levying officer's statutory fees and allowable costs for doing the levy.

For example, if you instruct the sheriff to levy on the judgment debtor's bank account, you pay a statutory fee as well as actual costs. If the levy is successful, the levying officer will recover the deposit that you advanced and as much of the amount owing under the judgment as he can.

If a levy is unsuccessful because a claim of exemption is filed, or the levying officer doesn't collect enough even to cover your deposit, you are temporarily out of the money. You may even have to pay the levying officer more, if the deposit didn't cover his costs.

However, you are entitled to recover these amounts from the judgment debtor if you file a Memorandum of Costs. Then, unless the debtor successfully objects to a specific cost (which is rare), the documented costs are fully collectable as part of your judgment.

Example: *You instruct the sheriff to levy against the debtor's car, and put up a $400 deposit, only to find out after the car has been seized that it is essentially worthless. Until you discover assets that you can successfully collect, you will be $400 poorer for your effort (assuming the levying officer used up the deposit—it is possible some of it was refunded to you).*

What, however, if you later discover a juicy bank account that will not only satisfy your judgment but also cover your $400? The levying officer will not be able to collect that $400 as part of the bank levy, since it is unrelated. To make the $400 collectable, you'll have to file a Memorandum of Costs with the court. Then the $400 can be collected as part of the judgment.

Exemptions Note: If you attempt a levy and the assets are determined to be exempt (for example, the debtor files a claim of exemption which is upheld), you can still, generally, recover costs of the levy from the judgment debtor. This is because the levy itself was proper; the fact that a levy is later disallowed doesn't mean that you weren't entitled to try. (A notable exception is levying against homesteaded real estate—see Chapter 14.C.2.)

2. Other Collection Costs

A California judgment creditor is entitled to "the reasonable and necessary costs of enforcing a judgment" (CCP § 685.040). However, unless the cost is one of those specified above, you must file a motion with the court, give the judgment debtor notice of the hearing on the motion, and convince the judge that the cost is reasonable.

> ***Example:*** *You use a registered process server in a levy on the judgment debtor's bank account because the levying officer has a two-week backlog and you're afraid the funds will evaporate if you don't act quickly. The process server's fees turn out to be $105. Fees and costs paid to a registered process server aren't listed in the statute—only fees and costs charged by the levying officer are collectable through a Memorandum of Costs. However, if you can convince a judge that a registered process server was necessary, the judge will award you the cost. Generally, judges are lenient in awarding this type of cost when the judgment creditor demonstrates good faith.*

In this chapter, we don't explain how to file a motion for costs. However, in Chapter 18, we tell you how to bring a noticed motion for an Assignment Order. That discussion should be helpful if you prepare a costs motion. (See Chapter 23 on doing legal research.) If the costs warrant it, get help from an attorney.

Reality Note: Many creditors claim costs in a Memorandum of Costs that are not authorized by statute—such as process servers' fees. It is up to the debtor to get these costs disallowed. We do not recommend that you add in extravagant costs of collection. However, if you're not sure if your costs can be claimed through a Memorandum of Costs, and you believe that they're reasonable, you can try including them and see what the debtor does.

B. Post-Judgment Interest

YOU CAN RECOVER INTEREST on the unpaid portion of your judgment and on unpaid costs that have been claimed on a Memorandum of Costs. If your original judgment was appealed and you won the appeal, interest accrues from the date judgment was first entered. If the judgment is an installment judgment, interest accrues on each installment as it becomes due.

Interest accrues at the rate of 10% per year.[2] If none of the judgment has been paid, it is fairly easy to compute the interest. If, on the other hand, you have received some payments and costs have been incurred, figuring the interest due on the judgment may get a little tricky. We explain how to do this in Section C, below.

For collection purposes, there are two types of interest:

- interest that accrues between the time the judgment is entered and the time the Writ of Execution is issued and
- interest that accrues between the date of issuance of the Writ of Execution and the actual levy.

The first type of interest must be properly documented before it can be collected by the levying officer. You do this first by claiming the interest due on a Memorandum of Costs (see Section D, below), and indicating the amount of interest due on a Writ of Execution.

The second type of interest can be collected by the levying officer without prior documentation by you, since the Writ of Execution directs the levying officer to collect interest on the amount remaining on the judgment. A Writ of Execution lasts for 180 days, so it's possible that several months' worth of interest will mount up by the time a levy is completed. It the levying officer collects enough to cover that interest, he will forward it to you.

C. Keeping Track of Post-Judgment Costs, Interest and Credits

WHEN IT COMES TIME to prepare a Memorandum of Costs to claim your costs and interest, you will need to have accurate records that show:

[2] The statutory post-judgment interest rate went up January 1, 1983. If you got your judgment before then, you collect interest at the rate of 7% annually before January 1, 1983, and at 10% after that date. However, a judgment against the State of California or any of its agencies is collectable at only 7% per year.

- when specific costs were incurred, and for what reason
- when specific payments were made on the judgment (voluntary and involuntary) and
- what costs and interest you previously claimed on Memoranda of Costs filed with the court.

We provide you with one method of keeping track of post-judgment costs, interest and credits. In the Appendix are forms to keep track of these items. You may want to make several copies in case it takes a while to collect your judgment. Although the information in these samples is typed in, you can handwrite your own forms.

1. Keeping Track of Costs

You'll find the Keeping Track of Costs form in the Appendix. If you keep the form up to date, when it comes time to prepare your Memorandum of Costs, you'll have all the information you need at your fingertips.

We suggest you keep your receipts for all costs incurred—especially if you paid cash. That way, if the judgment debtor raises any questions about the cost, you'll have proof it was a legitimate claim. Here's how to fill in the form.

Date Expended: Enter the date you paid each cost.

Cost Amount: Enter the amount of each cost.

Type of Cost: Enter the kind of cost. For example, it might be a filing fee for a Writ of Execution, a sheriff's deposit for a wage levy or a recording fee for an Abstract of Judgment.

Expense Record: Put how you paid the cost. If you paid by check, put the check number.

Date Costs Claimed: Leave this blank until you actually claim this cost on a Memorandum of Costs. At that time, fill in the date. (This record will ensure that you don't claim the same cost twice.)

If you've already been reimbursed, you cannot claim the cost on a Memorandum of Costs. For example, this might occur if the sheriff repaid your Writ of Execution filing fees and deposit from the proceeds of a bank levy. Make a note of any reimbursed costs.

KEEPING TRACK OF COSTS

Date Expended	Cost Amount	Type of Cost	Record	Costs Claimed
2/4/93	$3.50	Writ of Execution—Alameda	Cash	9/21/93
3/15/93	$28.00	Bank levy—sheriff's fees	#202	"
5/21/93	$15.00	Process server—debtor's exam	#231	"
6/18/93	$3.50	Writ of Execution—San Francisco	#235	"
6/30/93	$21.50	Wage levy—sheriff's fees	Cash	"

2. Keeping Track of Collecting Your Judgment

The Keeping Track of Collecting Your Judgment form in the Appendix gives you a handy record of everything that has happened on your judgment. Follow the instructions and keep the form up-to-date.

Top of form: Enter the judgment date and the judgment amount.

Date of Transaction: Enter the date each payment on the judgment was made or each Memorandum of Costs was filed with the court.

Type of Transaction: Say what kind of transaction was involved, such as voluntary payments, kind of levies and Memoranda of Costs.

Record: For payments, state how they were made. Include check numbers.

Amount Received: Enter the amount you received for each payment on the judgment.

Subtotal Received: Enter the total amount you have received to date as payment on the judgment.

Costs Filed: Each time you file a Memorandum of Costs with the court, enter the amount of costs you claim.

Interest Filed: Each time you file a Memorandum of Costs with the court, enter the amount of interest you claim.

Total Now Due: Enter the total amount now due. This is the amount remaining on the judgment less payments received (Subtotal Received), plus all costs (all amounts under Costs Filed) and interest (all amounts under Interest Filed) claimed on Memoranda of Costs.

KEEPING TRACK OF COLLECTING YOUR JUDGMENT

Judgment Date: 1/10/93

Judgment Amount: $6,000

Date of Transaction	Type of Transaction	Record	Amount Received	Subtotal Received	Costs Filed	Interest Filed	Total Now Due
3/28/93	Bank levy	#251211–Ala. Sheriff	$621	$621	–	–	$5,379
7/15/93	Wage levy	#8884A–SF Sheriff	$420	$1,041	–	–	$4,959
8/18/93	Wage levy	#8892A–SF Sheriff	$420	$1,461	-	-	$4,539
9/21/93	Voluntary	Cash	$250	$1,711	–	–	$4,289
9/21/93	Memo Costs	–	–	–	$71.50	$372.81	$4,733.31

3. Keeping Track of Interest (Calculation Sheet)

Interest may be collected on the judgment and on costs claimed in a Memorandum of Costs filed with the court. However, you cannot collect interest on interest that has previously accrued and been claimed in a previously filed Memorandum of Costs. (To collect interest on accrued interest, you must renew your judgment. See Chapter 20.)

The interest that accrues on a judgment depends not only on the size of the judgment, but also on how long it remains unpaid.

> ***Example:*** *A $3,000 judgment that is paid off within three months produces $75 in interest (calculated at an annual rate of 10%). A $500 judgment will produce the same amount of interest if it remains unpaid for 18 months.*

If a judgment is paid in a lump sum, computing interest is relatively easy. But it's more common for payments to dribble in, either voluntarily or through levies and wage garnishments. You must make a separate interest calculation for each period between payments. Unfortunately, there's no short-cut for doing this, although a computer spreadsheet can be a real timesaver.

If you're not using a computer, your efficiency can be greatly increased if you systematically complete the Keeping Track of Costs form (Section C.1, above) and Keeping Track of Collecting Your Judgment form (Section C.2, above). You shouldn't need to add up the interest amounts until you're ready to fill out a Memorandum of Costs (Section D).

We provide instructions for computing interest on a 360-day year in order to keep the process of calculating interest as easy as possible. That means that interest is based on a 12-month, 30-day per month year. If you want to be more accurate, substitute 365 days for 360.

Payments on a judgment are technically applied first to interest, then to the unpaid principal balance, including costs that were claimed on a Memorandum of Costs. You can apply payments in that order, rather than using the simplified method shown. Remember that you cannot claim interest on accrued post-judgment interest unless you renew the judgment.

Before getting started, you'll probably want to make several copies of the Keeping Track of Interest (Calculation Sheet) form. Here is how to use the form to calculate interest. You can refer to our completed sample for reference.

Starting Date (column A): Fill in either the date your judgment was entered (only if you haven't completed and filed a Memorandum of Costs before), or the date you last completed a Memorandum of Costs.

Ending Date (column B): Fill in either the date you are completing the form (only if you haven't received any payments on the judgment), or the date you first received a payment after the Starting Date (column A).

Number of Days (column C): Enter the number of days in the period between the Starting Date (column A) and Ending Date (column B). You can assume there are 30 days per month. For example, if the calculation period starts on 1/10/93 and ends on 3/28/93, we can figure two months from 1/10/93 to 3/10/93 (60 days) plus 18 days from 3/11/93 through 3/28/93, for a total of 78 days.

Balance (column D): Enter the original amount of your judgment (if you haven't completed and filed a Memorandum of Costs before). Otherwise fill in the balance due on the date you last completed a Memorandum of Costs, less interest previously claimed.

Payment (column E): Indicate the payment amount you received on the Ending Date (column B), if any.

New Balance (column F): Subtract the Payment (column E) from the Balance (column D), and enter this amount.

Interest Due (column G): In the interest blank, fill in either 10% (if you are calculating interest after 1/1/83), or 7% (if you are calculating interest before 1/1/83 or on a judgment against the State of California or any of its entities).

Now perform the equation and enter the amount in the blank at the right. In the sample provided, we multiply our Balance (column D) of $6,000 by an annual interest rate of 10%, by 78 days (column C), then divide by 360 (days per year). The result, $130, is the amount of interest that accrued on the judgment from 1/10/93 through 3/28/93.

You are now ready to calculate interest for the next period, which will commence as of the Ending Date (column B) above. Follow the same instructions based on the new balance.

(Sub)Total: When you have calculated interest for each period, add up the Interest Due (column G), and enter this amount at the bottom of the form. Naturally, if you use more than one calculation sheet, you'll need to add up the totals from the bottom of each page to get a grand total.

If you're not clear about the interest calculation process, you might want to study the sample we provide. This sample is consistent with all of the forms provided in this chapter, so you can see where we obtained the information necessary to complete the form.

KEEPING TRACK OF INTEREST (CALCULATION SHEET)

A Starting Date	B Ending Date	C No. of days	D Balance (F from line above)	E Payment	F New Balance	G Interest Due (D x 10 % · x C/360)
1/10/93	3/28/93	78	6,000.00	621.00	5,379.00	130.00
3/29/93	7/15/93	106	5,379.00	420.00	4,959.00	158.38
7/16/93	8/18/93	32	4,959.00	420.00	4,539.00	44.08
8/19/93	9/21/93	32	4,539.00	250.00	4,289.00	40.35
					(Sub)total	372.81

D. Memorandum of Costs

TO CLAIM AND COLLECT post-judgment costs and interest, you must periodically complete and file with the court a form that documents these amounts. We refer to this form as the Memorandum of Costs. It varies from court to court—a few courts require two forms[3]—and goes by different names, including:

- Memorandum of Costs After Judgment
- Cost Bill After Judgment
- Declaration for Accrued Interest After Judgment
- Memorandum of Credits, Accrued Interest and Costs After Judgment.

In the Appendix, we provide a form that can be used in many courts. If your court has its own form or forms, use them instead. You can easily adapt the instructions provided here.

You don't have to file a Memorandum of Costs at any particular time, as long as you do it within two years

[3] For instance, one court may have you document costs and credits on one form, and interest on another, whereas another may require costs and interest on one form but no documentation of credits.

of the date the costs were incurred (CCP § 685.070b). However, having your costs documented means that they are added to the judgment itself, and you can recover interest on them. Therefore, it makes sense to file a Memorandum of Costs whenever you incur significant costs (say $50 or more) that you don't recover.

Counties Where Service Is Not Done by Levying Officers

It used to be that the sheriff, marshal or constable served all levying papers and collected and forwarded funds to the judgment creditor. But budget cuts have pushed levying officers in some counties to drop those tasks.

In those counties, you must hire a private process server to serve wage garnishments and bank levies. The problem for the judgment creditor is that because the levying officer isn't serving papers and tacking his fee onto the total collected at the end of the levy, the process server's fees aren't recovered.

One practical way to get around this is to:

- get an estimated price quote from the process server before the papers are served, and
- claim that amount in a Memorandum of Costs that you file simultaneously with the Writ (see "Simultaneous Writ and Memorandum of Costs," below). Technically, you're not supposed to claim costs before they're incurred. Listing them on a Memorandum of Costs, however, does allow the debtor to contest them. And it keeps you from getting stuck paying the process server's fees.

After the debtor's time to respond has elapsed (15 days if service was by mail), you'll need to send a certified copy of the Memorandum of Costs to the levying officer. (See Section D.4.)

We suggest that you file a Memorandum of Costs at least once a year, unless you don't want the judgment debtor to know that you're actively pursuing the judgment (if you're planning to take the debtor by surprise), since you must have the debtor served with a copy of this document.

Once you have filed a Memorandum of Costs, make sure that you don't claim interest on post-judgment interest. Thus, the second time you prepare a Memorandum of Costs, subtract the interest previously claimed on a Memorandum of Costs from the total due before you start calculating. (On the Keeping Track of Collecting Your Judgment form, this would be the Total Now Due less all amounts claimed in the Interest Filed column.) If you want to earn interst on the interest you've claimed, you must renew your judgment—an option that's available once every five years. (See Chapter 20.)

Simultaneous Writ and Memorandum of Costs

If you file a Writ of Execution at the same time as a Memorandum of Costs, you can claim up to $100 in statutory costs on the Writ if those costs are documented in the Memorandum of Costs, along with this statement: "The fees sought under this memorandum may be disallowed by a court upon a motion to tax filed by the debtor notwithstanding the fees having been included in the writ of execution." (CCP § 6895.070(e)). However, if the judgment debtor successfully contests these costs, you will not be allowed to keep them.

1. Complete the Memorandum of Costs

Using information from the record-keeping forms you completed in Section C, above, you can now prepare a Memorandum of Costs to file with the court. A blank form is provided in the Appendix.

Caption: Fill in your name, address and telephone number, court name, case name and case number.

Memorandum of Credits: Enter the amount you have received on the judgment. You will find this sum in the column entitled Subtotal Received on the Keeping Track of Collecting Your Judgment form. If you haven't collected anything, put "None."

Pam Plaintiff
123 North Street
Berkeley, CA 94704
(415) 999 -9999
In Pro Per

MUNICIPAL COURT OF CALIFORNIA

COUNTY OF SAN FRANCISCO

PAM PLAINTIFF, Plaintiff, vs. DAN DEFENDANT, Defendant.

Case No. 12345

MEMORANDUM OF CREDITS, ACCRUED INTEREST AND COSTS AFTER JUDGMENT AND SUPPORTING DECLARATION

MEMORANDUM OF CREDITS

CREDIT for payments and partial satisfaction of judgment, including direct payments and executions partially satisfied: $ 1,711.00 (if none, state NONE).

INTEREST ACCRUING AFTER JUDGMENT

INTEREST ACCRUING AFTER JUDGMENT at 10% from date of judgment on balances due after dates of payments or credits acknowledged above: $ 372.81

(Plus $ -0- claimed on Memoranda of Costs filed previously).

MEMORANDUM OF COSTS AFTER JUDGMENT

1. Costs After Judgment Claimed on Memoranda Filed Previously .... $ -0-
2. Clerk's Fees .... $ 3.50
3. .... $ 3.50
4. Levying Officer's Fees .... $ 28.00
5. .... $ 21.50

-1-

6. Serving Supplementary Proceedings .... $ 15.00
7. .... $
8. Notary Fees .... $
9. .... $
10. .... $
11. .... $
12. .... $
13. .... $
14. .... $
15. .... $

TOTAL: $ 71.50

DECLARATION SUPPORTING MEMORANDUM OF CREDITS, ACCRUED INTEREST AND COSTS AFTER JUDGMENT

I, the undersigned, declare that I am the plaintiff/judgment creditor in this action; the post-judgment costs and accrued interest as set forth in the Memoranda above are true and correct to the best of my knowledge and belief, the costs incurred are reasonable and necessary, and have not been satisfied.

I declare under penalty of perjury under the laws of the State of California that the foregoing is true and correct. Executed on September 21, 19 —, at Berkeley, California.

Pam Plaintiff
[Signature]

Print name: Pam Plaintiff

/////////
/////////
/////////

-2-

Interest Accruing After Judgment: Enter the amount of interest you have calculated. (See Section C.3, above.) If you previously filed Memoranda of Costs, also fill in the amount you claimed, as indicated in the Interest Filed column on the Keeping Track of Collecting Your Judgment form (enter the total of all amounts in that column).

Memorandum of Costs After Judgment: Enter the costs you are claiming. You can obtain these from your Keeping Track of Costs form. As you enter them on the Memorandum of Costs, make a note on the Keeping Track of Costs form in the column entitled Date Costs Claimed (so you don't claim them twice).

Item 1: If you have filed previous Memoranda of Costs, enter the total amount claimed for costs, but do not claim them again. You will find this amount in the Costs Filed column on the Keeping Track of Collecting Your Judgment form (enter the total of all amounts in that column). If this is the first time you're claiming costs, put "None."

Items 2-3: Enter any clerk's fees you have paid for having papers filed or issued with the court, provided you did not already recover them from a successful levy. Additional clerk's fees can be entered in the blanks in Items 9-15.

Items 4-5: Enter any fees you paid the levying officer for acting on your Writ of Execution, provided you did not already recover them from a successful levy. Additional levying officer's fees can be entered in the blanks in Items 9-15.

Items 6-7: Enter any payments you made for service of additional papers (such as an Application and Order of Examination or Subpena Duces Tecum).

Item 8: If you had a notary notarize any documents in this case, enter the fees paid.

Items 9-15: Use these spaces for items you didn't have room to list above. Remember that you cannot claim attorneys' fees, fees for hours you spent trying to collect or out-of-pocket expenses incurred except as provided by statute. (See Section A, above.)

Total: Fill in the total amount of the costs.

Finally, fill in the date and city where you are signing the document and sign your name.

2. Have Debtor Served

You must have a copy of the Memorandum of Costs served on the judgment debtor by mail to his last known address. Then have the person who serves the debtor complete a Proof of Service by Mail. Instructions are in Chapter 22, Sections F and G.

3. File the Memorandum of Costs

After the judgment debtor is served, make two copies of the Memorandum of Costs and signed proof of service. Send the court the original and one copy of the Memorandum of Costs and signed proof of service and a self-addressed, stamped envelope. There is no filing fee. You'll find a generic cover letter in the Appendix.

4. Wait 15 days (Service by Mail)

The debtor has 15 days (ten days when he is served personally) to contest your Memorandum of Costs. If he doesn't, the Memorandum of Costs is considered final, and you are entitled to the amount claimed.

If the debtor contests the amounts you claim—which rarely happens—you can either argue against his motion in court, or forget about it and let him have his way. (See Chapter 18 for more information on motions.)

If the debtor doesn't contest your Memorandum of Costs, you can recover the amounts claimed. If you are in the midst of a levy and want to recover costs that were incurred after your Writ was issued, send a certified copy of the Memorandum of Costs (available from the court clerk for a small fee) to the levying officer, who can then recover the amount indicated. Or add the costs and interest to the Writ of Execution you obtain the next time you initiate a levy.

Chapter 16

If the Debtor Files for Bankruptcy

IF THE JUDGMENT DEBTOR FILES for bankruptcy, you may very well be at the end of the collections line. Through the bankruptcy process, the debtor may get rid of all or many of his debts—including yours. As of the bankruptcy filing date, all creditor collection activity must stop and funds collected shortly before the filing must usually be turned over to the bankruptcy court.

But creditors also have some rights. The debtor may have to surrender property that can be used to pay at least a portion of his debts. Certain types of debts and judgments survive bankruptcy fully intact. And if more than 90 days elapsed between the time you created a lien on the debtor's property and the date she filed for bankruptcy, you may be able to collect on your lien even if the debt underlying it is canceled in the bankruptcy. Finally, if the debtor lied in his bankruptcy papers, you may convince the bankruptcy court to throw out the debtor's case.

While bankruptcy can be a major setback, you may learn in this chapter that you're in better shape than you thought.

A. Types of Bankruptcy

THERE ARE DIFFERENT KINDS of bankruptcy, which are named after specific chapters of a federal set of statutes, called the Bankruptcy Code.

- **Chapter 7 Bankruptcy:** Also referred to as "liquidation" or "straight" bankruptcy, this is the most common form of bankruptcy used by individuals and small businesses. A debtor asks the court to cancel (discharge) her debts, in exchange for which she gives up all property—or its equivalent value—that isn't exempt from bankruptcy. The property is sold and proceeds are distributed to creditors under applicable bankruptcy rules. In "no asset" cases, there are no nonexempt assets—which means that creditors won't get paid anything. However, some types of debts and liens will survive the bankruptcy and can be collected after the bankruptcy case is closed.
- **Chapter 13 Bankruptcy:** A debtor creates a plan under which she pays a portion of her debts over a three- to five-year period. The percentage of debts that the debtor must pay depends on her after-expense income and can vary from a few cents on the dollar to pretty near full payment. A debtor's Chapter 13 plan must provide that her unsecured creditors (which

usually include judgment creditors) receive, as a group, at least the same amount as they would have had she filed a Chapter 7 bankruptcy. If the debtor successfully completes the plan, the balances still owing on her debts are wiped out and she need not surrender property for the benefit of the creditors. As with a Chapter 7 bankruptcy, however, some types of debts and liens will survive a Chapter 13 bankruptcy unscathed.

- **Other Bankruptcies:** Chapter 11 bankruptcy is primarily designed to let a business restructure its debt—that is, pay its creditors less than it owes them—while it continues to operate. Although individuals are permitted to file this type of bankruptcy, few do. Chapter 12 bankruptcy is a repayment plan designed especially for farmers. Creditors' remedies for Chapter 11 and Chapter 12 bankruptcies are beyond the scope of this book; see a lawyer.

Steering the Debtor to Alternatives

If bankruptcy is looming large, but the debtor hasn't yet filed, it is in your interest to prevent that from happening. If your judgment debtor is sincerely looking for an alternative to bankruptcy, here are two basic suggestions.

- **Consumer Credit Counselors:** This national organization helps debtors avoid bankruptcy and work out a voluntary plan with their creditors under which all of their debts are paid over time. If the number isn't in the phone book, the debtor can call 800-388-2227 or write National Foundation for Consumer Credit, 8611 2nd Ave., Suite 100, Silver Springs, MD 20910. Also, if you are contacted by this organization and asked to agree to a private voluntary repayment plan, cooperating will probably be more beneficial than bankruptcy court or formal collection measures.
- **Read About Alternatives:** *Money Troubles: Legal Strategies to Cope With Your Debts,* by Robin Leonard (Nolo Press), helps debtors calmly assess their debt situation and take the most sensible steps available. The book is available in most major books stores and public libraries, or may be ordered directly from Nolo Press.

B. Bankruptcy Overview

THIS SECTION GIVES AN OVERVIEW of Chapter 7 and Chapter 13 bankruptcies.

1. Timeline of Chapter 7 and Chapter 13 Bankruptcies

The accompanying timeline shows the major events in a Chapter 7 or Chapter 13 bankruptcy. In the sections that follow, we discuss these events and your potential remedies as a judgment creditor in more detail.

Timeline of Chapter 7 and 13 bankruptcies
(local procedures may vary)

Debtor files bankruptcy petition	Collections stayed (frozen) by bankruptcy court Trustee appointed by bankruptcy court
7 to 21 days later	Notice of bankruptcy mailed to creditors Proof of Claim may be filed, starting now
20-40 days after notice sent to creditors (may be later)	Creditors' meeting Confirmation hearing for repayment plan (Chapter 13 only)
30 days after Creditors' Meeting	File objections to exemptions, if any
60 days after Creditors' Meeting	File other objections, if any
90 days after Creditors' Meeting	Last day to file Proof of Claim
Debtor files Statement of Intention Re Secured Debts	Negotiate and sign Reaffirmation or Redemption Agreement with debtor within 45 days of the date the Statement of Intention is filed[1]
Chapter 7 Discharge	Discharge hearing if reaffirmation agreement is filed by debtor
Up to 1 Year After Chapter 7 Discharge	Objections to discharge may be filed based on late discovered fraud
3-5 years after Chapter 13 plan confirmed	Discharged if plan successfully completed

2. The Automatic Stay

At the instant a debtor files a bankruptcy petition, the court issues an order for relief that stays—that is, mandates a stop to—all collection activities against the debtor and his property (11 USC § 362). The stay, called an "automatic stay," remains in effect until the case is closed or the court lifts it for a particular creditor.

If you know of the bankruptcy and try to collect anyway, you can be held in contempt of court and fined—and possibly be sued by the debtor for damages (11 USC § 362(h)). The moral is, if you get even a whiff that the judgment debtor has gone bankrupt, immediately stop your collection efforts until you determine otherwise or, if the debtor has filed, until the court says you may proceed with collection efforts.

a. *If Levy Proceedings Were Initiated*

If you started levy proceedings before the automatic stay, immediately inform the levying officer about the bankruptcy. Give him the case name and number, and tell him to release to the bankruptcy trustee any funds collected as a result of your levy. You may later be required by the trustee to turn over funds collected during the 90 days directly preceding the bankruptcy filing date.

b. *Collecting From Co-debtors*

After the automatic stay goes into effect, your right to collect from co-debtors depends on the type of case.

- **Chapter 7:** A creditor may collect from any co-debtor before, during or after the bankruptcy proceeding.
- **Chapter 13:** The automatic stay prevents collection activity against a co-debtor while the bankruptcy case is proceeding—which can be up to five years. However, if the debtor's repayment plan indicates that less than 100% of your judgment will be paid, you may petition the court for relief from the stay to collect the unpaid portion from the co-debtor (11 USC § 1201(c)). That is beyond the scope of this book.

[1]Reaffirmation of a debt usually occurs when a debtor wants to hold onto property such as a car or a mortgage (that will be taken away if the payments on the property are not made), when the debtor wants to hold onto a credit card (and reaffirmation of the debt is a condition for doing this) or when the debtor wants to avoid a court contest over whether a particular debt was fraudulently incurred. The debtor must attend a discharge hearing if she agrees to reaffirm a debt that otherwise would be discharged. At the hearing, the court is supposed to make sure the debtor fully understands the consequences of reaffirming, and to disallow the reaffirmation if the debtor doesn't have this understanding.

C. Examine Bankruptcy Notice

IF THE DEBTOR LISTED your judgment in her bankruptcy petition, the court will mail you a document that notifies you of the debtor's bankruptcy. You will receive one of these notices:

- **Chapter 7 "no asset" notice:** used for Chapter 7 debtors who claim that all their assets are exempt—that is, not legally available to pay their creditors. Unless you receive further instructions from the bankruptcy court, there's no point in making a claim.
- **Chapter 7 "asset" notice:** used for Chapter 7 debtors with non-exempt assets. You may get paid a portion of your judgment, depending on the value of the assets, the rights of other creditors and whether you created liens on the debtor's property. But you must file a claim.
- **Chapter 13 notice:** used for debtors who intend to repay a portion of their debts through a Chapter 13 repayment plan. Again, you must file a claim.

The rest of this section takes you through the notice in detail. By the end of this section, you will have a good idea of your rights and remedies.

If you don't recognize the name of the debtor on the bankruptcy notice, contact the trustee. It may well be the judgment debtor, going under an entirely different name.

If You Didn't Receive Notice

If the debtor filed for bankruptcy but you didn't receive written notice from the bankruptcy court, one of two things might have happened: it got lost in the mail, or you weren't listed on the petition as a creditor. Either way, if you know about the bankruptcy, you should take steps to assert your rights. Contact the bankruptcy court and ask whether the debtor has filed bankruptcy. If so, find out which trustee is handling the case. Then contact the trustee and say that you are a judgment creditor and want notice of the bankruptcy so that you can properly respond. Be aware that reaching the bankruptcy court by telephone can be difficult. You may have to visit in person.

If you are completely unaware of a bankruptcy and were not listed on the bankruptcy petition, your judgment can legally survive the bankruptcy. However, while it may be tempting to pretend you don't know about the bankruptcy (if you received no notice) and hope your judgment survives, the better practice is to report in as a creditor and pursue whatever remedies the bankruptcy process affords you.

1. Court, Case and Debtor Information

The top of every notice states the name of the court and the bankruptcy case number.

Next is a heading that indicates what type of bankruptcy was filed. After the words "NOTICE OF COMMENCEMENT OF CASE UNDER CHAPTER" will be either "Chapter 7" or "Chapter 13." For Chapter 7 cases, one of two statements will follow: "(Individual or Joint Debtor No Asset Case)" or "(Individual or Joint Debtor Asset Case)." Make sure you understand exactly which type of case was filed. (See Section A, above.)

The next boxes are for the most part self-explanatory, with these exceptions:

Date Case Filed or Converted: For new cases, this will be the date the case was filed in bankruptcy court. If

FORM B91
(6/90)

United States Bankruptcy Court

Case Number

______________ District of ______________

NOTICE OF COMMENCEMENT OF CASE UNDER CHAPTER 13 OF THE BANKRUPTCY CODE, MEETING OF CREDITORS, AND FIXING OF DATES

In re (Name of Debtor)	Address of Debtor	Soc. Sec. /Tax ID. Nos.
	Date Case Filed (or Converted)	
Name and Address of Attorney for Debtor	Name and Address of Trustee	
Telephone Number	Telephone Number	

☐ This is a converted case originally filed under chapter ______ on ______________ (date).

FILING CLAIMS

Deadline to file a proof of claim:

DATE, TIME, AND LOCATION OF MEETING OF CREDITORS

FILING OF PLAN AND DATE, TIME, AND LOCATION OF HEARING ON CONFIRMATION OF PLAN

☐ The debtor has filed a plan. The plan or a summary of the plan is enclosed. Hearing on confirmation will be held:

______________ (Date) ______________ (Time) ______________ (Location)

☐ The debtor has filed a plan. The plan or a summary of the plan and notice of the confirmation hearing will be sent separately.

☐ The debtor has not filed a plan as of this date. Creditors will be given separate notice of the hearing on confirmation of the plan.

COMMENCEMENT OF CASE. An individual's debt adjustment case under chapter 13 of the Bankruptcy Code has been filed in this court by the debtor or debtors named above, and an order for relief has been entered. You will not receive notice of all documents filed in this case. All documents filed with the court, including lists of the debtor's property and debts, are available for inspection at the office of the clerk of the bankruptcy court.

CREDITORS MAY NOT TAKE CERTAIN ACTIONS. A creditor is anyone to whom the debtor owes money. Under the Bankruptcy Code, the debtor is granted certain protection against creditors. Common examples of prohibited actions by creditors are contacting the debtor to demand repayment, taking action against the debtor to collect money owed to creditors or to take property of the debtor, and starting or continuing foreclosure actions, repossessions, or wage deductions. Some protection is also given to certain codebtors of consumer debts. If unauthorized actions are taken by a creditor against a debtor, or a protected codebtor, the court may punish that creditor. A creditor who is considering taking action against the debtor or the property of the debtor, or any codebtor, should review §§ 362 and 1301 of the Bankruptcy Code and may wish to seek legal advice. The staff of the clerk of the bankruptcy court is not permitted to give legal advice.

MEETING OF CREDITORS. The debtor (both husband and wife in a joint case) is required to appear at the meeting of creditors on the date and at the place set forth above in the box labeled "Date, Time, and Location of Meeting of Creditors" for the purpose of being examined under oath. Attendance by creditors at the meeting is welcome, but not required. At the meeting, the creditors may examine the debtor and transact such other business as may properly come before the meeting. The meeting may be continued or adjourned from time to time by notice at the meeting, without further written notice to creditors.

PROOF OF CLAIM. Except as otherwise provided by law, in order to share in any payment from the estate, a creditor must file a proof of claim by the date set forth above in the box labeled "Filing Claims." The place to file the proof of claim, either in person or by mail, is the office of the clerk of the bankruptcy court. Proof of claim forms are available in the clerk's office of any bankruptcy court.

PURPOSE OF A CHAPTER 13 FILING. Chapter 13 of the Bankruptcy Code is designed to enable a debtor to pay debts in full or in part over a period of time pursuant to a plan. A plan is not effective unless approved by the bankruptcy court at a confirmation hearing. Creditors will be given notice in the event the case is dismissed or converted to another chapter of the Bankruptcy Code.

Address of the Clerk of the Bankruptcy Court	For the Court:
	Clerk of the Bankruptcy Court
	Date

FORM B9A
(6/90)

United States Bankruptcy Court

Case Number

______________ District of ______________

NOTICE OF COMMENCEMENT OF CASE UNDER CHAPTER 7 OF THE BANKRUPTCY CODE, MEETING OF CREDITORS, AND FIXING OF DATES
(Individual or Joint Debtor No Asset Case)

In re (Name of Debtor)	Address of Debtor	Soc. Sec. /Tax ID. Nos.
	Date Case Filed (or Converted)	
Name and Address of Attorney for Debtor	Name and Address of Trustee	
Telephone Number	Telephone Number	

☐ This is a converted case originally filed under chapter ______ on ______________ (date).

DATE, TIME, AND LOCATION OF MEETING OF CREDITORS

DISCHARGE OF DEBTS

Deadline to File a Complaint Objecting to Discharge of the Debtor or to Determine Dischargeability of Certain Types of Debts:

AT THIS TIME THERE APPEAR TO BE NO ASSETS AVAILABLE FROM WHICH PAYMENT MAY BE MADE TO UNSECURED CREDITORS. DO NOT FILE A PROOF OF CLAIM UNTIL YOU RECEIVE NOTICE TO DO SO.

COMMENCEMENT OF CASE. A petition for liquidation under chapter 7 of the Bankruptcy Code has been filed in this court by or against the person or persons named above as the debtor, and an order for relief has been entered. You will not receive notice of all documents filed in this case. All documents filed with the court, including lists of the debtor's property, debts, and property claimed as exempt are available for inspection at the office of the clerk of the bankruptcy court.

CREDITORS MAY NOT TAKE CERTAIN ACTIONS. A creditor is anyone to whom the debtor owes money or property. Under the Bankruptcy Code, the debtor is granted certain protection against creditors. Common examples of prohibited actions by creditors are contacting the debtor to demand repayment, taking action against the debtor to collect money owed to creditors or to take property of the debtor, and starting or continuing foreclosure actions, repossessions, or wage deductions. If unauthorized actions are taken by a creditor against a debtor, the court may penalize that creditor. A creditor who is considering taking action against the debtor or the property of the debtor should review § 362 of the Bankruptcy Code and may wish to seek legal advice. The staff of the clerk of the bankruptcy court is not permitted to give legal advice.

MEETING OF CREDITORS. The debtor (both husband and wife in a joint case) is required to appear at the meeting of creditors on the date and at the place set forth above for the purpose of being examined under oath. Attendance by creditors at the meeting is welcomed, but not required. At the meeting, the creditors may elect a trustee other than the one named above, elect a committee of creditors, examine the debtor, and transact such other business as may properly come before the meeting. The meeting may be continued or adjourned from time to time by notice at the meeting, without further written notice to creditors.

LIQUIDATION OF THE DEBTOR'S PROPERTY. The trustee will collect the debtor's property and turn any that is not exempt into money. At this time, however, it appears from the schedules of the debtor that there are no assets from which any distribution can be paid to creditors. If at a later date it appears that there are assets from which a distribution may be paid, the creditors will be notified and given an opportunity to file claims.

EXEMPT PROPERTY. Under state and federal law, the debtor is permitted to keep certain money or property as exempt. If a creditor believes than an exemption of money or property is not authorized by law, the creditor may file an objection. An objection must be filed not later than 30 days after the conclusion of the meeting of creditors.

DISCHARGE OF DEBTS. The debtor is seeking a discharge of debts. A discharge means that certain debts are made unenforceable against the debtor personally. Creditors whose claims against the debtor are discharged may never take action against the debtor to collect the discharged debts. If a creditor believes that the debtor should not receive any discharge of debts under § 727 of the Bankruptcy Code or that a debt owed to the creditor is not dischargable under § 523(a)(2), (4), or (6) of the Bankruptcy Code, timely action must be taken in the bankruptcy court by the deadline set forth above in the box labeled "Discharge of Debts." Creditors considering taking such action may wish to seek legal advice.

DO NOT FILE A PROOF OF CLAIM UNLESS YOU RECEIVE A COURT NOTICE TO DO SO

Address of the Clerk of the Bankruptcy Court	For the Court:
	Clerk of the Bankruptcy Court
	Date

a case was converted from one chapter to another,[2] the notice will show the date the conversion papers were filed, and the original filing date will be listed after "This is a converted case, originally filed under Chapter __."

Name, Address and Telephone Number of Trustee: The trustee is the court-appointed official who represents the unsecured creditors in a bankruptcy case. He tries to make sure that the debtor coughs up as much property (Chapter 7) or payments (Chapter 13) as the law allows. You may have a number of occasions to call the trustee.

Role of the Bankruptcy Trustee

When a debtor files for bankruptcy, the court appoints a bankruptcy trustee to handle the case. Until the court closes the case, the trustee has control of the debtor's assets. The debtor can't dispose of any property without the trustee's permission. It is the trustee's job to question the debtor's exemption claims and to ferret out all property that might be available for the benefit of the creditors.

2. Claims and Meeting Information

The next few boxes differs slightly, depending on the type of bankruptcy.

FILING CLAIMS: This item only appears on asset cases (not on Chapter 7 no asset notices). You must file a Proof of Claim form with the court within the date specified in this box. (This is covered in Section D, below.)

DATE, TIME AND LOCATION OF MEETING OF CREDITORS: Every bankruptcy debtor must personally appear in the bankruptcy court. This routine meeting normally consists of the trustee asking the debtor a few perfunctory questions about ambiguities in her papers. Creditors rarely choose to attend, but see Section C.3, below, to help make a decision about attending.

DISCHARGE OF DEBTS: This item appears on Chapter 7 notices only. It gives the deadline for challenging the discharge (cancellation) of certain categories of debts. If you believe that the debtor acted fraudulently prior to filing for bankruptcy or made serious misstatements in her papers, you can either ask the court to deny the bankruptcy altogether, or request the trustee look into the matter. (We discuss the grounds for objections in Section F, below.)

FILING OF PLAN AND DATE, TIME AND LOCATION OF HEARING ON CONFIRMATION OF PLAN: This item appears on Chapter 13 notices only. The confirmation hearing gives the court and creditors a chance to raise objections to the plan. Once the plan is confirmed by the court, it starts operating immediately. If the first or second box is checked, there should be a date, time and place for the hearing at which the court will accept or reject the debtor's repayment plan. You will either receive the plan with this notice or at a later date. If the third box is checked, the plan hasn't been filed yet and you will receive notice of the hearing at a later date as well as a copy of the plan. (See Section F.7, below, for how to interpret a Chapter 13 plan.)

3. General Case Information

The large box on the notice contains a lot of little writing. Here we help you decipher it.

AT THIS TIME THERE APPEAR TO BE NO ASSETS...: For Chapter 7 no asset cases only, you'll find a statement indicating that there are no assets from which payment may be made to unsecured creditors (as mentioned, judgment creditors are usually considered unsecured creditors). You'll be directed not to file a Proof of Claim—because it probably won't do any good. However, if later on it appears that the debtor did have some non-exempt resources, you should receive a notice indicating that there are assets and allowing you to file a Proof of Claim. (Proofs of Claim are covered in Section D, below.)

[2] The most common conversions are from Chapter 13 and Chapter 11 to Chapter 7. Essentially, the debtor starts out believing that a repayment or restructuring plan will work, but then finds out that it won't, and that a liquidation bankruptcy is required.

COMMENCEMENT OF CASE: This paragraph invites you to inspect the debtor's papers on file in the bankruptcy court. If the size of your judgment justifies the time it will take, we strongly recommend that you accept this invitation. (See Section F, where we discuss how to search for information that may result in dismissal of the bankruptcy.)

CREDITORS MAY NOT TAKE CERTAIN ACTIONS: This statement informs you that the automatic stay is in effect. It is important to understand that the stay goes into effect the moment bankruptcy is filed, even though you may not receive a notice for a while. For Chapter 13 debtors, the automatic stay may extend to co-debtors who have not filed for bankruptcy. (The automatic stay is discussed above in Section B.2.)

MEETING OF CREDITORS: This meeting is usually scheduled between 20 to 40 days after the filing of the bankruptcy petition, but sometimes it doesn't happen for months. It may be held at the court or any other convenient place. Despite its name, few creditors ever attend the meeting. Instead, they rely on the trustee to question the debtor about various aspects of her bankruptcy petition.

If you examine the bankruptcy court papers, as we recommend in Section D, below, and want to ask some follow-up questions of the debtor, the meeting of creditors is the place to do it. Or you can attend if you're simply curious about the process. But if you want to object to some aspect of the debtor's papers, the meeting of creditors is not the place. The trustee has no power to rule on disputes. Objections must be formally brought before a bankruptcy judge, which usually requires the aid of a bankruptcy attorney.

LIQUIDATION OF THE DEBTOR'S PROPERTY: This paragraph only appears on Chapter 7 notices. For no asset cases, it reminds you that there does not appear to be any non-exempt assets for the trustee to sell. For cases with assets, it states that you may be entitled to some of the proceeds from assets that the trustee will sell.

EXEMPT PROPERTY: This item appears on Chapter 7 cases only. As a creditor, you have the right to challenge the debtor's claims that certain property is exempt. The wise creditor won't leave this matter to chance—but will closely examine the debtor's bankruptcy papers for exemption claims that should be disallowed. (See Section F, below, for more on what property is exempt and how to search papers in the bankruptcy court.)

DISCHARGE OF DEBTS: This item appears on Chapter 7 cases only. You must act within the time limit set in this box for making an objection to the bankruptcy itself or to the discharge of a particular debt. (See Section F for more information on when and how a bankruptcy or the discharge of a specific debt may be opposed.)

PROOF OF CLAIM: This notice appears on Chapter 13 and Chapter 7 asset cases only. It explains what the Proof of Claim is and where to file it. (See Section D, below, for instructions.)

PURPOSE OF A CHAPTER 13 FILING: This self-explanatory notice appears on Chapter 13 cases only.

4. Court and Address Information

The blank at the bottom left shows the court's address. The clerk's signature or stamp and date are at the bottom right.

D. File Proof of Claim

IF THE DEBTOR FILED A CHAPTER 7 asset bankruptcy, you are entitled to file a Proof of Claim to get your share of non-exempt assets that are sold. And if the debtor filed a Chapter 13 bankruptcy, you'll need to file a Proof of Claim to receive payments under the plan. But don't get too excited. In a Chapter 7 case, the assets may produce only a few cents on the dollar. And even if there are valuable assets, there is a specific order in which proceeds are distributed to creditors—you may collect a lot or nothing, depending on your status. In a Chapter 13 plan, priority creditors and secured creditors are entitled to 100% payment over the life of the plan, which frequently leaves unsecured and nonpriority creditors with only a few cents on the dollar. (Most judgment creditors are unsecured and nonpriority creditors, as we explain in

Section D.2, below. And even creditors with liens may end up as unsecured creditors if those liens are avoided. See Sections F.1 and F.7.)

As you complete your Proof of Claim, you'll learn more about these categories of creditors and get some general guidelines for assessing your chances of getting paid.

If the debtor who files for bankruptcy is not the judgment debtor, but is married to the judgment debtor, you should still file your Proof of Claim. This is because:

- Bankruptcy filed by one spouse discharges all community debts (debts incurred in the course of the marriage) and
- the community property owned by a couple (property acquired during marriage) is available for distribution to the creditors of either spouse in a bankruptcy (assuming the property is non-exempt).

1. When to File Proof of Claim

Study your bankruptcy notice (Section C), which shows the deadline for filing your claim. If the case is a no asset case and you later receive a notice that assets have been discovered, comply with the deadline on that notice. Failure to file a Proof of Claim by the deadline usually means you get nothing.

2. How to Fill in Proof of Claim

You should receive a blank Proof of Claim form with the bankruptcy notice. If you don't, use the form contained in the Appendix or get a copy from the bankruptcy court.

The instructions that follow are based on official bankruptcy Form 10. Some courts may alter the form slightly, but you should be able to conform our instructions to any variances in the form.

Caption: Follow the format of the debtor's bankruptcy papers.

Name of Creditor: Enter your name. If it was misspelled on the notice, correct it here.

Name and Address Where Notices Should Be Sent: Enter your name, mailing address and telephone number. Check one or more of the boxes at the right, if they apply.

Account Number: Enter the account number by which you identify the debtor, if any. Check the box at the right if you are amending or replacing a previous claim, and provide the date it was filed. If it's a standard judgment based on an accident or other activity for which there's no account, put the case number from the court case.

Item 1: If your judgment is based on one of the categories listed on the form, check the appropriate box. If your judgment is for wages, salaries or commissions, also fill in the requested information. If you don't know which category to select, check "other" and do your best to describe the basis for your judgment.

Item 2: Put in the date the debt first arose.

Item 3: Put in the date your judgment was entered in the court.

Item 4: Here you state what type of bankruptcy claim you have. Read the instructions for this item below before completing it.

Do You Have a Secured Claim?

Secured claims are held by creditors who have liens on the debtor's property. Usually secured claims are based on agreements that identify specific property as collateral for repayment of a loan. But secured claims can also be based on liens imposed on homes or that are a result of non-payment for work performed on the house (mechanics liens) and liens that are created as a result of judgment collection activities. (See Chapter 4 and Chapter 6.C.1.) If you created liens against the debtor's property, consider the amount of your judgment a secured claim. If the debtor's property subject to your liens doesn't fully pay off your judgment, the balance will be considered an unsecured claim. Unfortunately, as you will see below, this balance frequently approaches 100%.

FORM B10
(6/90)

FORM 10. PROOF OF CLAIM

United States Bankruptcy Court
Northern DISTRICT OF California

PROOF OF CLAIM

In re (Name of Debtor)
Dan Defendant, aka Daniel Defendant, individually and dba Danny-Boy's Deli

Case Number
OHN010U2

NOTE: This form should not be used to make a claim for an administrative expense arising after the commencement of the case. A request for payment of an administrative expense may be filed pursuant to 11 U.S.C. § 503.

Name of Creditor
(The person or other entity to whom the debtor owes money or property)
Pam Plaintiff

Name and Address Where Notices Should Be Sent
Pam Plainiff
123 North Street
Berkeley, CA 94704

Telephone No. (415) 999-9999

☐ Check box if you are aware that anyone else has filed a proof of claim relating to your claim. Attach copy or statement giving particulars.

☐ Check box if you never received any notices from the bankruptcy court in this case.

☐ Check box if the address differs from the address on the envelope sent to you by the court.

THIS SPACE IS FOR COURT USE ONLY

ACCOUNT OR OTHER NUMBER BY WHICH CREDITOR IDENTIFIES DEBTOR:

Check here if this claim ☐ replaces ☐ amends } a previously filed claim, dated: ________

1. BASIS FOR CLAIM
- ☐ Goods sold
- ☐ Services performed
- ☐ Money loaned
- ☐ Personal injury/wrongful death
- ☐ Taxes
- ☒ Other (Describe briefly) breach of contract

☐ Retiree benefits as defined in 11 U.S.C. § 1114 (a)
☐ Wage, salaries, and compensations (Fill out below)
Your social security number ________
Unpaid compensation for services performed
from ________ (date) to ________ (date)

2. DATE DEBT WAS INCURRED
2/6/__

3. IF COURT JUDGMENT, DATE OBTAINED:
1/10/—

4. CLASSIFICATION OF CLAIM. Under the Bankruptcy Code all claims are classified as one or more of the following: (1) Unsecured nonpriority. (2) Unsecured Priority. (3) Secured. It is possible for part of a claim to be in one category and part in another.

CHECK THE APPROPRIATE BOX OR BOXES that best describe your claim and STATE THE AMOUNT OF THE CLAIM.

☒ SECURED CLAIM $ 6,421.88
Attach evidence of perfection of security interest
Brief Description of Collateral:
☒ Real Estate ☐ Motor Vehicle ☒ Other (Describe briefly)
Personal property and business assets
Amount of arrearage and other charges included in secured claim above, if any
$ 378.38 post-judg interest, $43.50 post judg costs

☐ UNSECURED NONPRIORITY CLAIM $ ________
A claim is unsecured if there is no collateral or lien on property of the debtor securing the claim or to the extent that the value of such property is less than the amount of the claim.

☐ UNSECURED PRIORITY CLAIM $ ________
Specify the priority of the claim.
- ☐ Wages, salaries, or commissions (up to $2000, earned not more than 90 days before filing of the bankruptcy petition or cessation of the debtor's business, whichever is earlier)—11 U.S.C.§ 507 (a)(3)
- ☐ Contributions to an employee benefit plan—11 U.S.C. § 507(a)(4)
- ☐ Up to $900 of deposits toward purchase, lease, or rental of property or services for personal, family, or household use—11 U.S.C. 507(a) (6)
- ☐ Taxes or penalties of governmental units—11 U.S.C. § 507(a)(7)
- ☐ Other—11 U.S.C. §§ 507(a)(2), (a)(5)—(Describe briefly)

5. TOTAL AMOUNT OF CLAIM AT TIME CASE FILED: $ ________ (Unsecured) $ 6,421.88 (Secured) $ ________ (Priority) $ 6,421.88 (Total)

☒ Check this box if claim includes prepetition charges in addition to the principal amount of the claim. Attach itemized statement of all additional charges.

6. CREDITS AND SETOFFS: The amount of all payments on this claim has been credited and deducted for the purpose of making this proof of claim. In filing this claim, claimant has deducted all amounts that claimant owes to debtor.

7. SUPPORTING DOCUMENTS: Attach copies of supporting documents, such as promissory notes, purchase orders, invoices, itemized statements of running accounts, contracts, court judgments, or evidence of security interests. If the documents are not available, explain. If the documents are voluminous, attach a summary.

8. TIME-STAMPED COPY: To receive an acknowledgment of the filing of your claim, enclose a stamped, self-addressed envelope and copy of this proof of claim.

THIS SPACE IS FOR COURT USE ONLY

Date
June 4, 19–

Sign and print the name and title, if any, of the creditor or other person authorized to file this claim (attach copy of power of attorney, if any)
Pam Plaintiff
PAM PLAINTIFF

Penalty for presenting fraudulent claim: Fine of up to $500,000 or imprisonment for up to 5 years, or both. 18 U.S.C. §§ 152 and 3571

- **Secured Claim:** Check this box if you have a judgment lien on the debtor's property. Enter the total amount of your judgment, including costs and interest that accrued prior to the bankruptcy filing date, less any payments that have been made on the judgment. Then check the box for the type of property to which your lien is attached or describe the property in the blank space. For instance, if you have a lien on the debtor's personal property because the debtor was served with your Notice of Debtor's Examination, put "all personal property." If the lien is on the debtor's business assets, put "business assets." For real estate liens, specify the county where the lien is, followed by "real estate."
- **Amount of arrearage and other charges included in secured claim:** Enter the costs and interest included in the total amount entered above. Finally, attach to this Proof of Claim a copy of all documents that substantiate your secured claim: recorded Abstract of Judgment (Chapter 4.E), Notice of Judgment Lien on Personal Property registered with the Secretary of State (Chapter 4.F), or Proof of Service of Application and Order for Appearance and Examination (Chapter 6.E).
- **Unsecured Nonpriority Claim:** Check this box if you have no judicial lien on the debtor's property and the debt underlying your judgment is nonpriority. (See "Are You a Priority Creditor?" sidebar.)[3] Enter the amount of your judgment plus costs and pre-bankruptcy interest, less any payments that you received.
- **Unsecured Priority Claim:** Priority claims are explained in the accompanying sidebar. If your judgment is based on a priority debt, check this box. Then enter the amount of the judgment plus costs and pre-bankruptcy interest, less payments made. Check the appropriate box to specify the type of priority debt.

Are You a Priority Creditor?

In Chapter 7 bankruptcy, when property is sold by the trustee to pay creditors, priority creditors are entitled to be paid after lienholders. If some assets are left after these priority claims are paid in full, nonpriority unsecured creditors get paid. In Chapter 13 bankruptcy, priority claims may be paid off in full under the plan while nonpriority claims may only receive a few cents on the dollar. Briefly, priority claims that a judgment creditor might have against the assets are:

- **Wages, salaries and commissions:** If you were an employee of the debtor, you may be entitled to a maximum of $2,000. The money must have been earned within 90 days before the debtor filed a petition or within 90 days of the date the debtor ceased business. Because of the time constraint, few judgment creditors will be affected by this category.
- **Contributions to employee benefit plans:** This applies if the debtor owes contributions to an employee benefit fund. The contributions must have become due within 180 days before the debtor filed a petition or within 180 days of the date the debtor ceased business.
- **Deposits by individuals for personal, family or household use:** If the debtor took deposits from you for the purpose of purchasing, leasing or renting goods or services for personal, family or household use, you are entitled to a maximum of $900 per deposit for goods or services that were never delivered.
- **Certain grain producers and U.S. fishermen:** You may be entitled to up to $2,000 if the debtor operates or operated a grain storage facility and owes you money as a grain producer, or the debtor operates or operated a fish produce or storage facility and owes you money as a U.S. fisherman for fish or fish products.

Item 5: Enter the appropriate amount in each category, as listed in Item 4, above. If there are post-judgment costs and interest included in your claim, check the box as indicated. (See Chapter 15.)

Item 6: This is a statement that you have deducted all money received on the judgment.

[3] Even if part of your claim is unsecured, there is no reason to check this box if you've already checked the "secured claim" box because you have a lien on some or all the debtor's property.

Item 7: Attach to the Proof of Claim:

- a copy of your judgment
- a copy of your latest filed Memorandum of Costs
- your written computation of interest accrued and costs incurred after the last Memorandum of Costs was filed up until the bankruptcy filing date and
- a copy of any document that establishes the creation of a lien on the judgment debtor's property. (See Item 4, above.)

Item 8: Follow the instructions on the Proof of Claim.

Date and Signature: Fill in the date, and sign and print your name.

3. File Proof of Claim

Make a copy of the Proof of Claim for your records. If you attend the creditors' meeting, you can file your Proof of Claim there. If you file by mail, make sure it is gets to the court within the deadline stated in the notice. There is no need to serve the Proof of Claim on the debtor or his attorney.

4. If Debtor or Trustee Objects

The amount you list on your Proof of Claim will be deemed correct unless the debtor or the trustee objects. The most likely objections are:

- you failed to attach proper documentation in support of your claim
- the amount you claim is incorrect or
- you improperly stated that your claim was a priority claim (Item 4).

See a bankruptcy attorney if your claim is rejected for a reason that you are unable to fix and the amount you are seeking warrants the expense.

E. Discharge and Discharge Hearing

IN A CHAPTER 7 CASE, the case will be discharged once the trustee has determined what property the debtor is entitled to keep and has distributed any available funds to creditors. In a Chapter 13 case, a discharge happens after the debtor successfully completes her repayment plan. Occasionally, the court schedules a discharge hearing as a formality. There is no need for you to attend; you will receive notice of the discharge in the mail.

After the final discharge, the bankruptcy case is over and the automatic stay is terminated. The discharge voids any money judgments against the debtor (11 USC § 524). If you haven't collected your judgment by now, you can't do so, unless you have liens on the debtor's property that survive the bankruptcy, special permission from the bankruptcy court or your debt automatically escapes discharge. (See Section F, below.)

If you receive notice that the bankruptcy has been "dismissed," rather than "discharged," you're in luck. A "dismissed" case has been thrown out, and the debtor is not entitled to relief via bankruptcy—thus, you may resume your collections procedures. In some instances, the debtor can file again right away, which would again subject you to an automatic stay. In other situations—usually when the debtor hasn't cooperated with the bankruptcy court or trustee—the debtor won't be able to refile for at least six months.

F. What's a Creditor to Do?

IN ADDITION TO FILING A PROOF OF CLAIM, a number of possible avenues are open to judgment creditors in bankruptcy court. But before you invest serious time and money pursuing your rights, remember that the paramount purpose of bankruptcy is to give the debtor a fresh start. The debtor will almost always get the benefit of the doubt and the court will be inclined to discharge every allowable debt. Still, if you do your homework, you may be able to snatch victory from the jaws of defeat. The purpose of this section is to give you an overview of your rights and remedies.

Remember to file a timely Proof of Claim with the bankruptcy court, if it is allowed. This remedy is covered in detail in Section D, above.

1. Preserve and Enforce Liens

If you obtained a judgment lien far enough in advance of the debtor's bankruptcy filing date, you are entitled to treatment as a secured creditor.[4] The lien may be on the judgment debtor's real estate or business assets (Chapter 4), or on all the debtor's personal property under the one-year examination lien created when you properly serve the judgment debtor with a notice of debtor's examination (Chapter 6).

As a secured creditor, you will usually have a better chance of getting at least some of your judgment paid through the bankruptcy process. And, in some cases, you may enforce the lien after the bankruptcy is closed. As a general rule, liens survive bankruptcy unless the bankruptcy court orders them removed (avoided).[5] If a lien survives bankruptcy, whatever portion of the debtor's property is subject to your lien is still subject to it, even though the debt is technically canceled. As we saw in Chapter 4, this often means that you'll get paid when the debtor sells or refinances his real estate or business. It's harder to enforce the lien against property that doesn't carry a title. Consult a bankruptcy attorney if you have questions about lien priorities and whether it is worthwhile to initiate enforcement proceedings.

[4]The trustee or debtor can get the bankruptcy court to invalidate any judicial lien that was created within 90 days of the debtor's bankruptcy filing date. This 90-day period is stretched to one year if the debtor is a relative or a close business associate, such as partner or a partner's spouse.

[5]A court may order a lien removed if it interferes with the debtor's right to keep property that qualifies as exempt.

2. Pursue Co-debtors

See Section B.2.b, above, for rules on pursuing co-debtors.

3. Pursue Debts That Are Automatically Nondischargeable

Certain debts automatically survive the bankruptcy intact, and can be collected in the manner described throughout this book. The ones that may affect judgment creditors are:

- **Unlisted debts:** Debts not listed in the papers the debtor files with the bankruptcy court, unless you had "notice or actual knowledge of" the bankruptcy in time to file a Proof of Claim (11 USC § 523(a)(3)).
- **Alimony and child support:** Obligations and judgments based on these support obligations (11 USC § 523(a)(5)). Any debt owed to an ex-spouse that "is in the nature of alimony or child support" will survive even if the debt isn't labeled that way in the divorce decree. Attorney fees in a divorce action, pay-outs from a divided pension and even payments made to even up a property settlement have been labeled "in the nature of support," and thus nondischargeable in bankruptcy.
- **Judgments caused by debtor's intoxicated driving:** Debts based on a death or personal injury resulting from the debtor's intoxicated driving. (No conviction is necessary, as long as the fact of the drunk driving is proven to the bankruptcy court's satisfaction.)

Even if a debt is automatically nondischargeable, creditors commonly file an action in the bankruptcy court to have the debt recognized as nondischargeable. If this isn't done, you later may have to convince a state court judge that the debt still exists—which may prove difficult if the judge doesn't understand bankruptcy (many don't).

4. Pursue Debts Declared Non-dischargeable by Court (Chapter 7)

Debts that arise from a debtor's fraudulent behavior or from a debtor's willful and malicious behavior can survive a Chapter 7 bankruptcy. However, a creditor must formally contest the discharge of the debt in court with the timely filing of a Complaint to Determine Dischargeability of Debt within 60 days of the date set for the first meeting of creditors. Common examples of debts that creditors can successfully preserve through the bankruptcy process are:

- civil judgments for damages resulting from assault and battery, theft, intentional infliction of emotional distress, breach of fiduciary duty (such as embezzlement) and other intentional torts (personal wrongs) that would commonly be considered willful and malicious acts
- loans that were made in reliance on false or misleading written statements
- debts based on intentional oral misrepresentations and
- debts incurred for luxuries or non-necessary items for which the debtor had no intention of repaying (debts incurred shortly before bankruptcy where the debtor is clearly insolvent may fit in this category).

Even if your judgment is based on this type of debt, it may not be worth your while to pursue the matter in the bankruptcy court. While it's theoretically possible to handle this proceeding yourself, no good self-help materials are available, so you'll probably need to hire a lawyer. Also, if you object to the discharge on the basis of the debtor's fraud and lose, the court can order you to pay the debtor's attorneys fees.

5. Object to Exemptions (Chapter 7)

The key to getting paid in a Chapter 7 bankruptcy is for the debtor to have lots of valuable property that can be sold by the trustee to pay you and other unsecured creditors. Unfortunately for you, most individuals filing for bankruptcy in California can keep all or most of their property by claiming it to be exempt.

In California, an individual debtor has a choice of two sets of exemptions to choose from: "System 1" and "System 2." Either one system or the other may be used, but not both. If married people file jointly, both must choose the same system. In both systems, most property is exempted only to a certain value—for example, a car up to $1,200. Up to $100,000 in a home may be exempt under California homestead laws. Both systems also exempt some property regardless of its value.[6] Although exemption laws do not apply to businesses, an individual proprietor filing for bankruptcy may claim exemptions as an individual, even if the indebtedness arose from the conduct of her business.

You may want to visit the bankruptcy court to examine the debtor's case file. Exemptions will be listed on Form 6, Schedule C. If you discover obviously bogus exemptions, or that property has been greatly undervalued to bring it within the limit of an exemption, you're entitled to object. Written objections must be made within 30 days of the creditors' meeting. That is beyond the scope of this book. You can, however, informally report your findings to the trustee and hope that he'll do the job for you.

! Even if the exemption claimed by the debtor has no legal justification, it will still be honored by the court if no one objects within the 30-day deadline. So make sure you review the bankruptcy file and make any objections in a timely manner.

---

[6] A United States District Court has ruled that the California homestead exemption, which exempts between $50,000 and $100,000 of equity in a home, can't be used by bankruptcy filers. (*In Re Pladson*, N.D. Calif. May 7, 1993). Many bankruptcy experts believe this decision will ultimately be overturned on appeal. In the meantime, however, judgment debtors with equity in their homes may now have to cough most of it up for the benefit of their creditors if they choose to file for bankruptcy. For a complete explanation and listing of the California exemptions, we recommend *Money Troubles: Legal Strategies to Cope With Your Debts*, by Robin Leonard (Nolo Press).

6. Challenge the Bankruptcy (Chapter 7)

In every Chapter 7 bankruptcy case, the debtor must list all her property, debts, income and expenses and describe all property transactions that occurred during the year previous to filing.

This includes any:

- income or property to be received in the future, such as tax refunds, inheritances, life insurance payments and personal injury recoveries
- property that was given away or sold at less than full value prior to filing for bankruptcy and
- payments made to creditors prior to filing for bankruptcy that were outside of the ordinary course of business.

On the basis of the debtor's detailed information, the trustee decides whether there are non-exempt assets that can be sold and whether the bankruptcy should be allowed.

The bankruptcy law is very strict with Chapter 7 debtors who intentionally tried to cheat their creditors by hiding or unloading property prior to filing for bankruptcy or lied about their property or income in their bankruptcy papers.

If this type of behavior is brought to the attention of the bankruptcy court, the judge may order the bankruptcy dismissed. The court may also dismiss the bankruptcy if the debtor has enough income or non-exempt property to pay his debts. A dismissal would free you up to continue your collection efforts just as if the bankruptcy were never filed.

Creditors are often in the best position to discover fraud and deceit. By carefully inspecting the debtor's bankruptcy file and comparing the information there with what you already have, you may be able to dig up the evidence needed to stop the bankruptcy cold. You also can learn the names of other creditors and use them as additional resources in this endeavor. Even if you aren't sure about what you find in the bankruptcy papers, you can photocopy them and take them to a bankruptcy lawyer for analysis. Unfortunately, most creditors leave this type of investigation to the trustees, who rarely conduct independent checks on the truth of the information in the papers.

If you discover evidence of fraud or untruthfulness, you can hire a lawyer to challenge the bankruptcy, bring the information to the attention of the trustee and request that he file the challenge on behalf of you and the other creditors or negotiate with the debtor to reaffirm the debt in exchange for your willingness to not pursue your fraud claim in the bankruptcy court.

If the bankruptcy has already been discharged and you discover that the debtor committed fraud in filing the bankruptcy, you have one year after the discharge to file a complaint with the bankruptcy court. You'll need a lawyer to pursue such an objection. If you prove the fraud, the bankruptcy discharge will be nullified and you will be able to pursue the debt once again (11 USC §§ 727(e), 1228(d), 1328(d)). The catch is that if you do all the work and win, you'll still have to compete with any other creditors when you go to collect your judgment.

7. Chapter 13 Repayment Plans

Interpreting a Chapter 13 plan can be a little worky. Your main job is to find out under which category of creditor you are listed. This will depend on what you put in your Proof of Claim. (See Section D.) Most judgment creditors appear in the plan as unsecured creditors who are entitled to be repaid a percentage of the debt over the life of the plan. But you also may be classified as a priority creditor and be entitled to 100% repayment of the debt. Usually, priority creditors fall within one of the categories listed in Section D, but some bankruptcy courts also allow creditors who are owed non-dischargeable debts to be classified as priority creditors.

If you obtained liens on the debtor's property (see Chapters 4 and 6), examine the list of liens that the trustee or the debtor are avoiding. Your name is likely to show up here if the property is exempt or your lien was obtained within 90 days before the bankruptcy filing date. If your lien is avoided, you don't have it anymore and you will be treated like an unsecured creditor.

The portion of an unsecured claim that is likely to be paid under a Chapter 13 plan is determined by the amount of disposable income available to the debtor for repayment, the number of priority creditors who will be paid in full and the amount the unsecured creditors would have been paid in a Chapter 7 bankruptcy—the debtor's plan must pay out at least that amount. Disposable income is the difference between the debtor's net income and reasonable living expenses. Although the trustee can challenge specific expenses as being unreasonable, the usual result is that precious little disposable income is available. Nevertheless, if you can show that expenses have been improperly inflated, you may produce larger payments for yourself and other creditors under the Chapter 13 plan.

The plan will be accepted or rejected at a confirmation hearing, which creditors rarely attend. The judge's decision will be based primarily on the trustee's recommendation and established rules governing Chapter 13 plans. You can object to the confirmation of a debtor's plan on a number of technical grounds, including the arguments that the expenses listed on the form are improper or too high, that the debtor's disposable income should be computed at a higher level, that the debtor's non-exempt property requires a higher overall payment to unsecured creditors, that the debtor is not paying a high enough percentage of her unsecured debts or that one or more creditors has been improperly classified as a priority creditor. But objecting is seldom worthwhile, since the bankruptcy process is geared toward getting the plan approved.

It's up to the bankruptcy trustee—not you—to handle problems if the debtor doesn't meet the terms of the Chapter 13 plan. The trustee may give the debtor a month or two grace period or may even allow some minor adjustments in the plan. As long as the debtor appears to be acting in good faith, the trustee will try to be accommodating. If it looks like the debtor cannot complete the plan, the trustee has these options:

- Amend the plan to reduce the debtor's total monthly payments or extend the repayment period from three years to five years. This may also reduce the amount you receive under the plan.
- Arrange for the debtor to convert to a Chapter 7 bankruptcy, in which case you can expect a notice of the conversion.
- Seek a discharge (cancelling) of debts without converting to Chapter 7, on the basis of hardship if the debtor's inability to pay is due to circumstances beyond his control. This probably means your judgment will be wiped out.
- Dismiss the Chapter 13 petition outright. This means that you can take up your collection activities where you left off when the bankruptcy was filed.

If you wish to know more about your rights as a creditor in the Chapter 13 process, consult a bankruptcy attorney or see the discussion on legal research in Chapter 23.

Chapter 17

WHAT TO DO IF THE DEBTOR DIES

LEARNING OF A JUDGMENT DEBTOR'S DEATH can be deeply sobering. No matter how zealously you have pursued your rights, the final reality of the debtor's death will certainly slow you down some. But please realize that you still may be able to collect your judgment.

What happens to your judgment if the debtor dies before you collect it?[1] If the judgment debtor left property when she died, you may be in luck. How much luck depends on whether the assets pass through a formal court process known as probate, or instead pass directly to the debtor's heirs. The probate court process provides an orderly procedure for you to present your claim and be paid out of the assets passing through probate. But there is no special procedure for creditors to collect from assets that don't pass through probate. You must track down these assets one by one—much the same as when the debtor was alive.

This chapter explains how to protect your interests if a case is opened in the probate court, and makes some suggestions for how to proceed against assets that don't pass through probate.

[1]This chapter applies only to estates being handled in California. If the debtor's estate is being handled in another state, you must follow the procedures of that state.

Important Definitions

Decedent: Someone who has died.

Intestate succession: The rules under which property is passed to a person's heirs when he dies without a will or when a will fails to pass the property for one reason or another.

Joint tenancy: A way of holding title to property that avoids probate. Upon one joint tenant's death, her interest in the jointly held property automatically passes to the surviving joint tenant(s).

Living (inter vivos) trust: A probate-avoidance device that allows someone to transfer property to a trust with instructions that it be transferred, without probate, to a named beneficiary at the owner's death.

Non-probate property: Property that does not go through probate because the decedent, while alive, set up a mechanism to avoid probate. Examples are life insurance proceeds, property held in joint tenancy, property held in living trusts and property held in informal bank account trusts (pay-on-death accounts).

Personal representative: The person who is authorized to act on behalf of a decedent's estate. If named in the will, this person is called an executor; if there is no will, he is called an administrator.

Probate: The court-supervised process by which a decedent's assets are distributed and debts are paid.

Probate estate: Assets of the decedent that are distributed through the probate process.

A. Learning of the Judgment Debtor's Death

HOW DO YOU FIND OUT that a judgment debtor has died? If you are looking for the debtor or actively involved in collecting the judgment, you undoubtedly will learn of the death from relatives or employers. If you live in the same town and read the newspapers—especially the obituaries—you may learn of it that way. But if you don't live in the same area or aren't hot on the debtor's trail, how you will learn of the death, if ever, depends on whether the debtor's estate is probated.

1. If There Is a Probate Court Proceeding

If some or all of the judgment debtor's assets pass through probate, you will learn of the debtor's death in at least one and possibly two ways:

- **Notice of Petition to Administer Estate:** The proposed personal representative (the person, usually a close relative, who is responsible for winding up the deceased person's affairs) must file, in the probate court, a document called Petition to Administer Estate. At this time, a date for a hearing on the petition is set. The proposed personal representative then must publish a notice of the filing and hearing date in a general circulation newspaper in the city where the judgment debtor died. Judgment collection services read the legal section of all newspapers in the areas where their judgment debtors are likely to die. But no one else does—so as a practical matter, you are unlikely to learn of the judgment debtor's death this way.
- **Notice of Administration to Creditors:** A much more useful form of notice may show up in your mailbox. If the personal representative knows of your judgment against the judgment debtor, he is required to mail you—first class—a notice of the death. The notice will also inform you of your right to file a Creditor's Claim against the estate for the amount of your judgment, plus costs and interest. The Notice of Administration to Creditors must be mailed within four months of the date the personal representative is appointed to that position by the probate court.

2. If There Is No Probate Proceeding

If there are no assets left to pass through probate, formal notice will not be sent to the decedent's creditors. You may not learn of the judgment debtor's death until you try to collect the judgment.

Assets commonly pass through probate when they are left in a will or when the decedent has made no provision for how they should be passed. But in many situations, assets don't pass through probate. When the debtor's assets are worth less than $60,000, they can be passed to the debtor's heirs without using the probate court. Or the debtor may have arranged, before death, to pass assets through a probate-avoidance device such as a living trust, joint tenancy property or a pay-on-death account. In Section B.3, below, we explain how the absence of probate court proceedings affects your rights as a judgment creditor.

B. What To Do When Judgment Debtor Dies

ONCE YOU LEARN—by whatever means—that the judgment debtor is dead, your first step is to determine whether a probate case has been or will be opened. Of course, if your notice comes in written form from the personal representative or you happen to see the published Notice of Petition to Administer Estate, you already know. If you learn about the death from some other source, you will need to investigate further. Probably the best approach is to contact the Probate Division of the Superior Court for the county in which the judgment debtor died and find out whether a probate petition has been filed in that person's name. Or if the death is recent, you can start monitoring the newspapers that would be most likely to carry a Notice of Petition to Administer the Estate.[2]

[2]Often one newspaper in a particular area carries most of the legal notices for that area.

1. If Probate Proceeding Is Open or in the Works

If you learn that a probate proceeding has been—or is to be—opened for the estate of the judgment debtor, you should complete a Creditor's Claim form. This document asserts your right to have your judgment paid from the debtor's assets, if there are enough assets left over after higher priority creditors are paid. If you don't file a Creditor's Claim, you give up all right to collect your judgment. We tell you how to file a Creditor's Claim in Section C, below.

Here's how to calculate the deadline for filing a Creditor's Claim:

- If you receive a Notice of Administration to Creditor's from the personal representative, you must file a Creditor's Claim within four months of the date the personal representative is appointed by the court or thirty days after the date the notice was sent to you, whichever is later.
- If you saw the published Notice of Petition to Administer Estate in a newspaper, the deadline is four months after the date set for the hearing on the Petition.[3]
- If you learn from the court or another source that probate proceedings have been opened, contact the probate court and find out when the personal representative was appointed. File your Creditor's Claim within four months of that date.

Late Filings: If you find out about the probate proceedings after the deadline for filing a Creditor's Claim, see a probate attorney (Chapter 23). If you received no notice, the outer limits for filing a claim are one year from the date the personal representative is appointed, or the date the probate court makes a final order for distribution of the estate, whichever is earlier. However, you must file a petition with the court to file a late claim (Probate Code § 9103).

[3]On occasion, the appointment will occur after the date set for the hearing, which means the deadline is extended until four months after the actual appointment. But since you have no way of knowing this, it is wise to assume that no deadline extension has occurred.

2. If Probate Is Opened, But Some Assets Pass Outside of Probate

Many people pass some of their assets through probate avoidance devices such as a living trust or pay-on-death bank account, but also leave enough property in their will to require the opening of probate court proceedings. Property passed through any type of a trust is specifically made liable for payment of creditors, assuming that the property passing through probate court is insufficient for that purpose (Probate Code § 18201). If you discover, therefore, that the probate proceeding won't produce enough in assets to pay off your judgment, plus costs and interests, consider collecting from assets passed outside of probate. But first read Section B.3, just below, for some suggestions on how to approach this task.

3. If No Probate Proceeding Is Open or in the Works

If no probate proceedings are begun, you must basically follow the same strategy you used while the debtor was alive: find some assets and levy if you can. The only problem is that the assets are no longer owned by the debtor but rather by the debtor's heirs. That's just a practical problem, however, not a legal one.[4]

Community Property Note: If the debtor was married you can go after the spouse's share of any community property owned prior to the debtor's death as well as property inherited by the spouse. (See Chapter 1.D.4.)

The difficulty in tracing the assets is that, with the exception of real estate and business assets, there will seldom be a public record of what happened to the debtor's property. If the debtor was single but had children, then you can reasonably expect that the children got most of it. If the debtor lived with a mate or companion, then look to that person. To definitely locate assets owned by these and other probable heirs, you will have to use the procedures outlined in Chapter 6 or hire an asset tracing firm (Chapter 23.D).

If you created liens on the debtor's real estate or business assets as we suggest in Chapter 4, you will have an easier time of collecting. Liens remain on the property after the debtor's death, and they must be paid off for the property to be sold with clear title. Much inherited property is sold soon after it is received, and the lien will probably have to be paid off then.

There is one important exception to this rule: liens on joint tenancy property do not survive the joint tenant's death. This seeming anomaly is based on the legal principle that joint tenancy property isn't technically inherited; a joint tenant's interest (including the lien) simply ends when he dies.

Example: *You obtain a judgment against Joe. He doesn't pay the judgment, so you place a lien on the house he owns in joint tenancy with Sarah. Joe dies without paying you. Sarah, the surviving joint tenant, gets complete ownership of the house without the lien. If, however, Joe originally owned the property alone, and created the joint tenancy to avoid paying you, you could bring an action to void the joint tenancy and collect from the property. You would need a lawyer to do this.*

Caution: Collecting a deceased debtor's assets outside of probate can sometimes get tricky. If the size of your judgment warrants it, we recommend you work with an attorney.

C. Preparing a Creditor's Claim

IN THIS SECTION, WE TELL YOU how to file a Creditor's Claim in a formal probate proceeding.

Use the Creditor's Claim form located in the Appendix. You'll need this information, available from documents filed in the probate, to make a formal claim:

- title and address of the probate court
- probate case number and
- name and address of the personal representative.

Caption: Fill in your name, address, phone number, and indicate that you are appearing in pro per. Enter the name and address of the superior court handling the probate, the debtor's name and probate case number.

Item 1: Fill in the total amount of the judgment still due. Remember to deduct any payments you received and add on accumulated post-judgment interest and court costs. (See Chapter 15.) If you haven't filed a Memorandum of Costs recently, do that first and serve a copy on the personal representative.

Item 2: Fill in your name as claimant.

Item 2a: Check this box if you are making your claim as an individual.

[4] It is possible for a creditor to open a probate proceeding on behalf of a deceased debtor. When this might be helpful must be determined on a case-by-case basis, with the help of a lawyer.

ATTORNEY OR CREDITOR WITHOUT ATTORNEY *(Name and Address)*: TELEPHONE NO.: 415/999-9999

Pam Plaintiff
123 North Street
Berkeley, CA 94704

ATTORNEY FOR *(Name)*: In Pro Per

FOR COURT USE ONLY

SUPERIOR COURT OF CALIFORNIA, COUNTY OF SAN FRANCISCO
STREET ADDRESS: City Hall, Room 300
MAILING ADDRESS: 400 Van Ness Avenue
CITY AND ZIP CODE: San Francisco, CA 94102
BRANCH NAME:

ESTATE OF (NAME):
DAN DEFENDANT, DECEDENT

CREDITOR'S CLAIM*
(for estate administration proceedings filed after June 30, 1988)

CASE NUMBER: 098765430

You must file this claim with the court clerk at the court address above before the LATER of (a) four months after the date letters (authority to act for the estate) were first issued to the personal representative, or (b) thirty days after the date Notice of Administration was given to the creditor, if notice was given as provided in Probate Code section 9051. Mail or deliver a copy of this claim to the personal representative. A proof of service is on the reverse.

1. Total amount of the claim: $ 6,421.88
2. Claimant *(name)*: Pam Plaintiff
   a. [X] an individual.
   b. [ ] an individual or entity doing business under the fictitious name of *(specify)*:
   c. [ ] a partnership. The person signing has authority to sign on behalf of the partnership.
   d. [ ] a corporation. The person signing has authority to sign on behalf of the corporation.
   e. [ ] other *(specify)*:
3. Address of claimant *(specify)*: 123 North Street, Berkeley, CA 94704
4. Claimant is [X] the creditor [ ] a person acting on behalf of creditor *(state reason)*:
5. [ ] Claimant is [ ] the personal representative [ ] the attorney for the personal representative. *(Claims against the estate by the personal representative and the attorney for the personal representative must be filed within the claim period allowed in Probate Code section 9100. See the notice box above.)*
6. I am authorized to make this claim which is just and due or may become due. All payments on or offsets to the claim have been credited. Facts supporting the claim are [X] on reverse [X] attached.

I declare under penalty of perjury under the laws of the State of California that this creditor's claim is true and correct.

Date: August 8, 19___

Pam Plaintiff
(TYPE OR PRINT NAME AND TITLE)

Pam Plaintiff
(SIGNATURE OF CLAIMANT)

INSTRUCTIONS TO CLAIMANT

A. On the reverse, itemize the claim and show the date the service was rendered or the debt incurred. Describe the item or service in detail, and indicate the amount claimed for each item. Do not include debts incurred after the date of death, except funeral claims.
B. If the claim is not due or contingent, or the amount is not yet ascertainable, state the facts supporting the claim.
C. If the claim is secured by a note or other written instrument, the original or a copy must be attached (state why original is unavailable). If secured by mortgage, deed of trust, or other lien on property that is of record, it is sufficient to describe the security and refer to the date or volume and page, and county where recorded. (See Probate Code section 9152.)
D. Mail or take this original claim to the court clerk's office for filing. If mailed, use certified mail, with return receipt requested.
E. Mail or deliver a copy to the personal representative. Complete the Proof of Mailing or Personal Delivery on the reverse.
F. The personal representative will notify you when your claim is allowed or rejected.

(Continued on reverse)

* See instructions before completing. Use Creditor's Claim form No. DE-170 for estates filed before July 1, 1988.

Form Approved by the Judicial Council of California DE 172 (New July 1, 1988)

CREDITOR'S CLAIM (Probate)

Probate Code, §§ 9000 et seq., 9153

ESTATE OF (NAME): Dan Defendant, DECEDENT	CASE NUMBER: 098765430

FACTS SUPPORTING THE CREDITOR'S CLAIM

[X] See attachment *(if space is insufficient)*

Date of Item	Item and Supporting Facts	Amount Claimed
1/10/__	Judgment entered in Pam Plaintiff v. Dan Defendant in San Francisco Municipal Court, Case No. 12345. Judgment is based on a breach of contract. No payments have been received on the judgment, and post-judgment costs and interest to date amount to $421.88 (Copies of the judgment and Memorandum of Cost are attached). The following liens were created: Abstract of Judgment recorded in Alameda County 2/8/__, Book #1, Page #1; Abstract of Judgment recorded in San Francisco County 2/11/__, Book#2, Page #2; Notice of Judgment Lien On Personal Property filed with the California Seretary of State 2/18/__, #3873.	$6,421.88
	TOTAL	$ 6,421.88

PROOF OF [X] MAILING [ ] PERSONAL DELIVERY TO PERSONAL REPRESENTATIVE

(Be sure to mail or take the original to the court clerk's office for filing)

1. I am the creditor or a person acting on behalf of the creditor. At the time of mailing or delivery I was at least 18 years of age.
2. My residence or business address is *(specify)*: 123 North Street Berkeley, CA 94704
3. I mailed or delivered a copy of this Creditor's Claim to the personal representative as follows *(check either a or b below)*:
   a. [X] **First-class mail.** I deposited a copy of the claim with the United States Postal Service, in a sealed envelope with postage fully prepaid. I used first-class mail. I am a resident of or employed in the county where the mailing occurred. The envelope was addressed and mailed as follows:
      (1) Name of personal representative served: Gretl Goodrich
      (2) Address on envelope: 234 West Street San Francisco, CA 94118
      (3) Date of mailing: August 8, 19__
      (4) Place of mailing *(city and state)*: Berkeley CA
   b. [ ] **Personal delivery.** I personally delivered a copy of the claim to the personal representative as follows:
      (1) Name of personal representative served:
      (2) Address where delivered:
      (3) Date delivered:
      (4) Time delivered:

I declare under penalty of perjury under the laws of the State of California that the foregoing is true and correct.

Date: August 8, 19__

Pam Plaintiff (TYPE OR PRINT NAME OF CLAIMANT)

▶ Pam Plaintiff (SIGNATURE OF CLAIMANT)

DE 172 (New July 1, 1988)

CREDITOR'S CLAIM
(Probate)

Page two

Item 2b: Check this box if you are making this claim on behalf of an unincorporated company doing business under a fictitious name and enter the fictitious name.

Item 2c: Check this box if you are making this claim on behalf of a partnership—and are authorized to do so.

Item 2d: Check this box if you are making the claim for a corporation—and are authorized to do so.

Item 2e: Check this box if none of the above applies, and indicate your authority to make the claim. For example, you might be the judgment creditor's conservator or attorney in fact under a power of attorney.

Item 3: Enter your address.

Item 4: Check the first box if you are a creditor. Check the second box if you are acting on behalf of a creditor and state your authority.

Item 5: Leave this blank.

Item 6: This states that you're making a valid claim and have given the debtor all credits due him. Check both boxes in this item.

Fill in the date, print or type your name and sign the form.

Page Two: At the top, fill in the name of the deceased debtor and the case number.

Facts Supporting the Creditor's Claim: Check the "See attachment" box, since you'll be attaching a copy of your judgment and, if applicable, the most recent Memorandum of Costs.

Date of Item: Fill in the date your judgment was entered. If you have more than one judgment, list each separately.

Item and Supporting Facts: Provide a brief description of your judgment.[5] For example: "Judgment against [Name of Debtor] for [briefly describe what the judgment was for—such as breach of contract or failure to pay back a loan]." State if costs were claimed in Memoranda of Costs and the amount of these costs. Also describe any judicial liens that you created on the debtor's personal property (including examination liens—see Chapter 6) and real estate. If you provide sufficient information on the liens (date, book and page, and county where recorded), you are not required to attach copies of the liens. Otherwise, provide copies of the liens. See the sample.

Amount Claimed: Enter the total from Item 1 on the front of the form.

Total: List the total amount you are owed.

Proof of Mailing/Personal Delivery: Unlike most court documents, you are allowed to serve the Creditor's Claim yourself. Depending on whether you plan to mail or personally deliver the document, check the appropriate box before "Mailing" or "Personal delivery."

Complete the rest of the Proof of Service following the guidelines in Chapter 22—with the exception that you are allowed to serve the papers. Use the accompanying sample as a guide.

3. Serve and File the Claim

Make four copies of the Creditor's Claim, including all attachments. Mail or personally deliver a copy to the personal representative. Send the original and one copy to the court to be file-stamped and returned in a self-addressed, stamped envelope.

4. After You Submit a Claim

The personal representative should send you an Allowance or Rejection of Claim form indicating whether payment is approved. If payment of your judgment is approved, you may be paid immediately, or the personal representative may wait until the court issues a final order stating how estate property is to be distributed.

[5] You don't need a judgment to file a Creditor's Claim, but we don't cover other types of claims in this book.

How the Representative Pays Claims

The personal representative must pay off debts in the order set out below—except that debts owed the federal or state government have priority. The first five categories are paid as soon as the personal representative has enough money from the estate (Probate Code § 11421).

1. Expenses of administering the estate
2. Funeral expenses
3. Expenses of last illness
4. Family allowance to support the decedent's family during probate[6]
5. Wages due the decedent's employees
6. Mortgages, judgment liens and other liens.[7] These are paid from the proceeds of the property subject to the lien; if the proceeds aren't enough, the remaining amount is classed with general debts
7. General debts, including judgments that are not secured by liens.

5. Disputing a Rejected Claim

What if the representative rejects your claim, or ignores it, which is the same thing? You can dispute the decision formally by filing a lawsuit against the estate within three months from the date you receive your notice of rejection. If you don't receive an Allowance or Rejection of Creditor's Claim form, treat the 30th day after the claim was filed, plus five extra days if the personal representative was served by mail, as the date rejection was given.

If the claim is disputed, the estate pays the amount of the claim into court, where it remains until the matter is settled (Probate Code § 11427).

However, before you run to court, contact the personal representative by phone or letter. You may be able to work something out, or perhaps the personal representative can explain the reason for the rejection. For example, if she claims the judgment has been satisfied in whole or in part, you might be able to show that it hasn't. Or you might be able to compromise if there was an arrangement with the debtor, such as an agreement (disrupted by the debtor's death) that you would waive part of the judgment if voluntary payment were made by a certain time.

On the other hand, if the reason for nonpayment or partial payment is lack of money in the estate, check the court file to get a clear understanding of how funds are being disbursed. You may discover that there aren't enough assets to fight over. Generally, bringing a suit to challenge the denial of a claim isn't wise if the estate has insufficient funds to pay you, unless you have reason to believe this isn't true.

If you decide to sue, your next step depends on the amount in question. If it's relatively small (up to $5,000), you can probably handle it yourself in small claims court, although there are special notice requirements for suing an estate. Check with the small claims advisor, if the court has one, or someone knowledgeable about probate. If the amount is large enough for a municipal or superior court action, see a lawyer.

---

[6] Also, if the debtor's house had a declaration of homestead on file, family members will be entitled to the homestead exemption if they inherit all or part of the house, are living in it at the time of the debtor's death and don't have a homestead exemption on other property.

[7] If you recorded an abstract of judgment in a county where the debtor owned real property, you have a lien against it (Chapter 4). Other useful liens you may have created are liens on business personal property (Chapter 4) and examination liens (Chapter 6).

Chapter 18

HELP FROM THE JUDGE: SEIZURE, TURNOVER AND ASSIGNMENT ORDERS

FROM TIME TO TIME, the mainline collection processes outlined in this book are not sufficient to get your judgment collected. For instance, the debtor may own valuable property, but it can't be levied on, either because it's in the debtor's private residence or because the debtor is concealing it. Or, you may know that the judgment debtor receives periodic royalty payments but a levy is impracticable because it only collects what is due at the time the levy is made.

In these types of situations, it is normally possible to reach the assets in question if you first get permission from a judge. This chapter tells you how to bring a motion to obtain the following court orders.

- **Seizure Order:** allows a levying officer to levy on personal property in a private home
- **Turnover Order:** requires the judgment debtor to turn over specified property to the levying officer
- **Assignment Order:** requires the judgment debtor to assign certain rights to the judgment creditor—such as the right to receive royalties, payments due under a continuing contract or federal wages that are exempt from regular garnishment.

If you wish to file a type of motion that's not covered in this chapter, you will need to strike out on your own. You can still use the material in this chapter as a general procedural guide. (See Chapter 23 for information about legal research.)

A. Kinds of Motions

THERE ARE TWO BASIC WAYS to bring a motion.

1. Ex Parte Motions

With the ex parte approach, you don't give the debtor advance written notice. You prepare the necessary paperwork and then simply approach the judge through her clerk for an informal hearing, usually in the judge's office.

Ex parte motions are allowed in collections cases when giving notice to the judgment debtor might frustrate the purpose for the order. For instance, if you want an order permitting a levy on property in the debtor's home, giving the debtor notice of your intentions will most likely cause the property to disappear in a hurry.

In an ex parte hearing, you are required to provide the judgment debtor with 24 hours' oral notice unless you convince the judge that even this much notice would defeat the purpose of your motion. The samples in this chapter contain optional language asking the court to dispense with the 24-hour notice requirement. If the judge rejects this no notice option, you'll have to reschedule your hearing with the judge and provide oral notice. If you don't wish to risk this, leave the optional language out of your motion papers and provide the oral notice.

2. Noticed Motions

The other way to bring a motion is to prepare the necessary paperwork and schedule a formal hearing for a date that will let you give the judgment debtor at least 15 days' written notice (20 days, if service is by mail). This approach is termed a "noticed motion."

B. How To Bring a Motion

HERE IS WHAT YOU MUST DO to bring a motion and get an order signed by a judge.

Small Claims Court Note: In Small Claims Court, you can use a form, Notice of Motion and Declaration, which will simplify the paperwork. Check with the Small Claims Court for specific procedures.

1. Check Court Rules

The procedures governing motions are similar in every court, but some courts have their own rules of procedure. There is nothing terribly difficult about making motions, but courts normally insist that the rules be strictly followed.

Contact the court where you obtained your judgment. Find out whether the court has any special rules for bringing motions. The clerk will either refer you to the court's local rules, if they exist, or tell you that the court follows the statewide *Rules of Court.*

Local rules can be obtained from the court or your county law library. The statewide *Rules of Court* are also available in the law library and sometimes in large public libraries. *Rules of Court* rules that specifically affect motions are reprinted in Section D of this chapter for your reference. Study them and any local rules that you find.

Before you prepare any documents, check with the clerk or court rules to find out:

- the days and times your motion may be heard, the location and how you may schedule your motion. If you can get a hearing date over the phone, allow yourself time to prepare your papers and—for a noticed motion—at least 20 days to have the debtor served
- the filing fees—about $14 and
- how many copies of the documents are required.

2. Prepare Documents

If you think you've already been run through the mill on paperwork, grit your teeth and prepare for more. Even the simplest motion papers must be typed, double-spaced, on 8-1/2" x 11" numbered legal paper. A piece of lined paper is provided in the Appendix. Either photocopy it in abundance or buy numbered lined paper from an office supply store.

Court documents prepared on lined paper are referred to as "pleadings." Type or use a word processor to complete your documents. Number the pages of each document at the bottom.

On the first page of each pleading, fill in your name, address and phone number at the top left. Starting on line 8, center the title of the court in capital letters. Place the caption and case number several lines below. Fill in the title of the document, and place the date, time and location under the title.

Some courts, such as Los Angeles, require "bluebacks" for all pleadings. Bluebacks are simply blue paper stapled to the backs of court documents that identify the people involved in the legal action, the court and the document being filed. Bluebacks can be obtained from most large office supply stores.

To make a motion, you must prepare the following four documents, which can be physically combined into one continuous document:

- **Notice of Motion (if needed) and Motion:** This gives the court and judgment debtor written notice of what you are requesting and when the hearing on your motion will be held, so the debtor can appear at the hearing and contest your request. The notice part of this document is not necessary for ex parte motions.

- **Declaration:** This is a statement, under oath, of the facts that give the court a basis for acting on your motion. It is required for both ex parte and noticed motions. For most collection motions, only your statement is necessary. However, if you are relying on somebody else's observations to bring your motion, you must submit that person's statement in a declaration as well. For example, if you are seeking a Seizure Order, and the debtor's ex-roommate has information about property in the debtor's home, she will need to sign a declaration.
- **Memorandum of Points and Authorities:** This is a short statement of the facts of your situation and citations to the legal authority entitling you to your requested order. We provide some model language and tell you what citations to provide for the motions covered in this chapter. This document is required for both noticed and ex parte motions.
- **Proposed Court Order:** This document puts the judge's decision on your request into effect. It is used for both noticed and ex parte motions. If your request is granted, the judge signs the order that you have prepared, possibly with modifications.

Follow the samples in this chapter, modifying them to fit your situation. Do not copy instructions word-for-word into your document.

3. Photocopy Documents

Make at least three photocopies of your documents. Staple each set of documents in the upper left hand corner. Comply with any local court requirements, such as two-hole punching the documents or attaching tabs at the bottom for exhibits.

4. Have Debtor Served (Noticed Motions Only)

For noticed motions, have one copy of your papers served on the judgment debtor before you file them with the court. It is usually easiest to have the debtor served by mail at his last known address. Service by mail must take place at least 20 days before the hearing date. Include your proposed order with the motion papers being served. After your papers are served, complete a proof of service, have the server sign it and attach it to your motion papers. (Instructions for serving documents and preparing proofs of service are in Chapter 22.)

5. File Papers With Court

At least a week before the hearing date, take or send the court the original and the remaining copies of the documents. You may have to pay a fee at this time—approximately $14. If you mail your papers, send the following to the court clerk:

- cover letter requesting that you be assigned a hearing date if you don't already have one, that the original documents be filed and that the file-stamped copy be returned to you
- original of your motion papers and at least one complete copy
- motion fees (about $14) and
- self-addressed, stamped envelope.

The clerk will file or lodge (temporarily place the documents in the court file pending the hearing) the original, and file-stamp your copies.

For ex parte motions, the clerk will deliver the original and perhaps one of the copies to the judge, who will either hear your request or decide it on the basis of your papers.

6. Provide Notice (Ex Parte Motions Only)

For ex parte motions, you must give the judgment debtor 24 hours' oral notice of the hearing unless you convince the judge that even this much notice would defeat the purpose of your motion. Oral notice is provided by a polite telephone call telling the judgment debtor when and where the ex parte hearing will be held.

7. Examine Objections or Claim of Exemption (if Filed)

The debtor may file documents objecting to your motion. Look at them carefully, since you will need to counter the debtor's arguments at the hearing.

The judgment debtor is entitled to file a Claim of Exemption to contest a motion for an Assignment Order (CCP § 708.550). The debtor may claim that the payments you want assigned are exempt, or a portion is needed to support the debtor or her family.

The Claim of Exemption to an Assignment Order must be filed and served (in the form of a noticed motion) at least three days before the hearing scheduled on your motion. If a Claim of Exemption isn't filed by the judgment debtor, she waives the exemption, and the judge is entitled to order exempt payments assigned.

8. Attend Hearing

The day before the hearing, sit down and review your motion papers. On the day of the hearing, try to get to the court a little early. If your motion is ex parte, go to the designated room or courtroom. For noticed motions, there may be a bulletin board with a list of the cases to be heard. If your case isn't listed, check with the courtroom clerk.

Bring copies of all your documents, including the unsigned order and any proofs of service. Let the clerk or bailiff know you are present.

When your case is called, step forward. Always address the judge, "Your Honor." Some judges prefer to ask questions, but others will ask you to begin. Explain your request in your own words.

> ***Example:*** *Good morning, your honor. I am the judgment creditor in this case and I am seeking an order assigning to me certain payments due the judgment debtor from third parties. Specifically, the judgment debtor receives monthly payments from Katherine Piper on a promissory note, monthly rent from his tenant Paul Simon, and quarterly royalty payments from his publisher. The judgment debtor owes $6,000 on the judgment, plus costs and interest. If the assignments are ordered as I request, the judgment will be satisfied in approximately 15 months. Otherwise, I will have to repeatedly levy on these payments.*

If the judgment debtor has filed a Claim of Exemption or otherwise responded to your motion, he has an opportunity to speak after you. You then have a chance to reply. Your reply to a Claim of Exemption will have to be either that the payments are not exempt or that the payments are not needed to support the judgment debtor. (See Chapter 9.D.4, for how to oppose a Claim of Exemption based on need.)

Once your motion is heard by the court—either in the informal ex parte hearing or in the more formal hearing for noticed motions—the judge must make a ruling. She may grant your request in full or part, deny it, or take the matter under submission, which means she will decide later. If you lose, nothing happens, and you may proceed with other collection efforts.[1] You can still claim costs incurred, such as filing fees and any service of process fees. (See Chapter 15.)

If the judge grants your motion, she will sign your proposed Order, possibly with changes. Once the Order is signed, conform your copies by printing the judge's name below the signature line, and copying all other information and markings that the judge put on the original order.

9. If Required, Have Order Served on Debtor

Once you receive a signed order from the court and conform the copies, you will need to have a copy personally served on the judgment debtor for it to be valid, unless the judge orders otherwise. See Chapter 22, Section D, for instructions on personal service.

10. Have Affected Third Party Served With Notice of Order

Have any affected third parties served with a notice of the order. For an Assignment Order, have one notice mailed

---

[1] While it is possible to have a higher court review the judge's decision on your motion, it's almost never worth the time and expense.

to each source of payments being assigned (see sample below). Instructions for service by mail are in Chapter 22, Section F.

> *To Peter Publisher:*
>
> *NOTICE IS HEREBY GIVEN that under the terms of an Assignment Order dated ______ (a copy is attached to this notice) Dan Defendant's right to receive royalty payments from you has been assigned to Pam Plaintiff, 123 North St., Berkeley, California 94704 to the extent necessary to satisfy the judgment that Pam Plaintiff obtained against Dan Defendant.*
>
> *The amount necessary to satisfy this judgment is now $6,000 plus costs and accrued interest. Interest accrues on the unpaid balance of this judgment at the rate of 10% per year.*
>
> *If you make any payments to Dan Defendant after you receive this notice, you will not satisfy the obligation that has been assigned and will still be liable for full payment to the judgment creditor.*
>
> *Dated:*
>
> ______________________
>
> *Pam Plaintiff*

11. File Proofs of Service With Court

Prepare and file original proof of services with the court, showing that the orders have been served on the affected parties. See Chapter 22 for how to do this.

12. Follow Court Order

Once the order has been signed by the judge, you may go ahead with the approved action. Make sure you follow the instructions in the order. If the judge modified the order, you must comply with it as changed.[2]

[2] If circumstances change after an Assignment Order is made, either party can bring a noticed motion to amend or set aside the Order (CCP § 708.560). Examples of changed circumstances are that the debtor now needs the payments for support or if the debtor can now afford to relinquish a greater portion of the payments because of an increase in income.

If a third party is affected, he must comply with the order. For instance, once a third party receives notice of an Assignment Order, payments should be sent directly to you. If the third party doesn't comply with the assignment, send a letter reminding him of his obligation under the order. If he still doesn't comply, and there is enough at stake to justify pursuing the matter, consult an attorney. (See Chapter 23.)

C. Sample Motions and Orders

THIS SECTION GIVES EXAMPLES of three motions and orders. Using the samples as guides, prepare your own documents on lined pleading paper following the instructions in Section B.2, above.

1. Motion for Seizure Order (Ex Parte)

A levying officer cannot forcibly enter a judgment debtor's private residence to levy against assets there unless he has a seizure order from the court. You obtain this order by making a motion. To obtain a Seizure Order, you must convince the court that:

- the debtor has property that you need to seize to collect all or part of your court judgment
- your belief that the assets are on the premises in question is a reasonable one (you have "probable cause" for your belief) and
- you have no reasonable alternative methods to collect your judgment.

This motion may be brought ex parte unless the judge or a local court rule requires the noticed motion process. Examine any local rules to see whether this issue is addressed. If there is no rule, ask the court clerk if a motion for a Seizure Order can be brought ex parte. If you receive no clear answer, proceed ex parte. If it turns out that the court requires a noticed motion, you'll then need to comply. See the sample for how a motion might address these requirements in a hypothetical situation.

Pam Plaintiff
123 North Street
Berkeley, CA 94704
415/999-9999

Appearing In Pro Per

MUNICIPAL COURT OF CALIFORNIA

CITY AND COUNTY OF SAN FRANCISCO

PAM PLAINTIFF, Plaintiff,	NO. 12345
vs.	EX PARTE MOTION FOR SEIZURE ORDER, DECLARATION, MEMORANDUM OF POINTS AND AUTHORITIES, AND PROPOSED ORDER
DAN DEFENDANT, Defendant.	Date: May 26, 19__ Time: 3:00 P.M. Dept: A

MOTION FOR SEIZURE ORDER

Plaintiff, the judgment creditor, moves the court for an order authorizing a levy on the personal property of Dan Defendant, which is located inside his private home.

The specific items of personal property which will be subject to the levy are:

1) 1 Nikon FE Camera, lens, and equipment valued at approximately $4,000; and

2) Six paintings by the artist Arnold Williams valued at approximately $12,000.

The motion is made on the grounds that 1) the judgment creditor has a judgment against the judgment debtor with a balance due, including costs and accrued interest, of $6,000; 2) the property sought in the levy is valued well above the exemptions for this type of property; 3) the property is located in the judgment debtor's private home; and 4) there are no reasonable alternatives available for collecting the judgment .

This motion is based on the Declaration of Pam Plaintiff, the Memorandum of Points and Authorities, and the complete files and records of this action.

-1-

DECLARATION

I, Pam Plaintiff, declare as follows:

1. I obtained a judgment against Dan Defendant from the San Francisco Municipal Court on January 10, 19__ in the within-referenced action.

2. The balance due on the judgment is $6,000, plus post-judgment costs and accrued interest.

3. On April 16, 19__ I conducted a debtor's examination with Dan Defendant. In the course of this examination, Dan Defendant stated under oath that he possesses: 1) a Nikon FE Camera, lens, and equipment valued at approximately $4,000, and 2) six paintings by the artist Arnold Williams, valued at approximately $12,000. He said the camera is normally kept in his office located in his home, and that the paintings are on the walls of his living room and entry hall.

4. I also determined from the debtor's examination that these are the only non-exempt items of value which Dan Defendant currently possesses. His home has several major liens on it and his business has been liquidated. His bank account contains funds that are mostly exempt under the wage garnishment law.

5. Dan Defendant has been unwilling to make voluntary payments on this debt, despite my suggestions that he do so.

Comment: *As mentioned earlier, if you are bringing your motion ex parte you must either include in your Declaration a statement that you gave the judgment debtor 24 hours' notice of the hearing (the first phrase set out below), or a statement explaining why giving this notice would defeat the purpose of the motion (the second phrase set out below). After you decide which approach you want to use, select and adapt the appropriate phrase to your situation.*

6. At 3:00 P.M. on May 25, I spoke to the judgment debtor at his office at (415) 999-8888 and informed him that this ex parte motion would be heard by the above captioned court at 3:00 P.M. on May 26.

OR

6. I did not provide the judgment debtor with oral notice of this hearing because I believe that to give such notice would defeat the purpose of this motion. The judgment

-2-

debtor has previously taken evasive actions when I have attempted to collect this judgment. I am concerned that if he were given 24 hours' notice of this hearing, he would use that time to transfer the assets to another location, thereby avoiding the levy.

I declare under penalty of perjury under the laws of the State of California that the foregoing is true and correct.

> ***Comment:*** *This last sentence is mandatory on declarations. If you don't have this language, you must have your statement witnessed and signed by a notary public.*

Dated: May__, 19__

____
Pam Plaintiff

MEMORANDUM OF POINTS & AUTHORITIES

This is a motion for an order permitting a levy on assets located on the judgment debtor's private property. Under the provisions of Code of Civil Procedure Section 699.030, the court may issue an order authorizing the levying officer to levy on property located in a private place of the judgment debtor if, according to the best knowledge, information and belief of the judgment creditor, the application describes with particularity both the property sought to be levied upon and the place where it is to be found.

The judgment creditor has provided these descriptions in her Declaration, and the reasons why the order is required for her to collect her judgment. Accordingly, the judgment creditor requests that her motion be granted.

> ***Ex Parte Note:*** *If you are seeking an ex parte order without oral notice, as we recommend, use the following model paragraph.*

Under C.C.P. Section 699.030, the order sought in this motion can be obtained either ex parte upon 24 hours' notice to the judgment debtor or upon proof that the such notice would be self-defeating. The judgment creditor's Declaration supplies this proof, and the judgment creditor therefore requests that the 24-hour rule be dispensed with.

Dated: May __, 19__

Respectfully Submitted,

____
Pam Plaintiff
Judgment Creditor

-3-

ORDER

The motion of Pam Plaintiff was heard by this court ex parte on the date and at the time set forth above. The judgment creditor appeared in pro per. The judgment debtor did not receive notice and did not appear. The court finds that oral notice to the judgment debtor would have defeated the purpose of the motion and that this matter was therefore properly heard without oral notice.

> ***Comment:*** *If you plan on giving 24 hours' oral notice, the last two sentences of the preceding paragraph should be replaced with the following sentence:*
>
> The judgment debtor did/did not appear after being given 24 hours' oral notice of the ex parte proceeding.

The court having considered the motion and good cause appearing,

IT IS ORDERED that a levy is authorized to be made on the following property located in the home of judgment debtor Dan Defendant:

1) a Nikon FE Camera, lens, and related equipment; and

2) six paintings by the artist Arnold Williams.

IT IS FURTHER ORDERED that a copy of this order shall be personally served upon the judgment debtor and:

NOTICE IS HEREBY GIVEN THAT FAILURE BY THE JUDGMENT DEBTOR TO COMPLY WITH THIS ORDER MAY SUBJECT THE JUDGMENT DEBTOR TO BEING HELD IN CONTEMPT OF COURT.

Dated: _________

Signed: ______________________

Judge of the Municipal Court

-4-

2. Motion for Turnover Order (Ex Parte)

A Turnover Order requires the judgment debtor to turn over to the levying officer such assets as tangible personal property, certificates of title to personal property (for example, a motor vehicle), or stock certificates (CCP § 699.040). It can only be used if you have first obtained a Writ of Execution (see Chapter 7) and are able to show that you need it. A Turnover Order is useful if:

- you know the judgment debtor has specific items of property, but are having trouble locating them for the purpose of making a levy or
- property belonging to the judgment debtor is where it can't be reached by an ordinary levy (such as a judgment debtor's home, warehouse or garage), and you don't wish to, or can't, obtain a Seizure Order[3] (see Section C.1, above) or
- you want specific evidence, which you have good reason to believe the debtor possesses, of debts owed to the judgment debtor by third parties, and you would rather proceed this way than get the evidence through a subpena and debtor's examination (Chapter 6).

This order can customarily be obtained with an ex parte motion, although local rules or a judge may require a noticed hearing.

[3] A seizure order authorizes the levying officer to enter a private place to levy on assets. A turnover order requires the judgment debtor to deliver property named in the order to the levying officer. You use a seizure order if you want to levy on an item that couldn't easily be concealed (a grand piano, for instance), and a turnover order for tangible items that are easy to hide, such as jewelry and documents.

Pam Plaintiff
123 North Street
Berkeley, CA 94704
415/999-9999

Appearing In Pro Per

MUNICIPAL COURT OF CALIFORNIA

CITY AND COUNTY OF SAN FRANCISCO

PAM PLAINTIFF, Plaintiff, vs. DAN DEFENDANT, Defendant.	NO. 12345 EX PARTE MOTION FOR TURNOVER ORDER, DECLARATION, MEMORANDUM OF POINTS AND AUTHORITIES, AND PROPOSED ORDER Date: May 26, 19__ Time: 3:00 P.M. Dept: A

MOTION FOR TURNOVER ORDER

Plaintiff, the judgment creditor, moves the court ex parte for an order requiring the judgment debtor to turn over to the levying officer the following described property:

1. Certificates evidencing ownership of stock in Apple Computer Corporation;

2. One Apple LaserWriter printer; and

3. Certificate of title to one 1987 Ferrari Testarossa, California license plate #YRT567.

This motion is made on the grounds that 1) the judgment creditor has a judgment against the judgment debtor with a balance due of $6,000, plus post-judgment costs and accrued interest; 2) the property sought to be turned over is not exempt or is valued well above the exemptions for this type of property; and 3) the property is either located in the judgment debtor's private home or has been concealed from the levying officer so that a levy could not be made.

-1-

This motion is based on the Declaration of Pam Plaintiff, the Memorandum of Points and Authorities, and the complete files and records of this action.

DECLARATION

I, Pam Plaintiff, declare as follows:

1. I obtained a judgment against Dan Defendant from the San Francisco Municipal Court on January 10, 19__ in case # 12345.

2. The balance due on the judgment is $6,000, plus post-judgment costs and accrued interest.

3. On April 16, 19__ I conducted a debtor's examination of Dan Defendant. In the course of this examination, Dan Defendant stated under oath that he owns stock in Apple Computer Corporation, that he owns an Apple LaserWriter, and that he owns and drives a Ferrari Testarossa.

4. I obtained a Writ of Execution directed to the County of San Francisco from the San Francisco Municipal Court on April 28, 19__.

5. I transmitted the original issued Writ of Execution and instructions to the levying officer for San Francisco County to levy on the stock, LaserWriter and Ferrari. The levying officer reported back that the stock and LaserWriter are located in the judgment debtor's home, and that while he had seen the judgment debtor driving a Ferrari, he was unable to find it at the judgment debtor's house.

> **Comment:** *When bringing an ex parte motion you must either include in your Declaration a statement that you gave the judgment debtor 24 hours' notice of the hearing (the first phrase set out below), or a statement explaining why giving this notice would defeat the purpose of the motion (the second phrase set out below) Select and adapt the appropriate phrase to your situation.*

6. At 3:00 P.M. on May 25, I spoke to the judgment debtor at his office at (415) 999-8888 and informed him that this ex parte motion would be heard by the above-captioned court at 3:00 P.M. on May 26, 19__.

OR

6. I did not provide the judgment debtor with oral notice of this hearing because I believe that to give such notice would defeat the purpose of this motion. The judgment

-2-

debtor has previously taken evasive actions when I have attempted to collect this judgment. I am concerned that if he were given 24 hours' notice of this hearing, he would use that time to transfer the assets or items sought under this Turnover Order to another location or otherwise conceal them.

I declare under penalty of perjury under the laws of the State of California that the foregoing is true and correct.

> ***Comment:*** *This last sentence is mandatory on declarations. If you don't have this language, you must have your statement witnessed and signed by a notary public.*

Dated: May__, 19__

____
Pam Plaintiff

MEMORANDUM OF POINTS & AUTHORITIES

The judgment creditor is seeking a Turnover Order. Under the provisions of Code of Civil Procedure Section 699.040, upon a showing of need, the court may issue an order, after a Writ of Execution has issued, requiring the judgment debtor to turn over to the levying officer property, title to property and evidence of debt owed by third parties.

In the Declaration, the judgment creditor has shown that a Writ of Execution has been issued and has stated why she needs the order to collect the described property. Accordingly, the judgment creditor requests that her motion be granted.

> ***Ex Parte Note:*** *If you are seeking an ex parte order without oral notice, as we recommend, use the following model paragraph. If you are providing oral notice, don't use it.*

Under C.C.P. Section 699.040, the order sought in this motion can be obtained ex parte either upon 24 hours' notice to the judgment debtor, or upon proof that the such notice would be self-defeating. The judgment creditor's Declaration supplies this proof and the judgment creditor therefore requests that the 24-hour rule be dispensed with.

Dated: May __, 19__

Respectfully Submitted,

____
Pam Plaintiff
Judgment Creditor

-3-

ORDER

The motion of Pam Plaintiff was heard by this court ex parte on the date and at the time set forth above. The judgment creditor appeared in pro per. The judgment debtor did not receive notice and did not appear. The court finds that oral notice to the judgment debtor would have defeated the purpose of the motion and that this matter was therefore properly heard without oral notice.

> ***Comment:*** *If you plan on giving 24 hours' oral notice, the last two sentences of the preceding paragraph should be replaced with the following sentence:*
>
> The judgment debtor did/did not appear after being given 24 hours' oral notice of the ex parte proceeding.

The court having considered the motion and good cause appearing,

IT IS ORDERED that the following property be turned over by the judgment debtor Dan Defendant to the levying officer for San Francisco County:

1. Certificates of title to stock in the Apple Computer Corporation;
2. One Apple LaserWriter printer; and
3. One Ferrari Testarossa, California license plate #YRT567.

IT IS FURTHER ORDERED that a copy of this order shall be personally served upon the judgment debtor and:

NOTICE IS HEREBY GIVEN THAT FAILURE BY THE JUDGMENT DEBTOR TO COMPLY WITH THIS ORDER MAY SUBJECT THE JUDGMENT DEBTOR TO BEING HELD IN CONTEMPT OF COURT.

Dated: ________

Signed: ____________________
Judge of the Municipal Court

/////////
/////////
/////////
/////////

-4-

3. Motion for Assignment Order (Noticed Motion)

Suppose you discover that the judgment debtor receives regular payments that you can't readily intercept, such as:

- rents from tenants
- wages from the federal government (other than the U.S. Post Office and Federal Housing Administration, which can be reached through the regular wage garnishment procedure set out in Chapter 9)[4]
- sales commissions
- royalties, such as from a patent or copyright
- payments due on account (accounts receivable) or
- installment payments on judgments or promissory notes.

It is possible to have all or a portion of these payments go directly to you until your judgment is satisfied.[5] You do this with an order from the court that the judgment debtor assign to you some or all of her right to receive the payments. In essence, this assignment puts you in the shoes of the debtor for the purposes of receiving the payments, until your judgment is satisfied. Then the right to receive the payments returns to the debtor.

Example: *Justine is an author who receives royalties of approximately $1,000 from one of her publishers each quarter. Ira obtains a judgment against Justine for $15,000. He asks for a court order requiring Justine to assign to him the right to receive all of these royalties until the judgment is satisfied. If the royalties were Justine's sole or even primary source of income, the judge would probably order considerably less than 100% assigned.*

[4]If the judgment is for child or spousal support, wages of any federal employees may be reached through the normal garnishment procedure (see Chapter 9).

[5]The court may order that only a portion of payments due the debtor be assigned to you. This is the case with federal wages (25% is the limit) and when the debtor relies on the payments to make a living, as would be the case with an independent contractor gardener.

For federal wages reached through an Assignment Order, the judgment debtor must voluntarily forward the appropriate portion of his wages to you as described in an Assignment Order. If he doesn't comply, you can make a motion for contempt. We don't cover that motion here; you will probably need help from an attorney.

Assignment orders are particularly useful if the payments you are trying to receive are located outside of California. Otherwise you would need a sister-state judgment in that other state.

a. *What Assignment Order Can't Be Used for*

An Assignment Order can't be used for payments that are either nonassignable[6] or exempt from execution, such as:

- Social Security or Public Assistance benefits
- federal employee retirement benefits
- IRAs or Keogh plans
- payments from an irrevocable trust, the terms of which make payments to the beneficiary nonassignable or
- the portion of a payment from a retirement fund or pension that is exempt under the wage garnishment law. (See Chapters 8, 9 and 13 for more on exemptions.)

b. *Will Court Grant Assignment Order?*

The court is supposed to consider several key questions when deciding whether to grant an Assignment Order:

- What are the reasonable needs of the judgment debtor and his family? The court will not order an assignment that will strip the judgment debtor of income neces-

[6]A payment is nonassignable when it has been declared to be nonassignable by law—such as federal retirement pensions, or by the terms of an irrevocable trust—where money is irrevocably placed in trust under the control of a trustee to be handled on behalf of a beneficiary.

sary to meet the basic needs of the debtor and his family.

- How long are the payments likely to continue? If the payments will probably end in the near future (several months, perhaps), the court will be less likely to order an assignment.
- How large is the unsatisfied portion of the judgment in comparison with the payments sought to be assigned? If your judgment is nearly satisfied and only one or two payments are necessary to satisfy it, the court will be hesitant to order the assignment, since a levy will do the job. Conversely, if your entire judgment is outstanding and many payments will be needed to satisfy it, an Assignment Order is more likely.

When preparing your Assignment Order motion papers, keep those factors in mind.

c. *How To Prepare Assignment Order*

You must prepare two documents for the Assignment Order. The first contains a notice of motion and motion, declaration and memorandum of points and authorities. The second document is the Order and includes space for both the judge and debtor to sign.

Efficiency Note: Normally, the judgment debtor must sign the Assignment Order before the assignment takes effect. It may be possible, however, to short-circuit this requirement by changing the language of the Order slightly. This is desirable because it eliminates the considerable potential for noncompliance by the judgment debtor.[7] This has worked for some practicing lawyers and, while not strictly in compliance with the wording of the statute, is something you may want to try. If so, do the following:

- Eliminate the following (as shown in the sample Order):

I hereby make the assignments required by this Court Order.

____

Judgment Debtor

- Replace paragraph one of the sample Order with the following paragraph:

The judgment debtor Dan Defendant's right to receive the following payments shall be and hereby is assigned to the judgment creditor Pam Plaintiff until the judgment is satisfied or this order is amended.

Dated: __________________

[7] If the judgment debtor doesn't sign the assignment order, you may bring a motion for contempt. For this you will probably need the help of an attorney.

Pam Plaintiff
123 North Street
Berkeley, CA 94704
415/999-9999

Appearing In Pro Per

MUNICIPAL COURT OF CALIFORNIA

CITY AND COUNTY OF SAN FRANCISCO

PAM PLAINTIFF, Plaintiff, vs. DAN DEFENDANT, Defendant.	NO. 12345 NOTICE OF MOTION AND MOTION FOR ASSIGNMENT ORDER, DECLARATION, AND MEMORANDUM OF POINTS AND AUTHORITIES Date: May 26, 19__ Time: 3:00 p.m. Dept: A

NOTICE OF MOTION AND MOTION FOR ASSIGNMENT ORDER

TO THE JUDGMENT DEBTOR(S) AND TO ANY ATTORNEY(S) OF RECORD FOR THE JUDGMENT DEBTOR(S):

NOTICE IS HEREBY GIVEN that on May 26, 19__ at 3:00 p.m. in Department A of the court located at 400 Van Ness Avenue, San Francisco, California, Pam Plaintiff, judgment creditor, will move the court for an order instructing Dan Defendant, judgment debtor, to assign to her the judgment debtor's interest in, and all rights to payment under, the following assets to the extent necessary to satisfy the judgment:

a) copyright royalties from Peter Publisher on a quarterly basis;

b) rents from his tenant Paul Simon, on a monthly basis in the amount of $500; and

c) monthly installment payments of $247.21 on a promissory note executed by

-1-

Katherine Piper on July 6, 19__.

This motion is made on the grounds that:

a) the judgment creditor has a judgment against the judgment debtor;

b) the balance due on this judgment is $6,000, plus post-judgment costs and accrued interest; and

c) the judgment debtor has an assignable right to the payments described above.

This motion will be based on this Notice of Motion and Motion, the Declaration of Pam Plaintiff, the Memorandum of Points and Authorities and the records and file of this action.

DECLARATION

I, Pam Plaintiff, declare as follows:

1. I obtained a judgment against Dan Defendant, judgment debtor, from the San Francisco Municipal Court on January 10,19__ in the within-referenced case.

2. The balance due on this judgment is $6,000 plus post-judgment costs and accrued interest.

3. I am informed and believe that the judgment debtor is entitled to receive, or will be entitled to receive, the following payments:

a) copyright royalties from Peter Publisher on a quarterly basis;

b) rents from his tenant Paul Simon, on a monthly basis in the amount of $500; and

c) monthly installment payments of $247.21 on a promissory note executed by Katherine Piper on July 6, 19__.

I declare under penalty of perjury under the laws of the State of California that the foregoing is true and correct.

Comment: *This last sentence is mandatory on declarations. If you don't have this language, you must have your statement witnessed and signed by a notary public.*

Dated: May__, 19__

____
Pam Plaintiff

-2-

MEMORANDUM OF POINTS & AUTHORITIES

The judgment creditor's motion for an Assignment Order seeks an assignment of three categories of payments due the judgment debtor, as described in the Declaration of Pam Plaintiff.

Under Code of Civil Procedure Section 708.510, the court is authorized to order all or part of a judgment debtor's right to payments due, or to become due, assigned to the judgment creditor. This assignment may be ordered to the extent necessary to satisfy the money judgment. Accordingly, Pam Plaintiff, judgment creditor requests that the court issue an Assignment Order, and that the assignment made under this order continue until the judgment specified in Pam Plaintiff's Declaration, plus post-judgment costs and accrued interest is fully satisfied.

Dated: May __, 19__ Respectfully Submitted,

____

Pam Plaintiff
Judgment Creditor

-3-

Pam Plaintiff
123 North Street
Berkeley, CA 94704
415/999-9999

Appearing In Pro Per

MUNICIPAL COURT OF CALIFORNIA

CITY AND COUNTY OF SAN FRANCISCO

PAM PLAINTIFF, Plaintiff, vs. DAN DEFENDANT, Defendant.	NO. 12345 ASSIGNMENT ORDER

ASSIGNMENT ORDER

The motion of Pam Plaintiff came on regularly for hearing before this court on ______________________. Pam Plaintiff, judgment creditor, and Dan Defendant, judgment debtor, both appeared in pro per. The court having considered the motion and good cause appearing:

IT IS ORDERED THAT:

1. The judgment debtor, Dan Defendant, shall assign to Pam Plaintiff, the judgment creditor, the judgment debtor's right to receive the following payments until the judgment is fully satisfied or this Order is amended:

a) 100% of the copyright royalties owed to the judgment debtor by Peter Publisher on a quarterly basis.

b) 50% of the rents due the judgment debtor from his tenant Paul Simon, on a

-1-

monthly basis in the amount of $250.

c) 100% of the monthly installment payments in the amount of $247.21 on a promissory note executed by Katherine Piper on July 6, 19__.

2. The following parties shall make the payments specified in the first paragraph of this order to the judgment creditor, to be applied to the judgment creditor's judgment until the judgment is fully satisfied or this Order is amended: Peter Publisher, Paul Simon and Katherine Piper.

IT IS FURTHER ORDERED that a copy of this order shall be personally served upon the judgment debtor; and:

NOTICE IS HEREBY GIVEN THAT FAILURE BY THE JUDGMENT DEBTOR TO COMPLY WITH THIS ORDER MAY SUBJECT THE JUDGMENT DEBTOR TO BEING HELD IN CONTEMPT OF COURT.

Dated: ________ Signed: ______________________

Judge of the Municipal Court

I hereby make the assignments required by this Court Order.

____

Judgment Debtor

Dated: ________________

-2-

D. California Rules of Court

HERE ARE RELEVANT SECTIONS from the *Rules of Court*.

CIVIL LAW AND MOTION RULES

Rule 301. Applicability

The rules in this division apply to proceedings in civil law and motion in superior, municipal, and justice courts and to discovery proceedings in family law and probate.

Adopted, eff. Jan. 1, 1984. As amended, eff. July 1, 1984.

Rule 303. Definitions and Construction

(a) **[Law and motion defined]** "Law and motion" includes any proceedings:

(1) On application before trial for an order, except for causes arising under the Welfare and Institutions Code, the Probate Code, the Family Law Act (Civil Code, §§ 4000–5174), or Code of Civil Procedure sections 540–553 (concerning prevention of domestic violence); or

(2) On application for an order regarding the enforcement of judgment, attachment of property, appointment of a receiver, obtaining or setting aside a judgment by default, writs of review, mandate and prohibition, a petition to compel arbitration, and enforcement of an award by arbitration.

(b) **[Application of other rules]** Rules 235 and 249 apply to proceedings under this division.

(c) **[Application to demurrers]** Unless the context or subject matter otherwise requires, these rules apply to demurrers.

Adopted, eff. Jan. 1, 1984. As amended, eff. July 1, 1984.
[Source: New]

Rule 305. Application for Order Shortening Time

An application for an order shortening time shall be supported by a affidavit or declaration showing good cause for the order.

[Source: New]

Rule 307. Assignment of Matters

Except as provided in rule 375, the presiding judge or a judge designated by the presiding judge shall hear proceedings in law and motion.

[Source: New]

Rule 309. Notice of Determination of Submitted Matters

When the court rules on a demurrer or motion or makes an order or renders a judgment in a matter it has taken under submission, the clerk shall forthwith notify the parties of the ruling, order or judgment. The notification, which shall specifically identify the matter ruled upon, may be given by mailing the parties a copy of the ruling, order or judgment, and it shall constitute service of notice only if the clerk is required to give notice pursuant to Code of Civil Procedure section 664.5. The failure of the clerk to give notification shall not extend the time provided by law for performing any act except as provided in rule 2(a) or rule 122(a).

In a case having multiple parties, a clerk's notification made pursuant to this rule, or any notice of a ruling or order served by a party, shall name the moving party and the party against whom relief was requested, and specifically identify the particular motion, demurrer or other matter ruled upon.

[Source: Rules 204 and 504]

Rule 311. General Format

(a) **[Opening paragraph]** A notice of motion shall state in the opening paragraph the nature of the order being sought and the grounds for issuance of the order.

(b) **[Date of hearing; other documents]** The first page of each paper shall specify immediately below the number of the case (1) the date, time, and location, if ascertainable, of any scheduled hearing; (2) the nature or title of any attached document other than an exhibit; and (3) the trial date, if set. Documents bound together shall be consecutively paginated.

(c) **[Reference to previously filed papers]** Any paper previously filed shall be referred to by date of execution and title.

[Source: New]

Rule 313. Memorandum of Points and Authorities

(a) **[Notice of motion and demurrer—memorandum of points and authorities]** A party filing a demurrer or a notice of motion, except for a new trial, shall serve and file therewith a memorandum of points and authorities to be relied upon. The absence of the memorandum may be construed by the court as an admission that the motion or special demurrer is not meritorious and cause for its denial and, in the case of a demurrer, as a waiver of all grounds not supported.

(b) **[Contents of memorandum]** A memorandum of points and authorities shall contain a statement of facts, a concise statement of the law, evidence and arguments relied on, and a discussion of the statutes, cases, and textbooks cited in support of the position advanced.

(c) **[Case citation format]** A case citation shall include the official report volume and page number and year of decision.

(d) [When tables of contents and authorities and opening summary of argument required] A memorandum of points and authorities that exceeds 10 pages shall include a table of contents and table of authorities. A memorandum of points and authorities that exceeds 15 pages shall also include an opening summary of argument.

Adopted, eff. Jan. 1, 1984. As amended, eff. July 1, 1984.

[Source: New except subdivision (a) which is from rules 203(a) and 503(a) with additions from rules 202(a) and 502(a)]

Rule 315. Miscellaneous Papers

(a) [Caption of declaration or affidavit] The caption of the declaration or affidavit shall state the name of the declarant or affiant and shall specifically identify the motion or other proceeding which it supports or opposes.

(b) [Substitution of party as attorney] A substitution of a party as attorney in propria persona shall include the mailing address and telephone number of the party.

[Source: New]

Rule 317. Time for Filing Papers

(a) [In general] Unless otherwise ordered or specifically provided by law, all moving and supporting papers shall be served and filed at least 15 calendar days, all papers opposing the motion at least five court days, and all reply papers at least two court days before the time appointed for the hearing.

(b) [Time for filing proof of service] Proof of service of the moving papers shall be filed no later than five calendar days before the time appointed for the hearing.

[Source: New]

Rule 319. Place and Manner of Filing

(a) [Papers filed in clerk's office] Unless otherwise provided by local rule, all papers relating to a law and motion proceeding shall be filed in the clerk's office.

(b) [Requirements for lodged material] Material lodged with the clerk shall be accompanied by an addressed envelope with sufficient postage for mailing the material. After determination of the matter, the material may be mailed by the clerk to the party lodging it.

[Source: New]

Rule 321. Time of hearing

(a) [General schedule] The clerk shall post a general schedule showing the days and departments for holding each type of law and motion hearing.

(b) [Duty to notify if matter not to be heard] The moving party shall promptly notify the court if a matter will not be heard on the scheduled date.

(c) [Notice of nonappearance; action if no party appears] A party may give notice of nonappearance at a law and motion hearing and submit the matter without an appearance unless the court orders otherwise. If no party appears at a law and motion hearing the court may drop the matter from the calendar, to be reset only upon motion. In its discretion, the court may rule on a law and motion matter notwithstanding the failure of any party to appear at the hearing.

[Source: New]

Rule 323. Evidence at Hearing

(a) [Restrictions on oral testimony] Evidence received at a law and motion hearing shall be by declaration and affidavit and by request for judicial notice without testimony or cross-examination, except as allowed in the court's discretion for good cause shown or as permitted by local rule. A party seeking permission to introduce oral evidence, except for oral evidence in rebuttal to oral evidence presented by the other party, shall file, no later than three court days before the hearing, a written statement setting forth the nature and extent of the evidence proposed to be introduced and a reasonable time estimate for the hearing. When the statement is filed less than five court days before the hearing, the filing party shall serve a copy on the other parties in a manner to assure delivery to the other parties no later than two days before the hearing.

(b) [Judicial notice] A party requesting judicial notice of material under Evidence Code sections 452 or 453 shall provide the court and each party with a copy of the material. If the material is part of a file in the court in which the matter is being heard, the party shall (1) specify in writing the part of the court file sought to be judicially noticed; and (2) make arrangements with the clerk to have the file in the courtroom at the time of the hearing.

[Source: New]

Rule 379. Ex Parte Applications and Orders

An application for an order shall not be made ex parte unless it appears by affidavit or declaration (1) that within a reasonable time before the application the party informed the opposing party or the opposing party's attorney when and where the application would be made; or (2) that the party in good faith attempted to inform the opposing party and the opposing party's attorney but was unable to do so, specifying the efforts made to inform them; or (3) that for reasons specified the party should not be required to inform the opposing party or the opposing party's attorney.

[Source: Section 15, Standards of Judicial Administration]

Chapter 19

DEALING WITH AN OUT-OF-STATE JUDGMENT

IF YOU HAVE A JUDGMENT or support order from another state, but the debtor or her assets are in California, you must make your judgment enforceable in California before you can collect here. To do this, you must get a California court to issue a judgment based on the "sister-state judgment" (your original judgment).[1] Or, if you have an out-of-state support order, you must register it in California. Once you have completed the procedure, you are entitled to use all collection remedies available to California judgment creditors.

A. How To Obtain California Judgment for Sister-State Judgment

THIS SECTION APPLIES to money judgments issued in a state outside of California. Skip to Section B, below, if you have an order or judgment for child or spousal support from another state.

1. Determine Appropriate Court

If the amount of your judgment is $25,000 or less, you must file your sister-state judgment application in a California municipal or justice court. If the amount is over $25,000, you file in a superior court.

2. Decide in Which County To File

If the debtor lives in California, you must file your application in the county where he resides. If the debtor has assets in California but lives in another state, you can file in any county. If neither the debtor nor his assets are in California, you can't use this process in the California courts (CCP § 1710.20).

3. Get Authenticated Copy of Judgment

You must get an official copy of the sister-state judgment —called an authenticated copy—from the court that issued it.[2]

You can get a copy for a small fee by contacting the clerk of that court and requesting an authenticated copy of your judgment (some courts call them "exemplified copies"). Also take this opportunity to obtain some information that you will need to complete the sister-state judgment process. Specifically, find out:

[1] If the debtor moves to another state, you may need to get a sister-state judgment in the other state, which is beyond the scope of this book. (See Chapter 23.) Or an Assignment Order may be of help. (See Chapter 18.)

[2] This means that the clerk of the court that issued the out-of-state judgment puts the court seal or some other proof on the judgment to certify it as the real McCoy.

- how long judgments last in that state[3]
- the statutory post-judgment rate of interest for that state and
- the citations to the statutes of the other state that authorize the interest and set the duration of the judgment.

Below is a sample letter to send the clerk in the other state.

> *Date*
>
> *Clerk*
> *Chemicalzoo Justice Court*
> *One Justice Center*
> *Chemicalzoo, MI 48109*
>
> *Re: Pam Plaintiff v. Dan Defendant*
>
> *Case No. X100*
>
> *Dear Clerk:*
>
> *Enclosed please find a check in the amount of $__________ and a self-addressed, stamped envelope. Please send me an authenticated copy of the judgment entered on 8/8/88 in the above referenced case.*
>
> *I am seeking a sister-state judgment in the State of California. For that purpose, please provide me with the following information:*
>
> 1. *Duration of the judgment in my Chemicalzoo case (i.e., when will my judgment expire?)*
> 2. *Interest rate allowed on my Chemicalzoo judgment according to Michigan law*
> 3. *Citation to Michigan law as to the post-judgment interest rate.*
>
> *Thank you for your assistance.*
>
> *Sincerely,*
>
> *Pam Plaintiff*

[3]See a lawyer if your out-of-state judgment has expired, or if that judgment is more than ten years old. You may not be able to collect it in California (CCP § 337.5).

> **Research Note**
>
> If the clerk refuses to give you the information you request, you can find the answer in most California county law libraries. Locate the statutes for the other state, and use the index to find statutes that set the post-judgment interest rate and the duration of judgments. See Chapter 23.A, for more on using law libraries.

4. Prepare Application

In the Application for Entry of Judgment on Sister-State Judgment form, you request that your judgment from another state be made into a California judgment.

Caption: Fill in the requested information with these clarifications:

- Use the name and address of the court in which you are filing the Application.
- Enter the name of the plaintiff and defendant exactly as they appear on the out-of-state judgment. Leave the case number blank; the court will assign a number.
- Check the first box before "and issuance of Writ of Execution or other enforcement," unless you are in a hurry to obtain a Writ of Execution or the debtor is an individual who doesn't live in California, a foreign corporation (one not incorporated in California) not qualified to do business in California, or a foreign partnership (one formed in another state) that hasn't designated someone in California to receive service of

process on its behalf. If so, check the box before "and order for issuance of writ or other enforcement." (See Item 6, below, for further discussion of this option.)

Item 1: Enter your name exactly as shown in the sister-state judgment, as well as your current address.

Item 2a: Enter the name of the judgment debtor exactly as shown in the sister-state judgment.

Item 2b: Check this box if the judgment debtor is an individual, and enter the debtor's last known residence address.

Item 2c: Check this box if the debtor is a corporation, and enter the state of incorporation.

If it is a foreign (incorporated out-of-state) corporation, also check box 2c(1), and indicate whether it is qualified to do business in California.

Item 2d: Check this box if the judgment debtor is a partnership, and enter the full address of its principal place of business.

If it is a foreign (out-of-state) partnership, check box 2d(1), and indicate whether it has filed a statement designating an agent for service of process (filed a statement under Corporations Code § 15700).

Item 3a: Enter the name of the state in which the sister-state judgment was entered.

Item 3b: Enter the name and location (county, city or other local place) of the court that issued the sister-state judgment.

Item 3c: Fill in the date the sister-state judgment was entered.

Item 4: This item states that you are attaching an authenticated copy of the sister-state judgment. (See Section A.3, above.)

Item 4a: Enter the annual post-judgment interest rate allowed by the other state. (See Section A.3, above.)

Item 4b: Enter the citation to the law establishing the interest rate. (See Section A.3, above.)

Item 5a: Enter the amount still owing on the sister-state judgment.

Item 5b: Enter the filing fee for this application. (Check with the court in which you will be obtaining the California judgment—see Section A, above.)

Item 5c: Add up the accrued interest on the sister-state judgment, using the interest rate in Item 4a. See Chapter 15.C.3, for how to compute post-judgment interest. Make sure you calculate the interest at the rate indicated in Item 4a.[4]

Item 5d: Add up Items 5a, 5b and 5c and enter the total.

Now turn to the back of the form.

Short Title: Fill in the name of the plaintiff and defendant. Again, leave the case number blank.

Item 6: Ordinarily, you can't obtain a Writ of Execution or otherwise enforce a California judgment obtained through this procedure until 30 days after the judgment debtor is served with a Notice of Entry of Judgment on Sister-State Judgment. (See Section A.7 below.) Accordingly, you should leave this box blank unless one of the following is true:

(1) You want authority to get a Writ of Execution (Chapter 7) before serving notice of your California judgment on the judgment debtor, and the judgment debtor fits within one of the following categories:

- an individual who doesn't live in California
- a foreign corporation (one not incorporated in California) not qualified to do business in California[5] or
- a foreign partnership (one formed in another state) that hasn't designated someone in California to receive service of process on its behalf.[6]

---

[4]In Chapter 15, we tell you how to calculate simple interest, as California does not allow compound interest. If the sister-state allows compound interest, you may need some outside help to calculate it (an accountant, perhaps).

[5]A corporation organized under the laws of another state must register with the California Secretary of State as a foreign corporation if it wants authorization to do business in this state.

[6]A partnership based in another state is required to designate someone in California to accept court process (in case someone wants to sue them) as a condition of doing business in California.

ATTORNEY OR PARTY WITHOUT ATTORNEY *(Name and Address)*:	TELEPHONE NO.:	FOR COURT USE ONLY
Pam Plaintiff 123 North Street Berkeley, CA 94704	415/999-9999	
ATTORNEY FOR *(Name)*: In Pro Per		
NAME OF COURT: San Francisco Municipal Court STREET ADDRESS: City Hall, Room 300 MAILING ADDRESS: 400 Van Ness Avenue CITY AND ZIP CODE: San Francisco, CA 94102 BRANCH NAME:		
PLAINTIFF: PAM PLAINTIFF DEFENDANT: DAN DEFENDANT		
APPLICATION FOR ENTRY OF JUDGMENT ON SISTER-STATE JUDGMENT [X] **AND ISSUANCE OF WRIT OF EXECUTION OR OTHER ENFORCEMENT** [ ] **AND ORDER FOR ISSUANCE OF WRIT OR OTHER ENFORCEMENT**		CASE NUMBER:

Judgment creditor applies for entry of a judgment based upon a sister-state judgment as follows:

1. Judgment creditor *(name and address)*:
   Pam Plaintiff
   123 North Street
   Berkeley, CA 94704
2. a. Judgment debtor *(name)*:
   Dan Defendant
   b. [X] An individual *(last known residence address)*:
   234 West Street, San Francisco, CA 94118
   c. [ ] A corporation of *(specify place of incorporation)*:
      (1) [ ] Foreign corporation
         [ ] qualified to do business in California
         [ ] not qualified to do business in California
   d. [ ] A partnership *(specify principal place of business)*:
      (1) [ ] Foreign partnership which
         [ ] has filed a statement under Corp C 15700
         [ ] has not filed a statement under Corp C 15700
3. a. Sister state *(name)*: Michigan
   b. Sister-state court *(name and location)*: Chemicalzoo Justice Court, Chemicalzoo, Michigan
   c. Judgment entered in sister state on *(date)*: 2/31/__
4. **An authenticated copy of the sister-state judgment is attached to this application.** Include accrued interest on the sister-state judgment in the California judgment (item 5c).
   a. Annual interest rate allowed by sister state *(specify)*: 11.5%
   b. Law of sister state establishing interest rate *(specify)*: ML § 2(a)
5. a. Amount remaining unpaid on sister-state judgment: .... $ 8,654.21
   b. Amount of filing fee for the application: .... $ 56.00
   c. Accrued interest on sister-state judgment .... $ 1,019.79
   d. Amount of judgment to be entered *(total of 5a, b, and c)*: .... $ 9,730.00

(Continued on reverse)

Form Approved by the Judicial Council of California EJ-105 [Rev July 1, 1983]

APPLICATION FOR ENTRY OF JUDGMENT ON SISTER-STATE JUDGMENT

CCP 1710.15, 1710.20

SHORT TITLE: PAM PLAINTIFF v. DAN DEFENDANT	CASE NUMBER:

6. ☐ Judgment creditor also applies for issuance of a writ of execution or enforcement by other means before service of notice of entry of judgment as follows:
   a. ☐ Under CCP 1710.45(b).
   b. ☐ A court order is requested under CCP 1710.45(c). Facts showing that great or irreparable injury will result to judgment creditor if issuance of the writ or enforcement by other means is delayed are set forth as follows:

☐ continued in attachment 6b.

7. An action in this state on the sister-state judgment is not barred by the statute of limitations.
8. I am informed and believe that no stay of enforcement of the sister-state judgment is now in effect in the sister state.
9. No action is pending and no judgment has previously been entered in any proceeding in California based upon the sister-state judgment.

I declare under penalty of perjury under the laws of the State of California that the foregoing is true and correct except as to those matters which are stated to be upon information and belief, and as to those matters I believe them to be true.

Date: 12/21/__

Pam Plaintiff
(TYPE OR PRINT NAME)

▶ Pam Plaintiff
(SIGNATURE OF JUDGMENT CREDITOR OR ATTORNEY)

EJ-105 [Rev. July 1, 1983] **APPLICATION FOR ENTRY OF JUDGMENT ON SISTER-STATE JUDGMENT** Page two

If you don't know whether the second or third circumstance applies in your case, see Chapter 22.A.8, which tells you how to find out whether a corporation is qualified to do business in California and whether a foreign partnership has designated an agent to accept service of process.

(2) Your judgment creditor doesn't fit within one of the categories just listed, but you want to initiate collection activity before serving the judgment debtor with notice of your California judgment because you believe your efforts to collect will be frustrated if you don't.

If either of these situations applies, check Item 6a, which refers to California law that allows the court to issue a Writ of Execution before the debtor is served with a Notice of Entry of Sister-State Judgment. This is possible if "great or irreparable injury would result to the judgment creditor" if issuance of the Writ were delayed (CCP § 1710.45(c)). Then check Item 6b, which requests a court order allowing issuance of a Writ. In the space following explain why you can't wait until 30 days after you serve the judgment debtor. For instance, if past experience tells you that the judgment debtor is likely to conceal his assets if he learns of your California judgment before a Writ of Execution has issued, state this in the space provided. If any of the situations indicated in our explanation of Item 6, above, are true (for example, the debtor is a foreign corporation not qualified to do business in California), indicate this here. If you need additional room, check the box entitled "continued in attachment 6b" and prepare an attachment.

Item 7: This simply states that California can act on this request because the sister-state judgment has not expired. This is determined by the law of the state that issued the sister-state judgment. (See Section A.3.)

Item 8: This states that you know of no court order barring enforcement of the sister-state judgment.

Item 9: This states that you haven't filed court papers to obtain, or actually obtained, a California judgment based on the sister-state judgment. You can get a California judgment based on a sister-state judgment in only one California court.

Finally, enter the date, type or print your name and sign the document.

5. Prepare Notice of Entry of Judgment

The Notice of Entry of Judgment on Sister-State Judgment form is used to notify the debtor that you have obtained a California judgment based on the sister-state judgment.

Caption: Follow the format of the Application (Section A.4, above).

Item 1: Enter the judgment debtor's name exactly as it appears on the sister-state judgment.

Item 2a(1): Enter your name as judgment creditor exactly as it appears on the sister-state judgment.

Item 2a(2): Enter the total amount of the judgment (from Item 5d of your Application for Entry of Judgment).

Items 2b(1), (2) and (3): Enter here the information you put in Items 3a, 3b and 3c of the Application for Entry of Judgment.

Item 2b(4): Enter the name and case number of the original case of your sister-state judgment.

Item 3: Leave this item blank. This is a notice to the judgment debtor. The clerk will date and sign it.

Item 4: Check the first box.

Item 4a: Check this box if you are serving the person as an individual debtor.

Item 4b: Check this box if you are serving the judgment debtor under a fictitious name,[7] and enter the name.

Item 4c: Check this box if you are serving the debtor on behalf of another person or entity, and enter the name of that person or organization.

[7] If the debtor is an individual doing business as (dba) another name, put that other name here. Or, if the debtor is also known as (aka) someone else, put the other name (alias) here. If the debtor is using a fictitious name, putting it here will probably ease your levy efforts.

ATTORNEY OR PARTY WITHOUT ATTORNEY *(Name and Address)*:	TELEPHONE NO.:	FOR COURT USE ONLY
Pam Plaintiff 123 North Street Berkeley, CA 94704	415/999-9999	
ATTORNEY FOR *(Name)*: In Pro Per		
NAME OF COURT: San Francisco Municipal Court STREET ADDRESS: Room 300, City Hall MAILING ADDRESS: 400 Van Ness Avenue CITY AND ZIP CODE: San Francisco, CA 94102 BRANCH NAME:		
PLAINTIFF: PAM PLAINTIFF DEFENDANT: DAN DEFENDANT		CASE NUMBER:
NOTICE OF ENTRY OF JUDGMENT ON SISTER-STATE JUDGMENT		

1. TO JUDGMENT DEBTOR *(name)*: Dan Defendant

2. YOU ARE NOTIFIED
   a. Upon application of the judgment creditor, a judgment against you has been entered in this court as follows:
      (1) Judgment creditor *(name)*: Pam Plaintiff
      (2) Amount of judgment entered in this court: $ 9,730.00
   b. This judgment was entered based upon a sister-state judgment previously entered against you as follows:
      (1) Sister state *(name)*: Michigan
      (2) Sister-state court *(name and location)*: Chemicalzoo Justice Court, Chemicalzoo, Michigan
      (3) Judgment entered in sister state on *(date)*: 2/31/——
      (4) Title of case and case number *(specify)*: Pam Plaintiff v. Dan Defendant, #2001

3. **A sister-state judgment has been entered against you in a California court. Unless you file a motion to vacate the judgment in this court within 30 DAYS after service of this notice, this judgment will be final.**

   This court may order that a writ of execution or other enforcement may issue. Your wages, money, and property could be taken without further warning from the court.

   If enforcement procedures have already been issued, the property levied on will not be distributed until 30 days after you are served with this notice.

Date: Clerk, by ____________________, Deputy

[SEAL]

4. [X] NOTICE TO THE PERSON SERVED: You are served
   a. [X] as an individual judgment debtor.
   b. [ ] under the fictitious name of *(specify)*:
   c. [ ] on behalf of *(specify)*:

   Under:
   - [ ] CCP 416.10 (corporation)
   - [ ] CCP 416.20 (defunct corporation)
   - [ ] CCP 416.40 (association or partnership)
   - [ ] other:
   - [ ] CCP 416.60 (minor)
   - [ ] CCP 416.70 (conservatee)
   - [X] CCP 416.90 (individual)

(Proof of service on reverse)

Form Approved by the Judicial Council of California EJ-110 [Rev. July 1, 1983]

NOTICE OF ENTRY OF JUDGMENT ON SISTER-STATE JUDGMENT

CCP 1710.30, 1710.40 1710.45

Now check the box for the appropriate classification for service below (corporation, defunct corporation, individual, etc.).

Leave the proof of service on the back blank for now.

6. Prepare Judgment Form (if Required)

Some courts require a separate judgment form to be filled in. Ask the court clerk where you are filing your papers if your court does. If so, obtain the form from the court and fill it in. The information you have already entered in these forms should be sufficient.

7. File and Serve Papers

Make at least two photocopies of your forms, plus one for each judgment debtor.

a. *File the Papers*

Give or send the clerk of the court that will issue your California judgment the following documents:

- original Application for Entry of Judgment on Sister-State Judgment and two copies
- original Notice of Entry of Judgment on Sister-State Judgment and two copies and
- original and two copies of the judgment you prepared (if the court required this).

There will be a filing fee of approximately $30 to $180, depending on the court. The clerk should give you a certified copy of the Notice of Entry of Judgment on Sister-State Judgment and file-stamped copies of the other papers (one set to be served on the judgment debtor and one set for your records). If you mail the documents to the court, you can use the generic cover letter provided in the Appendix.

Unless the court requires you to file a separate judgment form, the Notice of Entry of Judgment on Sister-State Judgment serves as your California judgment.

b. *Have Papers Served*

Before you can initiate your collection activities, you must have the following papers served on the judgment debtor (unless you fall into one of the exceptions listed in Item 6 of the Application).

Service may be done by personal service or substituted personal service, discussed in detail in Chapter 22. You are also permitted to use two easy methods that we don't discuss in that chapter:

- Service by Acknowledgement (you mail the judgment debtor the papers and return envelope and have him sign a notice and acknowledgement of receipt (see CCP § 415.30 for particulars).
- If the debtor is outside the state, service by certified mail, return receipt requested (see CCP § 415.40 for particulars).

Because a debtor who wants to avoid service of process will refuse to sign, however, you may be better off having your papers served by a professional process server. (See Chapter 22.)

c. *File Proof of Service*

Once your papers are served on the judgment debtor, you must file a proof of service with the court. A proof of service form is on the back of the Notice of Entry of Judgment on Sister-State Judgment. Fill this in and then have your server sign it. (See Chapter 22 for instructions on completing a proof of service.)

If your service was accomplished by mail (acknowledgment or return receipt requested) you must attach the signed acknowledgment of receipt, or the return receipt showing actual delivery.

d. *Commence Collection*

With most judgment debtors, you may not obtain a Writ of Execution until 30 days after you have served the debtor with the sister-state judgment papers. This gives the judgment debtor 30 days to file a motion to vacate the judgment. If he doesn't, the California judgment based on the sister-state judgment is considered final, and you can now proceed as if you had an original California judgment. If the debtor does make a motion to vacate (this is pretty rare), the judge is not likely to grant it.

Your new judgment is subject to any time limitations and renewal restrictions of the issuing state—for example, it may expire sooner than ten years (the California expiration date).

If you obtained court authorization to obtain the Writ of Execution before the judgment debtor is served (Item 6 of the Application), you don't have to wait the 30 days. You can start collection activities (including getting a Writ of Execution) immediately. However, if a levy is made on the judgment debtor's assets, no sale or distribution can occur until the debtor has been served and you have filed a proof of service with the court.

B. How To Register Foreign Support Order in California

OUT-OF-STATE SUPPORT ORDERS can be collected in California the same as regular California judgments, provided they are first registered with the appropriate superior court registry.[8] There is no fee for this. Here is how to register an out-of-state judgment or order for:

- spousal support (alimony)
- child support[9]
- family support (combined spousal and child support) or
- wage assignment (for the satisfaction of a support order).

Your registration will automatically be referred to the District Attorney. If you want the DA to enforce your judgment, you will need to open a case with the DA's family support division. However, in most counties the district attorney's offices are backlogged. In other words, don't wait around for the DA to enforce your support order. (See Chapter 1.D.7.)

1. Determine County for Registration

This can be either the county where your ex-spouse lives, or the county in which a child who is the subject of the order lives.

2. Obtain Certified Copies of Order

You must obtain three certified copies of the foreign support order or judgment. If there were any modifications made, you'll need certified copies of these as well. You can get certified copies from the court that issued the foreign support order or judgment for a small fee, by

[8] If you are seeking to collect child or spousal support, you usually are entitled to collect amounts that are less than ten years overdue. However, if the child is under 24 years of age, you are entitled to collect the full amount of child support (Civil Code § 4383 prior to 1/1/94; Family Code § 5100 effective 1/1/94). And with court approval, even amounts that are more than ten years overdue are collectible. (See a lawyer.)

[9] To register an order for child support, you must have been entitled to receive payments under the support order.

either calling or writing to that court. Note that you cannot use photocopies of the certified support order—you must have three original copies that were certified by the court.

3. Obtain Copy of Support Act

Each state has passed a version of the reciprocal enforcement of support act. This act allows for the registration process described here. You must, however, attach a copy of your state's act to your registration form. The best way to do this is to take these steps:

- Go to the local law library (every county has at least one law library) and locate the statutes for the state in which you obtained the out-of-state judgment or order (the law librarian can help).
- Locate the reciprocal enforcement of support act for the state in which you obtained your support judgment or order (again, the law librarian can help).
- Photocopy the reciprocal enforcement of support act in its entirety (usually about five pages). You do not need to photocopy case annotations to the statutes.

4. Find Out Interest Rate in Foreign State

Each state has laws that govern what interest rate, if any, may be collected from a court order or judgment for money. To find this out, either:

- call the court in which you obtained the out-of-state judgment and ask the clerk for the interest rate for your support order or judgment or
- go to the local law library and find statutes for the out-of-state judgment which govern the post-judgment interest rate (a law librarian can help).

If you don't wish to collect interest, perhaps because your judgment is too recent to generate much interest, you could skip this step.

5. Fill in Statement for Registration

You'll need to fill in and complete a form called Statement for Registration of Foreign Support Order and Clerk's Notice. Here are line-by-line instructions.

Caption: Most required information is available from the court and the foreign support papers, with these clarifications:

- **Obligee:** Fill in your name, if you are owed money according to the foreign support order. If you are referred to in the support order as "wife," "husband," "plaintiff" or a similar descriptive term, list this in parentheses after your name. Also fill in the name of any child who is owed money according to the order. Make sure you fill in the names exactly as they appear on the foreign support order. After the child's name, fill in the word "son" or "daughter" in parentheses.
- **Obligor:** Fill in the name of your ex-spouse, exactly as it appears on the foreign support order. If your ex-spouse is referred to in the support order as "husband," "wife," "defendant" or a similar descriptive term, list this in parentheses after his name.
- **Title:** Check the first box if you are registering a support order. Check the second box if you are registering an order for assignment of wages for support.
- **Case Number:** Leave this blank.
- **Obligee's statement to register:** Specify the type of order you are registering.

Item 1: As in the "Obligee" portion of the caption, fill in your name and/or the name of any child who is owed money according to the foreign support order. Make sure you fill in the names exactly as they appear on the foreign support order.

Item 1a: Fill in the mailing address for you and/or the child listed in Item 1, above.

Item 1b: Fill in the street address for you and/or the child listed in Item 1, above.

ATTORNEY OR PARTY WITHOUT ATTORNEY *(Name and Address)*: TELEPHONE NO.: 415/999-9999

Pam Plaintiff
123 North Street
Berkeley, CA 94704

ATTORNEY FOR *(Name)*: In Pro Per

FOR COURT USE ONLY

NAME OF COURT: San Francisco Superior Court
STREET ADDRESS: Room 300, City Hall
MAILING ADDRESS: 400 Van Ness Avenue
CITY AND ZIP CODE: San Francisco, CA 94102
BRANCH NAME:

OBLIGEE: PAM PLAINTIFF, KATIE PLAINTIFF (daughter)

OBLIGOR: DAN DEFENDANT

STATEMENT FOR REGISTRATION OF FOREIGN SUPPORT ORDER AND CLERK'S NOTICE

[X] Support Order [ ] Order For Assignment of Wages For Support

CASE NUMBER:

Obligee's statement to register [X] foreign support order [ ] foreign order for assignment of wages for support is as follows:

1. Obligee *(name)*: Pam Plaintiff, Katie Plaintiff
   a. Mailing address:
      123 North Street
      Berkeley, CA 94704
   b. Residence address:
      Same

2. Obligor *(name)*: Dan Defendant
   a. Last known mailing address:
      234 West Street
      San Francisco, CA 94118
   b. Last known residence address:
      Same

3. Three certified copies of the following described support order or order for assignment of wages for support, with all modifications, are filed with this statement as required by Code of Civil Procedure section 1698.3.
   a. Name of state and title of court:
      Michigan: Chemicalzoo Superior Court
   b. Date of order and of all modifications of order:
      2/31/__. No modifications entered.

4. The order is registered in the following states *(specify the name and location of the court in each state and the type of order)*:
   None.

5. Amount of support now due and remaining unpaid: $8,654.21 principal, $1,019.79 interest (11.5% annual rate)

(Continued on reverse)

NOTICE TO OBLIGOR

If you wish, you have 20 days after the date of mailing of Notice of Registration to petition the court to vacate the registration of the Foreign Support Order or Foreign Order For Assignment of Wages or for other relief. *(See reverse for clerk's date of mailing.)* (Code of Civil Procedure, § 1699(b).)

The original and two copies of this statement, and one copy of the reciprocal enforcement of support act of the state in which the order was made, must be submitted for filing.

Form Approved by the Judicial Council of California EJ-120 (Rev. December 1, 1989)

STATEMENT FOR REGISTRATION OF FOREIGN SUPPORT ORDER AND CLERK'S NOTICE

CCP 1698.3, 1699
EJ-120/TEMP EJ – 12/5/89 (3)

OBLIGEE: Pam Plaintiff, Katie Plaintiff OBLIGOR: Dan Defendant	CASE NUMBER:

6. The obligee is informed and believes that the description and location of obligor's property subject to execution is as follows:

Real estate located at 234 West Street, San Francisco,CA

DECLARATION

I declare under penalty of perjury under the laws of the state of California that the foregoing is true and correct.

Date: 12/21/__

Pam Plaintiff
(TYPE OR PRINT NAME)

▶ Pam Plaintiff
(SIGNATURE OF OBLIGEE, PERSON HAVING LEGAL CUSTODY OF MINOR OBLIGEE, OR PERSON ACTING ON BEHALF OF OBLIGEE PURSUANT TO AN ASSIGNMENT OF RIGHTS)

NOTICE TO OBLIGOR

7. **To obligor** *(name)*: Dan Defendant

8. You are notified that a [X] Foreign Support Order [ ] Foreign Order For Assignment of Wages For Support has been registered with this court. A copy of the order is attached and the mailing address of the obligee is shown in this statement.

Date: Clerk, by ______________________, Deputy

CLERK'S CERTIFICATE OF MAILING

1. I certify that I am not a party to this cause and that a copy of the foregoing statement with a certified copy of the foreign order were sent to obligor by certified mail, return receipt from the addressee only requested. The copies were enclosed in an envelope with postage fully prepaid. The envelope was addressed to the obligor only at the address in the foregoing statement, sealed, and deposited with the United States Postal Service
at *(place)*:
on *(date)*:

Date: Clerk, by ______________________, Deputy

2. **Copy** sent to prosecuting attorney on *(date)*: by ______________________, Deputy

EJ-120 [Rev. December 1, 1989] **STATEMENT FOR REGISTRATION OF FOREIGN ORDER AND CLERK'S NOTICE** Page two

If you are hiding from the support provider and don't want to provide your home address, see a lawyer.

Item 2: As in the "Obligor" portion of the caption, fill in the name of your ex-spouse, exactly as it appears on the foreign support order.

Item 2a: Fill in the last known mailing address for your ex-spouse.

Item 2b: Fill in the last known street address for your ex-spouse.

Item 3: This item says that you're attaching three certified copies of the foreign support order along with any modifications. (We tell you how to get these copies in Section B.2, above.)

Item 3a: Fill in the state where the foreign support order was issued and the name of the court.

Item 3b: Fill in the date the support order was granted (signed by a judge). You'll find this information stamped, typed or written in on the support order. Also fill in the date that modifications, if any, were ordered. If modifications were not ordered, fill in the words "No modifications entered."

Item 4: This item applies only if you have registered the support order in any other states. If so, list each state, the name of the court, the city where the court is located and the type of order. Otherwise, specify "None."

Item 5: Fill in the amount of support due by first listing the principal balance owing on the support order, then accrued interest—if any, along with the percentage rate at which it was calculated. You can only add on interest if it is allowed by the law of the state where the foreign support order was made, and only at the percentage rate allowed by that state. (See Section B.4, above.) Make sure you have deducted any payments made, including money received from wage assignments.

Reverse side of form: In the caption, fill in your name after the word "obligee" and your ex-spouse's name after the word "obligor."

Item 6: If you know of any valuable property your ex-spouse owns in California, list a description and location of these assets. This might include bank accounts, vehicles or real estate. Only list major items of value in this item. If your ex-spouse owns real estate, on a blank full sheet of paper, attach a legal description of the property (which may be obtained from the recorder's office in the county where the property is located).

If you aren't sure what property your ex-spouse owns or don't want to tip him off about your collection plans, leave this item blank. Failure to list property in this item won't prevent you from going after the property once you start to collect your support order.

Declaration: Fill in the date, type or print your name as indicated and sign. This means you are signing under penalty of perjury, so the information on the declaration should be correct to the best of your knowledge.

Item 7: Fill in your ex-spouse's name, exactly as it appears on the foreign order.

Item 8: Check the first box if you are registering a foreign support order. Check the second box if you are registering a foreign order for assignment of wages for support.

Leave the rest of the form blank. It will be completed by the clerk of the court.

6. Copy and File Documents

Make three copies of the Statement for Registration of Foreign Support Order and Clerk's Notice. Also make an extra copy of everything else you're sending to the court for your own records. Then take or send to the clerk of the superior court:

- original and two photocopies of the Statement for Registration of Foreign Support Order and Clerk's Notice form
- three certified copies of the support order and any modifications to the support order and
- one copy of the reciprocal enforcement of support act of the state in which the order was made.

If you send your papers to the court, you'll need a cover letter requesting that your foreign order be registered and copies be returned to you in a self-addressed, stamped envelope you provide.

Once you've registered the Statement for Registration of Foreign Support Order and Clerk's Notice form, the clerk will send a copy by mail, return receipt requested, to the obligor. The obligor has 20 days after the mailing or other service in which to petition the court to formally object to the registration, regardless if he received and signed for the papers. If the obligor doesn't object by filing papers with court, the registered order stands as is, and may be enforced in California.

7. Collect Your Judgment

Technically you may start enforcing the judgment as soon as your foreign support order or judgment is registered, but we suggest you wait the full 20-day period. Often attempts to collect a judgment will cause an obligor to file objections with the court, whereas he otherwise might allow the 20-day period to lapse. If the obligor files objections with the court, you will need the help of an attorney. Otherwise, you may proceed with any collection techniques outlined in this book.

Chapter 20

RENEWING YOUR JUDGMENT AND REAL ESTATE LIENS

CALIFORNIA JUDGMENTS LAST FOR TEN YEARS. If all goes well, you won't need to renew your judgment, because you will collect it long before it expires.

You are entitled, however, to renew your judgment once every five years (CCP § 683.110). When you renew a judgment, all interest and costs you've claimed on Memoranda of Costs (Chapter 15) become part of the new judgment. In effect, this entitles you to receive compound interest on your judgment, because you'll be allowed to earn interest on accrued interest.

If your judgment isn't fully satisfied and it's getting close to ten years from the date your judgment was entered, you should renew it, along with any judgment liens you created on the debtor's real estate. The judgment can be renewed for successive ten-year periods. As a practical matter, that is seldom necessary.

There is one crucial requirement for renewal of a judgment: You must renew it *before* it expires. If you try to renew a judgment even one day after it expires, you are out of luck.[1]

[1] If you miss the deadline, see a lawyer. You may be able to bring a separate action to obtain a judgment on your judgment, if you file it within ten years of the date the original judgment became final (possibly months after it was entered—for example, if an appeal was filed). The ten-year statute of limitations may be extended if the debtor was out of the state for part of the ten years.

If you have a lien against the judgment debtor's real estate, you must also renew it before the current judgment expires. To be safe, you should renew your judgment several months before the expiration of the ten-year period, so you will have time to renew your lien. (See Section B, below.)

Example: *Jonathan obtains a $5,000 judgment against Vickie, which is entered on July 1, 1988. He records an Abstract of Judgment to establish a lien against Vickie's cabin in the Sierra. On April 1, 1998, Jonathan renews the judgment for another ten years. He also renews the lien. If Vickie continues to avoid payment, Jonathan can renew it again. If, however, Jonathan understandably forgets about or gives up on the judgment and fails to renew it by April 1, 2008, the judgment will be dead.*

Note for Support Orders: Judgments for child or spousal support do not need to be renewed. They are enforceable until paid in full. You may, however, opt to renew a support order if it has not previously been renewed as to past due amounts or at least five years have passed since it was renewed (CCP § 683.130(c)).

A. Renewing Your Judgment

HERE ARE THE STEPS you must take to renew a California judgment.

1. Get Current Renewal Forms

Obtain these two forms from the county court or law library:

- Application for and Renewal of Judgment and
- Notice of Renewal of Judgment.

The renewal forms are not provided in the Appendix, because it is imperative that you use the most current forms. When you renew your judgment, make sure you have the latest version of this book.

2. Fill Out Application

The Application for and Renewal of Judgment is your request for a ten-year extension of your judgment.

Caption: Follow the format of your other court papers. Check the box that says "judgment creditor." The "assignee of record" box is used only if the judgment has been assigned to someone else.

Item 1: Enter your name (exactly as it appears on the original judgment) and address as the applicant for the renewal.

Item 2: Enter the judgment debtor's name (exactly as it appears on the original judgment) and last known address.

Item 3a: Enter the case number of the original judgment.

Item 3b: Enter the date the original judgment was entered (it's on the original judgment or notice of entry of judgment).

Item 4: Fill this in only if you've previously renewed your judgment.

Item 5: Check this box.

Item 5a: Enter the total amount of the original judgment.

Item 5b: Enter the total post-judgment costs that you have claimed in Memoranda of Costs. (See Chapter 15.)

Item 5c: Add Items 5a and 5b and enter the subtotal.

Item 5d: Enter the total credits made on the judgment. (See Chapter 15.)

Item 5e: Subtract Item 5d from item 5c and enter the subtotal.

Item 5f: Enter the total post-judgment interest you have claimed in Memoranda of Costs. (See Chapter 15.)

Item 5g: Enter the fee for filing the renewal application. (Check with the court clerk.)

Item 5h: Add Items 5e, 5f and 5g and enter the total. This is the amount of your renewed judgment.

Item 5i: Leave this box blank unless your judgment is against different debtors, and each owes you different amounts. In this case, you must include an attachment, labeled Attachment 5, listing each debtor and the amount owed.

Now turn to the reverse side of the Application.

Short Title box: On the back of the form, enter the names of the plaintiff and defendant and the case number.

Item 6: Skip this entire item. It refers to a judgment for possession or sale. We only cover money judgments in this book.

Signature and date: Type or print your name, enter the date and sign the form.

ATTORNEY OR PARTY WITHOUT ATTORNEY *(Name and Address)*: TELEPHONE NO.: | FOR RECORDER'S USE ONLY

☐ Recording requested by and return to:

Pam Plaintiff 415/999-9999
123 North Street
Berkeley, CA 94704

ATTORNEY FOR *(Name)*: In Pro Per

NAME OF COURT: San Francisco Municipal Court
STREET ADDRESS: City Hall, Room 300
MAILING ADDRESS: 400 Van Ness Avenue
CITY AND ZIP CODE: San Francisco, CA 94102
BRANCH NAME:

PLAINTIFF: PAM PLAINTIFF

DEFENDANT: DAN DEFENDANT

CASE NUMBER: 12345

APPLICATION FOR AND RENEWAL OF JUDGMENT

FOR COURT USE ONLY

☒ Judgment creditor
☐ Assignee of record
applies for renewal of the judgment as follows:

1. Applicant *(name and address)*:
   Pam Plaintiff
   123 North Street
   Berkeley, CA 94704

2. Judgment debtor *(name and last known address)*:
   Dan Defendant
   234 West Street
   San Francisco, CA 94118

3. Original judgment
   a. Case number *(specify)*: 12345
   b. Entered on *(date)*: 1/10/—

4. ☐ Judgment previously renewed *(specify each case number and date)*:

5. ☒ Renewal of money judgment

a. Total judgment	$ 6,000.00
b. Costs after judgment	$ 681.50
c. Subtotal *(add a and b)*	$ 6,681.50
d. Credits after judgment	$ 2,060.00
e. Subtotal *(subtract d from c)*	$ 4,621.50
f. Interest after judgment	$ 1,046.41
g. Fee for filing renewal application	$ 2.25
h. Total renewed judgment *(add e, f, and g)*	$ 5,670.16

i. ☐ The amounts called for in items a–h are different for each debtor. These amounts are stated for each debtor on Attachment 5.

(Continued on reverse)

Form Approved by the Judicial Council of California EJ-190 (New July 1, 1983)

APPLICATION FOR AND RENEWAL OF JUDGMENT

CCP 683.140

SHORT TITLE:	CASE NUMBER:
PAM PLAINTIFF v. DAN DEFENDANT	12345

6. ☐ Renewal of judgment for ☐ possession.
☐ sale.

a. ☐ If judgment was not previously renewed, terms of judgment as entered:

b. ☐ If judgment was previously renewed, terms of judgment as last renewed:

c. ☐ Terms of judgment remaining unsatisfied:

I declare under penalty of perjury under the laws of the State of California that the foregoing is true and correct.

Date: 11/4/__

Pam Plaintiff
(TYPE OR PRINT NAME)

▶ Pam Plaintiff
(SIGNATURE OF DECLARANT)

3. Fill Out Notice of Renewal

This form notifies the debtor that you are renewing the judgment. Fill it out as follows.

Caption: Follow the format of your other court papers.

After "To judgment debtor (name)," enter the name of the judgment debtor exactly as it appears on the original judgment.

Leave the rest of the form blank.

4. File Papers With Court

Make at least three copies of the papers and give or send the clerk of the court that issued your judgment the following:

- original Application for and Renewal of Judgment and two copies
- original Notice of Renewal of Judgment and two copies and
- fee for renewing the judgment (about $14; check with the court).

If you send the documents to the court, use the generic cover letter provided in the Appendix, and include a self-addressed stamped envelope. The clerk will issue a Notice of Renewal of Judgment, which will serve as your renewed judgment, and file-stamp your copies.

If you're facing the ten-year renewal deadline, take your papers to the court for filing. That way, you can correct any problems on the spot.

5. Have Debtor Served

A copy of the Application for and Renewal of Judgment and of the Notice of Renewal of Judgment must then be served personally or by first-class mail on each judgment debtor before you can initiate collection activities under the renewed judgment (CCP § 683.160(a)). See Chapter 22 for how to make personal service or service by mail.

Once the judgment debtor has been served with the renewal papers, prepare a proof of service, following the instructions in Chapter 22. Have the server sign it and then file the proof of service with the court.

Note: The judgment is actually renewed once the clerk issues the Notice of Renewal of Judgment. You don't need to serve the judgment debtor to renew the judgment, but you must serve him before you can collect.

If the Debtor Objects to Renewal: After the debtor is served, he has 30 days to submit a motion asking the court to vacate or modify the renewal. If the debtor makes such a motion, he will serve a notice of motion on you personally or by mail, and there will be a court hearing on the motion. It is very unlikely that a debtor will object to renewal (he has few grounds to do so short of paying the judgment). It is similar to other noticed motion procedures covered in Chapter 18.

B. Renew Real Estate Liens

LIENS ON A DEBTOR'S REAL ESTATE EXPIRE when the underlying judgment expires. Installment support judgments are exceptions; real estate liens do not expire until the judgment is paid off (CCP § 697.320(b)). When you renew your judgment, also renew your real estate liens, following these steps:

- Obtain a certified copy of the Application for and Renewal of Judgment from the court. You'll pay a small fee.
- Record the certified Application with each county where you have recorded an Abstract of Judgment. (See Chapter 4.E.3 for information on recording documents.)

You must renew your lien *before it expires*. Otherwise, you won't be able to get another one under this judgment. As we pointed out in Section A, you should renew your judgment at least several months before it expires so you will have time to renew your real estate lien.[2]

---

[2] If the property subject to the lien was transferred and that transfer was recorded before your application for renewal was filed, you must take special steps to make the renewal valid. A copy of the renewal Application must be personally served on the transferee, and a proof of service must be filed with the court no more than 90 days after the filing of the renewal Application (CCP § 683.180).

ATTORNEY OR PARTY WITHOUT ATTORNEY *(Name and Address)*:	TELEPHONE NO.:	*FOR COURT USE ONLY*
Pam Plaintiff 123 North Street Berkeley, CA 94704	415/999-9999	
ATTORNEY FOR *(Name)*: In Pro Per		
NAME OF COURT: San Francisco Municipal Court STREET ADDRESS: City Hall, Room 300 MAILING ADDRESS: 400 Van Ness Avenue CITY AND ZIP CODE: San Francisco, CA 94102 BRANCH NAME:		
PLAINTIFF: PAM PLAINTIFF DEFENDANT: DAN DEFENDANT		
NOTICE OF RENEWAL OF JUDGMENT		CASE NUMBER: 12345

TO JUDGMENT DEBTOR *(name)*: DAN DEFENDANT

1. **This renewal extends** the period of enforceability of the judgment until 10 years from the date the application for renewal was filed.

2. **If you object** to this renewal, you may make a motion to vacate or modify the renewal with this court.

3. You must make this motion within **30 days** after service of this notice on you.

4. A copy of the *Application for and Renewal of Judgment* is attached *(Cal. Rules of Court, rule 986)*.

Date: Clerk, by ______________________________, Deputy

[SEAL]

See CCP 683.160 for information on method of service

Form Approved by the Judicial Council of California EJ-195 [Rev. July 1, 1989]

NOTICE OF RENEWAL OF JUDGMENT

CCP 683.160

Chapter 21

After the Judgment Is Paid

CONGRATULATIONS. You're probably reading this chapter because your collection activities have reached a happy end. Either you've collected your judgment in full, or you've agreed to settle and have been paid for less.

Before you get carried away celebrating, however, you must quickly fill out and file one or two forms to close the matter. This task is simple, but essential; if you don't do it promptly, you could end up in the unhappy position of owing the debtor money.

When your judgment is paid, you must:

- fill out an Acknowledgment of Satisfaction of Judgment form
- serve the debtor
- file the form with the court to show the judgment has been paid (technically, "satisfied") and
- if you created judgment liens on the debtor's real estate or personal business property, release them by filing a copy of the Acknowledgment with the Secretary of State and recording it with appropriate county recorders.

Small Claims Court Exception: If the debtor paid the Small Claims Court directly, the court clerk is responsible for filing a Satisfaction of Judgment. (See Chapter 1.D.1.) You must, however, release any liens you've created. (See Sections E and F, below.)

A. Why File an Acknowledgment?

THE DEBTOR HAS THE LEGAL RIGHT to demand that you file an Acknowledgment of Satisfaction of Judgment within 15 days after your judgment is satisfied—14 days for small claims judgments. A debtor also has the right to serve you with a written demand to file an Acknowledgment for partial satisfaction of the judgment if you have collected some payments on the judgment. Again, you must comply with the 15-day deadline. A debtor might want a partial Acknowledgment filed, for example, if she is selling or refinancing real estate and wants proof of how much she's paid on the judgment.

If you refuse, the debtor can take you to court. If she shows that you had no good reason not to file the Acknowledgment, you will be liable for any damages she sustains as a result of not having the Acknowledgment on file, plus her reasonable attorneys' fees and court costs. And on top of all that, you will have to pay the debtor ($50 for Small Claims Court judgment) $100 in damages. Although this scenario is unlikely to happen, there's no point in making it possible.

What harm can the debtor suffer if you don't promptly file your Acknowledgment? If the unsatisfied judgment shows up on the debtor's credit report, it might be used to deny credit, or prevent her from buying real estate or renting an apartment. If you have recorded a lien, she might not be able to sell her property.

Example: *Joe and Fred had a business dispute. Joe got a judgment against Fred for $10,000, which Fred paid over a 10-month period. However, Joe never filed a Satisfaction of Judgment, although Fred asked him to twice. Fred filed a small claims action of $1,500 against Joe, claiming his bad credit report lost him two profitable jobs. Joe ended up settling with Fred for $400.*

B. Fill Out Acknowledgment Form

AN ACKNOWLEDGMENT OF SATISFACTION of Judgment form is included in the Appendix. Fill it out as follows:

Caption: Follow the format of your previous court papers. Indicate how the judgment was satisfied:

- Check the first box if it is a full satisfaction of judgment. In this context, it means that you are willing to end the matter with regard to the debtor(s) you name. It doesn't necessarily mean that you received your full judgment.
- Check the second box if it is a partial satisfaction of judgment, meaning in this context that only part of the judgment has been paid and you're not willing to settle for that amount.
- Check the third box if the debtor has been paying you on an installment judgment, and all installments have been paid.

Item 1a: Check this box if the judgment has been fully satisfied, or at least one debtor doesn't owe you anything else on the judgment (see discussion just above).

Item 1a(1): Check this box if the judgment, costs and interest have been paid in full.

Item 1a(2): Check this box if you have settled for less than the total judgment, or for some other type of performance by the debtor (perhaps barter or service), but consider the judgment fully satisfied.

Item 1b: Check this box if the judgment has been only partially satisfied, and the debtor demanded that you file an Acknowledgment (see discussion above for the meaning of "partially satisfied" in this context). Enter the amount you have received to date.

Item 1c: Check this box if you had an installment judgment, and all installments have been paid. Enter the date the last installment was paid.

Item 2: Enter your full name and address as the judgment creditor. Your name must appear exactly as it appeared on the judgment.

Item 3: Leave this blank unless you have been assigned the right to collect this judgment.

Item 4: Enter the full name of the judgment debtor exactly as it appeared on the judgment and enter the debtor's address. If there is more than one judgment debtor, make sure you name only the debtor(s) being released.

Item 5a: Enter the date the judgment was entered.

Item 5a(1): Check this box and enter the book volume number and page number if you have this information. Otherwise, leave it blank.

Item 5b: Skip 5b unless you have renewed the judgment. If you have renewed the judgment, enter the date of renewal.

Item 5b(1): If you renewed the judgment, check this box and enter the book volume number and page number if you have this information.

Item 6: Check the box if you have recorded any Abstracts of Judgment or certified copies of the judgment anywhere. This almost always refers to liens you have placed on the judgment debtor's real estate.

Indicate whether you recorded an Abstract of Judgment or a certified copy of the judgment by checking the appropriate box. Then enter the county or counties where you recorded them, the date of recording, and the book and page number. You can get this information from the documents you recorded or from the recorder's office.

Item 7: Check this box if you created a judgment lien against the debtor's business personal property by filing a Notice of Judgment Lien with the Secretary of State, and enter the file number you were given.

Do not sign or date the Acknowledgment of Satisfaction of Judgment yet; you must sign in front of a notary public.

ATTORNEY OR PARTY WITHOUT ATTORNEY *(Name and Address)*: TELEPHONE NO.: 415/999-9999

Pam Plaintiff
123 North Street
Berkeley, CA 94704

ATTORNEY FOR *(Name)*: In Pro Per

FOR RECORDER'S OR SECRETARY OF STATE'S USE ONLY

NAME OF COURT: San Francisco Municipal Court
STREET ADDRESS: City Hall, Room 300
MAILING ADDRESS: 400 Van Ness Avenue
CITY AND ZIP CODE: San Francisco, CA 94102
BRANCH NAME:

PLAINTIFF: PAM PLAINTIFF

DEFENDANT: DAN DEFENDANT

CASE NUMBER: 12345

ACKNOWLEDGMENT OF SATISFACTION OF JUDGMENT

[X] **FULL** [ ] **PARTIAL** [ ] **MATURED INSTALLMENT**

FOR COURT USE ONLY

1. Satisfaction of the judgment is acknowledged as follows *(see footnote* before completing)*:
   a. [X] Full satisfaction
      (1) [X] Judgment is satisfied in full.
      (2) [ ] The judgment creditor has accepted payment or performance other than that specified in the judgment in full satisfaction of the judgment.
   b. [ ] Partial satisfaction
      The amount received in partial satisfaction of the judgment is $
   c. [ ] Matured installment
      All matured installments under the installment judgment have been satisfied as of *(date)*:
2. Full name and address of judgment creditor:
   Pam Plaintiff
   123 North Street, Berkeley, CA 94704
3. Full name and address of assignee of record, if any:
4. Full name and address of judgment debtor being fully or partially released:
   Dan Defendant
   234 West Street, San Francisco, CA 94118
5. a. Judgment entered on *(date)*: 1/10/__
      [ ] (1) in judgment book volume no.: (2) page no.:
   b. [ ] Renewal entered on *(date)*:
      [ ] (1) in judgment book volume no.: (2) page no.:
6. [X] An [X] abstract of judgment [ ] certified copy of the judgment has been recorded as follows *(complete all information for each county where recorded)*:

COUNTY	DATE OF RECORDING	BOOK NUMBER	PAGE NUMBER
San Francisco	2/11/__	2	2
Alameda	2/8/__	1	1

7. [X] A notice of judgment lien has been filed in the office of the Secretary of State as file number *(specify)*: 3873

NOTICE TO JUDGMENT DEBTOR: If this is an acknowledgment of full satisfaction of judgment, it will have to be recorded in each county shown in item 6 above, if any, in order to release the judgment lien, and will have to be filed in the office of the Secretary of State to terminate any judgment lien on personal property.

Date: 12/31/__ ▶ Pam Plaintiff
(SIGNATURE OF JUDGMENT CREDITOR OR ASSIGNEE OF CREDITOR OR ATTORNEY)

*The names of the judgment creditor and judgment debtor must be stated as shown in any Abstract of Judgment which was recorded and is being released by this satisfaction. A **separate notary acknowledgment must be attached for each signature.**

Form Approved by the Judicial Council of California EJ-100 (Rev. July 1, 1983)(Cor. 7/84)

ACKNOWLEDGMENT OF SATISFACTION OF JUDGMENT

CCP 724.060, 724.120, 724.250

C. Have Your Signature Notarized

YOUR NEXT STEP IS TO LOCATE a notary public. Banks and real estate offices are a good bet, or look in the yellow pages. There may be a fee for the notary's services; up to $10 is permitted (Government Code § 8211).

Take your original Acknowledgment of Satisfaction of Judgment form, and ask to have your signature notarized. The notary should ask you to provide some identification. After you sign, the notary will fill out a short form, which you attach to the Acknowledgment of Satisfaction of Judgment. The notary will enter your name, his signature and his official seal. That's it.

D. Serve and File Acknowledgment

THE DEBTOR MAY BE SERVED either personally or by mail with a copy of the Acknowledgment. See Chapter 22 for service instructions.

You can either file a copy with the court that issued the judgment or have the judgment debtor do it; if you physically deliver a copy to the debtor, he is responsible for filing the copy with the court. However, because you have responsibility for removing any liens you created, you're wiser to file the document yourself. Remember to keep a file-stamped copy of the Acknowledgment for your records.

E. Release Real Property Liens

IF YOU RECORDED AN ABSTRACT of Judgment with any county recorder, also record a certified copy of the Acknowledgment with that county recorder. This releases your judgment liens. The procedures and costs are about the same as recording the lien. (See Chapter 4.)

If you have recorded several liens, you may discover that this process costs you some money which you can't recover. Like it or not, you must still remove the liens. Just as you have a right to collect your judgment, the debtor has the right to have liens removed once the judgment has been paid.

F. Release Business Property Liens

IF YOU CREATED A JUDGMENT LIEN on any business personal property belonging to the judgment debtor, file a certified copy of the Acknowledgment with the Secretary of State. The fee for terminating the lien is generally about $4.

Chapter 22

Finding and Serving the Judgment Debtor

THROUGHOUT THIS BOOK we discuss procedures that require the judgment debtor, and occasionally third parties, to be served with legal documents. Service requirements—how, when and by whom documents must be delivered—must be followed to the letter. A person affected by a court action is constitutionally entitled to be notified of the nature of the action so that she can have her say.

It is important that you allow yourself enough time to have the debtor or another party served with papers. Collection procedures can easily get sidetracked if service is done incorrectly.

After proper service is made, the court must be notified, in writing, of how and when it was accomplished. This is done in a document called a proof of service, which is filed with the court.

A. Finding the Debtor

IF YOU CAN'T FIND THE DEBTOR, you may have to spend some time tracking her down—called "skip-tracing" in the collections trade. You'll have a number of resources at your disposal.

Massive amounts of information about virtually every individual in this country have been collected by a large number of government and private entities. Data about health, employment, taxes, real estate transfers, automobile registration, business or professional licenses, credit and voting are stored in files and computers.

Many government records on individuals are open to the public. (Notable exceptions are tax returns, Social Security and medical files, and investigation files compiled by law enforcement agencies.) You merely have to write, call or visit the appropriate office. Many privately organized systems, like crisscross telephone directories, are readily available, too, for free or a small charge. Other private records are obtainable by making a special request or by serving subpenas. (See Chapter 6.)

This section describes how to use and where to find the major public and private records likely to help you locate the debtor. For the most part, these records focus more on where the debtor lives than on what he owns. (For finding a debtor's assets, see Chapter 6 and the chapters that focus on specific types of assets.)

If you need skip-tracing ideas beyond the scope of this book, you may want to utilize another book on this subject. Three possibilities, written by investigators, are *Check It Out!*, by Edmund J. Pankau (Contemporary Books), *You, Too, Can Find Anybody*, by Joseph J. Culligan (Hallmark Press), and *A Private Eye's Guide to Collecting a Bad Debt*, by Fay Faron (Creighton-Morgan Publishing Group). You also might take a look at *Paper Trails: A Guide to Public Records in California*, by Barbara T. Newcombe (Center for Investigative Reporting and California Newspaper Publishers' Association). While not a "how-to" book, it gives detailed information on virtually every imaginable public record available.

1. The Telephone Company

To find the debtor's current address, begin with the obvious. Check the telephone directory and directory assistance to see if there is a new number.

If you have the debtor's phone number but can't find out the address from the phone book or operator, call—or have a friend call—the number from outside the calling area so you get it listed on a phone bill. Once the number is on a bill, contact the phone company and explain that you don't recognize the number and want to find out to whom the call was made. The representative will take a few minutes to trace the call and tell you the name to which the number is registered. In addition, unless the person has a private listing, the rep will tell you the address.

2. Crisscross Directories

Crisscross directories provide listings that are not normally available in telephone books. They are compiled by representatives who get information door-to-door rather than from phone customers.

The two major crisscross directories, the Polk Directory and the Haines Directory, are available for most major metropolitan areas. You can find them in major public libraries, title companies or the county tax assessor's or recorder's office.

If you know only the street where the debtor lives, you can pinpoint her exact address (unless the debtor isn't listed) by going down all the directory's listings for that street. The directory also lists the phone number for each address. You could also use the street listing to get the names, addresses and phone numbers of the debtor's neighbors so you can ask them for information about the debtor.

If you know just the debtor's phone number, you can find her address. The directory lists phone numbers in numerical order followed by the owner's name and address.

In addition to all this, the Polk Directory gives the occupation, if known, of each person listed. It also has a business section with the names of companies and ads by type of business.

3. Directories of Unlisted Phone Numbers

Even unlisted phone numbers may be included in a directory. These directories are put together surreptitiously and circulate in a sort of bill collector's underground, and thus are not readily available. You may, however, be able to gain access to one through a source such as an auto repossessor. They will probably charge you $50-$100 for a copy of a directory or for information on the number you need. If the information is good enough, it may be worth it.

Note: Occasionally, you'll see someone advertising that she can get you unlisted numbers. Make sure you get what you pay for.

4. Voter Registration Records

You can find these records at the registrar of voters for the city where you believe the debtor lives. If the debtor is a voter, the listing will include the debtor's name, address, phone number, birthdate, any party affiliation and date of registration. If the debtor has moved within the same county, the registrar will have the new address.

Even if the debtor isn't a voter, these records might be useful for finding out the names, addresses and phone numbers of relatives with the same last name as the debtor, as long as the name isn't too common.

5. U.S. Post Office

If the judgment debtor has moved and left a forwarding address, the post office will provide it. Send a request to the post office of the zip code where the debtor used to live. Following is a sample request.

> *Date*
>
> *Postmaster*
> *San Francisco, CA 94118*
>
> *Dear Postmaster:*
>
> *I am enclosing a check in the amount of $1.00 and a self-addressed, stamped envelope.*
>
> *Please provide me with the forwarding address on file for:*
>
> *Dan Defendant*
> *234 West Street*
> *San Francisco, CA 94118*
>
> *Sincerely,*
>
> *Pam Plaintiff*

If you only have a post office box number, the post office will release the street address and phone number of the box holder only if the box is listed in the name of a business. Some post offices will give you this information over the phone, but often you must request it in writing. You do not have to explain why you want the information.

The post office usually won't give out an individual box holder's address. There is one possible exception: if you give the post office a statement that the name, address and telephone number of a current box holder are required to serve legal papers in a pending proceeding. A form that may be used for this is shown below.

Whether this will work depends on the post office branch, and possibly whether the person presenting the request is a registered process server. You may even need a court order, which is beyond the scope of this book. (Chapter 18 covers court orders; Chapter 23 gives information on legal research.)

> *I, Pam Plaintiff, request the address of Dan Defendant, holder of P.O. Box 1 in the San Francisco, California 94118 Post Office.*
>
> *Pursuant to Postal Service Regulations (Administrative Support Manual, Section 352.44e(2)), I hereby certify that litigation has commenced or will soon commence and the address information is necessary to effect service of court process upon said box holder and for no other purpose.*
>
> *Names of all known parties: Pam Plaintiff (plaintiff), Dan Defendant (defendant).*
>
> *Court: San Francisco Municipal Court.*
>
> *Case No.: 12345.*
>
> *The box holder is served in the capacity of:*
>
> *[x] defendant, [ ] witness, [ ] other: ______.*
>
> *The nature of this litigation is as follows: Breach of contract by Dan Defendant.*
>
> *Dated: May 1, 19__*
>
> *Signature:______________*
>
> *Pam Plaintiff*

6. DMV Records

You are entitled to request the address of a California vehicle owner, as long as the purpose is to serve legal documents. But note that the DMV is increasingly hesitant to release information. As a result, the DMV sends a copy of your request to the debtor.

The fee is currently $5. You'll need to obtain a copy of DMV Form INF 1129, Information Request for Service of Legal Process. If your local DMV does not have the form, write the DMV, P.O. Box 944247, Sacramento, CA 94244-2470 or call 916-657-6474.

7. Credit Bureau Reports

Credit reporting agencies such as TRW, CBI/ Equifax and Trans Union may supply copies of a consumer's credit report to someone who needs the information for a legitimate business purpose involving the consumer. You are probably entitled to obtain the debtor's credit report if any of these situations applies (Civil Code § 1785.11):

- you intend to use the information to enforce a court order for support (Civil Code §1785.11(d)(1))
- you have an account for the debtor and wish to review it or collect on it
- you have a court order or subpena from the court
- you plan to employ the debtor
- you intend to rent a home or apartment to the debtor
- you are underwriting the debtor's insurance, settling a claim, granting credit or determining eligibility for government benefits
- you have a "legitimate business need for the information in connection with a business transaction" involving the debtor (Civil Code § 1785.11(d)(6)) or
- the debtor authorized in writing your receipt of the credit report (wishful thinking).

If you are entitled to a copy of the credit report, check with a credit reporting agency. It will charge you a fee ($12 is common) to provide a copy of the report.

If you illegally obtain the debtor's credit report, you may face a lawsuit and a judgment against you for thousands of dollars.[1]

8. Public Businesses Records

A business debtor may be licensed with various local or state agencies. The tax collector, assessor or Board of Equalization have information about most businesses. And the Department of Consumer Affairs, 916-322-5252, can provide referrals to various licensing agencies, if it doesn't maintain that data. Names of owners and business addresses should be listed in these records, but home addresses are generally confidential.

If the debtor is a sole proprietorship or general California partnership, a statement should be on file with the county clerk in the county where the principal place of business is located. Ask the county clerk for a copy of the Fictitious Business Name Statement, which lists the business's owners and their addresses.

If the debtor is a corporation, call the California Secretary of State's corporate status office at 916-445-2900. Or send a check for $1, a self-addressed, stamped envelope and request that includes the corporation's full name to: Secretary of State Corporate Status Division, 1230 "J" Street, Sacramento, CA 95814. All California Corporations and foreign corporations authorized to do business in California must register with the Secretary of State.

If the debtor is a limited partnership or a foreign general partnership authorized to do business in California, contact the California Secretary of State's Limited Partnership Division, P.O. Box 944225, Sacramento, CA 94244-2250, 916-324-6781. These partnerships must register with the Secretary of State.

B. Kinds of Service

SERVICE OF LEGAL DOCUMENTS is the process by which people are notified of legal proceedings that affect them. They have a constitutional right to object to those legal actions, so service must be accomplished on time and correctly.

There are three basic ways to serve legal papers:

- personal service
- substituted service and
- service by mail.

Each of these methods has its own rules, which must be carefully followed if your service is to be valid.

Documents can often be legally served in more than one way. To find out the specific type, or types, of service

---

[1] A consumer is entitled to at least $2,500 in damages plus costs and attorney fees if someone illegally obtains her credit report (Civil Code § 1785.31). She may also be entitled to $100 to $5,000 in punitive damages for each violation, court costs, attorney fees and whatever else the court awards.

required for a particular procedure, check the chapter covering that procedure.

Always have photocopies of your documents served. Keep originals for filing with the court.

C. Who Can Serve Your Papers

THE LAW PROVIDES that only a nonparty to the case—meaning someone other than you, the plaintiff/judgment creditor—may actually serve court papers. This person must be 18 or older and, if service is by mail, must be a resident or an employee in the county where he mails the papers.

1. Friend, Spouse or Relative

Your spouse, child 18 or older, relative, employee, friend or neighbor can serve papers for you as long as she is not a party to your case.

It's fine to use a nonprofessional when service is made through the mail (Section F, below). When documents are properly deposited in the U.S. mail, there is a presumption that they were received. In other words, the server shouldn't have to come into court to testify that service was properly made.

If, however, personal service is required (Section D, below), it may make sense to hire a professional process server (sheriff, marshal, constable or registered process server). Then, if the debtor claims he didn't receive the papers, having a neutral process server testify that they were delivered is more persuasive than a friend or relative. Another reason to hire a professional process server is that they have the experience and methods to find and serve evasive debtors.

2. Law Enforcement Officers

To have a law enforcement officer serve papers, call the sheriff's office in the county where the debtor is to be served. Ask whether the sheriff serves legal papers, or if it's done by a marshal or constable. In a few counties, law enforcement officers don't serve papers (due to budget problems).

When you find the right law enforcement officer, find out the fee for serving the papers—normally about $24 per person and per document. Then, either obtain and fill out the instruction form provided by the law enforcement officer, or draft your own instructions, giving such information as the best hours to find the party being served at home or work, general physical descriptions and so on. Note that law enforcement officers only serve papers during regular business hours. Finally, take or send the fee, instructions and papers to be served to the officer. (You can generally recover process servers' fees; see Chapter 15.)

3. Registered Process Server

When should you use a registered process server rather than a law enforcement officer? Registered process servers are appropriate when:

- the judgment debtor is hard to find
- you need service made fast
- the levying officer won't handle a particular levy, such as a bank levy or wage garnishment (this is uncommon, but a few counties have such restrictions)
- the debtor can't be served during normal business hours.

Professional process serving firms are commonly faster than law enforcement officers, and more resourceful at serving evasive persons. They work nights and weekends, too. They usually cost more, but the extra expense may be justified if your collection strategy demands quick service. For example, you might find out that the debtor is leaving the state and you want to conduct a debtor's examination before he leaves. Or you might want to initiate a levy ahead of someone else.

Some process servers charge a flat fee for a given geographical area; others charge for each attempted delivery. Shop around. If you know an attorney, ask her to recommend a good process-serving firm, or check the Yellow Pages for process servers in the area where the party is to be served. (You can generally recover fees paid to a registered process server; see Chapter 15.)

If you use a registered process server for a levy, you will probably have to prepare extra papers, such as a Notice of Levy. Check with the process server about those requirements or do your own research (Chapter 23).

D. Personal Service

IN THIS SECTION we tell you how to have legal papers personally served.

1. Personal Service on an Individual

If a court hearing has been scheduled or you think the judgment debtor might claim she wasn't served with the papers, personal service is the best type of service. You should hire a person who, if necessary, can come into court and testify that the judgment debtor actually received the papers.

If you use a professional, he will know how to make personal service. If you use a relative, neighbor or friend, however, you need to provide careful instructions.

Give your server a detailed description of the judgment debtor (for example, "he's 47, graying hair, about 5'10," medium build, looks a little like a bookish accountant"). Provide a photograph if you have one.

If a nonprofessional is serving papers for you, direct him to serve the papers on the debtor at the debtor's home. Service can be made on the judgment debtor at his workplace, but this is tricky, and we recommend you use a professional server if that's necessary.

The server should go to the debtor's house at a time he expects the debtor to be there—not 2 P.M. if the debtor works regular hours. Of course, the server shouldn't disturb the debtor very early or very late in the day. The best times are just before the debtor goes to work or just after he comes back.

Your server should understand that personal service is not made if he just leaves the papers on the debtor's porch or in the mailbox (which, incidentally, is illegal under Postal Service regulations).

The server must physically give copies of the legal papers to the debtor. This, of course, means that the server must actually see the debtor and be able to talk to him, whether or not he is willing to take the papers. A typical approach is to knock on the judgment debtor's door. If a person matching his description opens it, the server asks, "Are you Fred Anderson?" and if the response is affirmative, hands him the papers. If someone else answers the door, she would ask for Fred Anderson and hand the papers to him when he appears.

If the server is sure a debtor is home but not answering the door, the server has to do something to make the debtor either answer it or come to a window and identify himself. One server parks his car in the driveway at the debtor's house, knocks on the door, and then says, "Is that your car in the driveway?" When the debtor comes out to see what this is all about, the server says: "Say, are you Fred Jones?" (using a wrong name) At this point the debtor usually makes the appropriate correction ("I'm Fred Anderson"), confused about what this strange car has to do with him, and the server hands him the papers.

Whatever technique your server uses, he must make sure he is serving the right person. If the person being served does not respond to a direct question about his identity, the server will have to be a little creative. Maybe he could call the person's name and when the person reacts, say, "You are Fred Anderson, aren't you?" and then give him the papers if the response is affirmative. Or he might bring flowers or a gift-wrapped box—with the papers inside, of course.

Once the process server sees the debtor, makes personal identification and is close enough to make the service, it doesn't matter if the debtor refuses to take the papers, gets angry or tries to run away. The server can put the papers on the ground as close as possible to his feet, saying something like "This is for you," or "You have been served," and leave.

Under no circumstance should the server pick up the papers once they have been served in this manner. If he does, the service will be invalidated and have to be done again. And he should never try to force a defendant to take the papers. It's unnecessary and may subject the process server—or even you—to a lawsuit for battery.

If the server makes several (often three) unsuccessful attempts at personal service, he can try substituted personal service (Section E, below).

2. Personal Service on a Corporation

If your judgment debtor is a corporation, personal service must be made either on an officer of the corporation (president, vice-president, secretary or treasurer), or on the person who has been designated as agent for this purpose. Start by calling the corporation and asking who the officers are and which corporate office they are located in.

If this doesn't work, call the California Secretary of State's office (Corporate Status Unit, 916-445-2900) and ask for the corporation's Last Statement of Officers. The same phone number can be used if your corporate judgment debtor is a large national corporation doing business in California and you want to find out the name of the agent to be served.

If you know that the corporation's officers (or general manager) work out of a local office, it is easy to use substituted personal service, as discussed in Section E, below. And, unlike substituted personal service in other situations, you don't have to try personal service first.

If you cannot serve an agent or corporate officer, you may be able to serve the California Secretary of State instead. That requires a court order, which is beyond the scope of this book.

3. Personal Service on a Partnership

If your judgment debtor is a partnership, one of the partners must be personally served to serve the partnership as an entity. (See Section D.1, above.)

If you cannot serve one of the partners, you may be able to serve a limited partnership or foreign general partnership by serving the Secretary of State. That requires a court order, which is beyond the scope of this book.

E. Substituted Personal Service

WHAT IF PERSONAL SERVICE IS REQUIRED, but the process server can't find the party at home? If she attempts with "reasonable diligence" but can't serve the party, she can give the papers to an adult at the party's home[2] or workplace, with instructions to that person to give the papers to the party. In addition, she must mail a second copy of the papers to the party at the address where the papers were left (CCP § 415.20(b)). This method is called substituted personal service.

Some courts have specific requirements for how many and when personal service attempts must be made before substituted personal service is allowed. If you're using someone other than a professional server, ask the court if it has such requirements.

[2] The statute requires the papers to be left with a competent member of the household who is at least 18 years old.

Posting-and-Mailing Service

In rare instances, a server can post copies of the papers on the party's front door and mail a second set of copies to him at that address. For example, this type of service may be used when real property is being sold. We don't cover this procedure; a professional process server or attorney can handle it for you.

F. Service by Mail

IN SOME SITUATIONS, the debtor (or a third party) can be served by mailing the papers to her. Someone other than yourself who is over 18 and not a party to the action must do the mailing. It need cost no more than the first-class postage stamp.

Here's what you do to have papers served through the mail:

1. Complete and sign the legal papers.

2. Complete a proof of service by mail form (see Section G, below)—except for the signature.

3. Make copies of the papers, including the unsigned proof of service, keeping at least one set for yourself.

4. Put a copy of the papers, including a copy of the unsigned proof of service, in an envelope addressed to the person or business. You may use the debtor's residence address or the last office address given by him on any document he filed in your court case. If he has an attorney of record, send it to the attorney.

5. Put sufficient postage on the envelope for first-class delivery.

6. Have the server deposit the envelope in the mail box. Or, if the server is mailing the papers from her business, she may deposit them in the business's mail, as long as it will be taken for collection that day.

7. Have the server sign a proof of service. Then copy and file it with the court, following the instructions in Section G, below.

When service is made by mail, the person being served is usually entitled to an extra five days to respond.[3] For example, if you are required to give the judgment debtor 15 days' notice of a hearing, and you serve the judgment debtor with notice through the mail, the hearing must be scheduled at least 20 days in the future (CCP § 1013).

Certified Mail Note: Certified mail provides no advantage over first-class mail (unless, of course, a statute specifically requires this type of service). In fact, there may be a disadvantage to certified mail. When you mail something first-class, the party to whom it is addressed is presumed to receive it. But when you send something certified mail, it is not presumed received unless the recipient signs for it. Because certified mail is often signed for by other people in the house or isn't picked up at the post office, you are better off sending the papers first class.

G. Proof of Service Forms

WHEN PAPERS ARE SERVED, it is necessary to also fill out and file with the court a document called a proof of service, which states when and how service was made.

We tell you in the chapters on specific procedures when a proof of service must be filed. If you're notifying the debtor of a court hearing (with the exception of an ex parte motion, covered in Chapter 18), the proof of service must be filed before the hearing. How long in advance varies by court and procedure, but five business days is common.

Some documents have an official proof of service form on the back; sometimes you use your own form. Fortunately, the content of the various forms is pretty much the same. Below we show you sample forms for personal service and for service by mail. Blank copies of these forms are in the Appendix. Make plenty of copies before using them. Also make sure you keep copies of any completed proofs of service you file with the court.

[3] You are not given this extra five-day period when you are attempting a wage garnishment and the levying officer serves you with Claim of Exemption papers. (See Chapter 9.)

PARTY WITHOUT ATTORNEY (*My Name and Address*): Pam Plaintiff, 123 North Street, Berkeley, CA 94704 — MY TELEPHONE NO.: 415/999-9999	FOR COURT USE ONLY
NAME OF COURT: San Francisco Municipal Court STREET ADDRESS: City Hall, Room 300 MAILING ADDRESS: 400 Van Ness Avenue CITY AND ZIP CODE: San Francisco, CA 94102 BRANCH NAME:	
PLAINTIFF/JUDGMENT CREDITOR: PAM PLAINTIFF DEFENDANT/JUDGMENT DEBTOR: DAN DEFENDANT	
PROOF OF PERSONAL SERVICE (CCP Sections 1011, 2015.5)	CASE NUMBER: 12345

I declare that:

1. At the time of service I was at least 18 years of age and not a party to this legal action.
2. I am a resident of or employed in the county of San Francisco, California.
3. My business or residence address is: 4 Theway, San Francisco, CA 94114.
4. I served copies of the following paper(s) in the manner shown:
   a. Papers served [list exact titles of paper(s)]:

      APPLICATION AND ORDER FOR APPEARANCE AND EXAMINATION

   b. Manner of service: Personal Service. I personally delivered these papers to the following:

      (1) Name of person served: Dan Defendant

      (2) Address where served: 234 West Street, San Francisco, CA 94118

      (3) Date served: 9/21/—

      (4) Time served: 2:00 p.m.
5. I declare under penalty of perjury under the laws of the State of California that the foregoing is true and correct. Executed on 9/21/— at San Francisco, California.

Emma Frand
[Signature of Person Who Served Papers]

Print Name: Emma Frand

PROOF OF PERSONAL SERVICE

PARTY WITHOUT ATTORNEY *(My Name and Address)*: Pam Plaintiff 123 North Street Berkeley, CA 94704	MY TELEPHONE NO.: 415/999-9999	**FOR COURT USE ONLY**
NAME OF COURT: San Francisco Municipal Court STREET ADDRESS: City Hall, Room 300 MAILING ADDRESS: 400 Van Ness Avenue CITY AND ZIP CODE: San Francisco, CA 94102 BRANCH NAME:		
PLAINTIFF/JUDGMENT CREDITOR: PAM PLAINTIFF DEFENDANT/JUDGMENT DEBTOR: DAN DEFENDANT		
PROOF OF SERVICE BY MAIL (CCP Sections 1013a, 2015.5)		CASE NUMBER 12345

I declare that:

1. At the time of service I was at least 18 years of age and not a party to this legal action.
2. I am a resident of or employed in the county where the mailing occurred.
3. My business or residence address is: 4 Theway, San Francisco, CA 94114.
4. I served copies of the following paper(s) in the manner shown:

   a. Papers served [list exact titles of paper(s)]:

   MEMORANDUM OF CREDITS, ACCRUED INTEREST AND COSTS AFTER JUDGMENT AND SUPPORTING DECLARATION

   b. Manner of service: by placing true copies in a sealed envelope addressed to each person whose name and address is given below and:

   ☒ depositing the envelope in the United States Mail with the postage fully prepaid; or

   ☐ (If deposited at a business:) Placing for collection and mailing following ordinary business practices. I am readily familiar with the business practice for collection and processing of correspondence for mailing with the United States Post Office. The correspondence will be deposited with the United States Post office on the same date as the date of deposit (below) in the ordinary course of business.

   (1) Date of Deposit: September 21, 19—

   (2) Place of Deposit (city & state; business address if deposited at a business) : San Francisco, California

5. I declare under penalty of perjury under the laws of the State of California that the foregoing is true and correct. Executed on September 21, 19— at San Francisco, California.

Print Name: Emma Frand Emma Frand
[Signature of Person Who Served Papers]

Name and Address of Each Person to Whom Documents Were Mailed:

Dan Defendant
234 West Street
San Francisco, CA 94118

☐ Additional names and addresses on reverse.

PROOF OF SERVICE BY MAIL

Chapter 23

GETTING ADDITIONAL HELP

THE POINT OF THIS BOOK is to equip you to collect a judgment on your own. However, no matter how creative you are about locating the debtor and his assets, or how conscientious you are about sticking to the rules, at some point you may need information or assistance we don't provide.

In this chapter, we give some pointers on how to obtain help. There are several sources: the law library (Section A), collections attorneys (Sections B and C) and other collections professionals, such as paralegals, asset tracing firms, data search companies, investigators and collection agencies (Section D).

A. Doing Your Own Research

IF YOU NEED MORE LEGAL INFORMATION than this book provides, and can't get the answer from the levying officer or clerk, you may need to head to the law library. Here's how.

1. Find a Law Library

Each California county must have a law library that is open to the public without charge. Most law librarians are willing and even pleased to give you a hand, as long as you don't ask them to answer legal questions or interpret what you find in the books. If you encounter any difficulty because you are not a lawyer, you may need to give a gentle reminder that the California constitution requires public access to the law library.

How To Find and Understand the Law

If you decide to delve into the world of legal research, see *Legal Research: How To Find and Understand the Law*, by Stephen Elias (Nolo Press). This hands-on guide to the law library addresses the research methods discussed here in much more detail and will answer most of the questions that are likely to arise in the course of your research.

If you want a guided tour through the basics of legal research, you'll be interested in *Legal Research Made Easy: A Roadmap Through the Law Library Maze*, a 2-1/2 hour video by Nolo Press and Legal Star Communications.

2. Consult Background Resources

Resources such as encyclopedias, forms books or practice manuals are often helpful for beginning research on the law of collecting judgments, including:

- *California Practice Guide: Enforcing Judgments and Debts* (published by the Rutter Group). This resource describes in detail some of the basic procedures used in collecting judgments. It provides forms and legal references.

- *Debt Collection Manual*, Volume 2 (published by Continuing Education of the Bar). This book is probably not as useful (at least for non-lawyers) as the Rutter Group book.
- *California Forms of Pleading and Practice* (published by Mathew Bender). If you want guidance on a particular procedure not covered in this book, turn to this attorneys' forms book. It provides step-by-step guidance for many court procedures. Unfortunately, for the most part, these volumes do not comprehensively include judgment enforcement procedures.
- *California Jurisprudence*, Third Series (Cal. Jur. 3d), under "Enforcement of Judgments." This article outlines and cursorily discusses the entire Enforcement of Judgments Act.
- *Colliers on Bankruptcy*. It may take you a little time to orient yourself in this massive treatise, but once you do, you will find the answer to virtually any bankruptcy question that may arise.

Judicial Council Forms

To obtain copies of Judicial Council forms, check with the court clerk. Or go to the law library, which should have several resources for photocopying the forms, including these books:

- *California Forms of Pleading and Practice—Judicial Council Forms*
- *West's California Judicial Council Forms.*

3. Read Statutes and Cases

Background resources, including this book, are only discussions about law and procedure, not the law itself. That's why background resources provide citations to relevant statutes and court interpretations of these laws. Reading these statutes is a crucial step in doing legal research.

In California, a group of statutes (laws passed by the California legislature) collectively called the Enforcement of Judgments Act governs virtually every phase of each process we describe in this book. the "Enforcement of Judgments Act" is contained in § 680.010 to § 724.260 of the California Code of Civil Procedure (CCP).

If you are researching a bankruptcy question, you will be reading either federal statutes (located in Title 11 of the United States Code Annotated (USCA)) or the United States Code Service (USCS). You may also need to consult the Bankruptcy Rules (issued by the U.S. Supreme Court).

Unfortunately, reading these statutes may leave you less than fully enlightened. They tend to be difficult to understand and, sometimes, ambiguous. Thus, it often helps to read what a court has said about a statute. Unfortunately, there are very few court interpretations of the Enforcement of Judgments Act; it's relatively new, and the courts have not had much occasion to interpret it.[1]

B. Do You Need a Lawyer?

IF COLLECTING YOUR JUDGMENT starts to get complicated (for example, the debtor moves out of state or has assets that are hard to reach) *and* the stakes are high enough (say $5,000 or more), you may do better handing your case over to a lawyer who specializes in collecting judgments.

You will be entitled to recover your attorney fees if provided for in a contract or statute (CCP § 685.040).

1. How To Work With Lawyers

There are two ways to work with an attorney collecting your judgment. The first, traditional, way is to turn over the judgment to her. You pay the attorney's bills and wait

[1] Very few judgment collection cases are appealed, which is necessary if a case is to make it into the case books. The costs of bringing an appeal are almost always greater than the sum sought to be collected.

for her to collect the judgment and turn over the money to you.

An alternative, which will let you keep more of what you collect, is for you get help from the attorney but do most of the actual work yourself. You pay the attorney by the hour for her advice. Surprisingly, it may prove difficult to find an attorney who will work with you strictly on a consulting basis for an hourly fee.

2. Will a Lawyer Take Your Case?

If your judgment is worth less than $5,000, it probably isn't cost-effective to give your case to an attorney, whether you pay by the hour or make a contingency fee agreement. (See Section B.3, just below.)

That threshold level goes up if, after an initial review of the situation, the attorney thinks collection will be difficult (there are few reachable assets or they are cleverly concealed). In assessing how easy it will be to collect the judgment, the attorney will want to know whether the judgment debtor is an individual or a business, and what assets he has. In general, if a going business is involved, the attorney will be much more optimistic about the chances of collection.

For individual judgment debtors, the attorney will weigh the factors discussed in Chapter 1, including whether the individual is a settled member of the community, employed, the record owner of real estate or the owner of valuable non-exempt assets.

If the attorney agrees to handle your judgment, she will ask you to assign the judgment to her. This means, in essence, that the attorney will now own the judgment. You will be paid your share if and when part or all of the judgment is collected.

3. What Lawyers Charge

For consultations, collection attorneys' going rates are normally $90 to $150 an hour. Some lawyers charge up to $250 per hour. However, there is seldom any reason to pay a high-end fee. Shop around, both for an experienced lawyer and a reasonable fee.

If you want an attorney to take over your collection efforts, you normally have to pay a contingency fee—that is, a set percentage of what is collected. For individual judgment debtors, this percentage usually ranges from 33% to 50%, depending on the size of your judgment.

The smaller the judgment amount, the bigger percentage you can expect to pay. For business judgment debtors, the percentage is generally lower—both because of the greater likelihood of collection and because the lawyer hopes to get more business.

The nice thing about a contingency fee is that you don't have to pay the lawyer if nothing is collected (though you might have to pay costs that have been advanced). The down side of a contingency fee is that lawyers commonly refuse to take collection cases unless they see from the outset that collection is likely to be profitable to them. In those situations, the lawyer may end up being paid at the rate of hundreds of dollars an hour for taking a negligible risk.[2] Remember that you could probably use this book, obtain the same results and keep the lawyer's cut in your own pocket.

If you hire an attorney under a contingency fee agreement, you are entitled (under California law) to a

[2] Normally, the amount collected by an attorney under a contingent fee is much larger than what would be collected under an hourly rate. A rationale for this is that the attorney risks being paid nothing if she is unsuccessful, and that the extra amount collected under a contingency fee is compensation for this risk. As mentioned, however, this risk is normally illusory for the professional judgment collector.

written contract setting out the terms of the agreement. If you hire an attorney on a fee basis, and the attorney expects the bill to be more than $1,000, you are also entitled to a written contract. You should always request a written contract, even if the law doesn't require it.

Regardless of the fee arrangement, you may have to pay the costs of collecting the judgment. Make sure you agree on this in advance. If so, either the attorney will ask you to advance the costs or will advance the costs and have you reimburse him. Most collections involve at least $200 in costs; many, of course, cost much more. (See Chapter 15 for how costs are paid and how to keep track of them.)

C. How To Find a Collections Lawyer

BE SURE TO CHOOSE a collections lawyer rather than a general business lawyer. As you may have gathered from this book, the collections field is a specialty in itself. Some of the advantages of using a collections attorney:

- A collections attorney is in a better position to find out information on the debtor, since he is part of a network of collection lawyers who exchange information. A lawyer who is not actively involved in collections is an outsider and may have trouble getting needed information.
- A collections lawyer is set up to handle collection cases on a systematic, efficient basis. He can zero in on the problem and select the most productive strategies.
- An experienced collections lawyer has a valuable understanding of the normal debtor's psychology and uses it in the course of negotiations.

1. Where Should the Lawyer Be Located?

As a general principle, the attorney you select should be as geographically close as possible to the court where he will be doing his work. This normally means the county in which the court that issued the judgment is located. However, you may want an attorney where the debtor lives, works, has a business or has assets.

If the judgment debtor's home and assets are widely separated, you may have a difficult choice to make. Here are some helpful tips:

- If you are turning the judgment over to the attorney to collect, choose one close to where the judgment debtor lives.
- If you are hiring the attorney only to help you through a difficult moment in your collection effort (for instance, you need some guidance on bringing a particular motion), select an attorney in the same location as the court that issued the judgment.
- If assets you are seeking are in another state, find an attorney in that state. If you have a local attorney, get a recommendation.
- If you don't know where the judgment debtor is, or the debtor is temporarily judgment-proof and you plan to wait a year or two before trying to actively collect your judgment, find an attorney close to you.

2. Where To Get Referrals

To find a good collections attorney, check one or more of the following sources:

- **Friends or business associates:** The personal networking method works well if you have business and professional connections. However, when you get a recommendation, be sure the lawyer is a collections specialist. If so, she is likely to work on referral for collection agencies.
- **Lawyers who have served you well:** If you are satisfied with a lawyer who you used for some other purpose, that lawyer may be able to steer you to a good and honest collections lawyer.

- **Lawyer lists:** You can use a lawyer list (available in business and law libraries) to locate lawyers who specialize in collections. Some of these lists are:

  International Lawyers List
  Commerce Clearing House Quarterly
  American Lawyers Quarterly
  The Columbia List
  Campbell's List
  Forwarders List
  National List

- **A good local collections agency:** Since collection agencies refer their uncollected claims to attorneys, it makes sense to find out who handles their cases in your area and see if she will take your judgment. If the attorney is repeatedly used by an agency, you can be pretty sure she gets the job done more often than not.[3]

D. Other Collections Professionals

LAWYERS AREN'T THE ONLY PROFESSIONALS who may provide crucial assistance in your collection efforts. Others include:

- collection paralegals
- data search companies and
- asset tracing firms or private investigators.

If your main collection problem is locating the debtor or her assets, it might be worthwhile to hire a data search firm, collection agency or investigator instead of a lawyer, since they often have good skip-tracing departments.[4]

[3]Many collections attorneys rely heavily on paralegals. Some attorneys charge customers at attorney rates for paralegal work while others charge at a lower paralegal rate. You should consider only using an attorney who passes the paralegal rate on to the public.

[4]The term "skip-tracing" is used in the trade to mean tracking down a person and finding out about his personal and business affairs.

1. Collections Paralegals

It will come as no surprise to many of you that the real collection experts in law firms are lawyer assistants known as paralegals. Traditionally, a consumer could not work directly with these paralegals—instead, the law office itself had to be engaged, at lawyer rates.

However, an increasing number of paralegals are striking out on their own (as "independent paralegals"[5]) and offering assistance to members of the public who are undertaking their own legal tasks. Uncontested divorces, name changes, bankruptcies and child support modifications are all routinely handled by independent paralegals at a greatly reduced cost.

We anticipate that paralegals experienced in collections work will begin to deal directly with the public, too. If so, we suggest you first contact a paralegal if you simply desire some support or assistance with using this book. If, on the other hand, you need someone to actually handle your case, see a lawyer.

A recommendation by someone who has used a particular paralegal is the best way to find one in your area. You may also find a listing in the Yellow Pages under "typing services." Or contact the National Association for Independent Paralegals at 800-542-0034.

2. Data Search Firms

Data search firms specialize in using computers to efficiently ferret out from government and private databases information you need to carry out various collection activities. You may be a lot better off having one of these firms do your search than to spend hours trying to do it yourself. For example, a state-wide real estate search costs about $25-$35. It would take countless hours to get that information without use of a database.

Data search companies may be listed in the Yellow Pages under "searchers of records," "attorneys service bureaus" or "public records." Unfortunately, they're often

[5]For more information on independent paralegals, see *The Independent Paralegal's Handbook*, by Ralph Warner (Nolo Press).

difficult to locate (ironic as that may be), so here are the names of a couple of established companies. We don't specifically recommend or guarantee their services in any way.

- McCord Company 800-874-8820
- Prentice Hall Legal and Financial Services 800-222-2122

3. Investigators and Asset Tracing Firms

Probably the biggest impediment to collecting judgments is finding out what assets the judgment debtor owns and where they are located. Sometimes this information can be obtained cheaply through a computer database search (see Section D.2, just above); other times, it takes plain hard work by a skilled person.

Private investigators are skilled in locating individuals (and, sometimes, assets); asset tracing firms are skilled in locating assets. Both charge a fair amount for their services, but if your judgment is large enough to warrant the costs, you may save yourself a lot of grief in the long run by turning to them.

Perhaps the best place to find references to investigators or asset tracing firms are the advertisements in newspapers or periodicals that are directed to California attorneys. These can be found in your county law library (see Section A above). You can also find investigators in your area through the Yellow Pages, under "investigators" (if you don't live in a large city, you may need to go to the library and check the Yellow Pages of a city nearby).

4. Collection Agencies

We generally recommend against collection agencies because you often pay more to an agency than to a lawyer for much the same result. Collection agencies usually work hand-in-glove with attorneys, so they tack on an added fee. Agencies usually require a 50% commission on judgments. However, this percentage may include all court costs and levying fees—meaning you're not out anything if they don't collect. Make sure you're clear about this in advance.

Many agencies don't want to deal with judgments, since the collection techniques they are best at—telephone appeals and letters—usually aren't effective. After all, you only got a judgment because nothing else worked. In deciding whether to collect your judgment, the collection agency will probably assess the likelihood of success. If the debtor is employed, owns real estate or has a business, the agency will be likely to pursue your judgment. But remember, if you know about the debtor's assets, you can go after them yourself, using the instructions in this book.

Appendix

In this Appendix are most of the blank forms you'll need to complete the procedures covered in this book. Below is a complete listing of these forms followed by some important pointers on the next page.

Chapter	*Form*
General	Cover Letter to Clerk
General	Instructions to Levying Officer
General	Numbered Pleading Paper
4	Abstract of Judgment
4	Abstract of Support Judgment
4	Notice of Judgment Lien
5	Income and Expense Statement
6	Application for Appearance and Order of Examination
6	Debtor's Examination Questions
6	Order for Delivery of Property
7	Writ of Execution
9	Application for Earnings Withholding Order
15	Keeping Track of Costs
15	Keeping Track of Collecting Your Judgment
15	Keeping Track of Interest (Calculation Sheet)
15	Memorandum of Costs
16	Proof of Claim
17	Creditor's Claim
19	Application for Entry of Judgment on Sister-State Judgment
19	Notice of Entry of Judgment on Sister-State Judgment
19	Statement for Registration of Foreign Support Order & Clerk's Notice
21	Acknowledgment of Satisfaction of Judgment
22	Proof of Personal Service
22	Proof of Service by Mail

Tips On Using Forms

- Never fill out forms without making photocopies first. You may make a mistake, or you very well may need to use them again. While you can get new copies of most forms, making extra copies can save you considerable time and effort.
- Many forms have printing on both sides. Make sure you copy both sides. You do not have to copy the second side onto the back of the form; you can simply staple two pages together.
- Carefully follow the instructions in this book for completing the forms. Also look at the samples we provide to make sure you fill out the forms correctly.
- When possible, type. Otherwise, print clearly and neatly.
- When you send a completed form to the court or levying officer, keep copies for yourself. Spending the extra cents to make copies makes sense, since you never know if your forms will get lost in the mail, will be misplaced by a clerk, or will end up in the twilight zone.

Judicial Council Forms

Many of the forms you'll be using are "Judicial Council forms." These are standard forms that were designed by the California Judicial Council (an official body) for use in all California courts. Each Judicial Council form has a title in bold print at the bottom of the page and information in the lower left-hand corner that will help you identify the form and determine whether it is up-to-date. The number in the lower left hand corner is the Judicial Council's way of identifying the form.

Following the identifying number is a date of revision. The forms were current when this book was published. However, Judicial Council forms are subject to change approximately once a year, although some forms stay current for years. If you discover that a Judicial Council form we provide here is outdated (you will typically discover this when the court clerk sends your documents back to you), the new form should be available at the court where you have your judgment, either free or for a nominal fee. Or you can visit a law library and consult one of the sources we list in Chapter 23 for obtaining Judicial Council forms.

If you want to make sure the forms are up-to-date before you complete them, call the court and give them the name and number of the forms. Some courts are real sticklers about requiring the most up-to-date form; other courts are more lenient.

Date: ______________________

To:

Re: ____________________________ v. ____________________________

Court: ______________________________

Case No. ______________________________

Dear Clerk:

Enclosed please find:

1) Original and _____ copy/copies of the following document(s):

2) Check in the amount of $_______________ (if required);

3) Self-addressed stamped envelope; and

4) Other:

Please file, issue or record these documents and return conformed copies to me.

Sincerely,

____

Address:

____

____

____

Phone:

(_______) _________ - ________________

Date: ____________________________

Instructions to Levying Officer, County of ____

Please take the action described below to collect this court judgment. Please hold the Writ for its entire 180-day duration, or until the judgment has been satisfied, unless I contact and instruct you differently.

1. **Case Information:**

   Case: ____

   Court: ____

   Case No. ______________________________

   Levying Officer No. (on previous papers, if you have attempted levies in this county): ____________

2. **Enclosures:**

   ☐ Original Writ of Execution and ______ copy/copies

   ☐ Check or money order in the amount of $____________

   ☐ *(Check only if applicable.)* Separate written levy instructions

3. **Levy Instructions:**

   ☐ Type of levy: ____

   ☐ Please proceed as follows:

Sincerely,

____

(your signature)

Your Printed Name:

____

Your Address:

____

____

____

Your Phone Number:

(______) __________ - ______________

ATTORNEY OR PARTY WITHOUT ATTORNEY *(Name and Address)*: TELEPHONE NO.:

☐ Recording requested by and return to:

☐ ATTORNEY FOR ☐ JUDGMENT CREDITOR ☐ ASSIGNEE OF RECORD

FOR RECORDER'S USE ONLY

NAME OF COURT:
STREET ADDRESS:
MAILING ADDRESS:
CITY AND ZIP CODE:
BRANCH NAME:

PLAINTIFF:

DEFENDANT:

CASE NUMBER:

ABSTRACT OF JUDGMENT

FOR COURT USE ONLY

1. The ☐ judgment creditor ☐ assignee of record applies for an abstract of judgment and represents the following:
   a. Judgment debtor's

      Name and last known address

   b. Driver's license No. and state: ☐ Unknown
   c. Social Security No.: ☐ Unknown
   d. Summons or notice of entry of sister-state judgment was personally served or mailed to *(name and address)*:

   e. ☐ Additional judgment debtors are shown on reverse.

Date:

(TYPE OR PRINT NAME) (SIGNATURE OF APPLICANT OR ATTORNEY)

2. a. ☐ I certify that the following is a true and correct abstract of the judgment entered in this action.
   b. ☐ A certified copy of the judgment is attached.
3. Judgment creditor *(name)*:

   whose **address** appears on this form above the court's name.
4. Judgment debtor *(full name as it appears in judgment)*:

[SEAL]

5. a. Judgment entered on *(date)*:
   b. Renewal entered on *(date)*:
   c. Renewal entered on *(date)*:

This abstract issued on *(date)*:

6. Total amount of judgment as entered or last renewed: $
7. ☐ An ☐ execution ☐ attachment lien is endorsed on the judgment as follows:
   a. Amount: $
   b. In favor of *(name and address)*:
8. A stay of enforcement has
   a. ☐ not been ordered by the court.
   b. ☐ been ordered by the court effective until *(date)*:
9. ☐ This judgment is an installment judgment.

Clerk, by ______________________, Deputy

PLAINTIFF:	CASE NUMBER:
DEFENDANT:	

INFORMATION ON ADDITIONAL JUDGMENT DEBTORS

10. Name and last known address

Driver's license No. & state: ☐ Unknown
Social Security No.: ☐ Unknown
Summons was personally served at or mailed to *(address)*:

11. Name and last known address

Driver's license No. & state: ☐ Unknown
Social Security No.: ☐ Unknown
Summons was personally served at or mailed to *(address)*:

12. Name and last known address

Driver's license No. & state: ☐ Unknown
Social Security No.: ☐ Unknown
Summons was personally served at or mailed to *(address)*:

13. Name and last known address

Driver's license No. & state: ☐ Unknown
Social Security No.: ☐ Unknown
Summons was personally served at or mailed to *(address)*:

14. Name and last known address

Driver's license No. & state: ☐ Unknown
Social Security No.: ☐ Unknown
Summons was personally served at or mailed to *(address)*:

15. Name and last known address

Driver's license No. & state: ☐ Unknown
Social Security No.: ☐ Unknown
Summons was personally served at or mailed to *(address)*:

16. Name and last known address

Driver's license No. & state: ☐ Unknown
Social Security No.: ☐ Unknown
Summons was personally served at or mailed to *(address)*:

17. Name and last known address

Driver's license No. & state: ☐ Unknown
Social Security No.: ☐ Unknown
Summons was personally served at or mailed to *(address)*:

18. ☐ Continued on attachment 18.

ATTORNEY OR PARTY WITHOUT ATTORNEY *(Name and Address)*: TELEPHONE NO.:

☐ Recording requested by and return to:

☐ ATTORNEY FOR ☐ JUDGMENT CREDITOR ☐ ASSIGNEE OF RECORD

FOR RECORDER'S USE ONLY

SUPERIOR COURT OF CALIFORNIA, COUNTY OF

STREET ADDRESS:

MAILING ADDRESS:

CITY AND ZIP CODE:

BRANCH NAME:

PETITIONER/PLAINTIFF:

RESPONDENT/DEFENDANT:

ABSTRACT OF SUPPORT JUDGMENT

CASE NUMBER:

FOR COURT USE ONLY

1. The ☐ judgment creditor ☐ assignee of record applies for an abstract of a support judgment and represents the following:
   a. Judgment debtor's
   Name and last known address

   b. Driver's license No. and state: ☐ unknown
   c. Social Security number: ☐ unknown
   d. Birthdate: ☐ unknown

Date:

. . . .
(TYPE OR PRINT NAME)

▶ ______________________________
(SIGNATURE OF APPLICANT OR ATTORNEY)

2. I CERTIFY that the judgment entered in this action contains an order for payment of spousal, family, or child support.
3. Judgment creditor *(name)*:

   whose address appears on this form above the court's name.
4. ☐ The support is ordered to be paid to the following county officer *(name and address)*:

5. Judgment debtor *(full name as it appears in judgment)*:
6. a. A judgment was entered on *(date)*:
   b. Renewal was entered on *(date)*:
   c. Renewal was entered on *(date)*:
7. ☐ An execution lien is endorsed on the judgment as follows:
   a. Amount: $
   b. In favor of *(name and address)*:

[SEAL]

8. A stay of enforcement has
   a. ☐ not been ordered by the court.
   b. ☐ been ordered by the court effective until *(date)*:
9. ☐ This is an installment judgment.

This abstract issued on *(date)*:

Clerk, by ______________________________, Deputy

AIL TO:
ecretary of State
O. Box 1738
acramento, CA 95808

STATE OF CALIFORNIA
NOTICE OF JUDGMENT LIEN ON PERSONAL PROPERTY
(FOR FILING IN THE OFFICE OF THE SECRETARY OF STATE)

IMPORTANT—Read instructions on back before completing this form

REFERENCE: CODE OF CIVIL PROCEDURE SECTIONS 697.510, 697.550 AND 697.570

JUDGMENT DEBTOR (LAST NAME FIRST, IF AN INDIVIDUAL)

A. MAILING ADDRESS OF JUDGMENT DEBTOR	1B. CITY, STATE	1C. ZIP CODE

ADDITIONAL JUDGMENT DEBTOR (IF ANY) (LAST NAME FIRST, IF AN INDIVIDUAL)

A. MAILING ADDRESS OF ADDITIONAL JUDGMENT DEBTOR	2B. CITY, STATE	2C. ZIP CODE

. JUDGMENT CREDITOR

NAME:

MAILING ADDRESS:

CITY: STATE: ZIP CODE:

. ALL PROPERTY SUBJECT TO ENFORCEMENT OF A MONEY JUDGMENT AGAINST THE JUDGMENT DEBTOR TO WHICH A JUDGMENT LIEN ON PERSONAL PROPERTY MAY ATTACH UNDER SECTION 697.530 OF THE CODE OF CIVIL PROCEDURE IS SUBJECT TO THIS JUDGMENT LIEN.

A. Title of court where judgment was entered: ____________________

____

B. Title of the action: ____________________

C. Number of the action: ____________________

D. Date judgment was entered: ____________________

E. Dates of subsequent renewals of judgment (if any): ____________________; ____________________

F. Amount required to satisfy judgment at date of this notice: $ ____________________

G. Date of this notice: ____________________

. *I declare under penalty of perjury under the laws of the State of California that the foregoing is true and correct.*

Dated: ____________________ 19 ____ . (If not indicated, the date of declaration is the same as date in item 4G)

____
(SIGNATURE—SEE INSTRUCTION NO. 5)

FOR: ____________________

6. THIS SPACE FOR USE OF FILING OFFICER (DATE, TIME OF FILING AND FILE NUMBER)

7. ***RETURN COPY TO***

NAME
ADDRESS
CITY
STATE
ZIP CODE

NOTICE OF JUDGMENT LIEN—FORM J-1 (1/88)
PRESCRIBED BY THE SECRETARY OF STATE

FILING FEE $5.00

INSTRUCTIONS

This Notice of Judgment Lien should be filed only if the judgment is a money judgment that was first entered in this State after June 30, 1983 (see Code of Civil Procedure Section 697.510).

ITEM 1:	Enter name of judgment debtor as it appears in the judgment.
ITEMS 1A–1C:	Enter last-known mailing address of the judgment debtor.
ITEM 2:	Enter name of additional judgment debtor, if any. If there is more than one additional judgment debtor, continue Item 2 on an additional white sheet of paper 8½″ x 11″ in size.
ITEMS 2A–2C:	Enter last-known mailing address for any additional judgment debtor.
ITEM 3:	Enter the name and mailing address of the judgment creditor. The name of the judgment creditor should be as it appears in the judgment.
ITEMS 4A–4D:	Enter information from the judgment.
ITEM 4F:	Enter amount of the judgment adjusted for interest and payments to the date of the notice.
ITEM 4G:	The date of the notice will normally be the date the notice is executed.
ITEM 5:	This notice of judgment lien on personal property must be signed by the judgment creditor's attorney, if the judgment creditor has an attorney of record. If the judgment creditor does not have an attorney of record, then it must be signed by the judgment creditor. (Code of Civil Procedure Section 697.550) If the individual signing the notice signs on behalf of a law firm, which is the attorney of record, the name of the law firm should be entered BENEATH, not above, the signature. If the signature is for a judgment creditor, which is an entity, the name of the entity should be entered BENEATH, not above, the signature of the person signing for the judgment creditor.
ITEM 7:	If the attorney or judgment creditor wishes an acknowledgment of filing, the original and first copy of the notice of judgment lien must be presented for filing. Indicate in Item 7, the name and mailing address of the person who is to receive the acknowledgment of filing.

NOTICES

FILING PERIOD:	A Notice of Judgment Lien on personal property shall not be filed if it is presented for filing more than 10 days after the date of the notice (CCP Section 697.570). Receipt of the notice in the Secretary of State's Office shall be considered the date it is presented for filing. The date the notice is postmarked will not constitute presentation for filing.
NOTICE:	At the time of filing the Notice of Judgment Lien on personal property or promptly thereafter, the judgment creditor is required to serve a copy of the Notice of Judgment Lien on the judgment debtor (Code of Civil Procedure Section 697.560).
TERMINATION:	In order to terminate the judgment lien on personal property, an Acknowledgment of Satisfaction of Judgment or a court clerk's certificate of satisfaction of judgment will have to be filed with the Secretary of State's Office (Code of Civil Procedure Section 724.060(7)).
FILING FEE:	The Notice of Judgment Lien must be submitted with a filing fee of five dollars ($5) payable to the Secretary of State. DOCUMENTS NOT ACCOMPANIED BY THE FILING FEE WILL NOT BE FILED.
MAILING ADDRESS:	Mail the original and first copy of the notice to: Secretary of State P.O. Box 1738 Sacramento, CA 95808
COMPLETION OF FORM:	Please type the information on the form, if at all possible.

DEFENDANT/JUDGMENT DEBTOR: PLAINTIFF/JUDGMENT CREDITOR:	*(do not file with the court)*
COURT NAME:	
INCOME AND EXPENSE STATEMENT	CASE NUMBER:

(Attach additional sheets if you need more room)

EMPLOYMENT AND INCOME

1. What is your occupation?
2. Name and address of your business and employer:
3. How often are you paid? ☐ daily ☐ every week ☐ every two weeks ☐ twice a month ☐ monthly ☐ other:
4. Your gross pay for each pay period: $____________
5. Your take home pay for each pay period: $____________
6. If your spouse earns any income, give the name and address of the business or employer, and an estimate of your spouse's monthly take home pay:
7. Other income you and your spouse receive (support payments, public benefits, royalties, patents, business income, etc.):

Amount	When are payments received?	Source (name and address)

8. I, my spouse, and my other dependents own the following property:

   a. Cash: $____________

   b. Checking, savings, credit union, money market, CD and other financial accounts (specify below):

Account No.	Institution name and address	Type of Account	Co-owner, if any	Balance

   c. Stocks, bonds, and other liquid assets (specify below):

Account No.	Institution name and address	Type of Account	Co-owner, if any	Balance

   d. Cars, other vehicles, boat equity (specify below):

Make and year	Legal owner's name and address, if not you	Amount owed	Value

e. Real estate equity:

Address	Mortgage, trust deed holder	Amount owed	Value

f. Other personal property (jewelry, antiques, artwork, coin collections, furs, safety deposit boxes, equipment, machinery, livestock, etc.):

Description	Address where property located	Co-owner, if any	Value

EXPENSE INFORMATION

1. Monthly expenses for me, my spouse, and my other dependents

   a. Rent or house payment and maintenance $__________
   b. Food and household supplies $__________
   c. Utilities and telephone $__________
   d. Clothing $__________
   e. Medical and dental payments $__________
   f. Insurance (life, health, accident, etc.) $__________
   g. School, child care $__________
   h. Child, spousal support (prior marriage) $__________
   i. Transportation, auto expenses (insurance, gas, repair) $__________
   j. Laundry, cleaning $__________
   k. Entertainment $__________
   l. Other (specify): $__________

2. I, my spouse, and other dependents owe the following debts (include other judgments, loans, etc.):

Creditor's Name	For	Monthly Payments	Balance Owed	Owed By

3. The following persons depend, in whole or in part, on me or my spouse for support:

Name	Age	Relationship to me	Amount spent monthly

4. Other facts that affect my ability to pay this judgment:

I declare under penalty under the laws of the State of California that the foregoing is true and correct.

Date: ____________________ Signature: ____

ATTORNEY OR PARTY WITHOUT ATTORNEY (*Name and Address*): TELEPHONE NO.:	*FOR COURT USE ONLY*
ATTORNEY FOR (*Name*):	
NAME OF COURT: STREET ADDRESS: MAILING ADDRESS: CITY AND ZIP CODE: BRANCH NAME:	
PLAINTIFF: DEFENDANT:	
APPLICATION AND ORDER FOR APPEARANCE AND EXAMINATION ☐ **ENFORCEMENT OF JUDGMENT** ☐ **ATTACHMENT (Third Person)** ☐ **Judgment Debtor** ☐ **Third Person**	CASE NUMBER:

ORDER TO APPEAR FOR EXAMINATION

1. TO (*name*):
2. YOU ARE ORDERED TO APPEAR personally before this court, or before a referee appointed by the court, to
   a. ☐ furnish information to aid in enforcement of a money judgment against you.
   b. ☐ answer concerning property of the judgment debtor in your possession or control or concerning a debt you owe the judgment debtor.
   c. ☐ answer concerning property of the defendant in your possession or control or concerning a debt you owe the defendant that is subject to attachment.

Date:	Time:	Dept. or Div.:	Rm.:
Address of court ☐ shown above ☐ is:			

3. This order may be served by a sheriff, marshal, constable, registered process server, **or** the following specially appointed person (*name*):

Date: ▶ ______________________________
(*SIGNATURE OF JUDGE OR REFEREE*)

This order must be served not less than 10 days before the date set for the examination.

IMPORTANT NOTICES ON REVERSE

APPLICATION FOR ORDER TO APPEAR FOR EXAMINATION

1. ☐ Judgment creditor ☐ Assignee of record ☐ Plaintiff who has a right to attach order
   applies for an order requiring (*name*): to appear and furnish information to aid in enforcement of the money judgment or to answer concerning property or debt.
2. The person to be examined is
   ☐ the judgment debtor
   ☐ a third person (1) who has possession or control of property belonging to the judgment debtor or the defendant or (2) who owes the judgment debtor or the defendant more than $250. An affidavit supporting this application under CCP §491.110 or §708.120 is attached.
3. The person to be examined resides or has a place of business in this county or within 150 miles of the place of examination.
4. ☐ This court is **not** the court in which the money judgment is entered or (*attachment only*) the court that issued the writ of attachment. An affidavit supporting an application under CCP §491.150 or §708.160 is attached.
5. ☐ The judgment debtor has been examined within the past 120 days. An affidavit showing good cause for another examination is attached.

I declare under penalty of perjury under the laws of the State of California that the foregoing is true and correct.

Date:

.... ▶ ______________________________
(*TYPE OR PRINT NAME*) (*SIGNATURE OF DECLARANT*)

APPEARANCE OF JUDGMENT DEBTOR (ENFORCEMENT OF JUDGMENT)

NOTICE TO JUDGMENT DEBTOR If you fail to appear at the time and place specified in this order, you may be subject to arrest and punishment for contempt of court, and the court may make an order requiring you to pay the reasonable attorney fees incurred by the judgment creditor in this proceeding.

APPEARANCE OF A THIRD PERSON (ENFORCEMENT OF JUDGMENT)

(1) NOTICE TO PERSON SERVED If you fail to appear at the time and place specified in this order, you may be subject to arrest and punishment for contempt of court, and the court may make an order requiring you to pay the reasonable attorney fees incurred by the judgment creditor in this proceeding.

(2) NOTICE TO JUDGMENT DEBTOR The person in whose favor the judgment was entered in this action claims that the person to be examined pursuant to this order has possession or control of property which is yours or owes you a debt. This property or debt is as follows *(Describe the property or debt using typewritten capital letters)*:

If you claim that all or any portion of this property or debt is exempt from enforcement of the money judgment, you must file your exemption claim in writing with the court and have a copy personally served on the judgment creditor not later than three days before the date set for the examination. You must appear at the time and place set for the examination to establish your claim of exemption or your exemption may be waived.

APPEARANCE OF A THIRD PERSON (ATTACHMENT)

NOTICE TO PERSON SERVED If you fail to appear at the time and place specified in this order, you may be subject to arrest and punishment for contempt of court, and the court may make an order requiring you to pay the reasonable attorney fees incurred by the plaintiff in this proceeding.

APPEARANCE OF A CORPORATION, PARTNERSHIP, ASSOCIATION, TRUST, OR OTHER ORGANIZATION

It is your duty to designate one or more of the following to appear and be examined: officers, directors, managing agents, or other persons who are familiar with your property and debts.

QUESTIONS FOR DEBTOR'S EXAMINATION

1. What is your full name and your spouse's full name (if married)?
2. Have you ever used another name or nickname on any documents such as a driver's license, credit application or other important papers? If so:
   a. give name;
   b. give location and approximate time when name was used.
3. What is your current address and length of time lived there?
4. What is your current phone number?
5. What was your previous address?
6. What was your previous phone number?
7. What is your California driver's license (or California identification card) number?
8. What is your social security number?
9. What is your date of birth?
10. If married, what is your spouse's maiden name?
11. Are you employed as an employee, either part time or full time? If so:
    a. Name, address and phone number of employer;
    b. Frequency of payment (weekly, bi-weekly, monthly, etc.);
    c. Gross pay;
    d. Take home pay;
    e. commissions if any;
    f. how much is due you at the present time;
    g. how long on this job.
12. Where and with whom was your previous job?
13. Do you perform labor or services for someone else as an independent contractor rather than as an employee? If so:
    a. names, addresses, and phone numbers of persons or businesses for whom you perform services;
    b. nature of services performed for each such person or business;
    c. frequency of services;
    d. method of billing (e.g., flat rate, hourly rate, job rate).
14. Do you own a business (in whole, in part, as a partner, or as a corporation), or have you owned a business within the past five years? If so:
    a. describe business;
    b. who you do business with;
    c. describe major people or businesses who owe you money (names, addresses and telephone numbers);
    d. describe any business assets such as tools, equipment, computers, furniture, fixtures, machinery, etc. wholly owned by business;
    e. identify which of these assets you still owe money on and the approximate amount owed;
    f. describe, generally, method of doing business;
    g. provide names and addresses of partners (if the business is a partnership), and corporate officers (if the business is a corporation).
15. Do you own stock in any corporation or shares in a mutual fund? If so:
    a. name of corporation or mutual fund;
    b. form of ownership (certificates, computer account, etc.);
    c. location of certificates or account;
    d. amount of ownership and approximate value.
16. Do you maintain a brokerage account with any stock broker? If so:
    a. name and address of broker;
    b. account number(s);
    c. approximate amount in brokerage account.
17. Do you or your spouse have any funds in banks, savings and loans, money market accounts, certificates of deposit, escrow accounts, credit unions, or any other financial institutions, either in your name or jointly with any other individual? If so:
    a. name of each financial institution and address of branch possessing the funds;
    b. the account number of each account;

c. name(s) the account is under;
d. the approximate balance in the account;
e. date the last deposit was made;
f. source of the funds in the account;
g. when you typically make deposits and withdrawals.

18. Do you or your spouse own a safe deposit box? If so:
a. name of bank and address of branch;
b. name(s) of holder of safe deposit box;
c. contents of box.

19. Do you own any securities (that is, any document which grants a share of ownership in exchange for a loan or investment) such as bonds, annuities, etc? If so:
a. describe nature of security, bond, annuity, etc.;
b. institution or person issuing it;
c. approximate worth.

20. Do you own any whole life insurance policies? If so:
a. the name of the insurance company;
b. the name of your insurance agent;
c. the face amount of the policy;
d. the cash value of the policy, if any.

21. Do you own any of the following items? If so, describe the item, the item's location, approximate value, and any joint owner.
a. office equipment;
b. gemstones, gems or jewelry;
c. camera equipment;
d. computers;
e. antiques;
f. precious metals (gold, silver);
g. musical instruments including pianos and organs;
h. weapons (guns, swords, other);
i. furs;
j. watches;
k. stamp or coin collections;
l. china;
m. original art works;
n. crystal;
o. sports equipment, including exercise machines;
p. stereo or musical equipment;
q. any other items of value not mentioned above.

22. Do you own, in your own name, or jointly with others, an automobile, truck, motorcycle, RV, motor home, mobile home, boat or plane? If so:, provide the following information:
a. brief description (make, model and year);
b. approximate value;
c. legal owner;
d. registered owner;
e. license number;
f. vehicle identification number;
g. amount owed, if any, to a legal owner;
h. any other lienholder you are aware of.

23. Does a person, company or institution owe you money? If so:
a. name, address and telephone number of person or institution;
b. amount of each debt;
c. how each debt arose (e.g., judgment, loan, inheritance).

24. Do you owe money to anyone else besides this current judgment where you have been sued and the other person or business has received a judgment? If so:
a. to whom (address and telephone no.);
b. amount owed;
c. amount currently paid.

25. Did you ever file for bankruptcy? If so:
    a. when;
    b. where (district and branch);
    c. type of bankruptcy (Chapter 7 or Chapter 13, if you know);
    d. case number of the bankruptcy.
26. Are you a party (e.g., defendant or plaintiff) in any current action? This could be an action brought against you for a money judgment, an action in which you are the plaintiff, or any other action (including divorce, will contest, etc.)? If so:
    a. who are the parties in each action;
    b. who are the attorneys in each action (names, addresses and phone numbers; include information for parties if they are appearing in pro per);
    c. a brief description of each lawsuit;
    d. what is your position in the lawsuit, and do you expect to win.
27. Does your wife or husband receive any salary, commissions, or other income, as an employee or independent contractor, from an employer or business? If so:
    a. name, address and telephone number of employer;
    b. approximate amount and rate of income.
28. Any other sources of income? If so:
    a. amount of income;
    b. when do you receive income, and is it received on a regular basis;
    c. brief description of source.
29. Do you own any real estate individually or jointly (single family home, vacation home, co-op/condominium, duplex, rental property, business property, mobile home park, time share, undeveloped land, agricultural land, boat/marina dock space, airplane hangar, stationary mobile home)? If so:
    a. address and county;
    b. approximate fair market value;
    c. amount owed (first mortgage, second deed of trust) If so:
        1. to whom;
        2. amount and frequency of payments;
    d. when the property was obtained;
    e what names are on the deed;
    f. has title to the property been transferred since its acquisition by you;
    g. known debts or claims that affect the title (easements, tax liens, judgment liens, etc.);
    h. approximate amount of your actual ownership (equity) in the property;
    i. has a declaration of homestead been filed;
    j. does anyone live on the property;
    k. is the property developed, and if so, what kind of building(s).
30. Are you a landlord? If so:
    a. name and address of tenants;
    b. amount of rent paid and interval of payment.
31. Do you rent where you are now living? If so:
    a. amount of rent paid;
    b. landlord's name;
    c. landlord's address and phone number.
32. Are you the trustee for, or beneficiary of, any property held in trust for yourself or a third person? If so:
    a. briefly describe type of trust (e.g., living, bank account, spousal, Q-TIP);
    b. identify whether you are the trustee or beneficiary, or both;
    c. describe what the nature of the property is that is being held in trust (trust corpus).
33. Do you receive benefits from any government agency (e.g., unemployment insurance, disability insurance, workers compensation, social security, retirement, pension)? If so:
    a. name of agency;
    b. type of benefit;
    c. amount of benefit;
    d. frequency of benefit;
    e. the expected duration of the payments;
    f. basis for the benefit (e.g., unemployment, industrial injury, etc).

34. Do you receive benefits from or through a private business or entity such as an insurance company or financial institution (e.g., insurance, annuity, retirement, pension, worker's compensation benefits)? If so:
    a. name of provider;
    b. type of benefit;
    c. amount of benefit;
    d. frequency of benefit;
    e. the expected duration of the payments;
    f. the basis for the benefit.
35. Do you pay alimony/child support? If so:
    a. name address and telephone number of recipient;
    b. amount and frequency of support.
36. Do you receive alimony/child support? If so:
    a. name, address and telephone number of provider;
    b. amount and frequency of support.
37. Do you own any property (cash, tangible personal property items) that is currently in possession of others? If so:
    a. briefly describe the property;
    b. name, address and telephone number of possessor;
    c. purpose of possession;
    d. physical location of property.
38. Is there any reason why you can't pay on this judgment now or in the futureIf so, briefly describe reason.
39. Do you foresee your financial position changing in the future? If so, how?
40. Identify each item of property (cash, other personal property including motor vehicles, or real estate) you have sold or given away within the past three months, and when the transaction occurred.
41. Identify each service you have received from an individual or business (e.g., medical care, legal consultation, car repair) within the past three months, and when the service was provided. Also indicate whether you have paid for that service, and in what manner (cash, check, credit card, etc.).
42. Do you hold an occupational license of any type? If so:
    a. name of license;
    b. agency granting the license;
    c. expiration date of license;
    d. license number.
43. Do you own any mortgages or deeds of trust on any real estate? If so:
    a. property involved (address, county);
    b. approximate value of mortgage;
    c. date of mortgage or deed of trust;
    d. persons or institutions involved.
44. Do you own, solely or jointly, any copyrights, patents, trademarks, tradenames or trade secrets? If so:
    a. item protected by the copyright, patent, etc.;
    b. where registered (if registered) and registration number;
    c. co-owners, if any;
    d. royalties or other payments received under the copyright patent, etc.
45. Do you or your spouse have any personal property in pawn? If so:
    a. name and address of pawnbroker;
    b. brief description of property and approximate value.
46. Have you made a will? If so:
    a. describe bequests;
    b. physical location of will.
47. How much cash or traveller's checks do you have with you at this time? Identify specifically.
48. Any checks or money orders payable to you? If so, describe.
49. Do you or your spouse have an IRA or Keogh account? If so:
    a. institution and branch where account is maintained;
    b. amount in account.

____

____

____

(   )   -

___________________________ COURT OF CALIFORNIA

COUNTY OF ___________________________

________________________________,)) Plaintiff,) vs.)) ________________________________,)) Defendant.) ________________________________)	Case No.________________ ORDER FOR DELIVERY OF PROPERTY AFTER EXAMINATION [CCP Section 708.205] Examination Date:____________ Time:________________ Place:________________

The examination of ____ (judgment debtor or third person) was conducted on the date and at the time set forth above. It appearing from this examination that:

☐ the judgment debtor has an interest in property in the possession or under the control of ______________________________ (judgment debtor or third person); OR

☐ a third person owes the judgment debtor $_________________ (or property described as follows: ____),

and that the property described above is not exempt from enforcement of a money judgment;

IT IS ORDERED THAT ____ (judgment debtor or third person) shall ☐ immediately/ ☐ within ____ days of entry of this order deliver to ______________________________________ (judgment creditor or levying officer of ______________________ County at the following address: ____, California) the following property: __________________________________ ____________________________ which shall be applied toward the satisfaction of the judgment entered in this action on ___________, 19___.

DATED:

____
Judge/Commissioner of
the _________________ Court

/////////

/////////

/////////

ATTORNEY OR PARTY WITHOUT ATTORNEY *(Name and Address)*: TELEPHONE NO.:	LEVYING OFFICER *(Name and Address)*:
ATTORNEY FOR *(Name)*:	
NAME OF COURT, JUDICIAL DISTRICT OR BRANCH COURT, IF ANY:	
PLAINTIFF: DEFENDANT:	

APPLICATION FOR EARNINGS WITHHOLDING ORDER **(Wage Garnishment)**	LEVYING OFFICER FILE NO.:	COURT CASE NO.:

TO THE SHERIFF OR ANY MARSHAL OR CONSTABLE OF THE COUNTY OF
OR ANY REGISTERED PROCESS SERVER

The judgment creditor *(name)*:

requests issuance of an Earnings Withholding Order directing the employer to withhold the earnings of the judgment debtor (employee).

Name and address of employer

Name and address of employee

Social Security Number *(if known)*:

. The amounts withheld are to be paid to
a. ☐ The attorney (or party without an attorney) named at the top of this page.
b. ☐ Other *(name, address, and telephone)*:

. a. Judgment was entered on *(date)*:
b. Collect the amount directed by the Writ of Execution unless a lesser amount is specified here:
$

. ☐ The Writ of Execution was issued to collect delinquent amounts payable for the **support** of a child, former spouse, or spouse of the employee.

. ☐ Special instructions *(specify)*:

. ***(Check a or b)***
a. ☐ I have not previously obtained an order directing this employer to withhold the earnings of this employee.
—OR—
b. ☐ I have previously obtained such an order, but that order *(check one)*:
☐ was terminated by a court order, but I am entitled to apply for another Earnings Withholding Order under the provisions of Code of Civil Procedure section 706.105(h).
☐ was ineffective.

. . . . ▶ ______________________________
(TYPE OR PRINT NAME) *(SIGNATURE OF ATTORNEY OR PARTY WITHOUT ATTORNEY)*

I declare under penalty of perjury under the laws of the State of California that the foregoing is true and correct.

Date:

. . . . ▶ ______________________________
(TYPE OR PRINT NAME) *(SIGNATURE OF DECLARANT)*

KEEPING TRACK OF COSTS

Date Expended	Cost Amount	Type of Cost	Expense Record	Date Costs Claimed

KEEPING TRACK OF COLLECTING YOUR JUDGMENT

Judgment Date: ______________________________

Judgment Amount: ______________________________

Date of Transaction	Type of Transaction	Record	Amount Received	Subtotal Received	Costs Filed	Interest Filed	Total Now Due

KEEPING TRACK OF INTEREST (CALCULATION SHEET)

A Starting Date	B Ending Date	C No. of days	D Balance (F from line above)	E Payment	F New Balance (D-E)	G Interest Due (D x ____ % x C/360)
					(Sub)total	

____

____

____

(   )   -

______________________________ COURT OF CALIFORNIA

COUNTY OF ______________________________

______________________________, Plaintiff, vs. ______________________________, Defendant. ______________________________	Case No.______________ **MEMORANDUM OF CREDITS, ACCRUED INTEREST AND COSTS AFTER JUDGMENT AND SUPPORTING DECLARATION**

MEMORANDUM OF CREDITS

CREDIT for payments and partial satisfaction of judgment, including direct payments and executions partially satisfied: $______________________ (if none, state NONE).

INTEREST ACCRUING AFTER JUDGMENT

INTEREST ACCRUING AFTER JUDGMENT at 10% from date of judgment on balances due after dates of payments or credits acknowledged above: $______________

(Plus $__________________ claimed on Memoranda of Costs filed previously).

MEMORANDUM OF COSTS AFTER JUDGMENT

1. Costs After Judgment Claimed on Memoranda Filed Previously .... $_________
2. Clerk's Fees .... $_________
3. .... $_________
4. Levying Officer's Fees .... $_________
5. .... $_________

6. Serving Supplementary Proceedings .... $________

7. .... $________

8. Notary Fees .... $________

9. .... $________

10. .... $________

11. .... $________

12. .... $________

13. .... $________

14. .... $________

15. .... $________

TOTAL: $________

DECLARATION SUPPORTING MEMORANDUM OF CREDITS, ACCRUED INTEREST AND COSTS AFTER JUDGMENT

I, the undersigned, declare that I am the ________________________________ in this action; the post-judgment costs and accrued interest as set forth in the Memoranda above are true and correct to the best of my knowledge and belief, the costs incurred are reasonable and necessary, and have not been satisfied.

I declare under penalty of perjury under the laws of the State of California that the foregoing is true and correct. Executed on ______________________________, at ______________________________, California.

____
[Signature]

Print name:________________________

/////////

/////////

/////////

FORM B10
(6/90)

FORM 10. PROOF OF CLAIM

United States Bankruptcy Court ______________ DISTRICT OF ______________	PROOF OF CLAIM	
In re (Name of Debtor)	Case Number	
NOTE: This form should not be used to make a claim for an administrative expense arising after the commencement of the case. A request for payment of an administrative expense may be filed pursuant to 11 U.S.C. § 503.		
Name of Creditor *(The person or other entity to whom the debtor owes money or property)* Name and Address Where Notices Should Be Sent Telephone No.	☐ Check box if you are aware that anyone else has filed a proof of claim relating to your claim. Attach copy or statement giving particulars. ☐ Check box if you never received any notices from the bankruptcy court in this case. ☐ Check box if the address differs from the address on the envelope sent to you by the court.	THIS SPACE IS FOR COURT USE ONLY
ACCOUNT OR OTHER NUMBER BY WHICH CREDITOR IDENTIFIES DEBTOR:	Check here if this claim ☐ replaces ☐ amends } a previously filed claim, dated: ________	

1. BASIS FOR CLAIM
   - ☐ Goods sold
   - ☐ Services performed
   - ☐ Money loaned
   - ☐ Personal injury/wrongful death
   - ☐ Taxes
   - ☐ Other (Describe briefly)

☐ Retiree benefits as defined in 11 U.S.C. § 1114 (a)

☐ Wage, salaries, and compensations (Fill out below)

Your social security number ______________

Unpaid compensation for services performed

from ______________ (date) to ______________ (date)

2. DATE DEBT WAS INCURRED

3. IF COURT JUDGMENT, DATE OBTAINED:

4. CLASSIFICATION OF CLAIM. Under the Bankruptcy Code all claims are classified as one or more of the following: (1) Unsecured nonpriority. (2) Unsecured Priority. (3) Secured. It is possible for part of a claim to be in one category and part in another.

CHECK THE APPROPRIATE BOX OR BOXES that best describe your claim and STATE THE AMOUNT OF THE CLAIM.

☐ SECURED CLAIM $ ______________
Attach evidence of perfection of security interest
Brief Description of Collateral:
☐ Real Estate ☐ Motor Vehicle ☐ Other (Describe briefly)

Amount of arrearage and other charges included in secured claim above, if any
$ ______________

☐ UNSECURED NONPRIORITY CLAIM $ ______________
A claim is unsecured if there is no collateral or lien on property of the debtor securing the claim or to the extent that the value of such property is less than the amount of the claim.

☐ UNSECURED PRIORITY CLAIM $ ______________
Specify the priority of the claim.

- ☐ Wages, salaries, or commissions (up to $2000, earned not more than 90 days before filing of the bankruptcy petition or cessation of the debtor's business, whichever is earlier)—11 U.S.C.§ 507 (a)(3)
- ☐ Contributions to an employee benefit plan—11 U.S.C. § 507(a)(4)
- ☐ Up to $900 of deposits toward purchase, lease, or rental of property or services for personal, family, or household use—11 U.S.C. 507(a) (6)
- ☐ Taxes or penalties of governmental units—11 U.S.C. § 507(a)(7)
- ☐ Other—11 U.S.C. §§ 507(a)(2), (a)(5)—(Describe briefly)

5. TOTAL AMOUNT OF CLAIM AT TIME CASE FILED: $ ________ (Unsecured) $ ________ (Secured) $ ________ (Priority) $ ________ (Total)

☐ Check this box if claim includes prepetition charges in addition to the principal amount of the claim. Attach itemized statement of all additional charges.

THIS SPACE IS FOR COURT USE ONLY

6. CREDITS AND SETOFFS: The amount of all payments on this claim has been credited and deducted for the purpose of making this proof of claim. In filing this claim, claimant has deducted all amounts that claimant owes to debtor.

7. SUPPORTING DOCUMENTS: Attach copies of supporting documents, such as promissory notes, purchase orders, invoices, itemized statements of running accounts, contracts, court judgments, or evidence of security interests. If the documents are not available, explain. If the documents are voluminous, attach a summary.

8. TIME-STAMPED COPY: To receive an acknowledgment of the filing of your claim, enclose a stamped, self-addressed envelope and copy of this proof of claim.

Date	Sign and print the name and title, if any, of the creditor or other person authorized to file this claim (attach copy of power of attorney, if any)

Penalty for presenting fraudulent claim: Fine of up to $500,000 or imprisonment for up to 5 years, or both. 18 U.S.C. §§ 152 and 3571

ATTORNEY OR CREDITOR WITHOUT ATTORNEY *(Name and Address)*: TELEPHONE NO.:	*FOR COURT USE ONLY*
ATTORNEY FOR *(Name)*:	
SUPERIOR COURT OF CALIFORNIA, COUNTY OF STREET ADDRESS: MAILING ADDRESS: CITY AND ZIP CODE: BRANCH NAME:	
ESTATE OF (NAME): DECEDENT	
CREDITOR'S CLAIM* **(for estate administration proceedings filed after June 30, 1988)**	CASE NUMBER:

You must file this claim with the court clerk at the court address above before the LATER of (a) four months after the date letters (authority to act for the estate) were first issued to the personal representative, or (b) thirty days after the date Notice of Administration was given to the creditor, if notice was given as provided in Probate Code section 9051. Mail or deliver a copy of this claim to the personal representative. A proof of service is on the reverse.

1. Total amount of the claim: $
2. Claimant *(name)*:
   a. ☐ an individual.
   b. ☐ an individual or entity doing business under the fictitious name of *(specify)*:
   c. ☐ a partnership. The person signing has authority to sign on behalf of the partnership.
   d. ☐ a corporation. The person signing has authority to sign on behalf of the corporation.
   e. ☐ other *(specify)*:
3. Address of claimant *(specify)*:
4. Claimant is ☐ the creditor ☐ a person acting on behalf of creditor *(state reason)*:
5. ☐ Claimant is ☐ the personal representative ☐ the attorney for the personal representative. *(Claims against the estate by the personal representative and the attorney for the personal representative must be filed within the claim period allowed in Probate Code section 9100. See the notice box above.)*
6. I am authorized to make this claim which is just and due or may become due. All payments on or offsets to the claim have been credited. Facts supporting the claim are ☐ on reverse ☐ attached.

I declare under penalty of perjury under the laws of the State of California that this creditor's claim is true and correct.

Date:

. . . . ▶ ________________________________

(TYPE OR PRINT NAME AND TITLE) (SIGNATURE OF CLAIMANT)

INSTRUCTIONS TO CLAIMANT

A. On the reverse, itemize the claim and show the date the service was rendered or the debt incurred. Describe the item or service in detail, and indicate the amount claimed for each item. Do not include debts incurred after the date of death, except funeral claims.

B. If the claim is not due or contingent, or the amount is not yet ascertainable, state the facts supporting the claim.

C. If the claim is secured by a note or other written instrument, the original or a copy must be attached (state why original is unavailable). If secured by mortgage, deed of trust, or other lien on property that is of record, it is sufficient to describe the security and refer to the date or volume and page, and county where recorded. (See Probate Code section 9152.)

D. Mail or take this original claim to the court clerk's office for filing. If mailed, use certified mail, with return receipt requested.

E. Mail or deliver a copy to the personal representative. Complete the Proof of Mailing or Personal Delivery on the reverse.

F. The personal representative will notify you when your claim is allowed or rejected.

(Continued on reverse)

* See instructions before completing. Use Creditor's Claim form No. DE-170 for estates filed before July 1, 1988.

ESTATE OF (NAME): DECEDENT	CASE NUMBER:

FACTS SUPPORTING THE CREDITOR'S CLAIM

☐ **See attachment** ***(if space is insufficient)***

Date of Item	Item and Supporting Facts	Amount Claimed
	TOTAL	**$**

PROOF OF ☐ MAILING ☐ PERSONAL DELIVERY TO PERSONAL REPRESENTATIVE

(Be sure to mail or take the original to the court clerk's office for filing)

1. I am the creditor or a person acting on behalf of the creditor. At the time of mailing or delivery I was at least 18 years of age.
2. My residence or business address is *(specify)*:
3. I mailed or delivered a copy of this Creditor's Claim to the personal representative as follows *(check either a or b below)*:
   a. ☐ **First-class mail.** I deposited a copy of the claim with the United States Postal Service, in a sealed envelope with postage fully prepaid. I used first-class mail. I am a resident of or employed in the county where the mailing occurred. The envelope was addressed and mailed as follows:
      (1) Name of personal representative served:
      (2) Address on envelope:
      (3) Date of mailing:
      (4) Place of mailing *(city and state)*:
   b. ☐ **Personal delivery.** I personally delivered a copy of the claim to the personal representative as follows:
      (1) Name of personal representative served:
      (2) Address where delivered:
      (3) Date delivered:
      (4) Time delivered:

I declare under penalty of perjury under the laws of the State of California that the foregoing is true and correct.

Date:

. . . . ▶ ______________________________

(TYPE OR PRINT NAME OF CLAIMANT) (SIGNATURE OF CLAIMANT)

ATTORNEY OR PARTY WITHOUT ATTORNEY *(Name and Address)*: TELEPHONE NO.:	FOR COURT USE ONLY
ATTORNEY FOR *(Name)*:	
NAME OF COURT: STREET ADDRESS: MAILING ADDRESS: CITY AND ZIP CODE: BRANCH NAME:	
PLAINTIFF: DEFENDANT:	
APPLICATION FOR ENTRY OF JUDGMENT ON SISTER-STATE JUDGMENT ☐ **AND ISSUANCE OF WRIT OF EXECUTION OR OTHER ENFORCEMENT** ☐ **AND ORDER FOR ISSUANCE OF WRIT OR OTHER ENFORCEMENT**	CASE NUMBER:

Judgment creditor applies for entry of a judgment based upon a sister-state judgment as follows:

1. Judgment creditor *(name and address)*:

2. a. Judgment debtor *(name)*:

   b. ☐ An individual *(last known residence address)*:

   c. ☐ A corporation of *(specify place of incorporation)*:

      (1) ☐ Foreign corporation
         ☐ qualified to do business in California
         ☐ not qualified to do business in California

   d. ☐ A partnership *(specify principal place of business)*:

      (1) ☐ Foreign partnership which
         ☐ has filed a statement under Corp C 15700
         ☐ has not filed a statement under Corp C 15700

3. a. Sister state *(name)*:

   b. Sister-state court *(name and location)*:

   c. Judgment entered in sister state on *(date)*:

4. **An authenticated copy of the sister-state judgment is attached to this application.** Include accrued interest on the sister-state judgment in the California judgment (item 5c).
   a. Annual interest rate allowed by sister state *(specify)*:

   b. Law of sister state establishing interest rate *(specify)*:

5. a. Amount remaining unpaid on sister-state judgment: . . . . $
   b. Amount of filing fee for the application: . . . . $
   c. Accrued interest on sister-state judgment . . . . $

   d. Amount of judgment to be entered *(total of 5a, b, and c)*: . . . . $ ______

(Continued on reverse)

OBLIGEE: OBLIGOR:	CASE NUMBER:

6. The obligee is informed and believes that the description and location of obligor's property subject to execution is as follows:

DECLARATION

I declare under penalty of perjury under the laws of the state of California that the foregoing is true and correct.

Date:

. . . . ▶ ________________________________

(TYPE OR PRINT NAME) (SIGNATURE OF OBLIGEE, PERSON HAVING LEGAL CUSTODY OF MINOR OBLIGEE, OR PERSON ACTING ON BEHALF OF OBLIGEE PURSUANT TO AN ASSIGNMENT OF RIGHTS)

NOTICE TO OBLIGOR

7. **To obligor** *(name)*:

8. You are notified that a ☐ Foreign Support Order ☐ Foreign Order For Assignment of Wages For Support has been registered with this court. A copy of the order is attached and the mailing address of the obligee is shown in this statement.

Date: Clerk, by ________________________________, Deputy

CLERK'S CERTIFICATE OF MAILING

1. I certify that I am not a party to this cause and that a copy of the foregoing statement with a certified copy of the foreign order were sent to obligor by certified mail, return receipt from the addressee only requested. The copies were enclosed in an envelope with postage fully prepaid. The envelope was addressed to the obligor only at the address in the foregoing statement, sealed, and deposited with the United States Postal Service
at *(place)*:
on *(date)*:

Date: Clerk, by ________________________________, Deputy

2. **Copy** sent to prosecuting attorney on *(date)*: by ________________________________, Deputy

SHORT TITLE:	CASE NUMBER:

6. ☐ Judgment creditor also applies for issuance of a writ of execution or enforcement by other means before service of notice of entry of judgment as follows:

   a. ☐ Under CCP 1710.45(b).

   b. ☐ A court order is requested under CCP 1710.45(c). Facts showing that great or irreparable injury will result to judgment creditor if issuance of the writ or enforcement by other means is delayed are set forth as follows:

   ☐ continued in attachment 6b.

7. An action in this state on the sister-state judgment is not barred by the statute of limitations.

8. I am informed and believe that no stay of enforcement of the sister-state judgment is now in effect in the sister state.

9. No action is pending and no judgment has previously been entered in any proceeding in California based upon the sister-state judgment.

I declare under penalty of perjury under the laws of the State of California that the foregoing is true and correct except as to those matters which are stated to be upon information and belief, and as to those matters I believe them to be true.

Date:

. . . . ▶ ______________________________

(TYPE OR PRINT NAME) *(SIGNATURE OF JUDGMENT CREDITOR OR ATTORNEY)*

PROOF OF SERVICE

(Use separate proof of service for each person served)

1. I served the Notice of Entry of Judgment on Sister-State Judgment as follows:
   a. on judgment debtor *(name)*:

   b. by serving ☐ judgment debtor ☐ other *(name and title or relationship to person served)*:

   c. ☐ by delivery ☐ at home ☐ at business
      (1) date:
      (2) time:
      (3) address:

   d. ☐ by mailing
      (1) date:
      (2) place:

2. Manner of service *(check proper box)*:
   a. ☐ **Personal service.** By personally delivering copies. (CCP 415.10)
   b. ☐ **Substituted service on corporation, unincorporated association (including partnership), or public entity.** By leaving, during usual office hours, copies in the office of the person served with the person who apparently was in charge and thereafter mailing (by first-class mail, postage prepaid) copies to the person served at the place where the copies were left. (CCP 415.20(a))
   c. ☐ **Substituted service on natural person, minor, conservatee, or candidate.** By leaving copies at the dwelling house, usual place of abode, or usual place of business of the person served in the presence of a competent member of the household or a person apparently in charge of the office or place of business, at least 18 years of age, who was informed of the general nature of the papers, and thereafter mailing (by first-class mail, postage prepaid) copies to the person served at the place where the copies were left. (CCP 415.20(b)) ***(Attach separate declaration or affidavit stating acts relied on to establish reasonable diligence in first attempting personal service.)***
   d. ☐ **Mail and acknowledgment service.** By mailing (by first-class mail or airmail, postage prepaid) copies to the person served, together with two copies of the form of notice and acknowledgment and a return envelope, postage prepaid, addressed to the sender. (CCP 415.30) ***(Attach completed acknowledgment of receipt.)***
   e. ☐ **Certified or registered mail service.** By mailing to an address outside California (by first-class mail, postage prepaid, requiring a return receipt) copies to the person served. (CCP 415.40) ***(Attach signed return receipt or other evidence of actual delivery to the person served.)***
   f. ☐ Other *(specify code section)*:
      ☐ Additional page is attached.

3. The "Notice to the Person Served" was completed as follows:
   a. ☐ as an individual judgment debtor.
   b. ☐ as the person sued under the fictitious name of *(specify)*:
   c. ☐ on behalf of *(specify)*:
      under: ☐ CCP 416.10 (corporation) ☐ CCP 416.60 (minor) ☐ other:
      ☐ CCP 416.20 (defunct corporation) ☐ CCP 416.70 (conservatee)
      ☐ CCP 416.40 (association or partnership) ☐ CCP 416.90 (individual)

4. At the time of service I was at least 18 years of age and not a party to this action.
5. Fee for service: $
6. Person serving:
   a. ☐ California sheriff, marshal, or constable.
   b. ☐ Registered California process server.
   c. ☐ Employee or independent contractor of a registered California process server.
   d. ☐ Not a registered California process server.
   e. ☐ Exempt from registration under Bus. & Prof. Code 22350(b).
   f. Name, address and telephone number and, if applicable, county of registration and number:

I declare under penalty of perjury under the laws of the State of California that the foregoing is true and correct.

Date:

▶ ______________________________
(SIGNATURE)

(For California sheriff, marshal, or constable use only)
I certify that the foregoing is true and correct.

Date:

▶ ______________________________
(SIGNATURE)

ATTORNEY OR PARTY WITHOUT ATTORNEY *(Name and Address)*: TELEPHONE NO.:	*FOR COURT USE ONLY*
ATTORNEY FOR *(Name)*:	
NAME OF COURT: STREET ADDRESS: MAILING ADDRESS: CITY AND ZIP CODE: BRANCH NAME:	
OBLIGEE: OBLIGOR:	
STATEMENT FOR REGISTRATION OF FOREIGN SUPPORT ORDER AND CLERK'S NOTICE ☐ **Support Order** ☐ **Order For Assignment of Wages For Support**	CASE NUMBER:

Obligee's statement to register ☐ foreign support order ☐ foreign order for assignment of wages for support is as follows:

1. Obligee *(name)*:
   a. Mailing address:

   b. Residence address:

2. Obligor *(name)*:
   a. Last known mailing address:

   b. Last known residence address:

3. Three certified copies of the following described support order or order for assignment of wages for support, with all modifications, are filed with this statement as required by Code of Civil Procedure section 1698.3.
   a. Name of state and title of court:

   b. Date of order and of all modifications of order:

4. The order is registered in the following states *(specify the name and location of the court in each state and the type of order)*:

5. Amount of support now due and remaining unpaid: $

(Continued on reverse)

NOTICE TO OBLIGOR

If you wish, you have 20 days after the date of mailing of Notice of Registration to petition the court to vacate the registration of the Foreign Support Order or Foreign Order For Assignment of Wages or for other relief. *(See reverse for clerk's date of mailing.)* (Code of Civil Procedure, § 1699(b).)

The original and two copies of this statement, and one copy of the reciprocal enforcement of support act of the state in which the order was made, must be submitted for filing.

ATTORNEY OR PARTY WITHOUT ATTORNEY *(Name and Address)*: TELEPHONE NO.:	*FOR COURT USE ONLY*
ATTORNEY FOR *(Name)*:	
NAME OF COURT: STREET ADDRESS: MAILING ADDRESS: CITY AND ZIP CODE: BRANCH NAME:	
PLAINTIFF: DEFENDANT:	
NOTICE OF ENTRY OF JUDGMENT ON SISTER-STATE JUDGMENT	CASE NUMBER:

1. TO JUDGMENT DEBTOR *(name)*:

2. YOU ARE NOTIFIED

   a. Upon application of the judgment creditor, a judgment against you has been entered in this court as follows:

      (1) Judgment creditor *(name)*:

      (2) Amount of judgment entered in this court: $

   b. This judgment was entered based upon a sister-state judgment previously entered against you as follows:

      (1) Sister state *(name)*:

      (2) Sister-state court *(name and location)*:

      (3) Judgment entered in sister state on *(date)*:

      (4) Title of case and case number *(specify)*:

3. **A sister-state judgment has been entered against you in a California court. Unless you file a motion to vacate the judgment in this court within 30 DAYS after service of this notice, this judgment will be final.**

   This court may order that a writ of execution or other enforcement may issue. Your wages, money, and property could be taken without further warning from the court.

   If enforcement procedures have already been issued, the property levied on will not be distributed until 30 days after you are served with this notice.

Date: Clerk, by ______________________________, Deputy

4. ☐ NOTICE TO THE PERSON SERVED: You are served
   a. ☐ as an individual judgment debtor.
   b. ☐ under the fictitious name of *(specify)*:
   c. ☐ on behalf of *(specify)*:

   Under:
   ☐ CCP 416.10 (corporation) ☐ CCP 416.60 (minor)
   ☐ CCP 416.20 (defunct corporation) ☐ CCP 416.70 (conservatee)
   ☐ CCP 416.40 (association or partnership) ☐ CCP 416.90 (individual)
   ☐ other:

[SEAL]

(Proof of service on reverse)

Form Approved by the Judicial Council of California EJ-110 [Rev. July 1, 1983]

NOTICE OF ENTRY OF JUDGMENT ON SISTER-STATE JUDGMENT

CCP 1710.30, 1710.40 1710.45

ATTORNEY OR PARTY WITHOUT ATTORNEY *(Name and Address)*: TELEPHONE NO.:	FOR RECORDER'S OR SECRETARY OF STATE'S USE ONLY
ATTORNEY FOR *(Name)*:	
NAME OF COURT: STREET ADDRESS: MAILING ADDRESS: CITY AND ZIP CODE: BRANCH NAME:	
PLAINTIFF: DEFENDANT:	
ACKNOWLEDGMENT OF SATISFACTION OF JUDGMENT ☐ **FULL** ☐ **PARTIAL** ☐ **MATURED INSTALLMENT**	CASE NUMBER:

FOR COURT USE ONLY

1. Satisfaction of the judgment is acknowledged as follows *(see footnote* before completing)*:
   a. ☐ Full satisfaction
      (1) ☐ Judgment is satisfied in full.
      (2) ☐ The judgment creditor has accepted payment or performance other than that specified in the judgment in full satisfaction of the judgment.
   b. ☐ Partial satisfaction
      The amount received in partial satisfaction of the judgment is
      $
   c. ☐ Matured installment
      All matured installments under the installment judgment have been satisfied as of *(date)*:
2. Full name and address of judgment creditor:

3. Full name and address of assignee of record, if any:

4. Full name and address of judgment debtor being fully or partially released:

5. a. Judgment entered on *(date)*:
      ☐ (1) in judgment book volume no.: (2) page no.:
   b. ☐ Renewal entered on *(date)*:
      ☐ (1) in judgment book volume no.: (2) page no.:

6. ☐ An ☐ abstract of judgment ☐ certified copy of the judgment has been recorded as follows *(complete all information for each county where recorded)*:

COUNTY	DATE OF RECORDING	BOOK NUMBER	PAGE NUMBER

7. ☐ A notice of judgment lien has been filed in the office of the Secretary of State as file number *(specify)*:

NOTICE TO JUDGMENT DEBTOR: If this is an acknowledgment of full satisfaction of judgment, it will have to be recorded in each county shown in item 6 above, if any, in order to release the judgment lien, and will have to be filed in the office of the Secretary of State to terminate any judgment lien on personal property.

Date: ▶

(SIGNATURE OF JUDGMENT CREDITOR OR ASSIGNEE OF CREDITOR OR ATTORNEY)

*The names of the judgment creditor and judgment debtor must be stated as shown in any Abstract of Judgment which was recorded and is being released by this satisfaction. **A separate notary acknowledgment must be attached for each signature.**

PARTY WITHOUT ATTORNEY *(My Name and Address)*: MY TELEPHONE NO.:	**FOR COURT USE ONLY**
NAME OF COURT: STREET ADDRESS: MAILING ADDRESS: CITY AND ZIP CODE: BRANCH NAME:	
PLAINTIFF/JUDGMENT CREDITOR: DEFENDANT/JUDGMENT DEBTOR:	
PROOF OF PERSONAL SERVICE (CCP Sections 1011, 2015.5)	CASE NUMBER:

I declare that:

1. At the time of service I was at least 18 years of age and not a party to this legal action.
2. I am a resident of or employed in the county of ______________________________, California.
3. My business or residence address is: ____.
4. I served copies of the following paper(s) in the manner shown:

   a. Papers served [list exact titles of paper(s)]:

   b. Manner of service: Personal Service. I personally delivered these papers to the following:

      (1) Name of person served: ______________________________

      (2) Address where served: ______________________________________

      (3) Date served: ______________

      (4) Time served: ______________

5. I declare under penalty of perjury under the laws of the State of California that the foregoing is true and correct. Executed on ______________ at ______________________________, California.

____

[Signature of Person Who Served Papers]

Print Name: ______________________

PARTY WITHOUT ATTORNEY *(My Name and Address)*: MY TELEPHONE NO.:	***FOR COURT USE ONLY***
NAME OF COURT: STREET ADDRESS: MAILING ADDRESS: CITY AND ZIP CODE: BRANCH NAME:	
PLAINTIFF/JUDGMENT CREDITOR: DEFENDANT/JUDGMENT DEBTOR:	
PROOF OF SERVICE BY MAIL (CCP Sections 1013a, 2015.5)	CASE NUMBER

I declare that:

1. At the time of service I was at least 18 years of age and not a party to this legal action.
2. I am a resident of or employed in the county where the mailing occurred.
3. My business or residence address is: ______________________________________.
4. I served copies of the following paper(s) in the manner shown:

   a. Papers served [list exact titles of paper(s)]:

   b. Manner of service: by placing true copies in a sealed envelope addressed to each person whose name and address is given below and:

   ☐ depositing the envelope in the United States Mail with the postage fully prepaid; or

   ☐ (If deposited at a business:) Placing for collection and mailing following ordinary business practices. I am readily familiar with the business practice for collection and processing of correspondence for mailing with the United States Post Office. The correspondence will be deposited with the United States Post office on the same date as the date of deposit (below) in the ordinary course of business.

   (1) Date of Deposit: ______________________

   (2) Place of Deposit (city & state; business address if deposited at a business) : ______________________

5. I declare under penalty of perjury under the laws of the State of California that the foregoing is true and correct. Executed on ______________________ at ______________________, California.

Print Name: ______________________ ______________________

[Signature of Person Who Served Papers]

Name and Address of Each Person to Whom Documents Were Mailed:

☐ Additional names and addresses on reverse.

Index

A

B

C

D

E

F

G

M

N

O

P

R

S

T

GET 25% OFF YOUR NEXT PURCHASE

RECYCLE YOUR OUT-OF-DATE BOOKS

It's important to have the most current legal information. Because laws and legal procedures change often, we update our books regularly. To help keep you up-to-date we are extending this special offer. Cut out and mail the title portion of the cover of any old Nolo book with your next order and we'll give you a 25% discount off the retail price of ANY new Nolo book you purchase directly from us. For current prices and editions call us at 1-800-992-6656.

This offer is to individuals only.

MORE BOOKS FROM NOLO...

Everybody's Guide to Small Claims Court
by Attorney Ralph Warner
$18.95/CSCC

Everybody's Guide to Municipal Court
by Judge Roderic Duncan
$29.95/MUNI

Legal Research
by Attorneys Stephen Elias and Susan Levenkind
$19.95/LRES

Represent Yourself in Court
by Attorneys Paul Bergman and Sara J. Berman-Barrett
$29.95/RYC

TO ORDER CALL **1-800-992-6656** OR USE
THE ORDER FORM IN THE BACK OF THE BOOK

CATALOG

. . . more books & software from Nolo

ESTATE PLANNING & PROBATE

Plan Your Estate
Attorneys Denis Clifford & Cora Jordan. Nat'l 3rd ed.
Thoroughly revised and updated, this is the most comprehensive estate planing book available. It covers everything from basic estate planning to sophisticated tax saving stratagies. Includes information on federal estate and gift taxes, estate tax saving trusts, trusts used to control property left to beneficiaries, charitable remainder trusts, durable powers of attorney, living wills, funerals and burials. Good in all states except Lousiana.
$24.95/NEST

Make Your Own Living Trust
Attorney Denis Clifford. Nat'l 1st ed.
Find out how a living trust works, how to create one, and how to determine what kind of trust is right for you. Contains all the forms and instructions you need to prepare a basic living trust to avoid probate, a marital life estate trust (A-B trust) to avoid probate and estate taxes, and a back-up will. Good in all states except Louisiana.
$19.95/LITR

Nolo's Simple Will Book
Attorney Denis Clifford. Nat'l 2nd ed.
It's easy to write a legally valid will using this book. Includes all the instructions and sample forms you need to name a personal guardian for minor children, leave property to minor children or young adults and update a will when necessary. Good in all states except Louisiana.
$17.95/SWIL

Who Will Handle Your Finances If You Can't?
Attorneys Denis Clifford & Mary Randolph. Nat'l 1st ed.
Give a trusted person legal authority to handle your financial matters if illness or old age makes it impossible for you to handle them yourself. Create a durable power of attorney for finances with the step-by-step instructions and fill-in-the-blank forms included in this book.
$19.95/FINA

The Conservatorship Book
Lisa Goldoftas & Attorney Carolyn Farren. CA 2nd ed.
Provides forms and all instructions necessary to file conservatorship documents, appear in court, be appointed conservator and end a conservatorship.
$29.95/CNSV

How to Probate an Estate
Julia Nissley. CA 8th ed.
Save costly attorneys' fees by handling the probate process yourself. This book shows you step-by-step how to settle an estate. It also explains the simple procedures you can use to transfer assets that don't require probate. Forms included.
$34.95/PAE

audio cassette tapes

5 Ways to Avoid Probate
Attorney Ralph Warner with Joanne Greene. Nat'l 1st ed. 60 minutes
Provides clear, in-depth explanations of the principal probate avoidance techniques: joint tenancy, insurance, living trusts, savings account trusts and pension plans.
$14.95/KWL

Write Your Will
Attorney Ralph Warner with Joanne Greene. Nat'l 1st ed. 60 minutes
If you're getting ready to write your will, this tape is a good place to start. It answers the most frequently asked questions about writing a will and covers all key issues.
$14.95/TWYW

law form kits

Nolo's Law Form Kit: Wills
Attorney Denis Clifford & Lisa Goldoftas. Nat'l 1st ed.
All the forms and instructions you need to create a legally valid will, quickly and easily.
$14.95/KWL

software

Living Trust Maker
Version 2.0
Put your assets into a trust and save your heirs the headache, time and expense of probate with this easy-to-use software. Use it to set up an individual or shared marital trust, transfer property to the trust, and change or revoke the trust at any time. Its manual guides you through the process, and legal help screens and an on-line glossary explain key legal terms and concepts. Good in all states except Louisiana.
WINDOWS $79.95/LTWI2
MACINTOSH $79.95/LTM2

WillMaker®
Version 5.0
Make your own legal will and living will (healthcare directive)—and thoroughly document your final arrangements—with *WillMaker 5*. Its easy-to-use interview format takes you through each document step-by-step. On-line legal help is available throughout the program. Name a guardian for your children, make up to 100 property bequests, direct your healthcare in the event of coma or terminal illness, and let your loved ones know your wishes around your own final arrangements.
WINDOWS $69.95/WIW5
DOS $69.95/WI5
MACINTOSH $69.95/WM5

Nolo's Personal RecordKeeper
Version 3.0
Finally, a safe, accessible place for your important records. Over 200 categories and subcategories to organize and store your important financial, legal and personal information, compute your net worth and create inventories for insurance records. Export your net worth and home inventory data to Quicken®.
DOS $49.95/FRI3
MACINTOSH $49.95/FRM3

BUSINESS/WORKPLACE

The Legal Guide for Starting & Running a Small Business
Attorney Fred S. Steingold. Nat'l 1st ed.
An essential resource for every small business owner. Find out how to form a sole proprietorship, partnership or corporation, negotiate a favorable lease, hire and fire employees, write contracts and resolve disputes.
$22.95/RUNS

Sexual Harassment on the Job: What It Is and How to Stop It
Attorneys William Petrocelli & Barbara Kate Repa. Nat'l 2nd ed.
An invaluable resource for both employees experiencing harassment and employers interested in creating a policy against sexual harassment and a procedure for handling complaints.
$18.95/HARS

Marketing Without Advertising
Michael Phillips & Salli Rasberry. Nat'l 1st ed.
Outlines practical steps for building and expanding a small business without spending a lot of money on advertising.
$14.00/MWAD

Your Rights in the Workplace
Attorney Barbara Kate Repa. Nat'l 2nd ed.

The first comprehensive guide to workplace rights—from hiring to firing. Covers wages and overtime, parental leave, unemployment and disability insurance, worker's compensation, job safety, discrimination and illegal firings and layoffs.

$15.95/YRW

How to Write a Business Plan
Mike McKeever. Nat'l 4th ed.

This book will show you how to write the business plan and loan package necessary to finance your business and make it work.

$21.95/SBS

The Partnership Book
Attorneys Denis Clifford & Ralph Warner. Nat'l 4th ed.

Shows you step-by-step how to write a solid partnership agreement that meets your needs. It covers initial contributions to the business, wages, profit-sharing, buy-outs, death or retirement of a partner and disputes.

$24.95/PART

The California Nonprofit Corporation Handbook
Attorney Anthony Mancuso. CA 6th ed.

Shows you step-by-step how to form and operate a nonprofit corporation in California. It includes the latest corporate and tax law changes, and the forms for the Articles, Bylaws and Minutes.

$29.95/NON

How to Form Your Own Corporation
Attorney Anthony Mancuso. CA 8th ed.

This book contain the forms, instructions and tax information you need to incorporate a small business yourself and save hundreds of dollars in lawyers' fees.

California $29.95/CCOR
New York $29.95/NYCO
Texas $29.95/TCOR

The California Professional Corporation Handbook
Attorney Anthony Mancuso. CA 5th ed.

Health care professionals, lawyers, accountants and members of certain other professions must fulfill special requirements when forming a corporation in California. Contains up-to-date tax information plus all the forms and instructions necessary.

$34.95/PROF

The Independent Paralegal's Handbook
Attorney Ralph Warner. Nat'l 3rd ed.

Provides legal and business guidelines for anyone who wants to go into business as an independent paralegal helping consumers with routine legal tasks.

$29.95 PARA

books with disk

How to Form a Nonprofit Corporation
Attorney Anthony Mancuso. Nat'l 2nd ed.

Explains the legal formalities involved and provides detailed information on the differences in the law among all 50 states. It also contains forms for the Articles, Bylaws and Minutes you need, along with complete instructions for obtaining federal 501(c)(3) tax exemptions and qualifying for public charity status. Includes incorporation forms on disk.

DOS $39.95/NNP

How to Form Your Own Corporation
Attorney Anthony Mancuso.

Step-by-step guide to forming your own corporation. Provides clear instructions and all the forms you need including Articles, Bylaws, Minutes and Stock Certificates. Includes all incorporation forms on disk.

Florida DOS $39.95/FLCO
New York DOS $39.95/NYCO
Texas DOS $39.95/TCI

Taking Care of Your Corporation, Vol. 1: Director and Shareholder Meetings Made Easy
Attorney Anthony Mancuso. Nat'l 1st ed.

This book takes the drudgery out of the necessary task of holding meetings of the board of directors and shareholders. It shows how to comply with state laws for holding meetings, how to prepare minutes for annual and special meetings, take corporate action by written consent, hold real or paper meetings and handle corporate formalities using e-mail, computer bulletin boards, fax and telephone and video conferencing. Includes all corporate forms on disk.

DOS $26.95/CORK

How to Form Your Own California Corporation With Corporate Records Binder & Disk
Attorney Anthony Mancuso. CA 1st Ed.

How to Form Your Own California Corporation is also available in a handy new format. It includes all the forms and instructions you need to form your own corporation, a corporate records binder, stock certificates and all incorporation forms on disk.

$39.95/CACI

The California Nonprofit Corporation Handbook
Attorney Anthony Mancuso. Version 1.0

This book with disk package shows you step-by-step how to form and operate a nonprofit corporation in California. Included on disk are the forms for the Articles, Bylaws and Minutes.

DOS $39.95 NPI
MACINTOSH $39.95 NPM

Software Development: A Legal Guide
Attorney Stephen Fishman. Nat'l 1st ed.

Clearly explains patent, copyright, trademark and trade secret protection and shows how to draft development contracts and employment agreements. Includes all contracts and agreements on disk.

DOS $44.95/SFT

software

Nolo's Partnership Maker
Version 1.0

Prepares a legal partnership agreement for doing business in any state. Select and assemble the standard partnership clauses provided or create your own customized agreement. Includes on-line legal help screens, glossary and tutorial, and a manual that takes you through the process step-by-step.

DOS $129.95/PAGI1

California Incorporator
Version 1.0 (good only in CA)

Answer the questions on the screen and this software program will print out the 35-40 pages of documents you need to make your California corporation legal. A 200-page manual explains the incorporation process.

DOS $129.00/INCI

audio cassette tapes

How to Start Your Own Business: Small Business Law
Attorney Ralph Warner with Joanne Greene. Nat'l 1st ed. 60 minutes

This tape covers what every small business owner needs to know about organizing as a sole proprietorship, partnership or corporation, protecting the business name, renting space, hiring employees and paying taxes.

$14.95/TBUS

Getting Started as an Independent Paralegal
Attorney Ralph Warner. Nat'l 2nd ed. Two tapes, approximately 2 hrs.

Practical and legal advice on going into business as an independent paralegal from the author of *The Independent Paralegal's Handbook.*

$44.95/GSIP

GOING TO COURT

How to Change Your Name
Attorneys David Loeb & David Brown. CA 6th ed.

All the forms and instructions you need to change your name in California.

$24.95/NAME

Represent Yourself in Court

Attorneys Paul Bergman & Sara Berman-Barrett. Nat'l 1st ed.

Handle your own civil court case from start to finish without a lawyer with the most thorough guide to contested court cases ever published for the non-lawyer. Covers all aspects of civil trials.

$29.95/RYC

Everybody's Guide to Municipal Court

Judge Roderic Duncan. CA 1st ed.

Sue and defend cases for up to $25,000 in California Municipal Court. Gives step-by-step instructions for preparing and filing forms, gathering evidence and appearing in court.

$29.95/MUNI

Everybody's Guide to Small Claims Court

Attorney Ralph Warner. Nat'l 5th ed. CA 11th ed.

These books will help you decide if you should sue in Small Claims Court, show you how to file and serve papers, tell you what to bring to court and how to collect a judgment.

National $18.95/NSCC
California $18.95/CSCC

Fight Your Ticket

Attorney David Brown. CA 5th ed.

Shows you how to fight an unfair traffic ticket—when you're stopped, at arraignment, at trial and on appeal.

$18.95/FYT

Collect Your Court Judgment

Gini Graham Scott, Attorney Stephen Elias & Lisa Goldoftas. CA 2nd ed.

Contains step-by-step instructions and all the forms you need to collect a court judgment from the debtor's bank accounts, wages, business receipts, real estate or other assets.

$19.95/JUDG

The Criminal Records Book

Attorney Warren Siegel. CA 3rd ed.

Shows you step-by-step how to seal criminal records, dismiss convictions, destroy marijuana records and reduce felony convictions.

$19.95/CRIM

audio cassette tapes

Winning in Small Claims Court

Attorney Ralph Warner with Joanne Greene. Nat'l 1st ed. 60 minutes

Guides you through all the major issues involved in preparing and winning a small claims court case—deciding if there is a good case, assessing whether you can collect if you win, preparing your evidence, and arguing before the judge.

$14.95/TWIN

THE NEIGHBORHOOD

Dog Law

Attorney Mary Randolph. Nat'l 2nd ed.

A practical guide to the laws that affect dog owners and their neighbors. Answers common questions about biting, barking, veterinarians and more.

$12.95/DOG

Neighbor Law: Fences, Trees, Boundaries & Noise

Attorney Cora Jordan. Nat'l 2nd ed.

Answers common questions about the subjects that most often trigger disputes between neighbors: fences, trees, boundaries and noise. It explains how to find the law and resolve disputes without a nasty lawsuit.

$16.95/NEI

Safe Homes, Safe Neighborhoods: Stopping Crime Where You Live

Stephanie Mann with M.C. Blakeman. Nat'l 1st ed.

Learn how you and your neighbors can work together to protect yourselves, your families and property from crime. Explains how to form a neighborhood crime prevention group; avoid burglaries, car thefts, muggings and rapes; combat gangs and drug dealing; improve home security and make the neighborhood safer for children.

$14.95/SAFE

FAMILY MATTERS

The Living Together Kit

Attorneys Toni Ihara & Ralph Warner. Nat'l 7th ed.

A detailed guide designed to help the increasing number of unmarried couples living together understand the laws that affect them. Sample agreements and instructions are included.

$24.95/LTK

A Legal Guide for Lesbian and Gay Couples

Attorneys Hayden Curry, Denis Clifford & Robin Leonard. Nat'l 8th ed.

This book shows lesbian and gay couples how to write a living-together contract, plan for medical emergencies, understand the practical and legal aspects of having and raising children and plan their estates. Includes forms and sample agreements.

$24.95/LG

Divorce: A New Yorker's Guide to Doing it Yourself

Bliss Alexandra. New York 1st ed.

Step-by-step instructions and all the forms you need to do your own divorce and save thousands of dollars in legal fees. Shows you how to divide property, arrange custody of the children, set child support and maintenance (alimony), draft a divorce agreement and fill out and file all forms.

$24.95/NYDIV

Nolo's Pocket Guide to Family Law

Attorneys Robin Leonard & Stephen Elias. Nat'l 3rd ed.

Here's help for anyone who has a question or problem involving family law—marriage, divorce, adoption or living together.

$14.95/FLD

Divorce & Money

Violet Woodhouse & Victoria Felton-Collins with M.C. Blakeman. Nat'l 2nd ed.

Explains how to evaluate such major assets as family homes and businesses, investments, pensions, and how to arrive at a division of property that is fair to both sides.

$21.95/DIMO

How to Raise or Lower Child Support in California

Judge Roderic Duncan & Attorney Warren Siegal. CA 2nd ed.

Appropriate for parents on either side of the support issue. All the forms and instructions necessary to raise or lower an existing child support order.

$17.95/CHLD

The Guardianship Book

Lisa Goldoftas & Attorney David Brown. CA 1st ed.

Provides step-by-step instructions and the forms needed to obtain a legal guardianship of a minor without a lawyer.

$19.95/GB

How to Adopt Your Stepchild in California

Frank Zagone & Attorney Mary Randolph. CA 4th ed.

Provides sample forms and step-by-step instructions for completing a simple uncontested stepparent adoption in California.

$22.95/ADOP

Smart Ways to Save Money During and After Divorce

Victoria F. Collins & Ginita Wall. Nat'l 1st ed.

If you're going through a divorce, most likely you're faced with an overwhelming number of financial decisions. Here's a book packed with information on how to save money before, during and after divorce. It covers how to keep attorney's fees low, save on taxes, divide assets fairly, understand child support and alimony obligations and put aside money now for expenses later.

$14.95/SAVMO

California Marriage & Divorce Law

Attorneys Ralph Warner, Toni Ihara & Stephen Elias. CA 11th ed.

Explains community property, pre-nuptial contracts, foreign marriages, buying a house, getting a divorce, dividing property, and more. Pre-nuptial contracts included.

$19.95/MARR

Practical Divorce Solutions

Attorney Charles Sherman. Nat'l 1st ed.

Covers the emotional aspects of divorce and provides an overview of the legal and financial considerations.

$14.95/PDS

How to Do Your Own Divorce

Attorney Charles Sherman (Texas ed. by Sherman & Simons). CA 19th ed. & Texas 5th ed.

These books contain all the forms and instructions you need to do your own uncontested divorce without a lawyer.

California $21.95/CDIV
Texas $17.95/TDIV

MONEY MATTERS

Stand Up to the IRS

Attorney Fred Daily. Nat'l 2nd ed.

Gives detailed strategies on surviving an audit, appealing an audit decision, going to Tax Court and dealing with IRS collectors. It also discusses filing delinquent tax returns, tax crimes, concerns of small business people and getting help from the IRS ombudsman.

$21.95/SIRS

How to File for Bankruptcy

Attorneys Stephen Elias, Albin Renauer & Robin Leonard. Nat'l 4th ed.

Trying to decide whether or not filing for bankruptcy makes sense? This book contains an overview of the process and all the forms plus step-by-step instructions you need to file for Chapter 7 Bankruptcy.

$25.95/HFB

Money Troubles: Legal Strategies to Cope With Your Debts

Attorney Robin Leonard. Nat'l 2nd ed.

Essential for anyone who has gotten behind on bills. It shows how to obtain a credit file, negotiate with persistent creditors, challenge wage attachments, contend with property repossessions and more.

$16.95/MT

Simple Contracts for Personal Use

Attorney Stephen Elias & Marcia Stewart. Nat'l 2nd ed.

Contains clearly written legal form contracts to buy and sell property, borrow and lend money, store and lend personal property, release others from personal liability, or pay a contractor to do home repairs. Includes agreements to arrange child care and other household help.

$16.95/CONT

law form kits

Nolo's Law Form Kit: Power of Attorney

Attorneys Denis Clifford & Mary Randolph and Lisa Goldoftas. Nat'l 1st ed.

Create a conventional power of attorney to assign someone you trust to take of your finances, business, real estate or children when you are away or unavailable. Provides all the forms with step-by-step instructions.

$14.95/KPA

Nolo's Law Form Kit: Loan Agreements

Attorney Stephen Elias, Marcia Stewart & Lisa Goldoftas. Nat'l 1st ed.

Provides all the forms and instructions necessary to create a legal and effective promissory note. Shows how to decide on an interest rate, set a payment schedule and keep track of payments.

$14.95/KLOAN

Nolo's Law Form Kit: Buy and Sell Contracts

Attorney Stephen Elias, Marcia Stewart & Lisa Goldoftas. Nat'l 1st ed.

Step-by-step instructions and all the forms necessary for creating bills of sale for cars, boats, computers, electronic equipment, household appliances and other personal property.

$9.95/KCONT

Nolo's Law Form Kit: Personal Bankruptcy

Attorneys Steve Elias, Albin Renauer & Robin Leonard and Lisa Goldoftas. Nat'l 1st ed.

All the forms and instructions you need to file for Chapter 7 bankruptcy.

$14.95/KBNK

Nolo's Law Forms Kit: Rebuild Your Credit

Attorney Robin Leonard. Nat'l 1st ed.

Provides strategies for dealing with debts and rebuilding your credit. Shows you how to negotiate with creditors and collection agencies, clean up your credit file, devise a spending plan and get credit in your name.

$14.95/KCRD

PATENT, COPYRIGHT & TRADEMARK

Trademark: How to Name Your Business & Product

Attorneys Kate McGrath & Stephen Elias, with Trademark Attorney Sarah Shena. Nat'l 1st ed.

Learn how to choose a name or logo that others can't copy, conduct a trademark search, register a trademark with the U.S. Patent and Trademark Office and protect and maintain the trademark.

$29.95/TRD

Patent It Yourself

Attorney David Pressman. Nat'l 3rd ed.

From the patent search to the actual application, this book covers everything including the use and licensing of patents, successful marketing and how to deal with infringement. Includes all necessary forms and instructions.

$39.95/PAT

The Inventor's Notebook

Fred Grissom & Attorney David Pressman. Nat'l 1st ed.

Helps you document the process of successful independent inventing by providing forms, instructions, references to relevant areas of patent law, a bibliography of legal and non-legal aids and more.

$19.95/INOT

The Copyright Handbook

Attorney Stephen Fishman. Nat'l 2nd ed.

Provides forms and step-by-step instructions for protecting all types of written expression under U.S. and international copyright law. Covers copyright infringement, fair use, works for hire and transfers of copyright ownership.

$24.95/COHA

software

Patent It Yourself Software

Version 1.0

Patent It Yourself is also available in software. With separate tracks for novice and expert users, it takes you through the process step-by-step. It shows how to evaluate patentability of your invention, how to prepare and file your patent application and how to generate all the forms you need to protect and exploit your invention.

Windows $229.95/PYW1

HOMEOWNERS

How to Buy a House in California

Attorney Ralph Warner, Ira Serkes & George Devine. CA 3rd ed.

Effective strategies for finding a house, working with a real estate agent, making an offer and negotiating intelligently. Includes information on all types of mortgages as well as private financing options.

$24.95/BHCA

For Sale By Owner

George Devine. CA 2nd ed.

Everything you need to know to sell your own house, from pricing and marketing, to writing a contract and going through escrow. Disclosure and contract forms included.

$24.95/FSBO

Homestead Your House

Attorneys Ralph Warner, Charles Sherman & Toni Ihara. CA 8th ed.

Shows you how to file a Declaration of Homestead and includes complete instructions and tear-out forms.

$9.95/HOME

The Deeds Book

Attorney Mary Randolph. CA 3rd ed.

Shows you how to fill out and file the right kind of deed when transferring property. Outlines the legal requirements of real property transfer.

$16.95/DEED

LANDLORDS & TENANTS

The Landlord's Law Book, Vol. 1: Rights & Responsibilities

Attorneys David Brown & Ralph Warner. CA 4th ed.

Essential for every California landlord. Covers deposits, leases and rental agreements, inspections (tenants' privacy rights), habitability (rent withholding), ending a tenancy, liability and rent control. Forms included.

$32.95/LBRT

The Landlord's Law Book, Vol. 2: Evictions

Attorney David Brown. CA 4th ed.

Shows step-by-step how to go to court and evict a tenant. Contains all the tear-out forms and necessary instructions.

$32.95/LBEV

Nolo's Law Form Kit: Leases & Rental Agreements

Attorney Ralph Warner & Marcia Stewart. CA 1st ed.

With these easy-to-use forms and instructions, California landlords can prepare their own rental application, fixed term lease, month-to-month agreement and notice to pay rent or quit.

$14.95/KLEAS

Tenants' Rights

Attorneys Myron Moskovitz & Ralph Warner. CA 12th ed.

This practical guide to dealing with your landlord explains your rights under federal law, California law and rent control ordinances. Forms included.

$18.95/CTEN

JUST FOR FUN

Nolo's Favorite Lawyer Jokes on Disk

Over 200 jokes and hilariously nasty remarks about lawyers organized by categories (Lawyers as Vultures, Nobody Loves a Lawyer, Lawyers in Love...). 100% guaranteed to produce an evening of chuckles and drive every lawyer you know nuts.

IBM PC $9.95/JODI
MACINTOSH $9.95/JODM

Devil's Advocates: The Unnatural History of Lawyers

by Andrew & Jonathan Roth. Nat'l 1st ed.

A hilarious look at the history of the legal profession.

$12.95/DA

Poetic Justice: The Funniest, Meanest Things Ever Said About Lawyers

Edited by Jonathan & Andrew Roth. Nat'l 1st ed.

A great gift for anyone in the legal profession who has managed to maintain a sense of humor.

$9.95/PJ

29 Reasons Not to Go to Law School

Attorneys Ralph Warner & Toni Ihara. Nat'l 4th ed.

Filled with humor, this book can save you three years, $150,000 and your sanity.

$9.95/29R

OLDER AMERICANS

Social Security, Medicare & Pensions

Attorney Joseph Matthews with Dorothy Matthews Berman. Nat'l 5th ed.

Offers invaluable guidance through the current maze of rights and benefits for those 55 and over, including Medicare, Medicaid and Social Security retirement and disability benefits, and age discrimination protections.

$18.95/SOA

Beat the Nursing Home Trap: A Consumer's Guide to Choosing and Financing Long-term Care

Attorney Joseph Matthews. Nat'l 1st ed.

Guides you in choosing and paying for long-term care, alerting you to practical concerns and explaining laws that may affect your decisions.

$18.95/ELD

REFERENCE

Legal Research: How to Find and Understand the Law

Attorneys Stephen Elias & Susan Levinkind. Nat'l 3rd ed.

A valuable tool on its own or as a companion to just about every other Nolo book. Gives easy-to-use, step-by-step instructions on how to find legal information.

$19.95/LRES

Legal Research Made Easy: A Roadmap Through the Law Library Maze

2-1/2 hr. videotape and 40-page manual.
Nolo Press/Legal Star Communications. Nat'l 1st ed.

Professor Bob Berring explains how to use all the basic legal research tools in your local law library with an easy-to-follow six-step research plan and a sense of humor.

$89.95/LRME

CONSUMER/REFERENCE

Nolo's Pocket Guide to California Law

Attorney Lisa Guerin & Nolo Press Editors. CA 2nd ed.

Get quick clear answers to questions about child support, custody, consumer rights, employee rights, government benefits, divorce, bankruptcy, adoption, wills and much more.

$10.95/CLAW

Nolo's Pocket Guide to California Law on Disk

This handy resource is also available on disk. With this new format you can rapidly search through California law by topic and subtopic, or by using the key-word index. The program tracks and saves searches, and allows you to save text to a file for later use.

Windows $24.95/CLWIN
Macintosh $24.95/CLM

Nolo's Pocket Guide to Consumer Rights

Barbara Kaufman. CA 2nd ed.

Practical advice on hundreds of consumer topics. Shows Californians how and where to complain about everything from accountants, misleading advertisements and lost baggage to vacation scams and dishonored warranties.

$14.95/CAG

Nolo's Law Form Kit: Hiring Child Care & Household Help

Attorney Barbara Kate Repa & Lisa Goldoftas. Nat'l 1st ed.

All the necessary forms and instructions for fulfilling your legal and tax responsibilities. Includes employment contracts, application forms and required IRS forms.

$14.95/KCHLD

How to Win Your Personal Injury Claim

Attorney Joseph Matthews. Nat'l 1st ed.

Armed with the right information anyone can handle a personal injury claim. This step-by-step guide shows you how to avoid insurance company run-arounds, evaluate what your claim is worth, obtain a full and fair settlement and save for yourself what you would pay a lawyer.

$24.95/PICL

Fed Up with the Legal System: What's Wrong and How to Fix It

Attorneys Ralph Warner & Stephen Elias. Nat'l 2nd ed.

Forty common-sense proposals to make our legal system fairer, faster, cheaper and more accessible.

$9.95/LEG

IMMIGRATION

How to Get a Green Card: Legal Ways to Stay in the U.S.A.

Attorney Loida Nicolas Lewis with Len T. Madlanscay. Nat'l 1st ed.

Written by a former INS attorney, this book clearly explains the steps involved in getting a green card. It covers who can qualify, what documents to present, and how to fill out all the forms and have them processed. Tear-out forms included.

$22.95/GRN

Como Obtener La Tajeta Verde: Maneras Legitimas de Permanacer en los EE.UU.

Attorney Loida Nicolas Lewis with Len T. Madlanscay. Nat'l 1st ed.

The Spanish edition of *How to Get a Green Card.*

$24.95/VERDE

ORDER FORM

Code	Quantity	Title	Unit Price	Total

Subtotal

California residents add Sales Tax

Shipping & Handling ($4 for 1st item; $1 each additional)

2nd day UPS (additional $5; $8 in Alaska and Hawaii)

TOTAL

Name

Address

(UPS to street address, Priority Mail to P.O. boxes)

FOR FASTER SERVICE, USE YOUR CREDIT CARD AND OUR TOLL-FREE NUMBERS

Monday-Friday, 7 a.m. to 6 p.m. Pacific Time

Order Line 1 (800) 992-6656 (in the 510 area code, call 549-1976)

General Information 1 (510) 549-1976

Fax your order 1 (800) 645-0895 (in the 510 area code, call 548-5902)

METHOD OF PAYMENT

☐ Check enclosed ☐ VISA ☐ Mastercard ☐ Discover Card ☐ American Express

Account # Expiration Date

Authorizing Signature

Daytime Phone

MAIL YOUR ORDER WITH A CHECK OR MONEY ORDER MADE PAYABLE TO:
NOLO PRESS, 950 PARKER ST., BERKELEY, CA 94710

VISIT OUR STORE

If you live in the Bay Area, be sure to visit the Nolo Press Bookstore on the corner of 9th & Parker Streets in west Berkeley. You'll find our complete line of books and software—all at a discount. CALL 1-510-704-2248 for hours.

ALLOW 2-3 WEEKS FOR DELIVERY. PRICES SUBJECT TO CHANGE.

TO ORDER CALL 1-800-992-6656

JUDG 2.3

Get 25% off your next purchase

Recycle your out-of-date books

It's important to have the most current legal information. Because laws and legal procedures change often, we update our books regularly. To help keep you up-to-date we are extending this special offer. Cut out and mail the title portion of the cover of any old Nolo book with your next order and we'll give you a 25% discount off the retail price of ANY new Nolo book you purchase directly from us. For current prices and editions call us at 1-800-992-6656. This offer is to individuals only.

FREE NOLO NEWS SUBSCRIPTION

When you register, we'll send you our quarterly newspaper, the *Nolo News,* free for two years. (U.S. addresses only.) Here's what you'll get in every issue:

INFORMATIVE ARTICLES

Written by Nolo editors, articles provide practical legal information on issues you encounter in everyday life: family law, wills, debts, consumer rights, and much more.

UPDATE SERVICE

The *Nolo News* keeps you informed of legal changes that affect any Nolo book and software program.

BOOK AND SOFTWARE REVIEWS

We're always looking for good legal and consumer books and software from other publishers. When we find them, we review them and offer them in our mail order catalog.

ANSWERS TO YOUR LEGAL QUESTIONS

Our readers are always challenging us with good questions on a variety of legal issues. So in each issue, "Auntie Nolo" gives sage advice and sound information.

COMPLETE NOLO PRESS CATALOG

The *Nolo News* contains an up-to-the-minute catalog of all Nolo books and software, which you can order using our toll-free "800" order line. And you can see at a glance if you're using an out-of-date version of a Nolo product.

LAWYER JOKES

Nolo's famous lawyer joke column continually gets the goat of the legal establishment. If we print a joke you send in, you'll get a $20 Nolo gift certificate.

We promise *never* to give your name and address to any other organization.

Your Registration Card

Complete and Mail Today

COLLECT YOUR COURT JUDGMENT Registration Card

We'd like to know what you think! Please take a moment to fill out and return this postage paid card for a free two-year subscription to the *Nolo News*. If you already receive the *Nolo News*, we'll extend your subscription.

Name ______________________ Ph.( ) __________

Address ______________________

City ______________ State _____ Zip __________

Where did you hear about this book? ______________________

For what purpose did you use this book? ______________________

Did you consult a lawyer? Yes No Not Applicable

Was it easy for you to use this book? (very easy) 5 4 3 2 1 (very difficult)

Did you find this book helpful? (very) 5 4 3 2 1 (not at all)

Comments ______________________

____

____

____

____

THANK YOU **JUDG 2.3**

[Nolo books are]..."written in plain language, free of legal mumbo jumbo, and spiced with witty personal observations."

—ASSOCIATED PRESS

"Well-produced and slickly written, the [Nolo] books are designed to take the mystery out of seemingly involved procedures, carefully avoiding legalese and leading the reader step-by-step through such everyday legal problems as filling out forms, making up contracts, and even how to behave in court."

—SAN FRANCISCO EXAMINER

"...Nolo publications...guide people simply through the how, when, where and why of law."

—WASHINGTON POST

"Increasingly, people who are not lawyers are performing tasks usually regarded as legal work... And consumers, using books like Nolo's, do routine legal work themselves."

—NEW YORK TIMES

"...All of [Nolo's] books are easy-to-understand, are updated regularly, provide pull-out forms...and are often quite moving in their sense of compassion for the struggles of the lay reader."

—SAN FRANCISCO CHRONICLE

NO POSTAGE
NECESSARY
IF MAILED
IN THE
UNITED STATES

BUSINESS REPLY MAIL
FIRST-CLASS MAIL PERMIT NO 3283 BERKELEY CA

POSTAGE WILL BE PAID BY ADDRESSEE

NOLO PRESS
950 Parker Street
Berkeley CA 94710-9867